Leisure Cultures:
Values,
Genders,
Lifestyles

Edited by

Graham McFee

Wilf Murphy

Garry Whannel

LSA
Publication No 54

First published in 1995 by
Leisure Studies Association

A catalogue record for this book
is available from the British Library.

ISBN: 0 906337 65 8

Layout design and typesetting by Myrene L. McFee
Reproduction by University of Brighton
Binding by Kensett Ltd., Hove

Contents

Introduction

The study of leisure has always been a multidisciplinary and at times an interdisciplinary endeavour. Leisure studies, sports studies, and cultural studies (as fields of study) have previously emerged out of attempts to draw on a range of traditional disciplines in forging new intellectual configurations. One of the characteristics of this collection — exemplifying these characteristics — is the broad range of disciplinary contexts from which the papers have grown. The influences of economics, sociology, history, English, media and cultural studies, political science, and anthropology can all be detected in the papers in this volume. At the same time, there is plenty of evidence of a productive cross-fertilisation of ideas. For instance, many of the contributors work in institutional contexts that help to promote interdisciplinary work.

The collection is divided into three sections, which seem to the editors to reflect something fundamental about the topics/issues foregrounded in the papers in the volume. The abiding concern, reflected in the collection title, is with *leisure cultures*; and the section divisions make sense of that overall concern. More specifically, the *particular* aspects of the dynamic concerning *power-relations* explored in each paper seem usefully presented in this way.

The first section, **Gendered Constructions**, brings together work that has, at least in part, foregrounded the issues associated with the production of masculinities, of femininities, and of gender differences. The second section, **Values in Public and Private Spheres**, brings together a diverse range of papers that focus, in various ways, on the values that are brought into play in defining leisure cultures, and on the impact of these values on the provision and consumption of leisure time opportunity: in particular, on the public and private character of such values — characterised both in terms of the public and private economic spheres, and in the various contributions of individual and social group (perhaps understood via, say, Giddens' structure/agency dynamic [Giddens, 1984: pp. 25-28]). The nature of values themselves must be understood; but also the contestation of value, and its situated rebirth (Willis, 1982: p. 124). And central here will be concerns with the values that underpin both *leisure activity* and *leisure studies*. In the third section, **Lifestyles, Citizenship and Change**, the key concept is *change*, especially changes in leisure lifestyles — although without denying the importance of continuities. A focus on aspects of social change prompts re-analysis of *lifestyle* and *citizenship*, in terms of changing leisure consumption. Various conceptions of the nature and obligations of citizenship, and of the leisure-patterns which both support them and are supported by them, are explored.

However, the imposition of an over-neat taxonomy on these papers *could* serve to mask the extent to which there are very distinct differences in approach, method, and theoretical preconception between the papers in each section. Equally, there are inevitably continuities, overlaps, links and themes in common, between papers in different sections. For this introduction, we have singled out a number of themes having resonances in many of the papers both within and across sections, without in anyway implying that all these themes are of the same kind, or are suitable for a single taxonomy.

Masculinities and femininities

The issue of gender difference has been growing in prominence in work within leisure studies, a development some would consider long overdue. Until recently much of this work has been associated with examining the constraints upon women's leisure — but, increasingly, the impact of work on the construction of femininities in other intellectual contexts is having its impact within leisure studies.

Rosemary Deem's work in the field is well-known and her paper provides a valuable updating of the argument that women and men experience time, and consequently leisure, in different ways. Deborah Philips' analysis of girls' fiction in the 1950s draws out the presence of a concern with status, skill, and career that serves to challenge the image of the decade as one in which women were, unproblematically, returned to domesticity. Eleanor Peters and Nadina Prosser both offer vivid pictures of the ways in which young girls struggle to produce meaningful leisure against the social constraints of their circumstances. Garry Whannel's examination of young people's magazines explores ways in which gender differences are constructed. Jim Clough's (*et al.*) survey work on young girls' attitudes to sport (based on studies in an Australian context) offers fascinating and suggestive evidence to put alongside Whannel's.

Increasingly and belatedly, there is a growing research focus on the production of masculinities in sport and leisure. J. A. Mangan's historical overview analyses the ways in which masculinity and militarism have always been closely linked, and Karl Spracklen's fieldwork provides insights into the lived cultures of rugby league. Work on gender needs to examine the relation between masculinity and femininity, and Anne Flintoff, Sheila Scraton and Peter Bramham's study of aerobics explores the role of body image in leisure lifestyles and the ways in which (apparently health-related) physical activity contributes to the production of gender difference. John Sugden and Alan Tomlinson's evocative report on their fieldwork in Havana focuses on masculine street cultures and the managing of relationships with tourists (and researchers) in a beleaguered economy. Of course, gender is not the only significant form of stratification. Hanspeter Stamm and Markus Lamprecht's paper takes up the debate through its discussion of the continued significance of class in the formation of leisure practices and lifestyles.

Representation, fiction and the media

Three papers, those by Mangan, Philips and Whannel, focus specifically on representations, demonstrating ways in which popular literature, poetry, and magazines can be used as forms of evidence to provide clues to the cultural and ideological themes in play at specific historical moments. They illustrate both some of the epistemological diversity of leisure studies and the justified concern with the impact of such representations (especially mass-media representations) on patterns of leisure understanding and leisure consumption.

In giving due weight to the role of representations, these papers emphasise the variety of data-sources available to leisure studies. In this way, they have obvious connections with those papers where the methodological thrust is even more explicit.

Methods and research strategies

Most directly addressed in the paper by Sugden and Tomlinson, issues concerning the nature of inappropriate research strategies and methods are of primary interest in a number of papers. For Sugden and Tomlinson, some of the perils of practical ethnography are explicitly raised in the context of research into 'body tourism' in Cuba — in particular, the difficulties of negotiating an appropriate relationship with local 'gate-keepers': in the words of another of Tomlinson's papers (1995), a relationship characterised by "flattery and betrayal". But when, in the investigation described by Flintoff *et al.*, the male researcher enters the aerobics class, this is almost as much *terra incognita* as the backstreets of Havana: and, again, the research imperative must be negotiated in ways the paper addresses.

For Alan Clarke, too, the methodological questions are central; but now the context is provided by the need to make sense of suitable methods for pursuing leisure studies in our present (postmodern?/post-industrial?) situation. Crucial here are the values implicit in leisure-investigation, since they drive the kinds of questions appropriately asked.

Space and time

Several of the papers deal with the social organisation of space and time. Deem updates arguments that women and men experience time differently. David Crouch and Neil Ravenscroft analyse the relations of power, control and negotiation involved in land use, with reference to caravanning and rambling. Prosser's research reveals the special problems of space and time involved in the attempts of young girls in rural areas to construct leisure activities. Yohji Iwamoto discusses the threat to land produced by an intensely commercialised leisure culture in Japan. In Clarke's paper, also, concerns with the commodification of leisure can turn on the appropriation of spaces.

In addressing these issues, the papers remind us that the concept of *power* must be seen more expansively than might otherwise be the case: as ranging more widely than simply the direct influence of one person or group of persons on another. And here, of course, is a point crucial under the *representations* theme identified above.

Youth

Many of the papers have implications relevant to youth education in its broader sense. Ravenscroft discusses the emergence of a citizenship defined by consumption, with increasing differentiation between those with and without means. Peters' examination of young girls and their leisure patterns contrasts youth services and independent leisure practices. Clough's survey of school age girls offers a vivid picture of the kinds of sporting aspirations that develop within the context of formal education. Prosser's examination of the leisure patterns of young girls in a rural area illustrates the relative marginality of education in providing means of developing active leisure. Philips' study of girls' fiction in the 1950s illustrates the ways in which hopes and expectations are developed outside of, as well as within, formal education. Similarly, Whannel's discussion of images of sport in the print media explores ways in which media images serve to construct particular expectations of sport.

Given the importance of youth as a target market for much leisure provision, this theme represents an abiding concern. We see that youth are not necessarily powerless *even though* their (direct) economic power may be limited: leisure producers would be foolish to neglect them (as Iwamoto emphasises). And recognising that youth may have a place at the leisure 'negotiating table' is conceding that they may have some power after all.

Public/private

The distinction between the State and commercial provision, and the relation of public and private spheres is a concern in a number of papers. Stan Parker introduces four categories: commercial provision, public provision, mutual aid leisure, and individual leisure. Mike McNamee discusses the relation of personal commitment and ethical value to professionalism, by considering the possibility of professional ethical codes for sports coaches. Sarah-Louise Prime and Vic Kerton's discussion of General Practitioner referral schemes addresses the working of health provision during a period of reconstruction: what is private concern, what public? Sugden and Tomlinson's paper, examining as it does informal and semi-illicit cultural practices, portrays the ways in which such practices flourish in the interface between an affluent tourist influx and an impoverished culture of survival.

The variety of different questions (around the topic of 'public/ private') derive not merely from the variety of uses of the terms "public" and "private" in this context, but from the inter-connections between what is important when addressing *this* question rather than *that*. As the paper by Parker illustrates, we cannot simply and without discussion treat public and private (economic) sectors as though they were homogenous or unitary: there are important distinctions within such categories. Equally, as McNamee explores, a professionalisation of coaching cannot be achieved simply through the production of public rules — that the 'internalisation' of such rules depends on our learning how to make sense of them, in ways not guaranteed by attempts at ever tighter verbal formulation.

The economic and cultural

Several papers deal with both cultural and economic issues, and three focus specifically upon the economic. Clare Brindley and Richard Hud son-Davies analyse the impact of the National Lottery. Brian Davies, Paul Downward and Ian Jackson examine the relation between cultural and economic factors in patterns of rugby league support, and Iwamoto discusses the commercialisation of leisure in Japan.

Unless we are aware of the diversity of economic bases of leisure — as well as the diversity of its moral bases — we cannot make sense of the differential questions that arise: how, for example, the economic imperatives of professional sportsmen in Rugby League differs from (and how it resembles) that of other sportsmen, as conceptualised by Davies *et al*. Again, the place of gambling in the leisure-culture of the UK can no longer be explored without attention to the economic impact of the National Lottery. But, equally, consideration of the morality of gambling must be crucial to any understanding of its cultural impact. And the cultural impact of leisure economics, and its unique cultural context in Japan, is one motivation of Iwamoto's discussion: in particular, the shift in target group from the business community to a growing youth culture.

'Foreign' parts

While the majority of the papers concern sport, leisure and education in the British context, we are pleased to be able to include papers that allude to other national contexts. Sugden and Tomlinson's paper is based on fieldwork in Cuba, Stamm's upon Switzerland, Iwamoto's on Japan, and Clough's research is part of a cross-cultural comparison between England and Australia. In these ways, the papers emphasise the cultural specificity of leisure values, leisure activities and (some of) leisure studies. But they also emphasise the continuities within the field of leisure studies: these are matters where practitioners can usefully meet together for a productive peer-review of analytical ideas and methods as well as for the sharing of information.

Conclusion

The papers in this volume had their first 'life' as presentations at the Leisure Studies Association's 1995 Conference in Eastbourne (September 12-14). This provided a forum for discussion for the ideas here presented: presentations have been revised in the light of their reception at the Conference and — although some authors have preferred to acknowledge the paper's history by retaining something from the oral presentation — typically redrafted for publication to accommodate criticisms raised in discussion. The editors, too, have striven both to lead the authors towards clarity of expression (where necessary) and to excise passages which fail this test, while seeking to maintain the individual 'voice' of authors. And the Conference has yielded two other volumes in addition to this one — *Policy and Politics in Sport, Physical Education and Leisure* (eds Scott Fleming, Margaret Talbot and Alan Tomlinson), and *Professional and Development Issues in Leisure, Sport and Education* (eds Lesley Lawrence, Elizabeth Murdoch and Stan Parker).

The production of this volume incurs a number of debts, from the editorial points of view: to the authors, for presenting at the Conference and for bearing with (and meeting) our demands and deadlines; to all the members of the Conference organising committee, for generating such an interesting collection of presenters and presentations; and especially to Myrene McFee who, in addition to her hard work administering the Conference and her master-minding of the schedules for authors and editors, has designed and prepared the pages from which this text was produced.

Graham McFee *(University of Brighton)*
Wilf Murphy *(University College Salford)*
Garry Whannel *(Roehampton Institute London)*

November 1995

References

Giddens, A. (1984) *The constitution of society.* Cambridge: Polity Press.

Tomlinson, A. (1995) 'Flattery and betrayal: Observations on qualitative and oral sources', in A. Tomlinson and S. Fleming (eds) *Ethics, sport and leisure; Crises and critiques.* Chelsea School Research Centre Topic Report 5. Eastbourne: University of Brighton, pp. 244-264.

Willis, P. (1982) 'Women in sport in ideology', in J. A. Hargreaves (ed) *Sport, culture and ideology.* London: Routledge and Kegan Paul, pp. 117-135.

Part I

Gendered Constructions

Time for a Change? Engendered Work and Leisure in the 1990s

Rosemary Deem

University of Lancaster

Introduction

In this paper I want to explore a number of ideas about time, work, leisure, and gender relations. In particular, I am concerned to subject to critical examination, the notion of 'spare' time as an aspect of people's lives which supposedly takes place in the interstices of paid and unpaid work. I shall argue that 'spare' time is a problematic and gendered concept (Deem, 1996) which may turn out to be unhelpful to present and future ideas about leisure and work. In so doing I shall also examine critically other aspects of conceptions of time in social theory, and their significance for different kinds of paid and unpaid work, space, choices about consumption, perceptions of the speed and pace of life, and the possible contribution of education to changing leisure and work practices. In concluding the paper, I shall suggest that unless radical changes do take place in the organisation of the paid and unpaid work done by women and men in western societies (and the discourses about gender underlying these forms of work), then it is likely that many women in such societies will continue to experience their lives as more hectic, more work dominated, and less full of pleasure and enjoyment than the lives of many men.

Issues related to time, space, consumption, pace of life and life styles are important features of much recent social theory (Featherstone, 1990; Shields, 1991; Keat, Whiteley et al., 1994; Lash and Urry, 1994; Massey, 1994; Adam, 1995; Mulgan and Wilkinson, 1995; Urry, 1995), particularly amongst those theorists who argue that we are living in a post modern and globalised world. It is indeed partly this recognition of substantial world change which has had such a dramatic effect on social theory itself. However, as Massey notes, some contemporary social theorists have failed to grasp the significance of gender to their analyses (Massey, 1994). Although this does not mean that their work is therefore rendered totally flawed, omission or down-playing of gender relations has serious consequences for the applicability of social theories to issues concerning the quality of life and multiple uses of time.

By contrast, in the fields of employment, household work, and education, issues of gender identity and gender relations have long been recognised as important aspects of theoretical and empirical analysis. In the field of leisure, the importance of gender issues is gradually being recognised by a wider group of researchers. However, though research on leisure often includes matters related to employment and households, the role of education has not always been taken fully into account. Hence my analysis here also includes looking at what is happening to young women and men currently in education. Education is often marginalised or ignored by prominent social theorists, with the prominent exception of Bourdieu (Bourdieu, 1987a; Bourdieu, 1987b; Bourdieu, 1990; Bourdieu, 1993), yet it is a key arena for identifying and shaping cultural change.

Women and leisure — changing directions

Since I last did any sustained work in this field (Deem, 1986; Deem, 1988), the analysis of women and leisure has changed quite considerably, although some of the political impetus and excitement seems to have gone. The field has changed in three ways. Firstly new theoretical approaches and changing social, cultural, economic and political conditions have caused feminists themselves to look anew at how gender relations in leisure may be studied. Post modernist and post structuralist theories have attempted to undermine universal 'grand' theories, questioned concepts of power in which some are seen to be powerful and others are not, dispensed with concepts of social class, and dedifferentiated or deconstructed gender and gender categories (Butler, 1990; Nicholson, 1990; McNay, 1992; Clough, 1994). Some of these new modes of theorising have given rise to a focus on difference, notions of multiple performances of gender, as well as a shift away from thinking that women have anything in common with each other or that the category woman has any useful purpose.

As with all theoretical debates in which academic careers are formed or progressed, and status differentials established, there is a tendency for some protagonists of new approaches to overstate their case. This has certainly happened in the field of leisure. Thus, Le Feuvre alleges that many gender and leisure researchers writing in the 1980s believed that all women desired autonomous leisure (Le Feuvre, 1994). Wearing claims that many studies of women's leisure, especially those emanating from a socialist feminist perspective, were overly deterministic and paid little or no attention to the meanings of leisure or to the capacity of leisure to provide a space for resistance to traditional ideas about gender identity (Wearing, 1992). Bella developed a similar critique suggesting that relationships were more important in women's leisure than activities or achievements (Bella, 1989).

There are certainly theoretical differences between these critics and those whose work is being critiqued. The latter group principally includes the research done by Green, Hebron and Woodward (Green, Hebron *et al.*, 1990),Wimbush and Talbot (Wimbush and Talbot, 1988), Henderson, Bialeschki *et al.* (Henderson, Bialeschki *et al.*, 1989) and myself (Deem, 1986). However, the notion that none of us were aware of any significant differences between women, that we failed to understand the importance of individual women's identities or that we did not see in women's leisure any opportunities for resistance, is a convenient (for the purposes of polemic) but also inaccurate, fiction. Furthermore, as Scraton points out, the mere fact of recognising differences between individual women does not bracket away or make insignificant, shared material disadvantages which affect groups of women (Scraton, 1994).

The second distinctive feature of gender and leisure studies in the 1990s is that some malestream theorists have seized upon recent feminist critiques of previous research on women and leisure. They have used these to show that feminist researchers with political convictions and purpose, including those working from a socialist feminist perspective, misunderstood the nature of leisure. Such researchers are accused of missing the point that many women do not feel oppressed by men and enjoy male company during their leisure and their work (Rojek, 1995). It is perhaps not always recognised that some of the research being criticised was carried out in response to and as a partial counter against, such claims. Rojek rounds on feminist leisure researchers for having argued that women shared a common world of leisure and for thinking that leisure was something that could usefully be analysed as a separate cultural phenomenon (Rojek, 1995). Had Rojek read some of the most recent work by feminist writers discussing space, place and time, instead of relying only on the malestream literature in this area, he might have realised that some of his assumptions are misconceived precisely because of his failure to engage fully with issues of gender relations. Thus, he writes confidently about the significance of the concept of the flâneur (an observer and stroller) in the city. This analysis, despite the use of his and her as personal pronouns relating to flâneurs, utilises a gendered and masculine concept which as Massey notes, cannot be applied to women since women are always observed (Massey, 1994). However, in a climate of post feminism, where feminists are warned that their both their analysis and their political strategies are outdated (Wilkinson, 1994), and when it is frequently noted that both women and men recoil from the label of feminism despite embracing some of its values and concerns (Griffin, 1989; Pilcher, 1992; Sianne, 1994; Wilkinson, 1994), it is easy for malestream researchers and think tank gurus to dismiss feminist writing and the politics which accompanies it. Yet it is precisely the link between politics and theory which distinguishes some feminist writing from many of the other recent contributions to social theory (Deem, 1994b).

There is also a third and further aspect of the 1990s debate about gender and leisure, which appears both in the malestream critique of women and leisure research, and in recent feminist critiques of the same research. This is the argument that analyses which talk about male power or women struggling for leisure are pessimistic, whereas new post structuralist or post modernist forms of analysis of leisure are optimistic (Wearing, 1992; Rojek, 1995). It is tempting to invoke a rapid scanning of recent national or international news bulletins here, in order to suggest that the globalised, polluted and conflict ridden world does not give much grounds for optimism. Surely that is one of the messages of those who warn of environmental risks (Beck, 1992)? However, undoubtedly the need to emphasise the positive aspects of women's leisure, whatever forms it takes and whosoever it involves and whether it is separated from or overlaps with work, is important and was well recognised by precisely those writers accused of ignoring it (Deem, 1986; Wimbush and Talbot, 1988; Henderson, Bialeschki *et al.*, 1989; Green, Hebron *et al.*, 1990). Having spent some time sketching current developments in social theory (including feminist theory) and theories about leisure as a prelude to considering 'whatever happened to spare time', I now want to turn to a consideration of how time relates to engendered leisure.

Clock time, own time, free time

Many leisure analysts have recognised the importance of time, just as have several generations of social theorists. However it is only relatively recently that the social theory of time has moved beyond using time as an explicit rather than implicit concept (Adam, 1990; Adam, 1995). Adam notes that time is "embedded in social interactions, structures, practices and knowledge, in artefacts, in the mindful body, and in the environment" (p. 6) but emphasises that it is the complexity, simultaneity and multiplicity of time which have often been missed. In leisure research, notions of clock, rational and commodified time, have been extensively used, as have notions of free time. Nevertheless, with a few exceptions (Urry, 1994a; Urry, 1995), insufficient attention has been paid to how these notions are embedded in and affected by social relations.

The idea of 'spare' time in relation to work and leisure is an unsatisfactory one from the viewpoint of gender relations, though the concept has some 'respectable' historical origins in accounts of the shortening of the male industrial working week (Thompson 1967). 'Spare' time principally refers to clock and commodified time, although it has often been used in a much wider sense than this. Adam observes that an analysis of 'free' time in the context of shortened working hours 'creates an appearance of ever increasing free time, even of 'time wealth' (p. 96). However she contends, this 'free' time arises through increased efficiency at work and does not belong to people in the first place. Thus, Adam notes, so called 'free' time is in fact 'produced' time, a '*not- work time*' that exists only in relation to the time of markets and employment' (p. 96) and so is less appropriate for those not in paid employment, including full time houseworkers, unemployed people and those who are retired. However Adam warns us about the importance of not retreating into a dualism which contrasts clock time with cyclical or process time, as some feminists have done (Davies, 1990)

Adam also draws to our attention the important concept of 'the unreflected backcloth of 'own' time, upon which 'other' times are constructed' (1995: p. 7) and which co-exists with other kinds of time. She further suggests that in the simultaneity of times, time hierarchies can be very significant. Gender relations play a key role in the relative prioritising of time hierarchies, as I have begun to discover in exploratory research on women and holidays (Deem and Tinkler, 1995; Deem, 1996). On holidays away from home taken by households with children, and during the preparations which precede these holidays, the time hierarchies and priorities of children and, where relevant, men, may sometimes be seen as more important than those of women. 'Spare' time is certainly referred to in holiday contexts but is something which may benefit women with male partners and dependent children somewhat less than those with whom they live. If, then, we want to know what has happened to 'spare' time in relation to work and leisure, one answer may be that it is just one of many concepts of time and perhaps one which bears a closer relationship to the past than to the present or the future. This proposition, however, also depends on making certain kinds of political choices.

Leisure, working hours and consumption

In the 1980s, and in several previous periods of industrialisation, particularly at times of high unemployment, some writers suggested that the future in the western world would be one with increased leisure and decreased paid work, leading to a leisure society (Jenkins and Sherman 1981; Seabrook, 1988). However, more recently, such arguments have come under critical scrutiny. It has now been claimed that people no longer aspire to a leisure society. Instead, they prefer to engage in paid work, which offers more challenges than leisure, permits increased consumption, and whose proponents have acquired the high status once accorded to the leisured classes (Cross, 1995; Lane, 1995). One of the claims made by critics of the leisure society notion is that recently people have tended to choose longer hours of work, which in turn enable increased consumption, rather than choosing fewer working hours and more leisure time (Dore, 1995; Lane, 1995).

However, this view is itself worthy of more detailed examination. First, as Schor shows from her research in a large USA based telecommunications firm, even those who want to work shorter hours may be deterred by fears about how to repay their debts, and the possibility that their career chances will be harmed (Schor, 1995). Although debts are incurred through consumption, they refer to past or present rather than future consumption. Second, the assumed boundaries of leisure and work are in flux. As Cannon (1995) demonstrates, young people may wish to work in more flexible ways than their parents or grandparents, may not perceive strong boundaries between leisure and work. They do not necessarily regard leisure as 'rest' or as a time for undertaking the unchallenging activities Lane regards as characteristic of contemporary leisure (Lane, 1995).

Third, so-called 'choices' about hours of work are affected by gender relations, as well as by other cultural, economic and generational factors. Many women, and a smaller number of men, in western societies, are engaged in substantial amounts of paid employment *and* in extensive un- paid household work. Whilst the decision to work shorter or flexible hours is more often made by women than men, this may be a rather constrained choice, governed by women's household responsibilities, what employment is available to them, their qualifications, and employer attitudes to female workers (Hewitt, 1993; Wilkinson, 1994). It does not necessarily relate to women's wish to forego consumption or to engage in more leisure and 'spare' time. Indeed, economic necessity is often a major factor shaping women's engagement in paid work, especially if they are mothers.

For women who live with men, children or other dependants, the 'choice' to do less *unpaid* work involves an even more limited range of options Typically, such women either stop doing the work (a difficult choice when relationships and responsibilities are involved), encourage other members of their household to do it or pay an outsider to do the work. These solutions are dependent on cultural and economic resources and the capacity to negotiate successfully with the rest of the household (Hochschild, 1989; Gregson and Lowe, 1993; Goodnow and Bowes, 1994; Gregson and Lowe, 1994a; Gregson and Lowe, 1994b). Desaulniers and Théberge, in a secondary analysis of the 1985 Canadian Labour Force survey, found that of the relatively small proportion of people who were interested in a reduction in working hours, women wanted to use the time for household and family *obligations* and responsibilities, in other words for unpaid work. Men, on the other hand, wanted to use their extra 'spare' time for their own and/or family *leisure* but not unpaid work (Desaulniers and Théberge, 1992). Only by recognising the importance of gender rela- tions to decisions about working hours, the division of unpaid tasks and responsibilities, and choices about the relative merits of leisure and con- sumption or extra 'spare' time, can we begin to understand the social and cultural context of the multiple uses of time.

Paid and unpaid work — whose time is at stake?

As we have already seen, much of the discussion about work, leisure and so-called 'spare time' still focuses on paid work. This is not necessarily because all commentators recognise the link between the concept of spare time and paid work time as noted by Adam (1995). It is also because many social policies in western societies are still based round the notion that 'real' work is something done by males between the hours of 9am and 5pm or its equivalent, for 48 weeks a year (Hewitt, 1993). Yet as Hewitt observes, there are many forms of paid work which are neither 9am-5pm and permanent, nor done all year round. These include short term contracts, part time work, flexi-work, term- time-only contracts and twilight shifts. Not all of these are new, nor are they only done by women. However, it is worth noting Hewitt's point that there are now many more such jobs in the UK, as employers seek to loosen their dependence on a full time, permanent, and expensive, work force.

Simultaneously with shifts in kinds of paid work contracts, or perhaps as a consequence, many employees, whatever their contractual status, and job, perceive that they are experiencing an intensified pace of life, in which everything is speeded up (Gershuny, 1995; Mulgan and Wilkinson, 1995; Pahl, 1995; Tyrell, 1995). Not that everyone finds this a problem. Younger people may take simultaneity and multi tasking for granted (Tyrell, 1995). Blurring of the boundaries between work and leisure may be seen as positive by a young generation of adults eager to escape what they see as the boring lives of their parents (Cannon, 1995). The media regularly make use of three minute time slots (Tresilian, 1995), and video time, now so familiar to many in western societies, is very different to some other kinds of time to which we are accustomed, in that it can speed up, slow down and move backwards as well as forwards (Gray, 1992; Urry, 1994a).

For many people intensification of pace of life is something about which they feel ambivalent or anxious. However, we have to set changes in paid work in a wider social and cultural context. Despite the evidence that people experience pace of life as stressful, irrespective of whether it is or not, there is also evidence that speed and busyness are highly valued (Shaw, 1995; Young, 1995). But there may still be, as Shaw notes, a gender element in this, which affects both 'produced' or 'spare' time, and the extent of guilt which accompanies any freed time. Shaw uses research based on contemporary Mass Observation data analysis to show that women tend to be task rather than time-oriented, are often grateful to have a job at all, and may strive for unrealistic objectives and targets in paid work. This orientation to conscientious performance or even over-work may be encouraged by new forms of management, using techniques such as work targets or performance related pay. The uncertainty of flexible and casualised short term contract working may also encourage over-work. Thus, whilst Wilkinson (1994) applauds feminisation at work for its potential to transform gender roles *and* work efficiency, Shaw suggests it may have deleterious consequences for women, by increasing the intensity of their paid work at a point when it is not clear that their unpaid work responsibilities have reduced significantly (Shaw, 1995). Davies makes a similar point about stress levels and ways of coping with work loads in relation to the approach of female nurses to management in health care services (Davies, 1992).

Flexible work then, may turn out to be to the greater advantage of employers rather than employees, since workers often have little say in the matter and may end up trading flexibility for job insecurity (Hewitt, 1995). Such insecurity is likely to have an effect on all aspects of people's lives, despite Handy's contention that flexible work, networked decentred organisations and a portfolio of job skills are offering people fresh opportunities for self development (Handy, 1995a; Handy, 1995b). Handy seems to downplay the relevance of cultural or informational capital to life style, something which a knowledge of Bourdieu's work might have remedied (Bourdieu, 1987a; Bourdieu, 1993).

So far as women are concerned, there is evidence that even where job flexibility has enhanced their chances of remaining in or returning to paid employment, there has not been a concomitant change in the social and cultural organisation of the workplace. Employers and organisations are still failing to fully address equal opportunities issues (Cockburn, 1991; Wilkinson, 1994), though in those in the public sector seem to have been somewhat more successful than their private sector counterparts (Farish, McPake *et al.*, 1995; Shaw and Perron, 1995). Although women are entering and remaining in the paid work force in larger and larger numbers than ever before in many western countries, they often find little recognition of the issues facing them in many of the organisations and amongst many of those with whom they have to work (Tanton, 1994; Wilkinson, 1994). This in itself can be a source of problems and difficulties, whether for discharge of household responsibilities, enjoyment of life, or job advancement and fulfilment.

Wilkinson (1994) suggests that organisations and men will gradually change their attitudes and approach, for two reasons. Firstly she claims that more employers will see the competitive advantage to be gained from being family friendly, flexible, emphasising empowerment of employees and developing corporate targets on equal opportunities. Second, she cites evidence that those under 35 years old, of both sexes, have more flexible and androgynous attitudes towards the organisation of paid work than older generations, particularly men. Thus, Wilkinson notes that both younger men and women are attracted to jobs in organisations which have "a strong female presence and effective equal opportunities policies: these are taken as markers of being smart and leading edge" (Wilkinson, 1994: p. 24). However, what Wilkinson does not take fully into account is the well recognised gap between attitudes and behaviour. There is also the possibility that attitudes change as people grow older (i.e. there are intragenerational value shifts as well as intergenerational ones). It remains an open question as to whether the attitudes expressed by young adults in the recent survey to which Wilkinson refers will remain unchanged, or if they do, whether they will influence actual behaviour as those respondents grow older.

Theories of gender and leisure which suggest considerable variation in the subjectivities of different women (Wearing, 1992; Le Feuvre, 1994) and changed attitudes or resistance to conventional gender stereotypes, come up against some problems when we come to look at evidence on who actually does housework and childcare, though to be fair Le Feuvre recognises this. It may be that here we should invoke Adam's (1995) concept of implication, which can help link these different levels of the local and the global, or the individual and the whole, by accepting that there are complex interrelations, mutual impermeability and inseparability of the two phenomena. Studies in the UK (Hewitt, 1993; Wilkinson, 1994; Central Statistical Office, 1995) and the USA (Hochschild, 1989), indicate that although the attitudes of both women and men to domestic divisions of labour are changing, behaviour still lags behind apparent attitudinal shifts. This is not to say that no changes have occurred in behaviour. Thus, recent research in Australia (Goodnow and Bowes, 1994) and the USA (Hood, 1993) suggests that in some countries more men are taking on a bigger share of domestic and caring work. However there is still a long way to go before work at home is equally shared between both genders.

We also need to be cautious about research data purporting to show changes in domestic divisions of labour or in attitudes to gender stereotypes. Typically, attitudinal data derive from large scale surveys (Wilkinson, 1994; Central Statistical Office, 1995), essential for giving a broad overview and providing a snap shot of representative groups drawn from large populations, but giving little indication of the link between attitudes and behaviour. Information about behaviour in relation to domestic work is often derived from time budget studies (Shaw, 1991; Hewitt, 1993), which give us some indication of time spent on tasks and the outcomes of negotiations over domestic labour, but tell us little or nothing about how those negotiations were conducted. Only those studies which are qualitative and small scale give us any sense of what meanings and processes underlie attitudes about and behaviour in relation to the domestic division of labour.

Goodnow and Bowes's Australian study of fifty male/female couples, half with children living at home, who share their domestic work on an equitable basis, provides some rich insights into what is at stake when heterosexual couples negotiate how to conduct their domestic and caring work (Goodnow and Bowes, 1994). The processes of negotiation over household work both inside and out (since these two researchers are sensitive to the importance of including in their analysis all jobs in the home, from cooking and washing to servicing of cars, mowing of lawns and house/flat maintenance) are particularly well documented by Goodnow and Bowes. They show how tasks are divided up and why this happens. Their typology of women's speciality, man's speciality, fluid shifts (jobs which couples do together or are done by whoever is around when they need doing), off the list (jobs that a couple either decide not to do any more or pay someone else to do them),and 'to each their own' (p. 66), give a sense of the complexity of household work which is not matched by most previous research in this area. The authors' discussion about couples who develop a shared sense of the 'right kinds of place' in relation to house/ garden work, and the notion of 'good and fair relationships' are also useful in that they provide insights into the motivations that both women and men have for sharing household work (p. 95).

However, Goodnow and Bowes' research also demonstrates that the equal or relatively equal sharing of domestic work is based on continual, rather than once and for all negotiations. It also rests on personal identities which do not depend only on associations between gender and the kinds of paid or unpaid work done. Importantly, the division of domestic work also depends on the integration or assimilation of a multiplicity of times, from the rational distribution of time via employment, through different individuals' sense of own times, to the ordering of different time hierarchies. Certainly Wilkinson's (1994) evidence suggests that attitudes more favourable to such androgynous gender roles are developing in the UK. The work of Hood and others indicates that in the USA also, changes in attitudes to gender roles are matched by some changes in behaviour in respect of the gendered division of domestic work (Schor, 1992; Hood, 1993). Nevertheless, there is still a long way to go before shifts in attitudes and behaviour have any marked effects on women and men's lives and life styles at home and work.

Yet unless the domestic burden starts to fall more evenly on both men and women, many women's quality of life and 'own time' are likely to remain inferior to that of men. What women choose to do with their lives and 'own time' when they are freed from the major or sole responsibilities of the second shift will undoubtedly vary considerably, even within a given society. As Le Feuvre notes in her study of French mothers, social class and cultural capital have a considerable effect on how different women regard autonomous and family based leisure (Le Feuvre, 1994). She found evidence that working class women in paid employment would have preferred to exchange the time spent on their jobs for time spent on their families and domestic obligations. Middle class mothers, on the other hand, who were temporarily or more permanently outside paid work were prepared to pay for childcare or domestic help in order to engage in autonomous leisure. Middle class women in employment wanted some autonomous leisure but did not want to take yet more time away from their families. If women wish to combine work and leisure and engage in playfulness in a way consistent with post modern consciousness (Rojek, 1995) there is surely a better chance of this occurring if women do not have to shoulder almost the entire burden of domestic work on their own.

The ways in which domestic work and caring are shared between women and men may also affect women's decisions about marriage, something that women in the UK are increasingly opting out of, preferring to cohabit or live alone, even if they have dependent children (Wilkinson, 1994). This is not to say that women are necessarily oppressed by their circumstances. Indeed some seem to have benefited from the chance to be more autonomous. The UK-based market research on shifting cultural values to which Wilkinson (1994) refers, suggests that amongst very young women, there is a greater optimism about the future, and higher aspirations, than there are amongst very young men. Whilst one piece of research evidence, particularly since it makes little or no reference to social class, might well be misleading, the question of the role of young people and education in changing notions of 'own time' and domestic work is a central concern.

Does education have a role in changing gendered divisions of work and time?

As Adam (1995) notes, clock and rational time are extremely dominant at all stages of formal education. This is so whether we refer to the way educational institutions are organised through age cohorts and terms related to seasons of the year, the curriculum which often contains notions of the stages when particular kinds of knowledge are thought appropriate, or teaching and learning, which are usually divided by time slots and require the meeting of deadlines. 'Own time' and autonomous, self-directed learning are encouraged, if at all, only in the later stages of secondary education or in post compulsory education. In any case, cultural and informational capital affect the extent to which such opportunities are available and utilised.

Despite education's concern with clock and commodified time, in the public sector at least, it is one arena which could help people to cope with the pace and overload of modern lifestyles by using leisure or 'own time'. But these idea about 'own' time and slowing down are antithetical to the kinds of cultural changes which have recently been sweeping public sector services in western democracies. New managerialism, supported by left, centre and right political groupings, has tried to destabilise the caring professions by introducing more public surveillance and greater job insecurity (Clarke, Cochrane *et al.*, 1994; Clarke and Newman, 1994; Deem, Brehony *et al.*, 1995). Attempts to introduce so called 'enterprise cultures' to public sector organisations (Fairclough, 1991; Keat and Abercrombie, 1991), cultures which valorize speed of work as well as emphasising risk and profit, and prioritise the needs of consumers over producers, have been widely used in a number of countries. These attempts at cultural change have been accompanied by attempts seeking to introduce market principles and greater efficiency to public sector services, including education (Chubb and Moe, 1990; Le Grand and Bartlett, 1993; Deem, 1994a).

Currently, formal education does not appear to have much of a role in relation to leisure, though undoubtedly leisure occurs in the interstices of schooling (Griffin, 1985; Mac an Ghaill, 1989; Gilligan, Lyons *et al.*, 1990; Gaskell, 1992; Mirza, 1992; Wearing, 1992; Jones, 1993; Lees, 1993). So far as formal acknowledgement of leisure is concerned, and despite a long-standing debate about education for leisure, this occurs mostly, if at all, in adult education, the Cinderella of the education world (Thompson, 1983; Payne, 1991; Deem, 1993; Coats, 1994; Stacey, 1995). Some might want to make an argument that sport, which can be part of leisure, *is* an integral part of formal schooling. For a proportion of young people this is undoubtedly the case. However, as Scraton has demonstrated, for some young women, school sport does not correspond to something they want to do either before or after leaving school (Scraton, 1987; Scraton, 1992). Thus formal education, except for those forms of adult education which have so far escaped the pressures for all publicly funded education to be vocationally relevant, may not offer every young person ways of coping with the simultaneity of times and the pleasurable use of 'own' time.

However, this still leaves perceptions of and attitudes to gender roles as a major factor influencing use of 'own time'. Feminists have long suggested that schools were potentially good places to tackle these issues (Byrne, 1978; Deem, 1978; Arnot, 1985; Weiner, 1985). More recently, it has been suggested that whilst equal opportunities policies may have been a good strategy for achieving more favourable attitudes in the past, they may no longer be so appropriate in conditions of post modernity and post modernism (Arnot and Weiler, 1993; Middleton, 1993; Yates, 1993; Blair, Holland *et al.*, 1995). Indeed, some might argue that the pressing issue for gender relations in schools at present is that of boys, not girls. The under-achievements of the latter relate mostly, as we have seen earlier in the paper, to what happens after they leave education and enter the labour market. Instead of focusing on underachieving and unconfident school girls, some writers are suggesting that we turn our attention to under-achieving, pessimistic, introverted school boys (Wilkinson, 1994). This view and evidence of its existence is not a phenomenon confined to the UK; Weiss's USA based research on young women and men in an area of high industrial decline and unemployment also identified a growing mismatch between the future expectations and aspirations of girls and boys (Weiss, 1990). However Weiss's work may be distinguished from that of Wilkinson by the former's acute awareness of class and economic differentials and their relationship to the attitudes and aspirations of young people. Wilkinson herself suggests, though her evidence is flimsy, that generation is now a better predictor of attitudes and values than social class. There will, however, need to be much better empirical grounding of this claim if it is to be convincing.

Making boys rather than girls centre stage is not new in itself (Arnot, 1984; Askew and Ross, 1988). But as a growing literature on theoretical and empirical dimensions of masculinity inside and outside schooling has demonstrated (Brittan, 1989; Hearn and Morgan, 1990; Mac an Ghaill, 1994; Seidler, 1994), we can no more afford to ignore the cultural, social and economic dimensions of masculinity than we can those of femininity. Cultural capital is a central feature of the kinds of masculinities that young men develop, just as it is a key element in the gender identities adopted by young women. Whilst highly educated young men may acquire attitudes that favour androgynous gender roles and support a more equal division of labour in the home (Wilkinson, 1994; Cannon, 1995), this is not so likely amongst working class males, particularly those in areas where traditional 'male' jobs are no longer available and what awaits male school leavers are unemployment and poverty. Teachers, and educational policies, in conjunction with politicians and employers and a range of other social and economic policies, need to start to challenge the ways in which many young males develop gender identities and their approaches to life, including the issue of gendered divisions of labour in the home and in employment, Unless this happens then we will not see a shifting and rebalancing of gender roles and nor will we see a change in the way women and men regard and make use of 'spare' and leisure.

Conclusion: time for a change

In this paper I have explored a range of recent social theorising and empirical research on the themes of time, leisure, paid and unpaid work, education, and inter-generational shifts in cultural values towards gender roles. The purpose of this analysis has been to discover whether issues to do with gender relations are still relevant to issues of work, leisure and 'spare' time. Alternatively, have recent post structuralist and post modernist concerns focusing on difference and diversity reduced, or eliminated, the utility of perspectives on work and leisure which take gender relations and gender identities as a central feature? I have suggested that moves to eliminate gender and dismiss the utility of the concept of women, are not well supported by empirical evidence. These categories do still have significance for people in contemporary western societies.

I have also examined the extent to which, within formal education, there has been a transition from seeing equal opportunities concerns as connected to girls' under-achievement, low aspirations and pessimism, to a situation in which boys' under-achievement, low aspirations and pessimism have come to be perceived by some as a more intractable problem for educationists, politicians, employers, girls and women. I have suggested that whilst this view has some empirical support, attention still needs to be paid to social class differences; the concept of generation is not yet all-conquering. Furthermore, as I have shown, many women are still struggling in the home and at work to achieve the possibilities open to many men for more than a few decades.

In addition I have endeavoured to ask what has happened to the so called 'spare time' of women. This is a key question in the face of a perceived faster pace of life, and many other changes to our social condition and consciousness, particularly since there is evidence from many western societies that gender segregated divisions of labour have persisted both in the home and in employment. Those women (and a few men) who carry out the 'second shift' in the home may not share a common world, nor always feel oppressed. Enjoyment, autonomy and playfulness are, of course, not necessarily excluded by the need to do domestic labour and caring work. However, the scope of such obligations and responsibilities is likely to affect the quality of life of those who carry them. In particular, it may influence the extent to which those who do domestic work can prioritise 'own time' against clock time and the time hierarchies of others.

Finally, I have suggested that 'spare time' is not a concept that applies to everyone, since it is so closely linked to time 'produced' from what is left over after employment obligations have been fulfilled. Focusing on 'spare time' not only allows the perpetuation of the myth that work and leisure are binary opposites but also fails to draw our attention to the extent to which quality of life is linked both to values and behaviour in respect of gendered divisions of labour in the home. It is now time to act for change which challenges once and for all sharply divided gender relations, and the divisions of labour which are linked to them. Only then will both women and men be able to benefit fully from the novel and still changing conditions of life which dedifferentiate leisure and work, and which post modernists tell us are such a striking feature of life in contemporary societies.

Bibliography

Adam, B. (1990) *Time and social theory*. Cambridge: Polity Press.

———— (1995) *Timewatch: The social analysis of time*. Cambridge: Polity Press.

Arnot, M. (1984) 'How shall we educate our sons?', in R. Deem (ed) *Co-education reconsidered*. Milton Keynes: Open University Press.

———— (1985) *Race and gender; equal opportunities policies in education*. Oxford, Pergamon.

Arnot, M. and K. Weiler (eds) (1993) *Feminism and social justice in education*. London: Falmer Press.

Askew, S. and C. Ross (1988) *Boys don't cry: Boys and sexism in education*. Milton Keynes: Open University Press.

Beck, U. (1992) *Risk society: Towards a new modernity*. London: Sage.

Bella, L. (1989) 'Women and Leisure—beyond androcentrism', in E. Jackson and T. Burton (ed) *Understanding leisure and recreation: Mapping the past, charting the future*. State College, PA: Venture Publishing.

Blair, M., J. Holland, *et al.* (eds) (1995) *Identity and diversity*. Buckingham: Open University Press.

Bourdieu, P. (1987a) *Distinction*. London: Routledge.

———— (1987b) 'What makes a social class? On the theoretical and practical existence of groups', *Berkeley Journal of Sociology*, Vol. XXXII: pp. 1- 17.

———— (1990) *In other words.* Cambridge: Polity.

———— (1993) *Sociology in question.* London: Sage.

Brittan, A. (1989) *Masculinity and power.* Oxford: Blackwell.

Butler, J. (1990) *Gender trouble: Feminism and the subversion of identity.* London: Routledge.

Byrne, E. (1978) *Women and education.* London: Tavistock.

Cannon, D. (1995) 'The post modern work ethic', in Demos (ed) *The time squeeze.* London: Demos, pp. 31-2.

Central Statistical Office (1995) *Social focus on women.* London: HMSO.

Chubb, J. E. and T. M. Moe (1990) *Politics, markets and America's schools.* Washington DC: The Brookings Institute.

Clarke, J., Cochrane, A. et al. (eds) (1994) *Managing social policy.* London: Sage.

Clarke, J. and Newman, J. (1994) 'The managerialisation of public services', in J. Clarke, A. Cochrane and E. McLaughlin (eds) *Managing social policy.* London: Sage, pp. 13-31.

Clough, P. (1994) *Feminist thought.* Oxford: Blackwell.

Coats, M. (1994) *Women's education.* Buckingham: Open University Press.

Cockburn, C. (1991) *In the way of women.* London: Macmillan.

Cross, G. (1995) The all consuming work ethic, in Demos (eds) *The time squeeze.* London: Demos, pp. 21-2.

Davies, C. (1992) Gender, history and management style in nursing; towards a theoretical synthesis, in M. Savage and A. Witz (eds) *Gender and bureaucracy.* Oxford: Blackwell.

Davies, K. (1990) *Women, time and the weaving of the strands of everyday life.* London: Avebury.

Deem, R. (1978) *Women and schooling.* London: Routledge.

———— (1986) *All work and no play: The sociology of women and leisure.* Milton Keynes: Open University Press.

———— (1988) *Work, unemployment and leisure.* London: Routledge.

———— (1993) Popular education for women; a study of four organizations, in R. Edwards, S. Sieminski and D. Zeldin (eds) *Adult learners, education and training.* London: Routledge, pp. 235-250.

——— (1994a) 'Free marketeers or good citizens? Education policy and lay participation in the administration of schools', *British Journal of Educational Studies*, Vol. 42, No. 1: pp. 23-37.

——— (1994b) 'A Feminist Educator's Peregrination Through Sociology'. Inaugural lecture. Lancaster: Lancaster University.

——— (1996) 'No time for a rest? An exploration of women's work, engendered leisure and holidays', *Time and Society*, Vol. 5, No. 1: pp. 5-24.

Deem, R., K. J. Brehony, *et al.* (1995) *Active citizenship and the governing of schools*. Buckingham: Open University Press.

Deem, R. and P. Tinkler (1995) 'Women, the city and holidays'. Paper presented to British Sociological Association Conference, Leicester.

Desaulniers, S. and N. Théberge (1992) 'Gender differences in the likelihood that work reduction will lead to an increase in leisure', *Loisir et Societe*, Vol. 15, No. 1: pp. 135-154.

Dore, R. (1995) 'Who is actually in a hurry?'. Paper presented to annual meeting of the Association for the Social Studies of Time, Dartington Hall, Devon.

Fairclough, N. (1991) What might we mean by 'enterprise discourse'?, in Keat, R. and N. Abercrombie (eds) *Enterprise culture*. London: Routledge, pp. 38-57.

Farish, M., J. McPake, *et al.* (1995) *Equal opportunities in colleges and universities*. Buckingham: Open University Press.

Featherstone, M. (1990) 'Perspectives on consumer culture', *Sociology*, Vol. 24, No. 1: pp. 5-22.

Gaskell, J. (1992) *Gender matters from school to work*. Milton Keynes: Open University Press.

Gershuny, J. (1995) Time Keynsianism, in Demos (eds) *The time squeeze*. London: Demos, pp. 42-44.

Gilligan, C., Lyons, N. P. *et al.* (1990) *Making connections — the relational worlds of adolescent girls at Emma Willard School*. Cambridge, Mass: Harvard University Press.

Goodnow, J. J. and J. Bowes (1994) *Men, women and household work*. Oxford: Oxford University Press.

Gray, A. (1992) *Video playtime; the gendering of a leisure technology*. London: Routledge.

Green, E., S. Hebron, *et al.* (1990) *Women's leisure, what leisure*. London: Macmillan.

Gregson, N. and M. Lowe (1993) 'Renegotiating the domestic division of labour? A study of dual career households in north east and south east England', *Sociological Review*, Vol. 41, No. 3: pp. 475-505.

Gregson, N. and M. Lowe (1994a) *Servicing the middle classes*. London: Routledge.

——— (1994b) 'Waged domestic labour and the renegotiation of the domestic division of labour within dual career households', *Sociology*, Vol. 28, No. 1: pp. 55-78.

Griffin, C. (1985) *Typical girls*. London: Routledge.

——— (1989) 'I'm not a women's libber but ...', in S. Skevington and D. Baker (eds) *Feminism, consciousness and identity: The social identity of women*. London: Sage, pp. 189-91.

Handy, C. (1995a) *Beyond certainty: the changing worlds of organisations*. London: Hutchinson.

——— (1995b) *The empty raincoat: Making sense of the future*. London: Arrow Books.

Hearn, J. and D. Morgan (eds) (1990) *Men, masculinities and social theory*. London: Unwin Hyman.

Henderson, K. A., M. D. Bialeschki, *et al.* (1989) *A leisure of one's own*. University Park, AV: Venture Publishing.

Hewitt, P. (1993) *About time: The revolution in work and family life*. London: Rivers Oram Press.

——— (1995) 'Whose flexibility?', in G. Mulgan and H. Wilkinson (eds) *The time squeeze*. London: Demos.

Hochschild, A. (1989) *The second shift*. New York: Avon Press.

Hood, J. C. (ed) (1993) *Men, work and family*. Newbury Park California, London, Sage.

Jenkins, C. and B. Sherman (1981) *The leisure shock*. London: Eyre Methuen.

Jones, A. (1993) 'Becoming a "girl": post structuralist suggestions for educational research', *Gender and Education*, Vol. 5, No. 2: pp. 157-166.

Keat, R. and N. Abercrombie (1991) *Enterprise culture*. London: Routledge.

Keat, R., N. Whiteley, *et al.* (eds) (1994) *The authority of the consumer*. London: Routledge.

Lane, R. E. (1995) Time preferences: the economics of work and leisure, in Demos (eds) *The time squeeze*. London: Demos, pp. 2-11.

Lash, S. and J. Urry (1994) *Economies of signs and space*. London: Sage.

Le Feuvre, N. (1994) 'Leisure, work and gender: A Sociological Study of Women's Time in France', *Time and Society*, Vol. 3, No. 2: pp. 151-178.

Le Grand, J. and W. Bartlett (eds) (1993) *Quasi-markets and social policy*. London: Macmillan.

Lees, S. (1993) *Sugar and spice: Sexuality and adolescent girls*. London: Penguin.

Mac an Ghaill, M. (1989) *Young, gifted and black*. Milton Keynes: Open University Press.

—— (1994) *The making of men*. Buckingham: Open University Press.

Massey, D. (1994) *Space, place and gender*. Cambridge: Polity Press.

McNay, L. (1992) *Foucault and feminism*. Cambridge: Polity Press.

Middleton, S. (1993) 'A Post modern pedagogy for the sociology of women's education', in M. Arnot and K. Weiler (eds) *Feminism and social justice in education*. London: Falmer Press.

Mirza, H. (1992) *Young, black and female*. London: Routledge.

Mulgan, G. and H. Wilkinson (1995) *The time squeeze*. London: Demos.

—— (1995) 'Well being and time', in Demos (eds) *The time squeeze*. London: Demos.

Nicholson, L. (ed) (1990) *Feminism/postmodernism*. London: Routledge.

Pahl, R. (1995) 'Finding time to live', in Demos (eds) *The time squeeze*. London: Demos.

Payne, J. (1991) 'Understanding adult education and leisure', *Leisure Studies*, Vol. 10, No. 2: pp. 149- 162.

Pilcher, J. (1992) Social change and feminism: Three generations of women, feminist issues and the Women's Movement. Unpublished PhD. Cardiff: University of Wales.

Rojek, C. (1995) *Decentring leisure theory; rethinking leisure theory*. London: Sage.

Schor, J. (1992) *The overworked American*. New York: Basic Books.

—— (1995) 'The new American dream', in Demos (eds) *The time squeeze*. London: Demos.

Scraton, S. (1987) 'Boys muscle in where girls fear to tread — girls' sub cultures and physical activities', in J. Horne, D. Jary and A. Tomlinson (eds) *Sport, leisure and social relations*. London and Keele: Routledge.

Scraton, S. (1992) *Shaping up to womanhood: Gender and girls physical education.* Milton Keynes: Open University Press.

——— (1994) 'The changing world of women and leisure: "postfeminism" and leisure', *Leisure Studies,* Vol. 13, No. 4: pp. 249-261.

Seabrook, J. (1988) *The leisure society.* Oxford: Blackwell.

Seidler, V. (1994) *Unreasonable men: Masculinity and social theory.* London: Routledge.

Shaw, J. (1995) 'Why the rush?'. Paper presented to annual meeting of the Association for the Social Studies of Time, Dartington: Devon.

Shaw, J. and D. Perron (eds) (1995) *Making gender work.* Buckingham: Open University Press.

Shaw, S. M. (1991) 'Women's leisure time — using time budget data to examine current trends in future predictions', *Leisure Studies,* Vol. 10, No. 2: pp. 171- 181.

Shields, R. (1991) *Places on the margin.* London: Routledge.

Sianne, G. (1994) *Gender, sex and sexuality.* London: Taylor and Francis.

Stacey, C. R. (1995) *Experiences of women's education: Perceptions of change.* Unpublished Ph.D. thesis, University of Northumbria.

Tanton, M. (ed) (1994) *Women in management: A developing presence.* London: Routledge.

Thompson, E. P. (1967) 'Time, work discipline and industrial capitalism', *Past and Present,* Vol. 38 (December): pp. 52-97.

Thompson, J. (1983) *Learning liberation.* London: Croom Helm.

Tresilian, N. (1995) 'The three minute culture revisited'. Paper presented to annual meeting of the Association for the Social Studies of Time, Dartington: Devon.

Tyrell, B. (1995) 'Time in our lives: Facts and analysis on the 90s', in Demos (eds) *The time squeeze.* London: Demos. 2-11.

Urry, J. (1994a) 'Time, leisure and social identity', *Time and Society,* Vol. 3, No. 2: 131-149.

——— (1995) *Consuming places.* London: Routledge.

Wearing, B. (1992) 'Leisure and women's identity in late adolescence', *Loisir et Societe* Vol. 15, No. 1: pp. 323-342.

Weiner, G. (ed) (1985) *Just a bunch of girls.* Milton Keynes: Open University Press.

Weiss, L. (1990) *Working class without work.* New York: Routledge.

Wilkinson, H. (1994) *No turning back — generations and the gender quake*. London: Demos.

Wimbush, E. and M. Talbot (eds) (1988) *Relative freedoms:Women and leisure*. Milton Keynes: Open University Press.

Yates, L. (1993) 'Feminism and Australian State Policy: Some questions for the 1990s', in M. Arnot and K. Weiler (eds) *Feminism and social justice in education*. London: Falmer Press, pp. 167-185.

Young, M. (1995) 'Hurry sickness — a major disease of modern society?'. Paper presented to annual meeting of the Association for the Social Studies of Time, Dartington: Devon.

Athleticism: Origins, Diffusion, and Legacy in the specific context of Militarism, Masculinity, and Mythology[1]

J. A. Mangan
University of Strathclyde

Over recent years much time and effort, certainly on my part, have been devoted to stress the moral essence, and the astounding global consequences, of the curricular revolution in the influential late Victorian and Edwardian public school system of Imperial Britain.

> Athleticism, as this curricular revolution (and its corruptions) was termed, constituted a innovation, creating shock waves that travelled the length and breadth of the British Empire, leaving in their wake transformed educational policies and practices. In short, the ideology comprised in pure form an idiosyncratic reconstruction of the curriculum with playing fields as a major (but not an exclusive) setting for moral rehabilitation and redirection. (Mangan, 1989: end cover)

The ideology proved to be a major force for educational and social change, and its significance has been inexcusably neglected in studies of the making of the imperial, and, indeed, the global curriculum and society.

David D. Gilmore's *Manhood in the making: Cultural concepts of masculinity* is concerned with the way different cultures conceive and experience manhood: "the approved way of being an adult male in any given society" (Gilmore, 1990: p. 1). Gilmore is intrigued by the fact that so many societies construct an exclusionary image of manhood through trials of skill and endurance, by the fact that there seem to be "parallels in male imagery around the world" constituting "a ubiquity rather than a universality", and finally, by the fact that there appear to be continuities of masculine expectations across cultural boundaries; in particular, the demand made upon males to "be a man" or "act like a man" (p. 90) — an expectation of aggressive assertion.

23

Gilmore's attention has been caught by the apparently similar and the often dramatic manner in which cultures, past and present, non-literate and literate, define manhood. Can we speak, he asks, of a global masculine archetype born of trials and testing. "If there are archetypes in the male image," he surmises, "they must be largely culturally constructed as symbolic systems, not simply as products of anatomy, because anatomy determines very little in those contexts where the moral imagination comes into play. The answer to the manhood puzzle must lie in culture; we must try, therefore, to understand why cultures use or exaggerate biological potentials in specific ways" (Gilmore, 1990: p. 23).

It is appropriate at this point to note the conclusions of Clark McCauley in *The Anthropology of War*:

> ... Twenty years ago, Lorenz and Ardrey ... popularised the idea of an aggressive or killer instinct for aggression in warrior societies, but which was present to some degree in all humankind.... Anthropologists then and now find the hypothesis of a killer instinct not so much wrong as irrelevant to the kind of facts they want to explain. The Vikings of some hundreds of years ago are the notably peaceful Danes of today. The horse and gun made some people of the Shoshonean Basin — the Utes and Snakes — into warriors, and other people of the same basin — the poor Diggers — into fearful refugees. The gun and the market for sales made both the Miskito kingdom and its Sumo victims 'out of identical aboriginal material. (McCauley, 1990: p. 2)

In these examples, the rate of cultural change is too great to be a function of genetic differences. So McCauley (1990: p. 7) advances the notion of *pre-adaptation* — ecological change that leads to cultural adaptation mediated by human choice based on pre-existing culture. Historians of culture, claimed McCaulay, "are confident that the speed and direction of cultural change in relation to changed ecology could only be understood in terms of change consciously directed by the perceptions of human actors" (p. 8). Both directly and indirectly such arguments lead back to Gilmore who argues, unremarkably, that culturally endorsed ideals of manhood make an indispensable contribution both to the continuity of social systems and to the psychological integration of men into their communities. To understand the meaning of manhood from a sociological point of view, and, on occasion, as I hope to demonstrate, from a historical point of view, therefore, it is important to understand its social rather than individual functions *and* causes. And to Gilmore, it is clear that acts of manhood are frequently related to the extent of disciplined aggression required of the male In his opinion this simply demonstrates that life is mostly hard — and men, historically, have been given the dangerous tasks in the interest of the survival of the group. Thus while there may be no "Universal Male" it is possible to speak of a Ubiquitous Male — a quasi-global personage: "Man-the-Impregnator-Protector-Provider" (Gilmore, 1990: p. 223).

These three moral injunctions 'seem to come repeatedly into focus' whenever and wherever the word "manhood" is valued. They represent danger: "they place men at risk on the battlefield, in the hunt, or in confrontation with their fellows" (Gilmore, 1990: p. 223). Consequently if the group is to survive, boys must steel themselves to undertake such activities, must be prepared by various sorts of tempering and toughening, *and* must accept the fact that they are expendable Thus, states Gilmore, in a crucial passage, men too, nurture their society "by shedding their blood, their sweat, their semen..., by producing children, by dying if necessary in faraway places to provide a safe haven for their people" (p. 230). In short, manliness is a cultural construct with the important concomitant of martial expendability. And in Gilmore's words — most apt for my immediate historical purpose here (I will deal with the relationship to contemporary society later) — "in Victorian England, a culture not given over to showy excess, manhood was an artificial product co-axed by austere training and testing" (p. 18). In other words, an imperial masculinity consonant with empire building became a sexual imperative.

The making of masculinity is the focus of this paper. It is concerned with the cultural creation of a self-sacrificial warrior — an imperial elite — and with the conditioning of this elite — on the public school playing fields of the privileged; those important locations of an indoctrination into martial, moralistic manhood with eventually serendipitous global ramifications.

The morality associated with the games field inculcated and promoted Darwinian militaristic attitudes. Michael Howard has warned against subscription to "an alarming picture of pre-1914 Britain as a proto-Fascist society" (Howard, 1981: p. 352). While patriotic militarism existed, in his view, it was without bitterness or fanaticism and was "underpinned by a strong Christian ethic and leavened by the values of Victorian liberalism" (Howard, 1981: 352). This is a somewhat fanciful view — certainly as regards the British public school. In fact, there was little Christianity or liberalism in the Victorian or Edwardian public school pupil. Playing fields symbolised calculated subscription to harsh Social Darwinism and righteous Christian militarism. The one sustained the other — and society sustained them both.

One outcome was that "an epidemic of martial feeling"[2] attacked the young — outside and inside the schools. Geoffrey Best (1975) sought to discover the extent of this epidemic within the public schools where the officer elite of the British army was trained (p. 130). Discovery, he argued, was important not only to an understanding of the public school system but also to an understanding of far more profound and difficult questions such as the nation's attitude to war. It might permit detection of the sources of the militarism so conspicuous in pre-1914 European thought which, in his view, far more than 'incidents' and assassinations, telegrams and ultimata, were responsible for the Great War (p. 130). Within the schools Best noted a close relationship between militarism and sport, and suggested, certainly now uncontentiously, that public school games provided a "training in the qualities of the officer", while sport in general, was the direct road to the health and strength indispensable to the good soldier (p. 131). Best also noted that the language of the playing field was a marked feature of public school speech writing on military matters (p. 142). This was well illustrated by Baden-Powell in his book *Sport and War* published in 1900:

> 'What sort of sport did you have out there?' is the question with which men have, as a rule, greeted one on return from the campaign in Rhodesia; and one could truthfully say, 'We had excellent sport.' ... The work involved in the military operations was sufficiently sporting in itself to fill up a good measure of enjoyment. (Baden-Powell, 1900: p. 17)

Over and above the aggressive rhetoric of the playing field, the public schoolboy was exposed to a consistent martial rhetoric in the form of lectures from visiting speakers, headmasters' speeches, and chapel sermons. The words of Lord Esher to an Eton master were certainly heeded:

> It is most necessary that their minds as well as their bodies should be trained on military lines when they are young. It is just as important to be taught early to think correctly upon matters affecting the defence of our country and the Empire as to be taught the truths of history and science. (quoted Howard, 1981: p. 351)

Precept was translated into practice in unequivocal terms by General Sir Ian Hamilton who, on unveiling the Boer War memorial tablet at Glenalmond College, exhorted the boys to be ready to fight "for Glenalmond, Scotland and the Empire" and urged on them the adoption of the Japanese spirit of self-sacrifice: a willingness to meet a patriotic death "as a bridegroom goes to meet his bride" (Best, 1975: p. 145). With Field Marshall Roberts, Hamilton visited many British public schools to impress on their inhabitants the importance of military sacrifice, duty and enthusiasm. Without doubt this proselytism had its effect. There was a chauvinistic mutiny at Haileybury in 1900 at the time of the relief of Ladysmith touched off by the headmaster, Edward Lyttelton's refusal to grant a half holiday in celebration: "some 500 boys marched to Hertford singing 'Rule Britannia' and other patriotic songs" (Cecil, 1969: p. 143). And shortly before the Great War Robert Graves recalled a debate at Charterhouse in his last year, "that this House is in favour of compulsory military service" in which a mere "six votes of one hundred and nineteen were noes" (Graves, 1972: p. 53).

Within this new climate, a rhetoric of jingoistic conceit in poetry, prose and printing now coalesced into a triadic instrument of propaganda in which the subject of this paper — *the self sacrificial subaltern* — was celebrated. The sons of the upper middle class could not escape, even if they wished which was often unlikely, its sustained attack. In his autobiography of the years before the Great War, Esmé Wingfield-Stratford provides graphic and startling evidence of the impact of a rampant militarism on the young:

> ...the whole atmosphere of the time seemed to be faintly redolent
> of gunpowder; ... among those who professed and called themselves
> gentlefolk in the *fin de siècle* — and I think this would apply to
> an even wider circle — everybody seemed to be talking about those
> two linked attractions of war and empire. (Wingfield-Stratford,
> 1945: p. 74)

What Thomas Carlyle had insisted, many had come to believe. The national hero was now a warrior and a patriotic death in battle was the finest masculine moral virtue.

Militaristic songs, doggerel and verse then were a pronounced feature of the literature associated with late Victorian and Edwardian public schools and their staff, pupils and advocates (see Mangan, 1989: Ch. 4).

The imagery of chivalry penetrated deeply into the fabric of late Victorian culture. The subaltern — the instrument of imperial force — was now frequently portrayed as a mystic pre-medieval paladin. Imperial heroes were regularly compared to Knights, and Empire was the Holy Grail. Baden Powell's *Scouting for Boys* is heavy with chivalric images. He had originally intended to call his scouts "The Young Knights of the Empire" (Richards, 1992 p. 87). Romantic impulse led Ruskin also to espouse colonial rather than modern war. It offered greater opportunity for individual chivalric heroism (MacKenzie, 1992: p. 6). In this view, he was at one with many of his contemporaries. In one regard, Ruskin, however, was quite out of step. In his view "the knight has a shield and sword, not a bat and ball." For Ruskin sport was not war and war was not sport. Many differed with him — not least the plethora of public school officers who considered colonial wars more or less as sporting events. Colonial battlefields were exotic versions of the playing fields of Eton and elsewhere (MacKenzie, 1992: p. 10).

For many subalterns, war was a game:

> It would be a mistake to imagine that this light-hearted playing
> with fire had anything in common with the grim blood lust of Continental militarism. Nations with open frontiers, and every fit man a
> soldier, did not think of war as a game, played between professional
> teams for the entertainment of the ordinary civilian. But that was
> just how we, in those roaring 'nineties, did think of it. And though
> the best, it was only one of many games. (Wingfield-Stratford,
> 1945: p. 78)

And while the Boer War and the subsequent military reforms of Lord Haldane from 1906 onwards, especially his creation of a Territorial Army reserve, stimulated more extensive and systematic military training in the public school, as E. S. Turner has explained, there was little danger of officers becoming boringly professional:

Year after year they were going in for an ever-widening range of
sports .... If in this period, as General Fuller would have it, sport
developed into a 'pestilence', then the blame must fairly be laid on
the officers. Many others have criticised the British officer on the
ground that his obsession with games encourages him to look on
war in a sporting light ... [but] Such critics have usually minimised
the effect played by sport in creating *esprit de corps*, and in revealing those individuals — both officers and men — with stamina and
mettle. Other nations failed abjectly to understand the British
officer's attitude to sport. (Turner, 1956: p. 269)

The most famous public school versifier, who sang loud and often of the
relationship between public school playing field and imperial battlefield,
was Sir Henry Newbolt. Newbolt's poems in praise of the public schoolboy
at war and the public school as a preparation for war: "Sacramentum
Supremum", "Clifton Chapel", "The Schoolfellow", "The School at War",
"The Best School of All", "The Vigil", "The Grenadier's Goodbye", "The
Echo", "Commemoration" and, of course, "Vitaï Lampada", arguably, are
too well known to be considered here, yet again, but collectively they
should not be overlooked for what they were — a sustained paean to the
public school boy as sacrificial imperial subaltern.

However, Newbolt's poem of
bravery, "He Fell Among Thieves", should not be overlooked here. It has
special relevance. In his monumental study, *Heroic Poetry*, C. M. Bowra
asserted that this poetry was "a poor substitute for history, and for the
most part, should not be approached as if it were a record of fact". Its
relevance to history lies elsewhere — in revealing what "men believed and
felt" (Bowra, 1952: p. 535). The same is true of what he calls "post-heroic
poetry" which he suggests has different but essential features: the hero is
now subordinate to chivalrous dreams or national destiny or something
else. He has become an instrument of high designs and situations,
allegorical or symbolic (Bowra, 1952: pp. 559-561).

In "He Fell Among Thieves" a young officer fights to the last bullet, is
captured by bandits, is condemned to death, dreams in his last hours
before dawn, untroubled by hope or fear, of English childhood, schooldays
and college, and "strong on his feet" at first light is executed. The poem is
based on fact — up to a point. The officer was Lieutenant George W. Hayward, who, on an expedition to the Pamirs in 1878, correctly fearing an
attack on his camp by a local chief, sat up all night with a loaded revolver
beside him only to fall asleep before dawn and be killed. Lord Curzon
investigated the facts of Hayward's death in 1918 at Newbolt's request and
wrote later to Newbolt that, while in certain facts Newbolt had been incorrect, his picture was, of course, an idealised one "neither claiming nor
requiring historical accuracy." (Newbolt, 1927: pp. 406-407). In short, for
Newbolt, Hayward was not an unfortunate explorer but a heroic icon —
and in that role an inspiration to Newbolt's admiring schoolboy audience,

who, as Lady Desborough told Newbolt in 1921, included her sons Julian and Billy Grenfell (Newbolt, 1927: p. 409) — dead officer heroes of the Great War.

In *The Book of the Happy Warrior* Newbolt also took up the chivalric theme. He addressed himself "To All Boys" informing them that he had made available to them, for the first time in the English language, stories of some of the great warriors of history including Roland, Richard Coeur de Lion, St. Louis, King of France, Robin Hood, Bertrand de Guesclin, the Black Prince and Bayard. In reality, however, these stories were merely a means to make a point about modern chivalry and the modern English public schoolboy who (in Newbolt's view) in the admirable pursuit of empire, had "fought without hatred, and conquered without cruelty, and while doing so had preferred death, and even defeat to the deliberate use of foul means" (Newbolt, 1917: pp. 222-3). There were two great principles of chivalry, Newbolt told his boys of the empire: service to country and membership of a warrior caste — a brotherhood, past and present — founded on chivalrous team games because their great merit was that they made men not bookworms.

This, of course, was a common belief at the time. It was not the exclusive ideological property of Newbolt. In *The New Elizabethans* celebrating the lives of heroes of the Great War, and published after it, E. B. Osborn wrote:

> Cricket and football and the other English team-games are modern substitutes for the hard exercises of the mediaeval knights, and if either the hardness or the chivalry goes out of them, then they cease to provide the training in *moral* which is the most vital part of true education. The fact remains that the most important element in war — and in peace for that matter — and the most difficult to make sure of, is the moral element, and for that there is nothing like the old English school tradition. (Osborn, 1919: p. 2)

Ours is not an age in any way sensitive or sympathetic to the potency of the militaristic mythologies of late Victorian and Edwardian Britain. Perhaps then it is time to attempt, however inadequately, to understand the passion, power and persuasiveness of the Victorian myths, mythologies and mythmakers as part of a wider attempt to comprehend the nature of common processes of cultural conditioning into masculinity. The lead should be taken from Roy Porter who attempted, in his elegant biography of Gibbon, "to probe the problems and principles of history as they appeared in Gibbon's own time" rather than simply assess him in terms of today's values (Porter, 1988: p. iv).

It is a truism to observe that all men, women and children are products of their time as well as of biology and psychology. To appreciate their cultural indoctrination from infant to adult they must be set carefully in the context of their times:

And the Late-Victorian public schoolboys had grown up at a time when Britain was at her apogee.... They would have been brought up in the nursery on the patriotic verse of Robert Southey and Thomas Campbell. At school their minds would have been moulded by men with the robust and simple-minded patriotism of Charles Kingsley and of William Johnson Cory, that vehement enthusiast who taught so many future members of the ruling class at Eton, not least among them Lord Rosebery and Lord Esher. From schools where they came under the influence of such teachers, this generation passed to universities where they came in contact with professors like John Ruskin. (Howard, 1981: p. 341)

I have written on an earlier occasion (Mangan, 1988) that the Victorian and Edwardian public schools "produced composers of doggerel in profusion" and in a gentle rebuke of the doyen of public school history, E. C. Mack, who claimed that it was mostly uninspired, I added, that in context more than Mack allows, some of it was inspiring, and it did inspire. Mack, I repeat again, failed to understand its fervour; he underestimated its appeal; he seemed unable to comprehend its purpose — "He dealt in absolutes when he should have dealt in relativities". Its versifiers were "the voices of a period subculture; the poetasters of an upper class community" (Mangan, 1988: p. 143). Certainly they were limited in vocabulary, technique, expression. They were parochial and could be banal. But they were not without influence (Mangan, 1988: p. 143). Mack was not impressed by these public school bards but accepted that the public schools produced "responsible, honourable boys, willing to give their lives unquestionably to the preservation of Empire" (Mack, 1941: p. 143). He saw the wood but failed to appreciate the importance of the trees.

Throughout the Age of the New Imperialism, through indifferent but impassioned verse the magazines of the British public schools urged the 'crown of self-sacrifice' on their young readers: "the beau idèal was the warrior and the ultimate glory, sacrificial" (Mangan, 1988: p. 152).

The *Cheltonia* (quoted in Mangan, 1986a: p. 61), for example, asserted:

> Thy sons are noble and brave
> Ready to kill and save
> Though the rewards be grave
> For they honour thee.
> The soldier as he wounded lies,
> Lifts up his cold and glassy eyes
> Upwards to the burning skies
> While a far off voice replies
> 'Cheltonia honours thee'.

And on the death of General Gordon, it published this inspirational quatrain (quoted in Mangan, 1986a: p. 61):

> Gone from our sight, in our heart he still lingers;
> Crown of self-sacrifice — death — he has won;
> Martyr to duty, with witless finger,
> Beckoning onwards, our hero has gone.

It was a period characterised by militaristic verse in schools and society. A notable feature of the period were the anthologies of poems of war. Many were published between 1875 and 1914. The most successful was certainly W. E. Henley's *Lyra Heroica* published in 1891, which was reprinted nine times. Publication included a special edition for schools. Its purpose was "to set forth ... the beauty and the joy of living, the beauty and blessedness of death, the glory of battle and adventure, the nobility of devotion, ... the sacred quality of patriotism" (quoted Richards, 1992: p. 82). Some idea of the popular support for militaristic patriotic verse can be obtained from the press notices of *Lyra Heroica*, subtitled modestly, incidentally, "An Anthology selected from the best English verse of the sixteenth, seventeenth, eighteenth and nineteenth centuries", and of which, Henley himself wrote, "The speciality of this collection is that all the poems chosen are commemorative of heroic action and illustrative of heroic sentiment" (quoted in Henley, 1893: p. 13). Notices included (quoted in Henley, 1893: pp. 14-17):

The Saturday Review
> "A very fine book, which will, we hope, help to keep the blood of many English boys from the wretched and morbid stagnation of modernity."

The Pall Mall Gazette
> "Every boy ought to have this book, and most men."

The National Review
> "A manly book, which should delight manly boys and manly men ..."

The Irish Daily Independent
> "... it would be hard indeed to make a milksop of a lad nourished on these noble numbers."

The Graphic
> "By far the best book of verse for boys."

The British Weekly
> "A collection of the noblest verse in our language."

The Scotsman
> "Never was a better book of the kind put together, ..."

The National Observer
> "On the whole ... the most inspiring anthology with which we are acquainted."

Henley published a book of his own poems, *London Voluntaries*, subtitled *The Song of the Sword and Other Verses*, in 1893. In it, his recitative, "The Song of the Sword", dedicated to Rudyard Kipling, celebrated the chivalric company of imperial warriors, the power of their weaponry, and the glory of imperial aggression (quoted Henley, 1893: p. 35) —

Follow, O follow, then,
Heroes, my harvesters!
Where the tall grain is ripe
Thrust in your sickles:
Stripped and adust
In a stubble of empire,
Scything and binding
The full sheaves of sovranty:
Thus, O thus gloriously,
Shall you fulfil yourselves:
Thus, O thus mightily,
Show yourselves sons of mine —
Yea, and win grace of me:
I am the Sword.

— and the ecstasy of the sword of empire: "edged to annihilate, hilted with government" and the efficient instrument of the Will of God (quoted in Henley, 1893: p. 35):

Clear singing, clean slicing'
Sweet spoken, soft 'finishing;
Making death beautiful.

Inspired by the Boer War, Henley published *For England's Sake: Verses and Songs in Time of War* in 1900. It was dedicated to:

Frederick Hugh Sherston Roberts, V.C.,
Lieutenant, Kings Royal Rifle Corps
and to the many valiant souls whose passing
for England's sake has thrilled the ends
of the world with pain and pride.

(Roberts, killed in action at Colenso, was the son of Lord Roberts of Kandahar.)

For England's Sake (Henley, 1900: p. 11) includes a psalm to imperialism:

We are the Choice of the Will: God, when He gave the word
That called us into line, set at our hand a sword;
Set us a sword to wield none else could lift and draw,
And bade us forth to the sound of the trumpet of the Law.
East and West and North, wherever the battle grew,
As men to a feast we fared, the work of the Will to do.

to effacing self-sacrifice (p. 126),

Ever the faith endures,
England, my England:-
Take and break us: we are yours,
England, my own!
Life is good, and joy runs high
Between English earth and sky:
Death is death; but we shall die
To the Song on your bugles blown,
England — To the stars on your bugles blown.

and to expendable heroes (p. 16).

> So long as the One Flag floats and dares,
> So long as the One Race dares and grows,
> Death — what is death but God's own rose?
> Let the bugles of England play
> *Over the hills and far away!*

Such moral mandates, stern admonishments and evocative fantasies survived the Great War. In 1919 George Herbert Clarke edited *A Treasury of War Poetry* in which the *Sonnenkinder* of the Edwardian summers were remembered in phrases of ethereal glory — very different from the bitter language of Owen, Sassoon and Graves. Herbert Asquith's "The Fallen Subaltern" (Clarke, 1919: p. 373) recorded the burial of a young officer on the battlefield with Apollonian tenderness:

> As goes the Sun-god in his chariot glorious,
> When all his golden banners are unfurled,
> So goes the soldier, fallen but victorious,
> And leaves behind a twilight in the world.
> And those who come this way, in days hereafter,
> Will know that here a boy for England fell,
> Who looked at danger with the eyes of laughter,
> And on the charge his days were ended well.

Mildred Huxley wrote triumphantly of undergraduate officers in "Subalterns: A Song of Oxford" (Clarke, 1919: p. 128):

> They who had all, gave all. Their half-writ story
> Lies in the empty halls they knew so well,
> But they, the knights of God, shall see His glory,
> And find the Grail ev'n in the fire of hell.

In a rhapsodic verse entitled simply "The Dead" (Clarke, 1919: p. 393), Sigourney Thayer dreamed of the glorious living dead:

> But now my nights are filled with flowered dreams
> Of singing warriors, beautiful and young;
> Strong men and boys within whose eyes there gleams
> The triumph song of worlds unknown, unsung;
> Grim earth has vanished, leaving in its stead
> The shining glory of the living dead.

Joyce Kilmer in her "The New School" (Clarke, 1919: p. 260) described the haunting silence of studies, river and pitches as boys who had learnt to live now learned to die:

> For many a youthful shoulder now is gay with an epaulette,
> And the hand that was deft with a cricket-bat is defter with a
>   sword,
> And some of the lads will laugh today where the trench is red
>   and wet,
> And some will win on the bloody field the accolade of the
>   Lord.

The well-established relationship between soldier and sportsman won subscription as in Owen Seaman's athletic anthem, *"Thomas of the Light Heart"* (Clarke, 1919: p. 201):

> He takes to fighting as a game;
> He does no talking, through his hat,
> Of holy missions; all the same
> He has his faith — be sure of that;
> He'll not disgrace his sporting breed,
> Nor play what isn't cricket. There's his creed.

And the "games" of war and cricket for some still had their similarities (Clarke, 1919: p. 286):

> Full sixty yards I've seen them throw
> With all that nicety of aim
> They learned on British cricket fields.
> Ah, bombing is a Briton's game!
> Shell-hole to shell-hole, trench to trench,
> "Lobbing them over" with an eye
> As true as though it *were* a game
> And friends were having tea close by.

While for some, Heaven, for dead heroes, could only be a cricket-field (Clarke, 1919: p. 286):

> They left the fury of the fight,
> And they were very tired.
> The gates of Heaven were open quite,
> Unguarded and unwired.
> There was no sound of any gun,
> The land was still and green;
> Wide hills lay silent in the sun,
> Blue valleys slept between.
> They saw far off a little wood
> Stand up against the sky.
> Knee-deep in grass a great tree stood ...
> Some lazy cows went by ...
> There were some rooks sailed overhead,
> And once a church-bell pealed.
> *"God! but it's England,"* someone said,
> *"And there's a cricket-field!"*

In fact, it is simply not recognised that well into the Great War, and indeed after it, ordinary and obscure men and women, deeply moved by tragic events, struggled to put a naive and intense patriotism into verse — of a sort, that owed nothing to the perceptions and experiences of the celebrated war poets, but spoke still of a sacrificial, obligatory duty (Letts, 1917: p. 16):

> For he died for England's sake
> If thou so live
> If thou so give
> That road thyself shall take.

and the nobility, honour and fearlessness of "golden boys" (*ibid.* p. 16):

> These happy boys who left the football field,
> The hockey ground, the river, the eleven,
> In a far grimmer game, with high elated souls,
> To score their goals.

The icons were preserved. Perhaps they needed to be. For the many, rather than the few, their retained sacredness was a means of existing with horror, death and loss.

Women versifiers of the Great War were numerous but have been mostly ignored. *Scars Upon my Heart*, edited by Catherine Reilly and published in 1981, sought to remedy this situation. Her voices from the past all mourn for the dead. Reilly admits, perhaps reluctantly, that "sentimentality and patriotism certainly went together during the Great War years". Now, she states correctly, "we have less time for Rupert Brooke and his solemn young heroism". We hear only Sassoon and Owen — "reluctant heroes [who] both stayed submissive to the high-minded macho ethic of the English officer". The self-protective emotional reticence of male combatants draws far less sympathy from Reilly than the expressed emotions of female non-combatants. In their verse, she writes, patriotism and religion became inter-changeable. The soldier became Christ crucified as in Alice Meynall's elegiac "Summer in England, 1914" (Reilly, 1981: p. xvi) which ends:

> Chide thou no more, O thou unsacrificed!
> The soldier dying dies upon a cross,
> The very cross of Christ.

"This," remarks Reilly, most perceptively in my view, "is the poetry of England, inalienable from Honour, Duty, God, Christ and Sacrifice", celebrating not war but the sacrifice of youth — a sacrifice expressed with gratitude: "All flows from Duty" (Reilly, 1981: p. xviii). Reilly, herself, read "many of these patriotic poems with mixed emotion". They read to her of neither superficiality nor hypocrisy but of 'fearsome desperate nobility'. She fails to make the point, however, but it should be made — that this acceptance of "the rightfulness of Sacrifice" was the legacy of history.

Reilly offers us poems of both patriotism and protest — and, as she says, "many thoughtful stirrings in between"; but patriotism received her closest attention — there is simply more of it, and she seems to find it inexplicable. She gives little space in her volume, however, to Katherine Tynan.

If Sir Henry Newbolt was the loudest songster of war as glorious fulfilment, Katherine Tynan[3] was the purest chantress of war as the source of sacrificial destiny. Tynan portrays the Great War as an opportunity for chivalric obligation (Tynan, 1916 p. 43):

> Pinks and syringa in the garden closes,
> And the sweet privet hedge and golden roses,
> The pines hot in the sun, the drone of bees,
> They die in Flanders to keep these for me.

In two volumes of war poems *Flower of Youth: Poems in War Time* published in 1915, and *The Holy War* published the following year, she never deviated from images of laughing and graceful boys, choosing" the steep way that Honour goes" and passing sweetly and seemingly painlessly into paradise (Tynan, 1916: p. 15):

> Straight to his death he went,
> A smile upon his lips,
> All his life's joy unspent,
> Into eclipse.

or from descriptions of boys of her class, boldly and bravely at war, treating 'soldiering as sport' (Tynan, 1915: p. 31):

> He plays the game, winning or losing,
> As in the playing fields at home;
> This picnic's nothing of his choosing,
> But since it's started, let it come.

and always light-heartedly (Tynan, 1915: pp. 14-15);

> Gay as at Eton or at Harrow,
> Counts battles as by goals and runs:
> God keep him from Death's flying arrow,
> To give his England fighting sons.

To Tynan the battlefields of the Great War were scenes of 'simple chivalry' (Tynan, 1915: p. 58):

> I can see you where you stand,
> Knightly soul, so clean, so brave,
> With a new sword in your hand,
> Where the lilied banners wave.

to which Britain's young knights went enthusiastically in a just cause (Tynan, 1916: p. 20):

> The boy's heart now is set on a star,
> A sword for the weak against the strong.
> A young knight riding forth to the War,
> Who dies to right the wrong.

She never confronted reality.

Perhaps an indication of the influence of the unremitting proselytising of militaristic versifiers and others, may be gauged from the *War Letters of a Public Schoolboy* by Paul Jones published, with a memoir, by his father in 1918. Paul Jones was killed in France on July 31st, 1917. He was remembered by a master of his public school, Dulwich, as the embodiment of all that was best in the public school spirit — "the very incarnation of self-sacrifice." (Jones, 1918). Jones, however, was more than the stereotypic public school ideal of the period. He was in essence a modest version of a twentieth century reincarnation of Renaissance Man, *uomo universale* a Dulwich scholarship boy, Head of Modern Side, Editor of the School Magazine, Captain of Football and Victor Ludorum, and a Brackenbury scholar of Balliol College, Oxford. He appears, like many of his generation, to have had a total lack of cynicism and was to the modern eye almost impossibly naive, idealistic, and patriotic (see, for example, Slater, 1973: p. 2).

A month before he was killed, Jones wrote to his brother, a schoolboy at Dulwich, a statement that was Newboltian in style and substance:

> Have you ever reflected on the fact that, despite the horrors of the war, it is at least a big thing? ... The follies, selfishness, luxury and general pettiness of the vile commercial sort of existence led by nine-tenths of the people of the world in peace time are replaced in war by a savagery that is at least more honest and outspoken ... in peace time one just lives one's own little life, engaged in trivialities, worrying about one's own comfort, about money matters, ... just living for one's own self. What a sordid life it is! In war, on the other hand, even if you do get killed, you only anticipate the inevitable by a few years in any case, and you have the satisfaction of knowing that you have "pegged out" in the attempt to help your country. You have, in fact, realised an ideal, which, as far as I can see, you very rarely do in ordinary life. The reason is that ordinary life runs on a commercial and selfish basis; ...
>
> Personally, I often rejoice that the war has come my way. It has made me realise what a petty thing life is. I think that the war has given to everyone a chance to "get out of himself".... (Jones, 1918: pp. 3-4)

And like many public schoolboys of the time, he was obsessed by his school and schooldays. Their influence was profound:

> The more I see of life the more convinced I am of the greatness of the old school. Wherever you meet a Dulwich man out here, you'll find he bears a reputation for gallantry, for hard work and for what may be termed 'the public school spirit' in its best form. (Jones, 1918: p. 240)

His father recalled that among the few cherished personal possessions that he took with him into the zone of death were two photographs — one of the College buildings, the other of the Playing Fields. In his letter home he never failed to note the military exploits of Dulwich athletes (Jones, 1918: p. 2) or indeed, athletes of a more exalted rank:

> Do you realise what a fine part amateur sportsmen are playing in this war? I really doubt if there will be many great athletes left if things go on as they are doing. On the same day I read that Poulton-Palmer and R. A. Lloyd are gone. Only last year, I remember seeing those two as Captains of England and Ireland respectively, shaking hands with each other and with the King at the great Rugby Football match at Twickenham. I see news is to hand also of

the death in action of A. F. Wilding, a great athlete who never drank nor smoked. So in three days we have lost the most brilliant and versatile centre three-quarter in Poulton, the cleverest drop-kick in the world in Lloyd, and the world's champion tennis-player in Wilding! (Jones, 1918: p. 24)

Some idea of the affect of this influence on his perception of events, is conveyed by a remark he made in 1916:

> "If we are to win this War it will only be through gigantic efforts and great sacrifices. It is the chief virtue of the public school system that it teaches one to make sacrifices willingly for the sake of *esprit de corps*. Well, clearly, if the public school man holds back, the others will not follow." (Jones, 1918: p. 221)

On one occasion, he recorded, "I am finding the War a boring business, the glamour has decidedly worn off" (p. 219) and on another, he wrote, "This is a war in which there is nothing picturesque or romantic" (pp. 145-146). Nevertheless, in 1917 on being transferred, at his own request, from supply duties to a tank corps he exclaimed, "I am keeping splendidly well and am absolutely happy. By far the happiest time of my life since leaving school has been the last six months" (p. 252).

Jones is a convincing voice of conventional patriotism: for king, country and school. He is a product of the system which made him. He was not unusual except that he was articulate and was recorded for posterity. A few others like him — also members of the warrior elite of the public school system — have been similarly captured. The most striking example is the soldier-poet Julian Grenfell, educated at Eton and Balliol, who, in October 1914 from the Menin Road, south-west of Ypres, wrote to his mother:

> "We're all awfully well, except those who have stopped something. We have been fighting night and day — first rest today — for about four days ... I've never been so fit or nearly so happy in my life before; I adore the fighting ...." (Moseley, 1976: p. 238)

Later in the same letter he added, "I *adore* war. It is like a big picnic without the objectivity of a picnic" (Moseley, 1976: p. 238). Later he wrote, "The fighting excitement revitalises everything — every sight and word and action. One loves one's fellow man so much more when one is bent on killing him" (Moseley, 1976: p. 238). His biographer, Nicholas Moseley, observes of this blunt remark that Grenfell said things that other people might have felt but did not say. Grenfell, like Jones, was no crass hearty but a complex, contemplative man and his considered verdict was: "It is all *the* best fun. I have never felt so well, or so happy, or enjoyed anything so much. It suits my stolid health and stolid nerves and barbaric disposition" (Moseley, 1976: p. 238). Grenfell, wrote Moseley, "accepted the war and enjoyed it. He killed and was soon killed himself" (Moseley, 1976: Introduction). As Jeffrey Richards has reminded us in a most fundamental re-appraisal, the Great War was celebrated by others from the public school system:

> Conventional cultural history tends to see World War I as a watershed, with the disenchanted war poets and memoirists drawing on their front-line experiences to paint a grimly anti-heroic picture of a futile, wasteful and pointless war, a view which by extension is seen to have been generally accepted. What is forgotten is that their works tended to have a small circulation and to be restricted to the high-culture circles from which they had usually emerged in the first place. It is also the case that the war poets were probably equalled in number by serving officers who drew on their experiences to create a large body of fiction which glorified and mythified World War I, particularly for juvenile readers. (Richards, 1992: p. 81)

Nicholas Moseley, in an equally important passage in his biography of Julian Grenfell, claims that in the book he had tried:

> ...not just to describe life in an aristocratic family before the First World War, but to suggest states of mind that drove many families to embrace such a war; because there is evidence that behind the machinations and confusions of politicians in 1914 people had been brought up to feel that war was desirable and so, simply, wanted it ... when war came they and their friends entered into it eagerly and most of the young men were killed as if death was their justification. (Moseley, 1976: Introduction)

These public school officers were late Victorian and Edwardian *Sonnenkinder*. A society admired them and a community focused passionate attention on them (Green, 1977: p. 36). Martin Green has called them England's last true Children of the Sun (Green, 1977: p. 67). "The public school and university novels of the period make a cult of the frail figure in white, whose tirelessly elegant strokes, all through a long, golden afternoon, saves the team — and who later, though in scarlet now, saves the regiment out in the desert, still crying play up and play the game!" (Green, 1977: p. 60).

The apotheosis of the romantic alliance between playing field and battle field occurred on July 1st, 1916 at 7.30 a.m. on the notorious morning of the Battle of the Somme. It was a moment of terrible romantic tragedy! Captain Wilfred P. Neville's B. Company of the East Surrey Regiment attacked Montauban. As the officers' whistles shrilled and the regiment went 'over the top', the first man climbed onto the rampart into No Man's Land and as he did so, he kicked off a football: "It was a good kick, the ball rose and travelled well towards the German line" (Middlebrook, quoted in Veitch, 1984: p. 1). However, it was a bizarre game — by nightfall there were 57,470 officers and men dead, including Neville and many of his men. Their deaths inspired this banal but not empty elegy:

> On through the heat of slaughter
> Where gallant comrades fall
> Where blood is poured like water
> They drive the trickling ball.
> The fear of death before them
> Is but an empty name.
> True to the land that bore them
> The Surreys play the game. (quoted Veitch, 1984: p. 9)

In the fuller context of a more completed consideration of the rhetoric of jingoistic conceit in poetry, prose and pictures which constituted the full process of militaristic, literary and other propaganda in the late Victorian and Edwardian years I was at pains to stress that it is impossible to assess with certainty the influence of the rhetoric on the minds of both adolescent and adult but I maintained that it was reasonable to argue that it was not without influence. Indeed, it may have been, and probably was, deeply influential. Some of the time certainly claimed this (see, for example, Wingfield-Stratford, 1945: pp. 73-79). Subscription to the rhetoric had a certain logic.

Alan Swingeword has argued that it is literature in literate societies, that carries a major responsibility for establishing and sustaining the communal symbolism necessary for the survival of ideologies: "the 'styles' and 'forms' of living, dying, fighting and mating, is taught us in modern society through literary depictions." The argument may also be usefully extended to include art — and now the media. Structuralists like Roland Barthes have argued that the 'language' of a culture, defined as its *whole* system of signs, reflects the culture. However, it has been suggested that 'refraction', with its implications of a more subtle relationship, is a more useful term than 'reflection'. Others yet again, press for a more active role of 'language' in society, as an agent of change, conservation, dominance or resistance. All these points of view are concerned with cultural 'signs' as forms of power — both direct and indirect: Lèvi-Strauss's aphorism, "we do not think with myths but myths think themselves in us" is apposite here (Burke and Porter, 1987: pp. 12-17).

These brief reflections raise the issue of the role of system of signs in creating social reality. More specifically, it raises the question of the influence of the militaristic 'language' of late Victorian and Edwardian Britain. There is no way, of course, to measure with any accuracy the impact of images of war as a game, battlefields as playing fields and conflict as a match on schoolboy minds just as "there is no way to measure precisely, ... the effect of militant literary [and artistic] outpouring upon actual historical events" (Eby, 1987: p. 7). Cecil Eby suggests that probably in most cases the writer, and we will add the painter, like sensitive radar, responds to frequencies already pulsating in the ether and that in the period before 1914 popular literature, and we will add art, was so steeped in militant nationalism that the Great War, when it finally arrived, came like an ancient prophecy at last fulfilled (pp. 7-8). Whatever the truth of this assertion, the intention here has been to present the ideals, arguments and images of the writers and painters of late nineteenth and early twentieth century military patriotism rather more fully than is customary today, but much more than this, to suggest that they played a not insignificant part in the indoctrination of an elite community of sacrificial subalterns from the upper middle class, and imbued them with an uncomplicated concept of patriotism, imperialism and masculinity.

Of course, within the elite and within society some responded avidly, some less avidly, some remained unconvinced, some became disenchanted, but it is reasonable, in my view, to claim that many were convinced of the appropriateness of the projected martial image of masculinity.

And this image was functional, in at least three critical respects: it produced young men confident of their duty to fight and die; it offered psychological support for the bereft; it provided a martial culture to facilitate and sustain imperial expansion.

It could be argued that in the age of empire the imagery of militarism was a cultural imperative and the nature of the imagery of militarism was a necessary deception. To revisit Gilmore, it socialised upper middle class schoolboys into a 'male nurturing role' appropriate to the period and it disguised, sanctified and glorified their death in battle, assuring society of the appropriateness of their sacrifice.

And now a coda: to the simple minded educationalist, imperial militarism and the sacrificial subaltern was all a long time ago, and to quote Michael Howard:

> The consciousness of being an 'Imperial Race' was not widespread among the British after 1918. After 1945 it disappeared altogether. The way was clear for a new, but no less moralistic, generation to castigate their forbears for ever having entertained such illusions. (Howard, 1981: p. 355)

Do these illusions have any modern relevance? John Hoberman, who has written so well on the male body as a political icon, recently reflected on Gillie Perrault's views on fascism and youth. For Hoberman, Perrault's most interesting proposal is that the *violent idealism* of fascist athletic militancy has a clear political genesis. Fascism signified both "the festival of youth" and "the festival of the body"; there was a compelling conjunction between the psychology of adolescence and "the simplicity of the commands and imperatives of Hitler's nazism, ... the romanticism of war and death, ... the cult of hardness, ... the love of tumult". Between youth and nationalist socialism there was a harmony of inclination and intent (Hoberman, 1984: p. 104). The ideology had powerful, simple, convincing messages of certainty for its young and impressionistic audience. Fascism dealt in absolutes. It gloried in racial superiority, promoted action over intellect and endorsed the authority of the body. (p. 104). Hitler's moral aphorism delivered in his address to the German Gymnastics Festival in

1933, "Life will not be protected by weak philosophers but by strong men, encapsulated a militaristic ideology and legitimatised a sacrificial warrior community (p. 104) — with all its terrible consequences for us all.

With some justification, it may be claimed, that the New Imperial Britain of the late Victorian and Edwardian eras and Nazi Germany of the Nineteen Thirties both attempted to socialise a young elite into attitudes fundamental to the ambitions of the respective political regimes:

> This conditioning, involved values based on four interlocking spheres of socio-political consciousness — the need to establish an ideal of selfless service to the state, the need to establish a sense of racial superiority as a cornerstone of this selflessness, the need to establish and maintain an imperial chauvinism, ... and the need to engender uncritical conformity to the values of the group ... a major purpose of this interlinked set of values, was to create a 'fighting community,' ready to serve the nation in the plethora of its imperial struggles, large and small. (Mangan, 1986b: p. 116)

In both societies there was an unrelenting bombardment onto the minds of the young of specified and selective images of manhood, duty, heroism — and martial self-sacrifice. This indoctrination is perhaps better known in the case of Nazi Germany. However, as we have seen, it was also prevalent in British imperial society.

Such indoctrination, is relevant to, and has implications for, the current concern with the defining and structuring of masculinity and femininity. Both Imperial Britain and Nazi Germany confidently constructed images of male and female, their "natural and appropriate" roles, and the strategies of necessary socialisation into these roles. Self-evidently, of course, sexual image construction is closely related to the nature and purpose of political regimes and, in consequence, to the ideals and structure of their education systems — formal and informal. While British imperialism is a thing of the past, Fascism, in various forms, is a living ideology. It exists today within the democratic communities of Western Europe — and elsewhere in the modern world. And it has access to more powerful instruments of persuasion than ever before. Thus this study of indoctrination into a recent militaristic masculinity has its modern relevance.

On the part of the subtle-minded educationalist with an interest in cultures and their reality as much as concepts and their unreality, there is a willingness to reflect on the words of Marina Warner (1994): "modern myths of masculinity still approach the enigma of sexual difference using very old and simple formulae", and there remains an emphasis on warrior strength in the prevailing popular image of masculinity in comics, street fashion, rock bands and Schwarznegger-type movies. The paradigm of the Darwinist warrior is still dominant and the cry is not 'beware' but 'aspire'.

In the powerful transmitters of modern images in contemporary culture — the television channel, the computer game, the toy shop —

traditional mythic figures of masculinity like the warrior circulate and recirculate — providing desirable and desired role models. There is, says Warner, still an exaggerated insistence on aggression as the defining characteristic of heroism. Imperial militarism and its versifiers have their modern equivalents who peddle a familiar model of masculinity — perhaps, however, more ego-centric than socio-centric. If Warner is correct in rejecting sweeping assertions posing as sovereign truths beyond history and society, which claim that "the swagger and the cudgel" come naturally to men — the product of testosterone — and equally correct in accepting that masculinity is a cultural construct, what relevance has David Gilmore in his implicit if not explicit argument that aggression appears to be a cultural constant *required* of men by virtually all societies which carefully establish agents and agencies to foster it, presumably in the perceived interests of survival (Gilmore, 1990: esp. Introduction and Conclusion).

If he is right, the aggressive emphasis on his "male nurturing role" will not easily disappear. Societies will continue to demand it. A sanctioned aggression will continue to have a place in the mythologies of culturally approved masculinity. It will remain part of a Gilmorian cultural imperative and the Sacrificial Subaltern — trained on and off playing fields — will serve as a model for future imitation as an illustration of effective social strategies for socialisation into militaristic masculinity *and* as a demonstration of the force of continuity as well as change in cultural history.

A final thought: in the face of both the retention and the resuscitation of the ancient alluvial fields of Eastern Confucianism, the seismic irruptions of Islamic Fundamentalism, the tremors of ethnic hostilities, the deserts of modern totalitarianism and above all, the recurring bloody floods of history, will an assertive minority, a surface layer perhaps on an ancient bedrock in modern technological, pluralistic democratic cultures, inside and outside their educational systems, *fundamentally* deconstruct *and* reconstruct cultural masculinity? Perhaps not. We must simply wait and see.

Notes

[1] Ideas and text for this article are drawn from material to be published respectively in 1996 in J. A. Mangan (ed) *Tribal identities: Europe, nationalism and sport* to be published by Cass, under the chapter title 'Duty unto death: English masculinity and militarism in the age of the New Imperialism'; and in J. Nauright and T. Chandler (eds) *Making men: Games and masculine identity in Britain and Empire* to be published by Cass, under the chapter title 'Gamesfield and battlefield: A romantic alliance in verse and the creation of militaristic masculinity'.

[2] Vividly described by Esmé Wingfield-Stratford (1945) *Before the lamps went out*, London: Hodder and Stoughton, p.73.

3 Many of her verses first appeared in newspapers and journals including *The Times, The Spectator, The Cornhill Magazine, The British Review, The Windsor Magazine, The Tablet and The Westminster Gazette.*

References

Baden-Powell, R. S. (1900) *Sport in war.* London: William Heineman.

Best, G. (1975) 'Militarism and the Victorian Public School', in B. Simon
and I. Bradley (eds) *The Victorian Public School.* London: Gill and
Macmillan, pp. 129-46.

Bowra, C. M. (1952) *Heroic poetry.* London: MacMillan.

Burke, Peter and Roy Porter (1987) *The social history of language.* Cambridge: Cambridge University Press.

Cecil, R., (1969) *Life in Edwardian England.* London: Batsford.

Clarke, George Herbert, (ed) (1919) *A treasury of war poetry.* London:
Hodder and Stoughton.

Eby, Cecil Debrotte (1987) *The road to Armageddon: The martial spirit
in English popular literature 1870-1914.* Durham: Duke University
Press.

Gilmore, D. D. (1990), *Manhood in the making: Cultural concepts of masculinity.* New Haven: Yale University Press.

Graves, Robert (1972) *Goodbye to all that.* Harmondsworth: Penguin.

Green, M. (1977) *Children of the sun.* London: Constable.

Henley, W. E. (1893) *London voluntaries.* London: David Nutt.

———— (1900) *For England's sake.* London: David Nutt.

Hoberman, J. (1984) *Sport and political ideology.* London: Heineman.

Howard, M. (1981) 'Empire, Race and War in pre-1914 Britain' in H. Lloyd-
Jones et al., *History and imagination.* London: Duckworth, pp. 340-
355.

Jones, P. (1918) *War letters of a public schoolboy.* London: Cassell.

Letts, W. M. (1917) *The spires of Oxford,* New York, E. P. Dutton,.

Mack, E. C. (1941) *Public schools and British opinion 1780-1860,* New York,
Columbia University Press.

MacKenzie, J. M. (1992) 'Introduction', in J. M. MacKenzie (ed) *Popular
Imperialism and the Military 1850-1950.* Manchester: Manchester
Manchester University Press.

Mangan, J. A. (1986a) *The games ethic and imperialism.* Harmondsworth:
Penguin/Viking.

—— (1986b) 'The grit of our forefathers: Invented traditions, propaganda and imperialism', in J. M. MacKenzie (ed) *Imperialism and popular culture*. Manchester: Manchester University Press, pp. 113-139. .

—— (1988) 'Moralists, metaphysicians, and mythologists: The 'signifiers' of a Victorian and Edwardian sub-culture', in S. J. Bandy (ed) *Coroebus Triumphs*. San Diego: San Diego State University Press, pp. 141-162 .

—— (1989) *Athleticism in the Victorian and Edwardian public school: The emergence and consolidation of an educational ideology*. Falmer: Falmer Press, 1989.

—— (1994) 'Duty unto death: The socialisation of a self-sacrificial warrior elite', Paper presented to the International Conference: 'Elites and Aristocracies', University of Toulouse, September.

McCauley, C. (1990) 'Conference overview', in J. Hass, (ed) *The anthropology of war. Cambridge:* CUP, 1990, pp. 1-10.

Middlebrook, M. (1986) *The first day on the Somme*, quoted in Colin R. Veitch, 'Sport and war in the British literature of the First World War 1914-1918', unpublished M.A. thesis, University of Alberta.

Mosley, N. (1976) *Julian Grenfell: his life and the times of his death*. London: Weidenfeld and Nicolson.

Newbolt, H. (1917) *The book of the Happy Warrior*. London: Longman's, Green and Co.

Newbolt, M. (1927) *The later life and letters of Sir Henry Newbolt*. London: Faber and Faber.

Osborn, E. B (1919) *The New Elizabethans*. London: John Lane.

Porter, J. (1988) *Gibbon*, London: Weidenfeld and Nicolson.

Reilly, C. (ed) (1981) *Scars upon my heart*. London: Virago.

Richards, J. (1992) 'Popular imperialism and the image of the army in juvenile literature', in J. M. MacKenzie, *Popular imperialism and the military 1850-1950*, Manchester: Manchester Manchester University Press, pp. 80-108.

Slater, G. (1973) *My warrior sons: The Borton Family Diary 1914-1918*. London: P. Davies.

Turner, E. S. (1956) *Gallant gentlemen: A portrait of the British officer 1600-1956*. London: Michael Joseph.

Tynan, K. (1915) *Flower of youth*. London: Sidgwick and Jackson.

—— (1916) *The holy war*. London: Sidgwick and Jackson.

Warner, M. (1994) *The Reith Lectures*, BBC Radio 4, January/February.

Wingfield-Stratford, E. (1945) *Before the lamps went out*. London: Hodder and Stoughton.

White Boots and Ballet Shoes — Girls Growing Up in the 1950s

Deborah Philips

Brunel University College

I write about sport not as someone who was ever an active participant: I was one of those girls who 'dreaded games', but I did read about it. Sport clearly means something beyond its immediate form of activity in fiction for young women; in this paper I want to address the question of what it is that sport comes to signify in popular writing for girls in the post war decade of the 1950s, a period in which gender roles are undergoing a radical transition. I refer particularly to two novels by Noel Streatfield, *Ballet Shoes: A story of three children on the stage* (1936) and *White Boots* (1951), texts which I can be almost sure have been read and remembered with affection by a majority of women readers, but which most men will probably not have heard of at all (unless they have daughters). *Ballet Shoes* and *White Boots* and girl's comics are part of a generally unacknowledged shared reading among women, a culture which has been spoken of by feminist critics as:

> ... a common store of juvenile literary experience, ... [a] collective cultural inheritance that ... is one in which men had generally not participated.... (Foster and Simons, 1995: p. ix)

The 1950s has been constructed by most journalists and by literary and cultural critics in very particular ways. It is now largely perceived as the decade of the 'Angry Young Man', a period in which femininity features only marginally, and in which the experience of becoming an adult is only really written about significantly by men. Boris Ford's *Pelican Guide to Literature: The Modern Age* first published in 1961 and still in print in 1991 (which remains a standard text in libraries and which continues to perform the function of a crib for students) lists only five women writers in its appendix of over 120 significant writers and works of the period. The essay on 'The Novel Today' refers only to Ivy Compton Burnett and Iris Murdoch in its account of the decade's important novelists (Phelps, 1961). More recently,

Alan Sinfield's 1983 key collection on the period *Society and Literature 1945–970* refers to only 32 women in an index of over 500 entries, Robert Hewison's *In Anger: Culture in the Cold War 1945–1960* (1988) in an even longer list only manages 43 (and those references include as wide a range as the Queen, Mary Whitehouse and Twiggy).

This representation of the 1950s as dominated by male writers and critics is mirrored in a great many taught courses on the period, in which Joan Littlewood, Shelagh Delaney, Iris Murdoch and Muriel Spark are often the only women writers who feature. And yet, as Elizabeth Wilson points out in her important corrective *Only Halfway to Paradise: Women in Postwar Britain* (1980), the decade of the 1950s is a key moment in the refiguration of gender roles in the period after the war, when women had made a major incursion into the world of the work. The post-war years saw substantially more working women, and these were often engaged in different forms of work than would have been available to them in the pre-war years. There now were now double the number of women working in engineering, transport and other forms of labour that had opened up to women through the need to employ them during the war (for a fuller version of this point, see Philips and Tomlinson, 1992).

I have been concerned with the way in which this social change was experienced and represented by women themselves. It seems that the best place to look for this is in texts we know to have been popular among women. Romance fiction, writing for children, magazines and comics may be ephemeral forms of culture which do not enjoy high status, but it is precisely because they are not read with very great seriousness and because they are frequently overlooked in historical accounts of the period that they can offer valuable clues to the contradictions, aspirations and dilemmas of growing up as a young woman in the 1950s.

I want to address here some of the ways in which girls entered into the Brave New World of the 1950s; and to do so by reference to a set of texts which were written and read exclusively by women.
In 1957 Richard Hoggart could refer to the reading of comics as:

> ... a passive visual taking-on of bad mass art geared to a very low mental age. (p. 164)

In fact, the comic of the 1950s for young women (and there is no distinction in these texts between the pre- and post-pubescent girl) is hardly designed as a passive experience; *Girl* magazine and *Girl's Crystal*, the two comics that I have been most concerned with, are full of injunctions to become involved in activities and in the community. And the majority of these activities are physical or sporting.

Hoggart is also appalled by the incursion into British culture of what he calls:

> American or American type serial-books or comics, where page after page big-thighed and big bosomed girls from Mars step out of

their space machines and gangsters' molls scream away in high powered sedans. (Hoggart, 1957: p. 164)

Hoggart is here referring (as he continues to throughout *The Uses of Literacy*) exclusively to children's comics addressed to boys; girls in comics for girls such as *Girl* and *Girl's Crystal* are represented rather differently. Some indeed may be big thighed, but they do not appear as big bosomed until the 1960s, a point I will take up later. Hoggart may be an easy target, but he is not alone as a contemporary cultural critic who completely ignores the equivalent form of popular reading for young women.

Titles like S*choolgirl*, *Girl's Crystal*, *Girl*, and annuals and comics for girls in this period in fact refer hardly at all to the male gender. What is foregrounded instead are the activities and achievements of young women, almost always represented in an all-female world (occasionally a father or brother may pass through the frame of the narratives, but these are not considered as particularly significant figures in the lives of their heroines). And those achievements are almost entirely portrayed as in the field of physical activity; stories from these comics consistently endorse a prevalent educational model of sporting and physical activities as both morally improving and as a means of arriving at a proper sense of citizenship and of maturity. Sporting and physical training is also frequently evoked in these texts explicitly as a preparation for a career, a position which is further supported by feature articles which advise young women on the exciting career prospects offered in the post war world.

Sporting prowess and/or physical ability are invariably shown in these stories to be the means by which the young woman can come to gain respect from a community that is wider than her immediate nuclear family or school environment. Whatever these physical skills might be (and they include swimming, running, rock climbing, riding and sailing among many others) they are shown to have an effect beyond the individual achievement of the heroine. Whether her prowess has contributed to the rescuing of a puppy, a human being, the saving of a lost manuscript or treasure (and these are all stories that can be found in the *Girl's Crystal* annual of 1951) matters very little. What is consistent is the final frame of the comic strip. These almost always depict a young woman being rewarded for her competence and for her contribution to the social good: the reward might consist of a trophy, a medal, a cup, a cheque, a major role with the ballet company — but it is awarded by a respected figure from outside the immediate community. This figure, and it is almost always (although, importantly, not invariably) a man, may be a mayor, a West End theatre producer, an eminent writer, or a chief constable, but he stands as a representative of a welcoming and suitably appreciative wider adult world.

In *The Uses of Literacy* Hoggart refers to sport as a culture of resistance. But what he does not refer to at all is a sporting culture for women. The benefits of sporting and physical activities for young women had had a long history by the time that these stories appear as popular narratives. In the pre-war period, active participation in sporting activities seems to have been very much part of the lives of ordinary women: the Women's League of Health and Beauty had 120,000 women members in 1937. The enormous popularity of the 'Keep Fit movement' is an example of the engagement of women in developing their physical skills: Keep Fit was a form of exercise specifically addressed to women which was originally based on Swedish Gymnastics, in being taken up by the National Council of Girls clubs it was to become part of a mainstream culture for young women. [For more on the history of women's involvement in fitness and sporting movements in this period, see Hargreaves (1994) and Fletcher (1984).]

The attractions of dance, slimness, health and fitness led to a move-ment of women's involvement in sporting activities which was quite clearly seen not only as a source of physical benefits, but also as a means of achieving emotional satisfaction. Schoolgirl achievement in the novels of Angela Brazil, who was writing her boarding school stories from 1906 to 1946, is marked out not in academic or social success, but in the achieve-ments of the lacrosse or hockey field, or in acts of bravery, which are con-tingent on physical ability (see Freeman, 1976).

Noel Streatfield's 1936 novel *Ballet Shoes*, although it continues to be widely read and was a key children's book throughout the 1950s, is very much a product of the 1930s, in its assumption that physical training is an absolutely appropriate form of activity for the proper development of young women. As a 1939 article in the *Journal of Physical Education* ex-plains:

> The contemporary dance form affords an excellent physical and functional training of the whole body with an immediate goal and purpose.... (quoted in McIntosh *et al.* 1981: p. 225)

The three young girls who are the central protagonists of *Ballet Shoes* all learn to dance, and dancing is the means by which they are all launched into a world of work. The Fossils grow up in an all-female world and are ef-fectively put to work to support their non-biological family (for a very com-plicated set of narrative reasons). Pauline, the eldest, finds her skills di-rected towards acting, while the middle child, Petrova, discovers a talent for understanding the complexities of car and finally aeroplane engines; these talents are quite clearly presented as recommendations that a young girl should develop her abilities and learn the skills for a professional fu-ture. It is, however, Posy's talent and commitment to her ballet classes that command the most narrative space in the novel (as most readers will re-member). Posy's ballet training, which is shared with her two sisters, com-bines creativity, aesthetics and cultural capital with physical prowess. Dancing is seen in *Ballet Shoes* as a means of controlling and training the girl's body into an appropriate form of adult womanhood. But it is also seen as the means of offering a secure and independent future.

Physical strength and prowess are attributes in women that were val-ued throughout the war years and which continued to be so in the post-war reconstruction. Women took over the entire field of physical education from men recruited into active service, and were professionally trained by their local authorities for the purpose. Physical activity and the importance of sport and recreations for both boys and girls are particularly specified in the 1944 Butler Education Act, which includes in its provisions for a new form of national education:

> ... adequate facilities for recreation and social and physical training.

The Butler Act's raising of the school leaving age to 15 meant that numbers of young people in the primary and secondary schools population rose by one million between 1951 and 1964. These increased numbers meant that secondary schools had to extend their provision and improve their facilities, including those for sports, while the 1952 Town Development Act privileged the building and improvement of schools and hospitals.

The increase in the number of children above the age of 14 also meant a rethinking of leisure and sporting provision. Games which had been appropriate to younger children had to be developed into new ways of thinking about sport for adolescents.

The provision of facilities and new forms of sporting activity and its benefits for physical well-being were clearly on the agenda in post-war Britain, and foregrounded as an issue in education for both boys and girls. In a 1962 statement (that could have been made just as well anywhere else in the country) the Medical Officer of Health to the London County Council could affirm, acknowledging the beneficial effects of sporting and recreational facilities:

> ... the general improvement in the health of London school children. Of the children inspected during 1961, 99.2 per cent were found to be in a satisfactory physical condition. (quoted in Lowe, 1988: p. 78)

Sporting activity was not however just about physical well being, it was also associated with social training. As Sir Edward Boyle, Conservative minister of Education, stated in 1958, acknowledging the influence of the physical education movements of the 1930s and their integration into the school curriculum:

> What we are concerned with in education is, first and foremost, the development of human personality. Here, as I see it, we have made very great strides in Britain since the war. It is impossible to ignore the very great effect which developments such as the introduction of free movement classes have made upon the post-war generation .... (quoted in Lowe, 1988: p. 87)

In practice however, the declared commitment to secondary level provision for school sporting facilities was not to survive for very long under the conservative government, and the promises inscribed in the Butler Act were pared down; 1954 saw the Swinton Committee set up to find ways of saving money in education, and it was secondary schooling that suffered in comparison to further and higher education.

The national foregrounding of the importance of physical activity for young people in the post war period nonetheless inevitably found its way into reading material for young women, and sports are a regular and important feature of contemporary comics and annuals. The frontispieces for annual compilations of stories for girls always picture young women engaged in the full range of sporting activities: they are to be seen jumping, sprinting, swimming, diving, sailing, pot-holing, ski-ing. Of the fifteen stories in the *Girl's Crystal* Annual of 1951, eight centre around a form of physical activity; its front cover features two young women steering a small yacht round perilous rocks, and its frontispiece depicts five girls skilfully negotiating a steep slope on skis.

The reading of fiction and of magazines had increased considerably throughout the war years; it is well documented that the reading of fiction had survived paper shortages and distribution difficulties to become a major form of the consumption of culture (see Philips and Tomlinson, 1992). Post-war versions of magazines and popular novels for young women are a very rich source for understanding the new gender roles that the post war reconstruction demanded, because they were so widely read, and so clearly touched on concerns that were shared by a great many female readers. It is impossible to arrive at accurate reading figures for comics and annuals: many of their publishers are now defunct and of those that survive, most no longer keep documentation from the post-war period. However, the continuing circulation of these texts, demonstrated in the fact that they continue to appear at bazaars, fêtes and second hand bookshops suggests that they were read very extensively, and that they had a readership that extended beyond the initial purchaser. My copy of the *Girl's Crystal* Annual for 1951 (see Figure 1) bears the handwritten inscription:

> "If this book should chance to roam, box its ears and send it home ...by 2nd July."

The precise date here is an indication that these texts were frequently borrowed, and often circulated in a form of unofficial library.

Girl's annuals and comics in this period consistently endorse the prevalent educational model of sporting and physical activities as both morally improving and as a means of arriving at a proper sense of citizenship and of maturity. It is important to remember that the 'teenager' is a construct of the late 1950s — the distinction between adolescence and pre- and post-puberty is not marked in fiction for young women in this period as it was to be from the 1960s. This is apparent in magazines and comics for girls too, where the cut off age of childhood is not defined as it would be in magazines marketed from the 1960s onwards.

The stories in these comics and annuals can be understood as what literary critics would define as *bildungsromans* (see Bullock *et al.* (eds)

Figure 1   "If this book should chance to roam…"

(1988: p. 79): that is, tales which chart a learning experience in which a young protagonist arrives at the end of the narrative at maturity and increased wisdom [Charlotte Bronte's *Jane Eyre* (1847) and Charles Dickens' *David Copperfield* (1850) are examples of *bildungsroman*]. This structure is clearly identified in contemporary novels for young women, many of which take sport as a central motif and as the arena in which their heroines learn the lessons of young adulthood.

Noel Streatfield's *White Boots*, first published in 1951 and in print ever since, is a particularly good example; in which a sporting activity can become a metaphor for the trials and tribulations of adolescent life. The narrative employs skating as a means by which Harriet experiences and finds her way through the complex emotional and psychological demands of growing up.

Skating, like ballet for Posy in Streatfield's earlier novel *Ballet Shoes*, offers a whole range of skills and knowledges to its young heroine Harriet; with increased physical confidence, she also achieves maturity and understanding. Dedication to a sport offers lessons beyond those of physical capabilities: the competitive arena and the possibilities that the sport offers are also seen as a means of negotiating increasingly complex sets of personal relationships; with the triumphs and failures of skating come the lessons of learning how to face disappointment, and of how to experience rivalry. The sport is also presented as a way for young girls to learn how to present themselves to the adult world, literally so in the case of skating, where self-presentation is one of the categories that is judged. As Hargreaves (1994) remarks, of sports that are construed as 'appropriate' forms for young women:

> Body presentation which makes more visible the form and sexuality of the female body has become increasingly noticeable in particular female sports. Those which emphasize balance, co-ordination, flexibility and grace (such as gymnastics, ice-skating and synchronized swimming) are characterized as 'feminine-appropriate' — they affirm a popular image of femininity and demonstrate their essential difference from popular images of sporting masculinity. (p. 159)

While it may be the case that these particular physical activities are confined to a particular ideology of femininity, the skills and dedication required of a sport such as skating are not underestimated in *White Boots*. The qualities of "balance, co-ordination, flexibility and grace" are seen to be not only important in themselves, but also as a means of increasing confidence and assertion in the personal lives of its young heroines. The chapter headings of the novel offer a direct structural analogy between the achievements and dramas of the sporting arena and of significant family events: domestic titles ("Lalla's House", "Aunt Claudia", "Sunday Tea") are alternated with titles that denote stages in a sporting career ["Inter Silver Medal", "Skating Gala", "Silver Test"].

Physical exercise is also clearly signalled as a means to health in *White Boots*. Harriet, the young heroine (her age is, significantly, unspecified — but she is referred to by adults in the novel as a child), takes up skating as part of a convalescence from an unspecified illness. Her mother is advised to send her to skating lessons by a male doctor who has clearly been influenced by ideas of the Keep Fit movement (p. 216). Despite the provisions of the 1944 Education Act, Harriet's school cannot provide the sporting facilities that she needs and she is sent to a local ice rink where she encounters a new friend, Lalla. From a genteel but impoverished family, Harriet is set against the wealthy but orphaned Lalla in ways which are very revealing about post-war shifts in class formation. For Lalla, skating explicitly represents a career path; the daughter of professional skaters, she is being groomed for international competition. Harriet, however, discovers a new confidence and set of skills in her own initially incompetent attempts at skating and, in the final chapter, both girls come to see skating as a forum for their ambitions for the future. The final lines of the novel are spoken by Lalla — "Don't you all want to know what happens to Harriet and me? Because I do" — an address to the reader that implies very serious ambition.

By the late 1950s, the 'girl's' magazine which dealt with adolescent experience no longer addressed the questions of growing up in terms of the sporting arena. From 1957 a host of new magazines for young women appear, whose titles clearly signal that the newly identified 'teenager' should concern herself with love, romance and male pop stars. In his study *The Teenage Consumer*, Mark Abrams (1959) had defined what the publishers of comics and popular fiction had already recognised; the post-adolescent girl was now an economically significant category, who could use her leisure time more profitably in the consumption of records, fashion and cosmetics than on the playing fields. And, as he explained:

> Teenagers more than any other section of the community are looking for goods and services which are highly charged emotionally.
> (quoted in Hall *et al.*, 1964: p. 278)

Ballet, skating and sporting prowess were clearly no longer seen by the publishers of popular fiction as sufficiently highly charged for the teenager of the late 1950s. 1957 saw the launches of *Romeo*, *Roxy* and *Valentine*, followed by *Boyfriend* and *Marty* (named for the singer Marty Wilde) in 1959 and by *Flair* and *Honey* in 1960. The swimsuited girl is featured in these new comic strips not as an active, healthy and fit achiever, but as an object of display. Her breasts and waist are emphasized in the drawings, she is much less likely to be depicted actually swimming than lounging by the side of the pool, waiting for the boys who suddenly begin to feature in these narratives. For the first time, boys figure prominently in the frontispieces and illustrations. The stories which had once carried titles which signal activity and adventure ["Jill of the Racing Stable", "Larks for the Madcap", "Rivals for the Sports Captaincy", "Lola the Outlaw's Daughter" (*Girl"s Crystal*)] have transformed by the late 50s into stories which foreground appearance and dress ["The Schoolgirl Wore Mink" (*Girl's Crystal* 1962), "Pam's Perm", "The Party Dress" (*The Book for Girls* 1960)]. Feature articles which had once focused on the achievements of women both historical and contemporary ["The Famous Women Crossword", "The Story of Pochohontas", "Margot Fonteyn"] or on the prospects for careers ["An Exciting Career" (*Girl* 1954 and Collins 1955 *Girl's Annual*)] have become in the next decade articles on fashion and deportment ["The ABC of Girl"s Grooming"] or they are centred around male musicians ["Secrets of the Stars" (*Girl's Crystal* 1962)].

The frontispieces which once featured young women as actively engaged in the whole range of sporting activities have become, by the end of the decade, images of languorous young women dreaming of rock stars around the Dancette record player (see Figure 2). The *Adventure Book for Girls* is a title which does not survive into 1960.

Figure 2   **Frontispiece, Collins *Girls' Annual* (1961)**

What can be learnt from the construction of 'sport' as a positive signifier of female energy, ability and skills? In the post-war reconstruction, in which gender roles are undergoing a process of transformation, popular writing for young women focuses very directly acquiring skills for the future, and to a very marked degree on careers for women. The *Careers* book for young girls is a genre that emerges in the fifties only to die in the early 1960s. The desires, skills and ambitions of women are continually suggested in popular fiction in a way that is at odds with received wisdom about gender roles in the decade of the 1950s.

Girls comics and annuals for pre-adolescents — a category that it is important to remember is not a distinction in these texts until the late 1950s — continue to evoke sport as a site for the proper placing of ambitions and personal achievement for girls. But as Mary Dunne (1982) has pointed out, this ceases to the case in contemporary magazines and comics for girls past puberty.

Ballet Shoes and *White Boots* have remained in print ever since their initial publication; *Ballet Shoes* was broadcast in the summer of 1995 as a serial for BBC children's radio. Their endurance as key texts for young women suggests that they still continue to answer to unfulfilled wishes and ambitions in young women.

References

Abrams, M. (1959) *The teenage consumer.* London: Press Exchange.

Bullock, A., Stallybrass, O., and Trombley, S. (1988) *The Fontana Dictionary of Modern Thought.* London: Fontana, 1988.

Butler Act [1944] *Public General Statutes* Chapter 31. London: HMSO: p. 36.

Dunne, M. (1982) 'Introduction to some of the images of sport in girls' comics and magazines', in C. Jenkins and M. Green (eds) *Sporting fictions.* Birmingham: Birmingham University PE Department and CCCS.

Fletcher, S. (1984) *Women first: The female tradition in English Physical Education 1880—1980.* London: Athlone.

Foster, S. and Simons, J. (1995) *What Katy read: Feminist re-readings of 'classic' stories for girls.* Hampshire: Macmillan.

Freeman, G. (1976) *The schoolgirl ethic: The life and work of Angela Brazil.* London: Allen Lane.

Girl's Crystal Annual (1951) London: Fleetway House.

Hall, S. and Whannel, P. (1964) *The popular arts.* London: Hutchinson.

Hargreaves, J. (1994) *Sporting females: Critical issues in the history and sociology of women's sports*. London: Routledge.

Hewison, R. (1988) *In anger: Culture in the Cold War*. London: Methuen.

Hoggart, R. (1957) *The uses of literacy*. Harmondsworth: Penguin.

Lowe, R. (1988) *Education in the post-war years: A social history*. London: Routledge.

McIntosh, P G., Dixon, J. G., Munrow, A. D., and Willets, R. F. (1981) *Landmarks in the history of physical education*. London: Routledge.

Phelps, G. (1961) 'The novel today', in B. Ford (ed) *The Pelican Guide to English Literature: The modern age*. Harmondsworth: Penguin, pp. 475-494.

Philips, D. and Tomlinson, A. (1992) 'Homeward bound', in D. Strinati and S. Wagg (eds) *Come on down: Popular media culture in post-war Britain*, London: Routledge, pp. 9-45.

Sinfield, A. (ed) (1983) *Society and literature 1945—1970*. New York: Holmes & Meier.

Streatfield, N. [1936] (1960) *Ballet shoes: A story of three children on the stage*. Harmondsworth: Puffin Books.

Streatfield, N. (1951) (1963) *White boots*. Harmondsworth: Puffin Books.

Wilson, E. (1980) *Only halfway to paradise: Women in postwar Britain 1945 –1968*. London: Tavistock.

Nothing To Do?: A Study Of Young Women's Health And Leisure In A Black Country Community

Eleanor Peters

Cheltenham and Gloucester College of Higher Education

Introduction

There is a prevalent 'common-sense' assumption particularly in the press, that young people are engaging in unhealthy behaviours and adopting lifestyles which will establish life-threatening patterns for adulthood (Department of Health, 1992; Plant and Plant, 1992; *The Guardian*, 22 September, 1994). There is a specific emphasis in the media on 'risk-taking' by young people, particularly in relation to smoking, sexual activity and the consumption of alcohol and drugs. One 'Health of the nation' target aimed to reduce the teenage smoking rate from 8% for boys and girls aged 11-15 by one third by 1993, although figures released by the Department of Health in December, 1994 showed 11% cent of girls and 8% of boys at secondary school smoked regularly in 1993. Another 'Health of the nation' target is "to reduce the rate of conception amongst the under 16s by at least 50% by year 2000 (from 9.5 per 1,000 girls aged 13-15 in 1989 to no more than 4.8)". The British teenage pregnancy rate is the highest in western Europe. There are 'Health of the nation' targets with respect to alcohol consumption although they do not specifically refer to young people, and again makes no recommendations with regard to young people and drug use, although reports suggest more young people are experimenting with drugs (*The Guardian*, 25 July, 1995).

An established research tradition exists of ethnographic studies of young people's lives (for example Whyte, 1955; Willmott, 1966; Patrick, 1973; Willis, 1977), but the majority concentrate on white, working class young men many of whom are involved in street gangs or 'deviant' behaviour. As such, the lives and experiences of young women have been largely ignored. Notable exceptions include Griffin (1985), McRobbie (1991), Lees (1986, 1993) whose work provides compelling accounts of young women's lives. However there are very few texts which focus upon young people's health in the context of their everyday lives. Studies on women's health and leisure such as Green, *et al.* (1990) focus very little on young women for a variety of reasons including lack of access to young women and there seems to be a belief that young women are too busy pursuing leisure activities to take part in research.

Background to the study

This paper draws on the preliminary findings from an exploratory ethnographic study concerning young women's health and well-being. The focus of the research is on young women's attitudes, beliefs and practices around health issues including the part leisure plays in their lives. Wolverhampton Borough Council's Youth Affairs Department allowed me access to two youth groups to conduct my research. I previously worked as a youth worker for both Wolverhampton Borough Council and Birmingham City Council working with girls' groups. Girls and young women have traditionally used youth services less frequently than boys and young men or have been excluded (Nava, 1984) but in an effort to counter this both Wolverhampton and Birmingham and many other youth services provide female only provision, an issue I will return to later.

Over a period of six months I have been in contact with twenty young women aged between 11 and 16 years. Both groups are female only, although towards the end of my study one was moving towards being mixed and, therefore, I also had some contact with young men during my research. I am now working with a girls' group in Malvern to gather information to compare with the data collected at Wolverhampton to look at the similarities and differences between young women in differing areas. I have used a variety of research techniques to gather data including participant and non-participant observation, interviews, group discussions and questionnaires.

The main focus of this paper will be upon the leisure pursuits of these young women both within and outside youth service provision. The methodology used enabled the research to explore the lives and world-view of these young women and in this respect it follows the Weberian tradition of *Verstehen* sociology. An explicitly feminist approach was adopted (Mies, 1983; McRobbie, 1991; Maynard and Purvis, 1994), to counteract the marginalisation of women's lives and experiences in both social science and health research. As Harding says:

> Critics argue that traditional social science has begun its analysis in men's experiences. That is, it has asked only the questions about social life that appear problematic from within the social experiences that are characteristic for men (white, Western, bourgeois men, that is). (Harding, 1987: p. 10)

It is not enough to study habits, beliefs, attitudes and perceptions in isolation from people's everyday lives. To gain insight into the place of health and leisure in the world view of young women, the research needed to be located in the context of their everyday lives. The point of ethnographic research is to render apparently irrational and inexplicable behaviour and attitudes intelligible through the use of *Verstehen.* In the words of a Native American saying 'Do not judge a man [sic] until you have walked a mile in his moccasins. '

Ethnographic research depends upon the researcher having privileged access to a specific social group for a period of time in order to acquire and share their view of their own social world. There were many roles I could have chosen to adopt, including that of covert researcher, that is a person who does not inform people that they are being researched. This obviously brings in issues of ethics and was an approach I rejected as unethical and unnecessary. Covert research is very useful if it is difficult to gain legitimate access to a particular group of people, and allows the researcher to view life without those under study guarding their behaviour. However, this approach conflicts with the norms and values of feminist research which stresses the need to empower women by regarding them as co-participants in the research endeavour and not to see them merely as sources of data (Oakley, 1981; Klein, 1983). As McRobbie says, feminists;

> have sought to treat 'subjects' with respect and equality. We have studiously avoided entering 'their' culture, savouring it and then presenting it to the outside world as a subject for speculation. Feminism forces us to locate our own autobiographies and our experience inside the questions we might want to ask, so that we continually do feel with the women we are studying. (McRobbie, 1991: p. 70)

I chose to use a youth work setting for my research. Many other researchers looking at young women chose to use schools as their method of obtaining contact (Griffin, 1984; Lees, 1986, 1993). Lees (1986) suggests that it is unfair to expect young women to give up their leisure time in youth clubs to take part in research. While I agree with this comment to a certain point, I had many reasons for not choosing to go to schools. Although I explained to the young women that I was a researcher and at no time pretended otherwise, I was giving them a choice to take part or not. They were told by myself and the youth workers concerned that they did not have to take part if they did not want to. Obviously any young women who did not want to take part but still attended the group is researched through observation and I felt this was a problem. However, if I had entered schools with the backing of the headteacher, I would have been viewed as an authority figure, leaving the young women with little option about taking part in the research. Although overt research in a youth work context inevitably confers some authority on the researcher, I believe from past experience as a youth worker that young people attending youth clubs do not view youth workers in the same light as they view teachers because attendance at a youth club is voluntary, whereas school attendance is not, in formal terms.

The young women in the study and their communities

I was allowed access to two girls' youth groups in Wolverhampton, one of which I shall call Poolside, and the other Parkside. The main contact of my research was with the group at Poolside in the south of Wolverhampton in a small working class community. Until boundary changes in the, 1960s this area was part of a neighbouring town and not in Wolverhampton's jurisdiction. I believe this area has a very different character to that of Wolverhampton as a whole. The area was very reliant on the nearby steel industry and various deprivation indices suggest that Poolside is signifi-cantly more deprived then Wolverhampton as a whole. Both Poolside and Parkside have poor housing, including many boarded up properties and houses very close to each other with little open space. Unemployment in these areas is quite high, and youth unemployment is particularly high in Wolverhampton (see Table 1). I believe youth unemployment affects young people detrimentally by depressing their job aspirations and level of

Table 1

Housing Tenure (%), 1991 Census				
	Poolside	**Parkside**	**Wolver-hampton**	**National**
Owner Occupier	34.1	42.0	57.7	66.4
Local Authority	60.6	---	33.7	21.4
	Poolside	**Parkside**	**Wolver-hampton**	**National**
Households with more than 1. 5 persons per room	0.4 %	1.2 %	0.5 %	0.5%
Households with no car	53.6 %	55.4 %	41.3%	33.4%

Wolverhampton, 1991 Unemployment Ages 16-19			
Total Residents	Economically Active	Unemployed	On Gov. Scheme
13,803	8,089 (58.6%)	2,053 (25.4%)	1,035 (12.8%)

Wolverhampton, 1991 Unemployment 16+		
Total Residents	Economically Active	Unemployed
191,020	112,003 (58.9%)	15,927 (14.2%)

expectations for their adult lives. My perception, which is shared by others, is that young people can hardly be expected to defer gratification by engaging in healthy behaviour now in order to maintain full health in later life, if their present circumstances leave little scope for optimism about their future prosperity and well-being. The outcome is a desire for hedonism and short-term pleasure, which is reflected in young people's health-related behaviour and their leisure patterns.

So how do young women living in relatively deprived circumstances carve out meaningful leisure for themselves?

Obviously youth service provision plays a part in the lives of the young women I researched, as this was my first point of contact with them. Both groups were club based, one located in rooms in a community centre, and one in a purpose built youth centre. Many of the young women who attend the groups I researched also attended other clubs on the premises at least twice a week. When asked what they spent most of their spare time on, youth club was the main leisure activity stated. Susan, a young woman attending Poolside group said:

> "All youth clubs should be open more. For instance, we don't have anything to do on Wednesdays as the club isn't open. They should be open every evening and all day Saturday and Sunday, that's what I think."

All the young women enjoyed the youth club and when asked what was the best thing about the club the main response was the workers, closely followed by day trips. It appears that the ability of the youth workers to tread the fine line between friendliness and authoritativeness was an important aspect of the young women's enjoyment of attending youth clubs. Young women did seem to accept the inevitability of a certain amount of restriction, but did not enjoy youth clubs where workers were deemed too authoritarian. Most young women enjoyed attending a girls only group, saying that they had a more relaxed atmosphere, making it possible for them to have a laugh without boys causing trouble. As Green, *et al.* state:

> Various studies have identified the strategies employed by teenage boys to control girls' freedom of movement and leisure. These include the monopolisation of space and facilities in youth clubs, verbal techniques of social control directed at the girls' sexuality and reputations and the effect that young men's violent behaviour ('trouble') had on girls' parents, of tightening their control on their daughters' mobility. (Green, *et al.*, 1990: p. 149)

The provision of girls only groups provided by some local authorities are designed to counteract these problems and to allow young women space for themselves. Girls only groups are also invaluable for young women who cannot take part in other outside interests for reasons such as parental restrictions, which now brings me to a discussion of the restrictions on young women's leisure.

Restrictions on young women's leisure

Authors such as McRobbie (1980) and Ganetz (1995) have stated that girls are more likely to have restrictions placed on them by parents because of the risks of unwanted pregnancy and the cultural disapproval of young women seen in public without escort. When I asked the young women what restricted them from doing what they wished with their leisure time, the answers were either parental restrictions or lack of finance. Obviously, there were parental restrictions on young women's leisure time mainly derived from their concern about their daughters being out late at night partly due to their safety, but also because of their concern about their daughters' perceived respectability.

Most young women indicated that they did some housework and baby-sitting for either family or friends. Often the young women would be paid for this work, although sometimes families expected them to do it for free, which appears to be part of the socialisation of young women into 'caring' as training for later lives as mothers themselves (Sharpe, 1976; McRobbie, 1991). Frequently young women would be unable to attend club activities due to domestic commitments, although some young men are also restricted by domestic commitments I saw relatively fewer restrictions placed on the young men attending the group. Young men seemed to be less restricted by parental concern about safety and respectability and although they too were restricted by lack of finance, evidence suggests that young men are able to earn more from part-time work than young women (Green, *et al.*, 1990: p. 149).

Public transport in Poolside is quite poor and although relatively cheap by national standards, still caused young women problems when they wished to go out. With poor public transport and low levels of car owner-ship, most leisure activity takes place within the neighbourhood. The cost of taxis is prohibitive to young women in this area. The young women in Parkside, who lived much closer to the town centre, were more likely to spend their leisure time in town. Some young Asian women who attended Parkside were restricted from other interests outside youth provision because of religious and cultural reasons. I will return to this later.

Having examined the restrictions faced by these young women in pur-suing leisure activities, let us now turn to looking at how they do spend their leisure time.

Young women's leisure activities

There were many young women who said that they spent much of their time 'dossing' (aimlessly hanging around, waiting for something to happen) either in town or in their local neighbourhood. Corrigan, in his study en-titled 'Doing Nothing', suggests that "what most adults see as an endless waste of time, an absence of purpose, is, from the viewpoint of the kids, full of incident" (Corrigan, 1976: p. 103).

Corrigan's study focused mainly on boys, finding that their leisure activities took place mainly outside the home. A number of authors have identified the importance of 'bedroom culture' in girls' leisure (McRobbie, 1991; Green, *et al.*, 1992), but others such as Griffin (1985) and Lees (1986) argue that for most young women, like young men, their leisure is not primarily home centred. The 'bedroom culture' obviously exists to certain degree, dependent upon cultural and parental restrictions to girls' activities outside the home.

> Within feminist youth culture research, the concept of 'bedroom culture' denotes the culture of young girls, which is developed in the girls' room where friends experiment with make-up and clothes, talk about boys and problems, use the media, dance, etc. (Ganetz, 1995: p. 88)

Most of the young women I researched had little privacy at home, often sharing a bedroom with a sister, and therefore preferred the street as the place to hang out with their friends. As Griffiths says in her study of young women in West Yorkshire:

> In spite of its limitations, dossing was generally seen by girls as a positive occupation, equated with 'having a laugh'. 'Just a right good doss' was the highest accolade. (Griffiths, 1988: p. 56)

Indeed, most of the girls studied in this research project use the youth club as a space to meet their friends and to develop friendships, to chat in relative privacy and to be allowed to play music and generally to make as much noise as they wish. This suggests that the youth club provides young women with a space of their own, whose relative safety in contrast to the street is a very important aspect of youth service provision.

If young women are prevented from hanging around the streets by parents, or have little privacy at home, the space provided by youth clubs is important in affording young women some measure of recreational autonomy. It has been noted by researchers such as McRobbie (1991) how young women seek out private spaces for themselves, such as school lavatories and corridors.

Some young women in Poolside attended a locally organised marching band which took up much of their time at week-ends and some evenings. Many of the young women who attended band also attended youth club suggesting that these young women are more responsive than many to organised leisure provision. Young women from both groups took part in sports such as swimming or netball, usually through school organised teams, or said they spent time playing with friends.

Each youth club provides a slightly different set of activities although most provide a wide range of day-trips, residential visits, arts and crafts activities, sports activities and more. Day-trips are usually organised on the basis of young women's suggestions about what they would like to do. I joined the group for day-trips to Drayton Manor Park and to Granada Studios Tours, and other trips included activities such as ice-skating, bowling, cinema and go-karting. Many residential visits are to activity centres where young people take part in activities such as rock climbing and pony trekking. I attended a residential visit to an activity centre in Wales with a mixed group where young women and men took part in the same activities. The young women particularly enjoyed the activities at the centre, especially pony trekking and gorge walking and were more enthusiastic about taking part than the young men.

Wolverhampton also provides borough-wide specialist and cultural activities for young people, for example music recording facilities and African dancing classes. Obviously an important part of youth provision is the capacity to inform and to educate young people especially in disadvantaged communities, above and beyond the simple provision of leisure activities. I believe the varied activities available to young people taking part in Youth Services in Wolverhampton is of paramount importance because of the high levels of deprivation in many areas of the town. This provision allows a range of cultural experiences for young people which would otherwise be circumscribed. Most youth groups charge a small amount of money weekly to attend. Although young people and their families are asked to contribute to the cost of day-trips and residentials, the main costs are met by youth services which enables young people from disadvantaged communities to benefit from taking part in new activities and experiences which would normally be barred to them through expense and lack of transport, as well as cultural barriers.

Youth club provision has been frequently criticised for being male-biased (Nava, 1984) and providing traditionally male activities. Youth work has traditionally focused on 'unruly' young men seeking to control social disorder by diverting young men's energies into organised leisure. Young women have never been as visible as young men on the streets, do not cause as much trouble and therefore have not attracted the same amount of provision. During the, 1970s pressure was applied on the National Association of Youth Clubs to re-introduce girls-only provision. I found that most young women were happy to attend a girls-only group and many preferred to stating that it was more relaxed without boys around. Young women frequently feel excluded and marginalised in mixed youth clubs, lacking the assertiveness to challenge successfully boys' dominance of the activities. As two young women from Parkside group said: (Jackie): "I prefer coming to girls' group because the girls don't cause as much trouble as boys"; (Tina): "Yes, 'cos most boys are trouble".

In my past experience of working in youth provision I frequently encountered hostility to girls-only provision, but I feel this is very worthwhile and of great advantage to the young women who attend. The girls' group in Poolside was becoming mixed towards the end of my research due to objections from young men in the area that they had no club to attend on that day and time. Although a mixed youth club operates later that evening a male worker was placed to run a boys' group at the same time as the girls' group, the consequences of which were that boys dominated the group in numbers and in use of the activities.

The girls' youth club in Parkside offers an opportunity for Asian young women to take part in youth provision. More traditional Asian families want to maintain family honour where daughters' reputations are preserved and this includes not socialising with boys. The girls' youth club is an opportunity for these girls to experience a leisure pursuit outside the home. The leader would collect the young women from their homes and take them home after club. The club was strictly female only, and assurances were given to parents that the club was a safe place for their daughters to attend. In a report produced for Wolverhampton Youth Service, Smith suggests that older young women were more likely to need parental approval if they were Asian or had a disability (Smith, 1995), although issues of safety and respectability are not just isolated to these groups. This report highlights that youth provision for women could be improved as 60% of users are male and 40% female, but the percentage of females using the service has improved over recent years.

Conclusion

To conclude I wish to stress the point that although these young women live in relatively deprived conditions in terms of housing, overcrowding, access to transport, spending power and employment prospects, they do enjoy their leisure time and are able to find many enjoyable activities to do. They all enjoyed attending youth clubs seeing them as providing an important focus for their leisure activities, and were happy to attend mixed and female only groups seeing different advantages in both types of youth service provision. Although it may seem to adults that these young women are 'doing nothing', to the young women themselves just hanging out with friends in the street or in youth clubs is a pleasurable activity full of fun and excitement. It is evident that these young women do have limitations placed upon their leisure activities. Lack of finance and parental restriction do impinge on what they would like to do, but they appear to make the best they can of these situations and use all opportunities to their advantage including attending youth clubs.

References

Department of Health (1992) *The health of the nation*. London: HMSO.

Corrigan, P. (1976) 'Doing nothing', in S. Hall and T. Jefferson (eds) *Resistance through rituals*. London: Harper Collins.

Ganetz, H. (1995) 'The shop, the home and femininity as a masquerade', in J. Fornas, and G. Bolin (eds) *Youth culture in late modernity*. London: Sage.

Green, E., Hebron, S. and Woodward, D. (1990) *Women's leisure, what leisure?*. London: Macmillan.

Griffin, C. (1985) *Typical girls?*. London: Routledge and Kegan Paul.

Griffiths, V. (1988) 'From playing out to "dossing out": Young women and leisure', in E. Wimbush and M. Talbot (eds) *Relative freedoms: Women and leisure*. Milton Keynes: Open University Press.

Harding, S. (ed) (1987) *Feminism and methodology*. Milton Keynes: Open University Press.

Klein, R. D. (1983) 'How to do what we want to do: Thoughts on feminist methodology', in G. Bowles and R. D. Klein (eds) *Theories of women's studies*. London: Routledge and Kegan Paul.

Lees, S. (1986) *Losing out: Sexuality and adolescent girls*. London: Hutchinson.

——— (1993) *Sugar and spice*. Harmondsworth: Penguin.

McRobbie, A. (1980) *Working-class girls and the culture of femininity*. University of Birmingham: MA Thesis.

——— (1991) *Feminism and youth culture*. London: Macmillan.

Maynard, M. and Purvis, J. (1994) *Researching women's lives from a feminist perspective*. London: Taylor and Francis.

Mies, M. (1983) 'Towards a feminist methodology' in G. Bowles and R. D. Klein (eds) T*heories of women's studies*. London: Routledge and Kegan Paul.

Nava, M. (1984) 'Youth service provision, social order and the question of girls', in A. McRobbie and M. Nava, M. (eds) *Gender and generation*. Basingstoke: Macmillan.

Oakley, A. (1981) 'Interviewing women: A contradiction in terms', in H. Roberts (ed) *Doing feminist research*. London: Routledge and Kegan Paul.

Patrick, J. (1973) *A Glasgow gang observed*. London: Eyre Methuen.

Plant, M. and Plant, M. (1992) *Risk-takers: Alcohol, drugs, sex and youth*. London: Routledge.

Schofield, G. (1994) *The youngest mothers*. Aldershot: Avebury.

Sharpe, S. (1976) *Just like a girl: How girls learn to be women*. Harmondsworth: Penguin.

Smith, D. (1995) 'The work of the Youth Service in 1994'. Unpublished paper for Wolverhampton MBC.

Whyte, W. F. (1955) *Street corner society*. Chicago: Chicago University Press.

Willis, P. (1977) *Learning to labour*. Farnborough: Gower.

Willmott, P. (1966) *Adolescent boys of East London*. Harmondsworth: Penguin.

A Cross-Cultural Comparison of Girls' Participation in Sport

Jim Clough and Ron Traill
University of Canberra

Rod Thorpe
Loughborough University

Introduction

The case for the benefits to be gained from increased participation in sport has been well researched and documented over recent years. Typical of such a case is that put forward in an Australian report entitled *Children in sport* (1983) which proclaimed that the benefits for involvement in physical activity would be noted through "...higher levels of fitness, better health, pleasurable social involvement and the satisfaction derived from skilled performance in individual and group activities" (*Children in Sport*, 1983). Support for such a viewpoint is provided by Shrapnel, who claims that sport increases children's self confidence, feelings of independence and their social maturity and that it is "the responsibility of all adults involved in children's sport to ensure that every child has this opportunity" (Shrapnel, 1989: pp. 10-11). More recently Reeder, Stanton, Langley and Chalmers (1991: p. 308) claimed that "Participation in sporting and similar physical activities has been identified as a potentially important factor in a range of health outcomes".

However, one of the alarming aspects of this research literature is that fewer girls than boys are involved in regular sport participation (e.g. Dahlgren, 1988) and that up to 60% of girls involved in sport at school, drop out on leaving school (Australian House of Representatives Standing Committee on Legal and Constitutional Affairs, 1982: p. 115). It is therefore important for those responsible for planning sport programmes for girls to have a clear understanding of what encourages and discourages girls from playing sport.

69

Methodology

Background

In 1992 two of the authors were commissioned to investigate the sport related behaviours and attitudes of school aged young people in the Australian Capital Territory (ACT) (Clough and Traill, 1992). In 1993 it became possible to replicate the study [as part of the Young People's Programme of the National Sports Centre supported by the Sports Council] in Nottinghamshire in the United Kingdom (Clough, Traill and Thorpe, 1994). This paper focuses on the results for the female participants.

Sampling

The ACT study was jointly commissioned by the Junior Sport Unit of the ACT Department of Sport and Recreation and the Australian Sports Commission and naturally focused on issues with which they were concerned, such as the impact of the AUSSIE SPORT[1] programme, and the sporting needs of local young people. It sought to sample the views of forty males and forty females at each of thirteen year levels in the school system, that is from kindergarten to year twelve, encompassing the ages of five to eighteen. This sample was drawn from 8 primary, 4 high schools (Years 7 to 10) and 4 junior colleges (Years 11 and 12), involving students from government and private schools in proportion to that in the total population of such schools. A sample of 1,034, comprising 525 males and 523 females was obtained and analysed. The distribution is shown in Table 1.

The Nottinghamshire study sought to obtain a comparable sample, except that a year thirteen exists in a number of senior secondary schools. Where this occurred, students from this year level were, as far as possible, included in the sample in equal numbers to those at the other year levels at that school.

Due to a variety of factors, there was considerable variability in the number of young people sampled at each year level, particularly at the extremes of age. Apart from the need to treat the results from the Nursery level and those from Years 11 and 13 with some caution, the lower sample size is not *prima facie* likely to bias the results.

Wherever relevant the means for the year groups have been used to combine scores, rather than the total score, to give equal weight to each year level. The sample was drawn from 9 primary schools, 1 independent girls' school (with both a primary and a secondary section), 1 independent boys' school (with both a primary and a secondary section), 8 comprehensive secondary schools and 1 secondary college (Years 11 to 13).

As with the ACT sample schools were selected to match the demographic characteristics of the population. The sample comprised 455 males, 441 females and 2 who did not identify their gender. The distribution of this sample is shown in Table 1.

Table 1:   Students Surveyed by School Year

	Australian Sample			English Sample		
School Year	Males	Females	Total	Males	Females	Total
Kinder-garten-Nursery	40	39	79 (7.5%)	12	19	31 (3.5%)
Year 1	40	40	80 (7.6%)	30	30	60 (6.7%)
Year 2	40	40	80 (7.6%)	28	33	61 (6.8%)
Year 3	41	41	82 (7.8%)	37	40	77 (8.6%)
Year 4	41	41	82 (7.8%)	37	40	77 (8.6%)
Year 5	39	42	81 (7.7%)	34	37	71 (7.9%)
Year 6	40	40	80 (7.6%)	40	36	76 (8.5%)
Year 7	41	43	84 (8.0%)	39	36	75 (8.4%)
Year 8	43	41	84 (8.0%)	42	41	84*(9.3%)
Year 9	41	44	85 (8.1%)	44	33	77 (8.6%)
Year 10	45	37	82 (7.8%)	34	36	71*(7.8%)
Year 11	39	36	75 (7.2%)	23	14	37 (4.1%)
Year 12	35	38	73 (7.0%)	36	32	68 (7.6%)
Year 13	0	0	0 (0.0%)	19	13	32 (3.6%)
Not Indicated	0	1	1 (0.1%)	0	1	1 (0.1%)
Total	525	523	1048 (100%)	455	441	898 (100%)
* Gender data not provided by one participant						

Data Collection

Information was gathered by means of an eighteen-item questionnaire, many of the eighteen items having sub-items. The same twenty page questionnaire was completed by all of the young people, with the youngest primary school children receiving assistance from older children in their school who had completed the questionnaire and who had received some additional guidance from the research assistants. The research assistants monitored this process and assisted as necessary. This process proved to be a cost effective means of obtaining the information.

Results of the Mapping Exercise

What are Their Sporting Aspirations

How do young people, particularly females, like to spend their leisure time? Is sport a preferred leisure activity? When asked to rank seven leisure activities (playing or listening to music; hobbies; reading or writing; playing sport; going to scouts, guides, a church or social group; being with your friends or watching television) the young women in both countries ranked "being with your friends" and "playing sport" virtually equal as their first choice. The males in both countries ranked sport unambiguously at number one. Thus sport is clearly a favoured leisure activity.

The students were also asked to indicate which of a list of eleven reasons motivated them to play sport, with the emphasis being on outcomes expected. Table 2 shows the responses to these questions. These data give a strong indication that there is very little difference in the expected outcomes of participating in sport reported by the two samples, with both the percentages choosing the various alternatives and the ranking resulting from these being remarkably close. The average difference in percentage is less than five percentage points, while the average difference in rank is one. It is also interesting to note that in both samples, four of the first five responses involved reasons which were likely to be achieved principally through sport as defined in this study (the exception being "make new friends") and to involve intrinsic motivation.

Table 2   Females' Reasons for Playing Sport (Australia n=523, England n=441)

Reason	Australian		English	
	%	Rank	%	Rank
Improve my sporting skills	88	1	84	1
Make new friends	84	3	83	2
Be physically active	86	2	74	3
Play close and exciting games	77	4	74	4
Compete against others	66	5	57	5
Please my parents	46	6	44	6
Please the coach	42	7	37	10
Beat others in sport	36	9	39	7
Get medals and trophies	38	8	37	9
Meet members of the opposite sex	34	10	38	8
Be like my sporting heroes or heroines	32	11	25	11

Another question sought to find out why they played their favourite sport, with twenty five alternatives being offered (see Table 3).

Table 3   Reasons Female Students Play their Favourite Sport (Australia n=523, England n=441)

	Australian		English	
Reason	%	Rank	%	Rank
It's fun	98	1	96	1
It makes you feel good	91	2	84	3
It's something to do	82	4	85	2
You make new friends this way	82	3	77	4.5
People in this sport are really friendly	79	5	77	4.5
I am really good at this sport	70	6	67	7
Girls and boys can play it together	62	8	71	6
The coach is good	66	7	54	9
My friends play it too	48	10	62	8
I saw it played on television	44	12	50	10
You can make a good living from playing this sport	46	11	44	11
I want to represent (my district) at this sport	49	9	40	13
Parents encourage me to play it	43	13	39	14
I do not have to travel far to play it	37	16	42	12
It does not cost a lot to play	40	14	37	15
It makes you look good	38	15	33	19
I am not likely to be injured in this sport	36	17	33	18
It could help me overcome a disability	34	18	30	22
I play this sport with my parents	27	22	37	16
Teachers encouraged me to play it	26	23	35	17
I do not have to go to training sessions	28	21	32	20
I knew the coach	32	20	27	23
It helps you do well at schoolwork	34	19	24	25
My mum plays/played this sport	25	24	31	21
My dad plays/played this sport	20	25	27	24

While there are clearly some quite large discrepancies between the two countries in the percentage choosing given reasons, and consequent differences in ranks, one is struck by how similar the distributions in the two countries are.

It is, however, interesting to note that where a distinctly higher percentage of English children favour a reason than their Australian counterparts social reasons predominate: friends playing, girls and boys together, mum playing and teachers encouraging. By contrast, when the Australian children favour a reason it tends to be associated with the structure of an activity; to represent at this sport, the coach being good and it helping with schoolwork.

We believe that the similarity of rankings for these reasons lends support to the notion that the aspirations of the two groups are similar, and that in both countries, sport is a desired leisure activity. Further support is given to the notion that sport is a highly desired leisure activity by the students' responses to a series of questions that sought their feelings towards playing sport in a variety of contexts. The responses to these questions are summarised in Table 4.

Table 4   Female Students' Feelings about Playing Sport in Different Contexts – Percent (Australia n=523, England n=441)

	In Class-time at School (%)		For the School (%)		With Family or Friends (%)		For a Sporting Club (%)	
How children felt about playing sport	Aust	Eng	Aust	Eng	Aust	Eng	Aust	Eng
Excited	43	49	65	76	56	47	61	51
Too organised	27	31	10	10	19	22	23	24
Boring	32	22	8	9	12	11	11	13
Fun	61	66	83	86	56	48	59	57
Satisfying	38	38	50	45	43	33	45	38
Too many rules	30	33	11	12	24	27	22	24
Dangerous	18	14	14	17	14	9	16	11
Others take it too seriously	44	44	18	18	35	31	33	32
Too competitive	23	25	11	10	29	26	30	26
Challenging	37	36	38	38	47	46	54	46
Develops skills	57	57	47	40	49	38	56	48

Clearly, the positive emotions of fun, excitement, satisfaction, a sense of challenge and an awareness of skill development strongly outweigh any sense of boredom, danger, over-organisation or too high a level of competition. It is interesting to note also how positively playing sport with family and friends is rated (highest on fun and excitement and lowest on boredom). Conversely, sport "in classtime at school" is not well rated on some characteristics. Overall, it seems reasonable to conclude that the girls and young women sampled had a positive attitude towards sport as a leisure activity, and that the aspirations of the respondents in both countries were very similar.

Sports Played

The participation rates of the girls and young women in twenty-five different sports, most of which had one or more modified versions, was assessed. This data was collected to take into account sports which the girls might have played in four different contexts – in classtime at school, with family or friends, as a representative of their school, or for a sporting club. This information is provided in Table 5 (overleaf). In some instances, the sports identified are the modified versions of sport which are widely played in Australia and/or England, e.g. the modified versions of cricket are Kanga cricket and Kwik Cricket, while the sports listed differ between the countries to reflect differences in the popular sports in each country.

It is clear that where direct comparisons are possible there is a remarkable similarity between the figures, although there is a slight tendency for the Australian females to participate in the less traditionally female sports, for example the football codes. It can also be noted that few have represented their school or a community club in a competition. Where this has occurred, it is likely to have been in the traditional "female" sports. A further point of interest is that "Dance" and "Gymnastics" are the only activities in which more than ten percent of the English sample have participated within the sporting club context. There is also a striking difference between the sports which are played in classtime at school and with family and friends.

If we sum the percentages for the 25 sports listed for each country and divide by 100 we will gain some idea of the number of sports in which these young females have participated in each of the four contexts. This data is given in Table 6 (overleaf). The results from the males are included for comparison. This table shows that for each of the four groups a wider variety of sports are participated in with family and friends than in classtime at school, which is in turn greater than the number of representative sports. English males and Australian females are more likely to represent their schools than a sporting club, while the opposite is true for English females and Australian males. In all categories of representative sport, males participate more than females and Australians more than English. The differences are quite large in percentage terms, with, for example, 57% more Australian young women representing their school than their English counterparts.

Table 5   Sports Played by Females by Context – Percent (Australia n=523, England n=441)

Sport	In Classtime at School (%)		For the School (%)		With Family or Friends (%)		For a Sporting Club (%)	
	Aust	Eng	Aust	Eng	Aust	Eng	Aust	Eng
Aerobs/Gyms	53		26		8		26	
Aerobs/F'ness		41		30		2		8
Aths/Ltl Aths	35		16		16		19	
Aths/Cross Cty		60		21		19		2
Aust Footbl	22		13		2		2	
Badminton		29		40		2		10
Baseball	27		12		5		2	
Bsbl/Sfbl		26		16		1		1
Cricket/KCrkt	48	28	27	34	7	2	2	3
Cycling	10	5	80	83	1	1	2	1
Dance		45		37		4		22
Golf	5	2	26	34	0	2	1	3
Gymnastics		34		17		1		17
Hockey	36	50	10	13	11	13	7	6
Horse Riding	7	3	51	40	2	1	9	10
Lacrosse	15	10	2	2	1	0	0	0
Netball	44	65	28	32	32	27	24	7
Orienteering	19	18	9	11	3	2	3	3
Rounders		71		35		10		3
Rugby League	12	3	16	6	1	0	1	1
Rugby Union	14	2	8	4	2	0	1	0
Skating	15	4	67	77	1	0	5	3
Skiing	7	5	32	21	2	1	2	2
Soccer	37	24	22	33	12	6	4	2
Softball	46		19		16		7	
Squash	15	11	18	29	1	0	2	2
Tee-ball	43		14		11		7	
Tennis	29	47	45	45	4	4	14	9
Touch F'ball	28		20		3		1	
Volleyball	47	30	24	27	10	1	3	3

Table 6   Average Number of Sports Played by Females and Males

Sport	In Classtime at School	With Family orFriends	For the School	For a Sporting Club
Aust. Female n=523	6.49	6.87	1.60	1.53
Eng Female n=441	6.43	7.09	1.02	1.21
Aust Male n=525	7.76	8.53	2.10	2.39
Eng Male n=455	8.12	9.08	1.78	1.65

Another measure of the degree of participation in sport resulted from the questions relating to representing their school in competition against another school, or representing a sporting club against another sporting club. The young people were asked to indicate in which sports they had represented their school or sporting club against another such club in the present or previous year. Table 7, gives the results of this question.

Table 7.   Percentage of Males and Females Playing Representative Sport.

Context	Australian			English		
	Male	Female	Total	Male	Female	Total
	n=525	n=523	n=1048	n=455	n=441	n=898
For School	53.3	44.0	48.7	43.7	33.3	38.6
For Club	54.0	37.7	45.8	39.3	21.5	30.6

This data shows an even stronger trend than that based on the number of sports played. Clearly the level of participation by males is greater than that of females in all contexts. Similarly, the level of participation of the Australian sample is greater than the English sample in all contexts. With the single exception of Australian males, representing one's school is more frequent than representing a sporting club.

The most pertinent comparisons for the purposes of this paper are those across countries for females, with about one third more Australians representing their school and about three quarters more Australians representing a community club. Now this may just indicate that the English young women have a wider range of interests than their Australian counterparts, however, given the similarity of their aspirations we would argue that this is not the case.

What Influences Girls' Participation in Sport?

Two questions addressed this issue, the first seeking to explore what would cause these students to drop out of sport, while the second sought to identify those factors which would encourage them to participate in sport to a higher degree.

Table 8   Reasons Female Students would be Discouraged from Playing Sport Percentage (Australia n=523, England n=441)

Reason	% agree	Rank	% agree	Rank
	Aust		England	
Having a part-time job	38.2	10	30.2	15
My studies (lots of homework)	50.3	4	53.3	3
Having a poor coach	51.4	3	45.6	7
It costs too much money	48.4	5	48.1	6
Having to practise too much	25.2	16	34.9	10.5
The risk of being injured	28.7	15	28.6	17
Having more interesting things to do	36.1	11	42.0	8
My team losing all the time	23.3	17	22.7	19.5
Poor umpiring	46.7	7	41.7	9
Having barrackers and coaches yelling at me all the time	48.2	6	49.2	4
The season being too long	19.5	20	23.1	18
Having to travel all over the place to matches	35.6	12	28.8	16
Coaches not really being interested in the players, but just in winning	63.1	2	61.9	2
The coaches only putting the good players in the game, so that I miss out	65.4	1	64.6	1
My friends are not interested in sport	22.0	19	32.4	13
My parents thinking I should not play so much sport	22.6	18	22.7	19.5
Having a disability and cannot play sport	40.0	9	30.6	14
Nowhere near where I live to play the sport I would like to play	45.3	8	48.5	5
Our school being more interested in academic subjects than sport	31.7	13	33.8	12
Having to do other things than play, for example, umpiring, scoring	30.8	14	34.9	10.5

While a concern to measure the impact of AUSSIE SPORT led to the questions relating to coaching being very specific and perhaps a little loaded, clearly, factors relating to the coaches' behaviours are foremost in the respondents' minds with the first two reasons for the English students, and the first three for the Australians, relating to coaches. Studies, excessive barracking, the cost, lack of opportunities to participate close to home and the quality of umpiring were also important considerations. They were relatively unconcerned by the length of the season, their parents being concerned they played too much or, their team losing all the time.

In comparing coutries, there were only three factors in which there was a difference of about ten percentage points. Two of these might suggest a slightly different approach between the girls and young women in the two samples. While only a quarter of the Australian participants saw "having to practise too much" as a disincentive, over a third of the English sample would be discouraged for this reason. Similarly only twenty two percent of the Australian females would be discouraged by "my friends not being interested in sport" whereas this seemed important for thirty two percent of the English participants. Together these two results may suggest that the Australian young women are more interested in sport per se than their English counterparts. Despite these differences, generally the rankings were very similar across the two samples. This suggests that similar approaches in both countries would result in greater involvement in sport by females, and suggest what some of these strategies might be. They also lend some incidental support to the view that the aspiration of the females in these two countries are very similar.

The young people were also asked to indicate (see Table 9) which of six alternatives would increase the likelihood of them playing more sport.

Table 9   Female Students Reasons for Playing More Sport Percentage (Australia n=523, England n=441)

	% agree	Rank	% agree	Rank
Reason	Aust		England	
An indoor area was available	51.8	6	57.4	3
I had transport available	54.5	5	50.3	6
Sport did not cost me anything to play	62.1	3	56.7	4
I could play when I want to and not at a set time	63.5	2	70.1	1
My parents allowed me to play	55.4	4	51.7	5
If there was a competition available in one of my favourite sports that I could do well in	70.9	1	64.4	2

Again, the results are very similar: with being able to compete near home in a sport in which they could do well and having freedom to choose when to play alternating as most and second most chosen (the exception is the availability of an indoor area being more chosen by the English sample, an understandable difference). It is interesting to note the narrow range of twenty percentage points which cover the six alternatives in the two samples, suggesting that a variety of strategies might need to be used to promote greater involvement.

Before making some final comments, it is worth reporting that when the students were asked whether their present sporting facilities were sufficient, 78.4% of the Australian females and 78.5% of their English counterparts, said they were. While this does not indicate a high level of dissatisfaction, it is pertinent to note that the degree of satisfaction is related to the expectations of the individuals, as much as to the provision of facilities.

Discussion

If we accept that regular physical activity which "raises a sweat" in the individual is a good thing, then there is cause both for satisfaction and for concern in the results of this study.

Reasons for satisfaction

1.   Ninety six percent of these English females believed that playing sport was fun, rating it alongside being with their friends as their favourite leisure activity. They also indicated that the positive emotions of fun, excitement, satisfaction, a sense of challenge and an awareness of skill development clearly outweigh any sense of boredom, danger, over-organisation or too high a level of competition when they play sport in a variety of contexts.

2.   They indicated a belief that sport was beneficial by ranking "It makes you feel good" third among reasons why they play their favourite sport, chose to "Be physically active" third among their reasons for playing sport and showed an interest in raising their sporting achievements, making "improve my sporting skills" their first choice in their reasons for playing sport.

3.   The comparatively large number of sports to which these students have been introduced suggests that there would be a large pool of potential participant if clubs established appropriate junior competitions.

Reasons for concern

1.   Only about one third of the Nottinghamshire females played sport for their school against another school in the current or previous year, while slightly more than one fifth were active in a sporting club. One sixth of this

activity was in some form of dance. This is considerably less than for the ACT females, and for males in both countries, and quite low on an absolute basis. Given that Nottinghamshire would be viewed as a progressive county offering a structured programme for children, it may be that results in some other parts of England might present a greater cause for concern.

2   Since most of the young women's sporting participation is based around the school, when this link is broken it will require positive action on their part to remain involved in competitive sport. Experience suggests that this occurs in only a minority of cases.

How might participation rates be raised?

1.   Having the freedom to choose when they played sport would motivate many girls and young women to play more, as would the availability of an indoor area.

2.   Having access to a competition in a favourite sport in which they could do well was also important. This seems to be a major problem for many English young people.

3.   Being treated well by their coach and other adults. This would include being given the opportunity to play, the coach showing interest in them as individuals, not being "yelled at" by coaches and spectators. Interestingly, "losing all the time" was not a major concern to the young people, with "competing" and "close and exciting games" being of greater importance.

4.   Being able to see sport as a means of interacting with their present friends and a basis for making new friends. While overall meeting members of the opposite sex is not a strong motivation for most of these female students, those in the middle years of secondary school (Years 9 and 10) rate it more highly.

Note

[1]   AUSSIE SPORT was originally a modified sports programme for primary school age children which has systematically expanded to include community based sport, those beyond the primary school age range and a number of countries other than Australia.

References

Australian House of Representatives Standing Committee on Legal and Constitutional Affairs (1991) *Equity for Women in Sport: A Discussion Paper prepared for the House of Representatives' Standing Committee on Legal and Constitutional Affairs for the Enquiry into Equal Opportunity and Equal Status for Women in Australia.* A.G.P.S., Canberra.

Children in sport (1983) A policy statement, Confederation of Australian Sport, The Australian Council for Health, Physical Education and Recreation, and the Australian Sports Medicine Foundation, November.

Clough, J. R. and Traill, R. D. (1992) *A mapping of participation rates in Junior Sport in the Australian Capital Territory*, Canberra, ACT: ACT Junior Sport Council, October.

Clough, J. R., Traill, R. D and Thorpe, R. D. (1994) *A mapping of participation rates in Junior Sport in Nottinghamshire*, Loughborough: Loughborough University, April.

Dahlgren, W. J. (1988). A Report of the National Task Force on Young Females and Physical Activity: The Status Quo and Strategies for Change. Fitness Canada and the Fitness and Amateur Sport Canada Women's Program, January.

Reeder, A. I., Stanton, W. R., Langley, J. D., and Chalmers, D. J. (1991) 'Adolescents' sporting and leisure time physical activities during their 15th year', *Canadian Journal of Sports Sciences*, Vol. 16, No. 4 (December): pp. 308-318.

Shrapnel, M. (1989) 'Children in sport', *Sportsmed News*, (December): pp. 10-11.

Another Aspect of Rural Deprivation — Spatial Aspects of Young Women's Leisure in a Rural Area

Nadina Prosser

Cheltenham and Gloucester College of Higher Education

Introduction

Traditionally leisure research has tended to use quantitative methods of investigation in order to make generalisations as to how individuals, particularly males, spend their leisure time. It was not until the early, 1980s that serious consideration was given to women's leisure and to the specific role played by gender determining in shaping women's leisure time and leisure activities. This omission has slowly begun to be rectified over the past ten years as growing numbers of sociologists have employed ethnographic methods in order to investigate the complexities that can either restrict or enhance women's lives and leisure. However there has not been equal consideration of how young women spend their leisure time; studies have tended to treat women as a homogeneous group, with the age of women not being considered important. Although the number of ethnographic studies of young women has increased, most have not dealt specifically with their leisure. As Nava points out because girls are less deviant and make less noise than boys they are simply not noticed in public spaces and thus they tend to be overlooked in the literature (Nava, 1992).

This paper will discuss young women's leisure patterns in a rural area, and the strategies they implement to negotiate their own space, both private and public, within the context of their rural environment, This topic forms part of my main research project on 'Teenage girls' drug use in a rural area.'

Before I begin on the main part of this paper I shall briefly explain the focus of my PhD. The following description of the project to date is made with specific reference to two locations, Waterside and Hillside. These are, of course, pseudonyms in accordance with promises of confidentiality that have been made. Examples will be drawn from the work in progress in order to illustrate the points made in the latter part of the paper.

The focus of my research is an investigation into the perceptions of and attitudes to drugs and their use by teenage girls in a rural area, and the exploration of their use of drugs (both legal and illegal) set within the context of their lives as a whole. It was apparent when reviewing the literature that sociological research directly relating to this topic was scarce. Although there has been a wealth of studies on adolescent drug use the majority of these have been conducted in urban areas (Weiner, 1970; Leech and Jordan, 1970; O'Connor, 1986), using self-reporting questionnaires in a school-based environment. In addition, little research has concentrated on girls' drug use, studies of youth culture generally tending to marginalise the female adolescent (McRobbie and Nava, 1984; Lees, 1993).

For my own research, I chose to employ ethnographic methods of enquiry in order to discover teenage girls' patterns of illicit substance use, including their consumption of alcohol and tobacco, to explore the influential factors that may lead to their experimentation with these substances and what part their use plays within these young girls' lives. Since March, 1995 I have been spending one evening a week at two local youth clubs in two different locations of the same district. Waterside youth club is attended by approximately ten girls aged between 13 and 15. The Hillside club is attended by approximately twenty girls aged between 15 and 16. I also recently participated in a week's holiday with ten girls from Hillside youth club. This gave me an ideal opportunity to establish a closer relationship with them and to gain a clearer insight into how they perceived themselves and how these perceptions affected their behaviour and their use of space. As MacKenzie asserts, "There is a need to understand the role of women in an attempt to explain their spatial behaviour" (MacKenzie, 1980 [pages unnumbered]).

A brief socio-economic overview of both towns will provide some perspective on the practical constraints that the girls face. Both towns are between fifteen to twenty miles away from the main city and are situated in areas of natural beauty. Hillside has a population of 7,658 with an average of 2.5 to each household. It was once a main business centre of the area, its main industry being mining and, although this began to decline in the late 1940s, the settlement of a world-wide manufacturer in the early 1950s continued to bring prosperity to the area. The housing boom of the mid 1980s brought a lot of business to the area, particularly in the building trade, as city dwellers and commuters bought up local property. Since the late 1980s the area has declined dramatically, with light industry and building companies struggling to survive; 9% of employable persons are out of work and most of those who are employed are in manual jobs.

The same economic situation is found in Waterside. This was once a small shipping town with good water and rail links to other major business areas. Its present population is 7,416, also with an average of 2.5 persons per household. However the employment prospects are grim, again with approximately 9% of workers unemployed and, like Hillside, the majority of those who are employed are in manual jobs. The lack of jobs and transport means that workers face bleak prospects. They must look outside the area for employment, which means that much valuable labour is being exported, but the lack of public transport restricts them to jobs in certain locations, which exacerbates competition for jobs. Nearly a third of households in both towns have no private transport, which again accentuates the problem. Both towns are serviced quite well by public transport along the main arteries, there is an hourly service to and from the city, but there is little chance of mobility between the surrounding areas. As one resident pointed out in a local survey:

> We have quite a dense pattern of small settlements and a diffuse pattern of trip needs. ... conventional buses can't be the answer. (FODMAP, 1995: p. 36)

Apart from the inadequate service to these areas, the bus fares are quite expensive: a return ticket can cost anything between two to four pounds depending where you live along their route. The service to Hillside and Waterside starts at 7 a.m. and finishes between 6 and 7 p.m. This creates many problems for all age groups: there is little hope of utilising the leisure facilities that the city has to offer, and those in employment are limited to jobs with working hours between 8 a.m. and 6 p.m. These same problems also extend on a larger scale to local areas, where it is extremely difficult to seek job or leisure opportunities away from one's home area.

With these transport problems in mind I should now like to briefly describe the leisure facilities that Hillside and Waterside areas have to offer. Waterside has a rugby and a football ground situated at the back of a housing estate near to the centre of the town. It has a local park half a mile from the town centre and an open air swimming pool, which is situated on its own three quarters of a mile from the town centre and half a mile from the sports centre. The youth club, situated about two minutes' walk from the main shopping area, provides such activities as table tennis, pool and football.

Hillside has a football pitch and a rugby ground, situated close to residential areas. There are also two recreation grounds which have parks attached to them which are situated at the edge of the fields. Hillside's school, sports centre and youth club are all on the same site, situated about fifteen minutes' walk from the town centre. The youth club offers activities such as table tennis, pool and a disco. It also has use of the school sports hall for indoor football, basketball or trampolining.

If these facilities are considered in relation to girls' leisure requirements, it is obvious that there is an abundance of space provided for boys' entertainment, but a lack of space for girls' activities. Girls face many difficulties in finding their own space and use many strategies to negotiate with peers, parents and others to overcome these restrictions. The remainder of the paper will discuss what consequences this lack of space has on girls' leisure and how they negotiate their own space within this environment, focusing specifically on five types of space, namely the park, the youth club, the town centre, the woods and the home.

The park

A few of the girls in my research group occasionally go to the park either to have a sneaky cigarette or watch the boys "mess around with the football". They rarely talk about this activity in positive terms. I asked one girl why she went to the park if she found it boring,

> Mary: "Dunno really nowhere else to go. Its somewhere to 'ave a fag and a chat if your mates are around".

I then asked: "Do you ever play football or ask if you can play?"

> Mary: "No way, you know what boys are like about their precious balls. I play women's rugby. They get all leggy about that and take the mick".

This particular girl was trying to break out of the confines traditional female activities and into the realm of the traditional male activity. However, even though she had legitimised her status within this space to herself and other members of the women's rugby team, she was still confined to the swings and roundabout when the boys were around. She also faced a certain amount of opposition from the girls who did not participate in rugby. Although they did not say it directly to Mary, they have referred to her as butch, lesbo and rough. Thus attitude of peers to certain spaces also has a direct effect on where girls decide to spend their time. As the example above showed, the rugby field was not considered by Mary's peers to be a desirable space for their leisure.

The boys, on the other hand, are allowed to 'mess around' on the swings but can also show off playing football, rugby or other ball sports. Girls are marginalised to the peripheries not only in physical terms, the park being placed at the edge of the recreation ground, but also in social terms. Boys have the capacity to exercise a certain amount of social control over certain spaces, because of their traditional associations, which are reinforced by schools, peers and parents. Even though Mary was prepared to take part in a non-stereotypical female sport, she was not prepared to challenge her male peers outside of her rugby practice. Nava stresses that the regulation of girls is largely reinforced by boys through reference to some notion of femininity which incorporates different modes of sexual behaviour, difference and compliance. Outside of the home girls are observers of boys activities and boys are observers of girls' passivity (Nava, 1992).

The youth club

These perceptions of certain spaces and their associations were exemplified when a few of the girls from Hillside and myself were sat discussing where there was to go and what there was to do in the area. It became apparent that where you 'hung out' was a direct reflection on how you were perceived as an individual. (It is important to remember this is a subjective view from those girls who attend the youth club.)

Girls who hung out at the youth club were okay, although you were either cool amongst this group or a sap (girls who do not conform to the behaviour of the 'in crowd'). The difference between these two identities was that to be cool you did not spend much time inside the youth club, but hung about outside smoking and chatting with each other, or the boys. The only time you go into the youth club is if it is raining or if there is some good music playing. The saps, on the other hand, spent most of their time within the building, never danced (the dance floor being the domain of the cool girls) and spent most of the evening away from the boys seated in a corner chatting amongst themselves. A girl may occasionally break out of the sap identity if she smokes and is asked for a light or 'two's' on a fag (when one girl has smoked half the cigarette, she then passes it on to somebody else to finish).

The dance floor is one place within the youth club that girls occupy in their own right. Boys may dominant all other areas and activities of the youth club but the girls will physically remove them if they interfere with their dancing. They even dictate what music should be played and will, if necessary, do their own DJ-ing if they are dissatisfied with the music that is being played. The dance floor is a space where they can express themselves and communicate their own individuality and style. Youth clubs' activities generally are geared to boys' interests. As Jephcott argues girls' club activities are often jettisoned in favour of activities for boys because girls are less delinquent and do not need to be kept out of trouble (Jephcott, 1967: p. 138).

However, even when the girls do dance they are still subject to certain types of social control. They cannot show too much abandon or individuality for fear of being jeered at by the boys and other members of their peer group. Thus as well as having to face physical and practical boundaries, there are also significant social boundaries that must not be crossed if you wish to remain part of the 'gang. '

The town centre

Another area where girls hang about is the town centre. Girls who occupied this space were viewed as the 'hard gang'; they hung around with boys much of the time and were therefore assumed to be 'right slags'. As Lees asserts "a girl must not hang around too much waiting for boys, but all girls must hang around sufficiently" (Lees, 1986: p. **??**). When two of these hard girls came into the club one evening, the cool gang went outside and started justifying their own territory to each other by making such comments as:

"Who the fuck do they think they are?"

"Dirty slags probably ran out of boys to shag everywhere else,"

"She better not start on Ben or I'll punch her face in."

When these girls came out of the youth club after about ten minutes, both groups of girls smiled at each other and said 'hi-ya'.

Green, *et al.* believe sexuality is a central factor in the representation of women pursuing their leisure. The notion of "respectability" enters into minds when there is a discussion of women's mobility and their use of space. contributing to the division between respectable women and whore (Green, *et al.*, 1990: p. 113).

Hence the associations and stereotypes that are attached to certain spaces have a major influence on what type of peer group one becomes a member of and where that peer group spends their time. Sexual associations are particularly important, especially for girls. The stereotypes and associations attached to certain spaces can therefore lead to informal exclusion, by girls of boys, and by girls of girls.

This is particularly true in relation to sexual reputations, as the example above shows. Girls who are assumed to be sexually active are constantly subject to derogatory comments and may be excluded from groups who participate in organised activities. In the case of Mary, she was not excluded so much by the girls even though she was stereotyped as butch for playing rugby, but was excluded by the boys because she was not considered to be active in gender-appropriate behaviour.

The woods

Thus many of the girls avoid certain places and activities because of their associations. Instead, they take advantage of their rural surroundings, to hide from disapproving eyes and experience the freedom that other spaces fail to offer. Although woods also have traditional associations with boys, many of the girls spend a lot of their time during evenings sitting in the woods, chatting and smoking. Weekends are also spent in the woods. If parents consent (and sometimes even if they have not), the girls will camp there overnight. I asked two of the girls who said they had been camping the previous weekend with three other friends if they had been scared in the woods on their own. They both said that they had not been and agreed that they were less likely to come to harm in the woods than on the street: "at least no-one can see you in the wood". I asked them how they spent the evening. Anna replied that:

"I lit a fire, cos the others wouldn't 'ave a clue, then we sat round smoking and drinking and 'aving a laugh. It was real good because we could get real pissed up with no-one around to tell us off or to shut up or nothin' and we kept it secret from the boys so they wouldn't come and find us".

The woods are also used in school hours as well. It is not unusual for the girls to spend their lunch money on cigarettes and to smoke them in the woods that back on to the school. The woods are also a perfect escape route, as one girl pointed out to me:

"sometimes if you don't feel like going to a lesson you can jump over the fence and sit in the woods till it's over".

The girls use the woods as a space where they can spend their leisure time on their own terms. It provides a hiding place where they can engage in activities that would be met with disapproval by some of their peers and parents. However, although many girls use this space, some are not allowed because of parents' perceptions of it as an unsafe area. At the time of the particular camping trip referred to previously two of the girls were not allowed to go due to their parents perceptions of the woods as being unsafe. The girls were allowed to spend time with their friends at the woods in the day, but they were out of bounds at night. Hence girls must also negotiate with their parents as well as their peers when attempting to find their own leisure space. On one occasion Rachel defied her parents and camped out in spite of their request not to. She was found out and grounded for the week. The next weekend she asked her parents if she could go to a local festival. They agreed to trust her and let her go as long as she was back at a reasonable time. Rachel ended up staying out until 6.30 a.m. and sleeping in the car with two of her male friends. When she told her mother, she couldn't understand why she was so angry. She told me:

"I mean first of all she complains that I'm out in the open where anything could happen to me, and is not as though a group of five girls could protect themselves, then she takes a fit because I sleep in a car that you can lock, with two boys who are pretty handy."

Obviously there is a conflict between the adolescent's view of safety and that of the parents'. Valentine notes how women avoid perceived dangerous places at dangerous times and have restricted use of space because of this. She also comments on the differences women associate with spaces and places depending on whether it is day or night time. Within the day time she suggests that women fear some places, but at night women fear all public spaces when they are alone, because of the decreased visibility and increased opportunities for attack (Valentine, 1989). If this is so it is not surprising that mothers of rural young women are unhappy about their daughters roaming the woods at night. Rachel failed to understand the danger that both situations presented. One of Rachel's friends pointed out that her mum might have been worried about her going to the festival because of the opportunity to be with boys and hence the risk of becoming pregnant. Rachel had not thought of this and justified her mothers anger on those terms. Pregnancy is a major concern of many of the parents. The girls constantly complain that their parents will not let them go to certain places. because those places are associated with boys and hence the danger of pregnancy in their parent's minds, which again determines where the girls spend their leisure time.

The home

Another issue which constrains girls' leisure is the problem of transport. As mentioned earlier, the possibility of getting from one place to another is extremely limited. There is a heavy reliance on parents or older brothers and sisters with cars to provide transport. Some of the girls who I have met at the youth club live between one to ten miles away and find it very difficult to go to the youth club every week. Their parents may not have a car or refuse to take them. In this instance they generally have four choices: they can either walk, depending on how far away they live and if anybody is willing to walk with them; ask a friend stay at their house for the night; persuade an older boy from the youth club to give them a lift; or ultimately stay at home. Few take the latter option. Each of these options has a number of consequences associated with it. Walking lays the girls open to a variety of dangers. Even if they live only half a mile away from their leisure destination they may have to walk across an open space such as a football pitch or through a wooded area. These spaces often represent symbolic boundaries to both the girls and their parents. Staying over at a friend's house depends on whether the particular friend shares a bedroom with siblings and whether parents permit it. One girl told me that she was no longer able to have her friend Nicola to stay on a school night because her mum said Nicola talked too loud and kept every one awake. Bedroom culture (McRobbie, 1984) depends on having your own private space, but even if girls do have their own room privacy is not guaranteed, as they can be invaded by younger brothers or sisters and parents at any time.

Getting a lift home with an older boy is sometimes possible, especially if you or your friend happen to be 'going out' with or 'seeing' one of these boys. One of the girls said she specifically went out with Dave so he would drive her and her friends around:

"It's brilliant. I can go any where now without 'aving to ask my parents for a lift".

The final option of staying at home is a last resort. If friends are unable to see their friends in the week, they will either stay over at the weekend or travel to the city to meet. Staying over at the weekend again depends upon the girl's access to private space within the home. The girls may have to share a bedroom with up to three sisters, which can prevent the so-called 'bedroom culture' taking place. If the option of travelling to the city is taken, it often means that after paying for your bus fare, a snack and possibly cigarettes there is no money left, so the rest of the day is spent hanging around the bus station or window shopping.

Transport is also a hurdle to financial gain. Many of the girls have complained that they could not get a job because they had no way of getting to and from work. Roberts suggested that:

> Between establishing independence from parental supervision and acquiring the incomes necessary for personal transport, young people are probably more confined than a generation ago with the motor car having reduced the availability of public transport and transformed the bicycle from a means of transport into a toy. (Roberts, 1978: p. 20)

One of the girls was lucky enough to find a job in a pub approximately two miles from her home, where there was an arrangement that if she could get the bus to work her employers would bring her home. Baby sitting is another option but it is usually for family or relatives and the rewards are often very small.

A final restriction that may be placed upon girls, opportunities for leisure and employment are the general domestic demands which seem to apply specifically to girls. As Hendry, *et al.* point out:

> For some girls in particular whose 'skills' are more marketable in the world of casual labour and of whom much is demanded at home, the idea of limitless leisure as free time may ring rather hollow. (Hendry, *et al.*, 1993: p. 2).

These restrictions are doubly problematic in the winter months. As the darker nights draw in and the weather gets worse, girls are even more restricted as to where they can spend their leisure time. They may decide to use the facilities the youth club has to offer, but this again depends on parents' willingness to drive in bad weather conditions and whether you are in with the 'right' crowd. Thus a rural environment can provide ways of escape from many of the restrictions that adolescents girls face generally, or it can restrain their activities to the extent that successful peer involvement eludes them.

The rural environment can either enhance or solve some of the problems that girls encounter in both their private and public lives. Ultimately depending on the perceptions of those around them, they face the possibilities of freedom or boredom, restriction or risk, inclusion or isolation. As Roberts (1978: p. 35) pointed out:

> If the very definition of the countryside as a leisure resource is a social construct, this applies equally to what counts as recreation.

References

Critcher. C., and Tomlinson. A. (1995) *Sociology of leisure.* London: E & FN Spon.

Deem. R. (1986) *All work and no play? The sociology of women and leisure.* Milton Keynes: Open University Press.

FODMAP (1995) *Report, Countryside and Community Research Unit.* Cheltenham and Gloucester College.

Green. E., Hebron. S., Woodward. D (1990) *Women's leisure, what leisure?.* London: MacMillan.

Hendry. L. B., Shucksmith. J., Love J. G., and Glendinning. A. (1993) *Young people's leisure and lifestyles.* London: Routledge.

Jephcott. P. (1967) *Time of one's own.* London: Oliver and Boyd.

Leech, K., Jordan, B. (1970) *Drugs for young people: Their use and misuse.* European Printing Company.

Lees, S. (1986) *Losing out: Sexuality and adolescent girls.* London: Hutchinson.

────── (1993) *Sugar and spice — sexuality and adolescent girls.* Middlesex: Penguin.

Lloyd, A. (1975) 'Women's place, mans place', *Landscape* Vol. 20, No. 1: pp. 10-13.

MacKenzie, S. (1980) 'Women's place, woman's space', *Area*, Vol. 12 (pages unnumbered).

Matrix. (1984) *Making space: Women and the man-made environment.* London: Pluto Press.

McRobbie. A., and McCabe. T. (1981) *Feminism for girls: An adventure story.* London: Routledge & Kegan Paul.

McRobbie. A., and Nava. M. (1984) *Gender and generation.* Bath: Pitman Press.

Nava, M. (1992) *Changing cultures: Feminism, youth and consumerism.* London: Sage Publications Ltd.

O'Connor, D. (1986) *Glue sniffing and solvent abuse.* Cheadle: Boys and Girls Welfare Society.

Roberts, K. (1978) *Contemporary society and the growth of leisure.* London: Longman.

Valentine, G. (1989) 'Geography of women's fear', *Area*, Vol. 21, No. 4: pp. 385-390.

Weiner, R. S. R. (1970) *Drugs and schoolchildren.* Longman, Harlow.

Wimbush. E., and Talbot. M. (1988) *Relative freedoms: Women and leisure.* Milton Keynes: Open University Press.

Stepping into Aerobics?

Anne Flintoff, Sheila Scraton
and Peter Bramham

Leeds Metropolitan University

Postmodern thinkers have developed an interest in the body and its cultural significance in these 'new times'. Following the work of Foucault (1979, 1980) whose diverse subjects included the body, sexuality, medicine and power, contemporary writers have celebrated individual agency, diversity, fragmentation and changing cultural tastes. Linked to this growing individualisation, there has been a sharper focus in social analysis on the individual, the body and their cultural significance in the construction of personal identities and in relationships in general (Featherstone, et al. 1991; Shilling, 1993). Within the media, the thin and toned body is one of the dominant cultural icons of postmodern tastes and there are growing and diverse armies of experts to encourage healthy lifestyles and body management regimes. It is not just that some people, usually women, are on some kind of diet to attain an acceptable body shape: most are on a individualised 'diet' or body regimen, which involves lifestyle, including physical exercise and body maintenance.

What makes these new times different is a growing moral and political economy of health around the body and body shape. It is articulated mainly by the middle-aged and the service classes who demand, and actively pursue, healthy lifestyles. The media and cultural industries sustain icons of the powerful body for each gender: the masculine muscular body and the feminine toned body. Agency and moral worth become fused into body shape and a thin, powerfully-defined body, gained through exercise is a symbolic good of much currency and distinction (Winter, 1995).

The centrality of the body in people's lives is cast in sharp relief by 'deviant' examples of bulimia and anorexia. The social pressures generating eating disorders are in part symptomatic of the centrality of the body and the contested terrain of the gender order (Bordo, 1993). Particularly in sport and in fashion, many individuals are prepared to take performance enhancing drugs, to undergo surgery, or to embark on rigorous and

93

compulsive regimes of exercising. During the 1980s and 1990s there have been substantial developments in physical conditioning and exercise programmes both in software (namely videos, magazines and books) and in hardware (viz. home multi-gyms, weights and conditioning machines). Nike and Reebok have invested huge sums to develop and market attractive clothing and footwear for step aerobics in particular. Media stars such as Jane Fonda and Cindy Crawford have popularised aerobics. It is no accident that Cindy Crawford's video is entitled 'Shape Your Body', and whilst Cindy works her way through various exercises, some of which are even thought to be unsafe, the voice over is that of 'Fitness Expert Radu, New York's toughest trainer'. The feminine supermodel and the tough male trainer are just one permutation of the ideologies of gender order constructed by 'working out' in these new times.

If any one item or commodity symbolises these aspects of post-modernity it must be the exercise bike — whether located in the privacy of ones own home or in the more public arena of the gym. The restlessness of postmodern tastes and experiences can also be symbolised in the home or the multi-gym. One cycles furiously to nowhere, inspired perhaps by some simulated image, but what is crucial is to 'work out', to work to maintain or change one's body shape (Scraton and Bramham, 1995).

This paper grows out of an interest in the broader context of leisure lifestyles, the gender order and the postmodern preoccupation with the body by defining its desired and desirable shape. It seeks to map out a research project to begin to address some of the salient issues around the body, body image and physical exercise. The particular focus of our research project is young people's participation within a range of physical conditioning activities, both within and out of the school context. The first part of the paper draws out some key themes from some ongoing ethno-graphic data collected within conditioning classes by the research team. It concludes with some key theoretical and methodological issues that must be addressed. The coda of the paper outlines ongoing substantive research for understanding people's involvement in aerobics and physical con-ditioning programmes.

Aerobics, enthusiasms and the "body shop"

The term "body shop" is either associated with Anita Roddick or with cars, car repairs and resprays. Indeed, the garage metaphor can be stretched to understand the individual's involvement with exercise regimes. Just as cars are not solely functional objects or vehicles but rather statements about gender identity, social prestige, and so on, the same may be said about the human body. Just as cars are polished, cleaned, waxed, main-tained serviced and lovingly cared for, the same interest and commitment can be shown in the body. The American anthropologist, Horace Miner (1955), has commented wryly upon the Nacerima's central belief that the human body is subject to decay and disease unless exorcised by ritual.

Bourdieu's (1984) research too has focused on the body as a site for social practices and class distinction. He argues that the (male) professional and *petite bourgeois* classes define the body and its diet as end in themselves, whereas the working classes have a more instrumental approach both to the body and food consumption.

In terms of postmodern tastes, for many, the body is a crucial signifier of one's social standing and well being. There is then a cultural exhortation amongst the new service class of cultural intermediaries to maintain and enhance its symbolic value, its shape and its performance. Car enthusiasts gaze upon, clean and polish, talk about cars, and similar work is undertaken on the human body. Just as the Body Shop chain prides itself on being politically and ecologically correct, there is a similar drive to find a sustainable exercise regime and body shape. Consequently, there are exercise enthusiasts, with missionary zeal who seek to convert people to exercise regimens.

This section of the paper draws upon the experience of participant observation over a six month period of two aerobics classes within very different community settings. One is a step aerobics class, led by a male instructor, in a suburban setting in Leeds; the other is an aerobics class, led by a female instructor, in a small rural, not particularly thriving village, near Skipton, North Yorkshire. Despite the differing location of the classes, the differing genders of both participant researchers and instructors and differing format of activities, certain common themes emerge from this research into physical conditioning.

Both instructors are part of a wider professionalising network, accredited by RSA training qualifications, sustained by the professional hardware of sound systems, personal microphones and commercially produced tapes. The step aerobics class is a private commercial venture: a self-employed trainer provides all the necessary hardware — the steps, weights, instructions for circuits, and so on. All are commercially produced with identifiable brand names. The cost of a step class is double the cost of the aerobics class. Interestingly, in both classes, participants are trusted to pay in their own fees and handle any change unsupervised from the communal pot. Yet one hour of step aerobic class will generate over £100 in income, whereas the aerobics class less than £30. The aerobics class is much closer to self-organised enthusiasms (Bishop and Hoggett, 1986). The group is local, inclusive and provides mutual aid in leisure. For example, each individual brings her own towel to lie down on (unlike the blue rubber mats in the step aerobics class), and 'weights' such as bags of sugar or tins of beans (unlike the dumbbells and ankle bracelets in the other class). The same group of participants always turn up to the aerobics class whereas there is approximately a 30 per cent turn over in the step class, which therefore has a much greater proportion of casual users or 'strangers', arriving singly by car. In contrast, the vast majority walk to the village-based aerobics class, chat in groups before the start and linger on afterwards to talk to friends or the instructor about this and that.

Safe spaces

The aerobics class is in essence a safe legitimate female world within which women of most shapes and sizes can engage with a range of physical activities forming familiar rituals and routines — warm-up and stretching exercises, sequences of movements to music, relaxation exercises, and physical conditioning exercises. As in Dixey and Talbot's study of bingo in Leeds (1982), women can attend aerobics classes of an hour's length that fit in with other aspects of their lifestyle and domestic routines, without fear of criticism from partners, husbands and families. It is a local legitimate feminine space and activity — an 'outing', like the bingo hall, the hairdressers, and the adult education class, as documented in other research in leisure activities (see Deem, 1986; Green, *et al.*, 1990; Little, *et al.*, 1988).

Another feature of the classes is one of health and safety — just as individuals trust certain hairdressers with their hair, so women trust instructors with their bodies. Instructors approach newcomers and question them about injuries, illnesses, physical conditions, etc. Before starting the class and throughout the routines and exercises, participants are encouraged to 'try it and see', to set their own pace and level of difficulty, to rest when required, to take drinks as necessary and not to participate in any activities and exercises that exacerbate old and current injuries.

Choice

Individuals have a choice of classes to attend in any locality; some are aerobics, some are hybrids of circuits and aerobics, step aerobics and high impact aerobics and exercises. As in other spheres of leisure, choice is mediated by a variety of acknowledged and unacknowledged conditions such as income, ethnicity, accessibility, cultural competence, gender and so on. At a simple micro level within the class itself, each individual can choose the intensity of the workout (for example, setting the height of the step, level of difficulty of the exercise in the circuit, or a low level of high level exercise). Such choices are often made in relation to friendship networks, access to transport, the location and the particular instructor involved. Wherever the class takes place, there is ample opportunity for individual agency. There is no strong collective pressure to perform as in formal team games and sports but rather one can work at one's own pace. One of the catch phrases of one of the aerobics instructors is "you choose": between low or high impact exercises (e.g. 'jacks'or 'half-stars'; 'marching' or 'jogging'; 'lunges' or 'spotty dogs' — always with the injunction "you choose"). The same applies within the step aerobics class as the instructor always offers high and low impact choices in exercise routines and the individual can always set the height of the step (one or two inserts) to determine the intensity and difficulty of the workout.

Compulsion

It would be a mistake to imagine that aerobics and step aerobics are completely individualised, personalised and arbitrary. There is a substantial element of compulsion and collective pressure on individuals to attend classes and to perform whilst there. Participants often depend on the instructor for motivation rather than relying on self-motivation as well as acquiescing trancelike to the routines the instructor has planned for the class. Part of the moral and political economy of physical exercise is that it legitimates other spheres of free time and consumption. Individual lifestyles construct a balance between healthy and unhealthy activities and ' working out' can be part of a complicated equation within people's lifestyles. Strict diets may be violated, weekly norms of alcohol consumption flouted provided one 'burns off the calories' or 'fights the flab' in the gym or in exercise classes. Even smoking, seen by conventional medical wisdom as extremely dangerous to health, may be condoned as it releases stress and maintains a thin body by controlling appetite. Physical exercise is an important ingredient in both accumulating and reducing guilt in people's lifestyles. Needless to say, in postmodern times the individual must negotiate the level of guilt, the intensity of physical activity, its relationship to other dimensions in the individual's lifestyle (both with his/her conscience, body image and so on and within the context of social conventions and other people's lifestyles).

In contrast to the elements of choice in physical exercise and conditioning is the compulsion as instructors encourage individuals and the group collectively to "keep going", "just six more", "as many as you can in thirty seconds". There is the collective pressure to work hard as a group, to have a good work out and to handle new moves and techniques competently, to synchronise moves and movements so that the whole group is in time with and mirrors the instructor's movements. The class itself is regimented, controlled and carefully constructed and monitored. In one sense it is competitive as individuals often attempt high impact work even if it is not appropriate, simply because everyone else is doing it.

Competence

A successful class at an individual and collective level is the skilled accomplishment of interaction between the instructor and class members working through a complex of exercise routines. The machine-like fluidity of the routines appears to be effortlessly achieved but is always subject to negotiation, subversion and possible collapse. Tutors never know precisely who will turn up for the class and whether there will be sufficient space for all class members or if the hall will be too crowded. Things can go wrong when new members are slow to learn routines, or class members lethargically work through exercise routines they do not particularly enjoy. Going with friends can minimise the embarrassment of going wrong. One ill-coordinated individual can cause substantial havoc with the confined space of a village hall; casual and new members may find it hard to remember or decipher particular moves in aerobics — funky steps, thunderbirds, hops without the scotch go west, grapevines. The same applies to particular steps in step aerobics — rocking horses, combinations, etc. The individual's confidence wanes when she cannot keep up with the rest of the class or consistently muddles up complicated moves — such as coming off the wrong side of the step, jumping from the step or starting on the wrong foot. Although the instructors patiently (and pointedly) count the class in — with extra counts and demonstrations, consistent misdemeanors by individuals are turned into jokes or irony, supported by knowing looks or comments directed towards the miscreant. The instructor has to strike a satisfactory balance between complicated and easy routines so as not to risk losing the newcomers whilst simultaneously stretching the experienced class members.

Body exposure

One of the central rationales of working out, or working on the body, is one of display. The body is exposed to the gaze of the subject, with the mirror as a crucial audience. The body matters: it is exposed in all physical activity but specially so in aerobics. The stereotypical clothing of the aerobics class exaggerates body shape and contours — the thong, the single top and the leotard provide no hiding place. The instructors of both classes wear minimal clothing (for example vests instead of short sleeved T-shirts) to expose legs, shoulders, body shape — the muscular definition of the body is too good to hide or must be wrapped in clothing that still depicts and defines body shape. Some participants model themselves on the instructors and wear similar tight-fitting and fashionable clothing They position themselves in the front line, directly in the line of vision of the instructor. Others wear the 'right' clothing but are unfit or overweight and the leotard exposes, parodies and displays their shape. It is almost as if wearing the correct garment will produce the desired body shape by magic. Again others wear loose clothing for comfort, to protect themselves from scrutiny, as a realistic assessment of how far they deviate from the aerobics ideal, or a resistance to the body shape on offer.

No matter how loose the clothing, the body is exposed to the gaze of others, particularly the instructor, who faces the class and issues instructions for the routines and exercises. The great fear of aerobics is to be caught under the gaze of others, to be at the front of the class under the surveillance of those participants working out behind one's back as well as being subject to the supervisory gaze of the instructor. Consequently, participants develop a range of strategies to deal with these contingencies. In the step class, people arrive early, collect their sets from the side of the hall, and position their steps at the back of the class. In the aerobics class, people tend to have their own place, alongside one or a group of their friends in the hall and are figuratively put out when anyone (for instance, a newcomer) takes up 'their' position. The aerobics instructor often innovates within the sessions, for example, making the whole class turn 90 degrees to the left, whilst she moves to the side of the hall. This means that those working out safely on the left hand side of the hall are suddenly exposed and are in the front row under scrutiny. The same risk of exposure occurs when the group is divided into three rows and after each exercise, the one at the front drops to the back of the hall. Equally with circuits inside the class, with the individual working in smaller groups of four, one is much more open to supervision. It is hardly surprising that most participants are most comfortable at the back of the class, anonymous, where they can see and not be seen, follow the movements of others and not be seen — unless they fall completely out of step with the rest of the group or stop to take a drink.

Sexuality

Linked to fear of body exposure is the embarrassment of difference, of not conforming to the cultural ideal of a thin toned body. But what precisely is the body on offer that one should aspire? To look to the instructors one should imagine it to be male — to be strong, lean, muscular, energetic, and in control. When working through routines, the female instructor emphasises being in control, placing one's arms or legs in the correct safe position, feeling the stretch and when working out emphasising "lots of power — I like power", as she enthusiastically bounces her way through the routines. In the step aerobics group, the instructor is male and has achieved his body shape through physical conditioning and multi-gym work. His body shape has not been achieved solely through aerobics and he seldom works out during sessions. Women in the sessions are keen not to become too muscly like the instructor but simply want to be toned up and to have a desirable feminine body shape. Indeed, when introducing body conditioning exercises to the group, the instructor stressed explicitly that it was not to make women muscular but simply to tone up one's body shape.

　　Embarrassment occurs when particular exercises carry suggestive undercurrents of heterosexual intercourse. Indeed, in one all-women aerobics group, the instructor used to shout "make it sexxy" for certain of the routines. For example, as the name implies, 'pelvic tilts' require thrusting and tightening movement of the groin area, just like a youthful Elvis Presley. In one session, a group of three or four young girls (14-15 year olds) burst out in giggles during the exercise and the instructor explained why we were doing the exercise to strengthen groin muscles, tighten stomach and so on. Equally, 'hula hoops' requires gyrating the pelvic area first left circles and then right. One can detect a particular seriousness, a delicate tension and focus during these sexualised exercises. There is an age and status dimension too; one does not expect to see 45-65 year old women, well-respected community leaders, engaging in what could be interpreted as sexually-explicit movements in public.

Men in women's world

Given that aerobics is about women engaging in physical exercise in a feminine world, precisely what relationship do aerobics play within the wider ideological and material practices of patriarchy and the gender order? How should one understand or read aerobics (Winter, 1995)? Is it best understood as direct expression of a hegemonic masculinity as women strive to achieve a desirable body shape to make them attractive to men and the legislators of the cultural industries? Do women compete with each other to have a desirable or satisfactory body shape, with male approval a secondary factor? Is aerobics particularly suited to diverse women's needs as a safe, locally accessible and healthy form of exercise, separate from the masculine gaze? Or are we looking at a complex mixture of social practices with overlapping and contradictory rationales and motivations?

If most men feel excluded from aerobics and define it as a women-only or feminine activity, what position do men occupy or negotiate if they choose to enter this type of physical activity? It is particularly instructive to look at the position of the male instructor in the step aerobics class, as he seems to personify many of the claims of a hegemonic masculinity. He is in the dominant position, providing a commercial service in an all-women world. He resists feminisation by a pronounced display of masculinity, a well-defined body shaped by weights, and clothing conspicuous by its absence (vest, lycra shorts, with no jock strap or sports support, all in dark colours, unlike the fluorescent or florid tops of female instructors). He calls the shots as he puts thirty or forty women in each class through the routines, and he provides a professional technical account of the benefits of particular exercises in terms of bio-mechanics, muscle groups and so on (whereas the female instructor uses everyday language about body shape to 'sell' activities to the group — "this one's good for your tummies").

The issues around gender order become more pressing for a man having to join an aerobics group for research purposes. This was a distinct research strategy since the research team was keen to explore how different masculinities and femininities were negotiated and constructed within aerobics classes. Going along to an aerobics class represents a challenge to men and their definitions of masculinity and masculinities. Aerobics is for women and is targeted at the 'problem areas' for women's bodies. Indeed, one gym in Skipton is called 'Bums and Tums'. If men want to work out, why not do so in the more competitive 'harder' male environment of the multi-gym or weights room? Why not stay within traditional male-dominated individual and team sports? Whatever happened to male bonding and the 'locker room' culture? Why expose one's self and one's body to what could easily be a discrediting experience? Why run the risk of accusations of voyeurism? Of more political significance, why spoil a women-only group by being the odd one out?

The male researcher gained access to the all-women group by being defined as a safe, supervised and accompanied male, as husband and father attending the class, and encouraged to do so by family members. The instructor's policy was to welcome all comers, including men, into the aerobics class and actually planned to have a full session with the village football team but interestingly no one turned up. So the male researcher's presence within the group was mediated by family networks, other local friendships and a great deal of humour. Once inside the class, the research strategy is one of being invisible, to focus on observation and to be as non-threatening as possible, to be located at the back of the hall, cocooned by family and friends. Invisibility is further sustained by gaining competence at the movements, routines, and the exercise programmes so that one becomes part of the class and collective synergy when routines run well. Invisibity is sustained by avoiding body exposure, wearing loose T shirts and legging throughout, resisting the temptation to appear as a Mr. Motivator look-alike, with baseball cap, lurid lycra top and leggings and the air Jordan Nike boots. Whilst women may join aerobics classes as an end in itself, men are out of place. Despite attending as part of a family group, the researcher still felt the need to explain his presence to the instructor at the first class in terms of an attempt to increase flexibility for fell running (rather than admit to being involved in a research project). Even so the researcher still felt it politic to sound out the instructor, partners and friends whether it was all right to continue attending the classes and whether they had noticed any negative comments from other members in the rest of the group.

It is interesting that, in the step aerobics group of 30-40 participants, only one or two are men. They too are out of place even in the more masculine world of step aerobics. In one evening session, apart from the researcher, there was a man, in his late fifties, sitting alone on his step, wearing a 1960s style tracksuit top, shorts, with blue knee support-bandage, staring into space, talking to no one, waiting resignedly for the class proper to start.

Heterosexual males within aerobics class present something of a problem. There is the masculine cultural imperative of patriarchy to judge women's bodies in terms of their sexual attractiveness, and to slip into a pornographic gaze. On the other hand women may attend classes to develop the correct body shape or 'the look' (Hargreaves, 1993).

Stepping into aerobics research

The above ethnography raises a plethora of interesting theoretical and empirical questions that require further investigation. Research completed in four Leeds secondary schools confirm many of the key themes outlined in our analysis of aerobics in an out-of-school community context. The school-based research generated questionnaire data in terms of gender attitudes to different sporting, recreational and physical conditioning activities and programmes (Milosevic, 1995). Data analysis highlighted a clear gender difference in attitudes towards body and self-image amongst the year 11 pupils included in the sample.

The theoretical and empirical questions are complex and comprehensive and must be cast in terms of social theory. One major area of exploration must engage with questions around the topics of self-identity, the body and sexuality. Although work has begun to explore the social construction of sexualities (Weeks, 1991, Tiefer, 1995), the complex relationship between physicality and sexuality requires closer analysis. There is a need to deconstruct the 'natural' ideologies of hegemonic masculinity and explore the ways in which individuals, groups and institutions contest, resist as well as reproduce and mediate dominant ideologies around the body, gender and identity. What is required is a sociology of the body and gender order. Postmodern analysis has been sensitive to the aesthetic and to detailed readings of particular texts, practices and cultural forms. What is now required is to test the generality of such readings by studying the social location and distribution of postmodern tastes, predilections and practices (Scraton, 1994).

A second topic for consideration revolves around activity and agency. Research needs to examine the relationship between activity, physical exercise, control and empowerment. What are the connections between working out in a women-only aerobics class, feeling good about one's body shape and other aspects of life — self confidence, educational aspirations, employment careers, political action and involvement, leisure tastes and so on?

A third topic for consideration is space. The nature of the relationship between private and public spaces has long been one of the cornerstones of feminist analysis and action. The presence and absence of women in public spaces provide a crucial topic for social analysis. Occupying and contesting spaces provides a crucial axis from which to grasp the nature of the gender order. Space is also linked to the issue of power and surveillance, an important focus of postmodern theorising. The gaze of a dominant heterosexuality on the body provides the major points of reference for physicality, sexuality, identity and gender. Young people have an ambivalence about public scrutiny; the phrase 'hiding in the light' neatly captures young people's desire to be noticed yet not interrogated by the gaze of adults and subsequent control (Hebdige, 1990).

These themes provide the backdrop to the research project, Stepping into Active Leisure, which is currently under way at Leeds Metropolitan University. The research will examine the transition of young people from school-based experience of physical activity to a physically active lifestyle. Phase One of the research studies the attitudes of young men and women (aged 15-16) to physical activity and school PE. The second phase of the research examines the attitudes and behaviour of young adults (20-25 year olds) towards physical 'conditioning' activities. In its school-based phase, the research seeks to understand the reasons why some people drop out of, or lack enthusiasm for school PE. It seeks to identify activities that are seen to be most enjoyable and explore the influence of gender on school and out-of-school activities. During the second community-based phase of the research, the project will map out how 'conditioning' activities fit into the lives of young adults, as well as exploring issues in relation to opportunity, body image, health and well being. The aim is to study 'conditioning' activities within different organisation settings in the private and public sectors. Finally, the research aims to relate current experiences of leisure 'conditioning' sessions to previous school experiences of physical activity and PE. The collection of such detailed empirical data makes it possible to ground some of the key theoretical concerns about the body, sexuality and gender suggested by the aerobics ethnography.

References

Bordo, S. (1993) *Unbearable weight.* Berkeley/Los Angeles/London: University of California Press.

Bourdieu, P. (1984) *Distinction: A social critique of the Judgement of taste.* London: Routledge.

Deem, R. (1986) *All work and no play?.* Milton Keynes: Open University Press.

Dixey, R. with Talbot, M. (1982) *Women, leisure and bingo.* Leeds: Trinity and All Saints College.

Featherstone, M., Hepworth, M. and Turner, R. (1991) *The body: Social processes and cultural theory.* London: Sage.

Foucault, M. (1979) *Discipline and punish: The birth of a prison.* New York, Random House.

Foucault, M. (1980) *The history of sexuality.* New York: Vintage Books.

Green, E., Hebron, S. and Woodward, D. (1990) *Women's leisure, what leisure?.* London: Macmillan.

Hargreaves, J. (1992) 'Bodies matter! Images of sport and female sexualisation', in C. Brackenridge (ed) *Body matters: Leisure images and lifestyles.* LSA Publication No. 47. Eastbourne: Leisure Studies Association, pp. 60-66.

Hebdige, D. (1990) *Hiding in the light.* London: Comedia.

Little, J., Peake, L. and Richardson, P. (1988) *Women in cities.* London: Macmillan.

Miner, H. (1955) 'Body ritual amongst the Nacirema', *American Anthropologist,* 58. pp. 503-507.

Milosevic, L. (1995) *Fair play: Gender and physical education.* Leeds: Leeds City Council Department of Education.

Scraton, S. (1994) 'The changing world of women and leisure: Feminism, post-feminism and leisure', *Leisure Studies*, Vol. 13, No. 4: pp. 249-261.

Scraton, S. and Bramham. P. (1995) 'Leisure and postmodernity', in M. Haralambos (ed) *Developments in sociology*. Ormskirk: Causeway Press, pp. 17-34.

Tiefer, L. (1995) *Sex is not a natural act.* Boulder, Colorado: Westview Press.

Weeks, J. (1991) *Against nature: Essays on history, sexuality and identity.* London: Rivers Oram Press.

Winter, T. (1995) 'An exercise in contradiction: Reading the aerobics video', in T. Adshead-Lansdale and C. Jones (eds) *Border tensions: Dance and discourse.* Proceeding of the 5th Study of Dance Conference: Guildford, University of Surrey.

Playing the Ball, or the Uses of League: Class, Masculinity and Rugby — a Case Study of Sudthorpe

Karl Spracklen

Leeds Metropolitan University

Introduction

> *I wouldn't die for my team, but I'd consider going into an extended coma for it.* [Laurie Daley, rugby league player for Canberra, New South Wales (Captain), Australia]

In Australia, where rugby league has the same kind of media exposure and following as soccer over here, the sports firm Nike recently launched a campaign using Laurie Daley and another Australian international, Paul Harragon. In it Harragon, a prop with a reputation for delivering "big hits" — hard tackles that use all the defender's strength and weight to knock the attacker to the floor, not always within the remit of the rulebook — "rattles off a list of injuries as long as your arm that he has suffered playing rugby league" (*Rugby League Week*, Vol. 26, No. 4). At the end of the advert Laurie Daley then proceeds to make the declaration cited at the start of this paper. When this sparked a debate within the Australian press, Daley's business manager said "I support what Nike have said in that the commercial was aimed at depicting sports competition at the highest possible level", (*Rugby League Week*, Vol. 26, No. 5).

Laurie Daley's comment, although scripted for an advert trying to sell trainers, carries with it some powerful messages: loyalty to the team, the overriding will to win, and the lack of concern (or indeed encouragement) of pushing the body to painful extremes. These are then equated by his manager's comments with the desired qualities an athlete needs to be at the top of the sporting ladder. One can see how through this advert the game of rugby league is associated with certain facets of "hardness", elements that become attached to the developing masculinities of young

105

players in Australia who look up to Daley: they see through the advert just what they have to be, what they have to learn, to succeed in the sport of their choice.

In this country the game is regionalised in the industrial areas that are linked by the M62 motorway, plus the towns of Western Cumbria and Furness. But there is a similarity between the game in both countries, and the game as it is played by people in Papua New Guinea, France and New Zealand: that of the dominance of men in terms of players, supporters and administrators. Rugby, of whatever code, in Beziers, Bradford, Brisbane or Bougainville, is a male-dominated game (e.g. see Grundlingh, 1994). The existence of women's union and league, and women fans on the terraces, does not   deflect from this one inescapable fact. Each code of rugby was developed by — and is still controlled by — men.

This paper looks at the social networks that surround the game of rugby league in an area of a northern city called Sudthorpe (a pseudonym). It is important to note that most rugby league is non-professional, a fact overlooked by Dunning and Sheard's work on rugby and professionalism (Dunning and Sheard, 1979). This area was once one of the most heavily populated parts of the city, but these days most of the residential and industrial buildings have disappeared from Sudthorpe for road projects and warehouses. The focal points for the social networks surrounding rugby league remain the pitches where amateur rugby league is played (though these are under threat: see Spink, 1989), the two clubhouses belonging to Chemicals Amateur Rugby League Football Club (ARLFC) and the Boys Club, and the pubs that have not been demolished.

Most of the people in the social networks that surround the game in Sudthorpe no longer live in Sudthorpe, and I have identified an imaginary community that has created its own symbolic boundaries around "the game" (Cohen, 1985), that originates in the days when Sudthorpe was a densely populated working class suburb. One aspect of this is the survival inside it of an expression of masculinity associated with this older, "real" working class community, which has been conflated with the masculinities projected by the game itself. If it can be seen that these expressions of dominant masculinity are passed via the game of rugby league to those men and boys seeking to enter the game, who then shape their own masculinities in an identical way, we can see how the imaginary community produces and maintains its identity. This paper attempts to draw out issues surrounding the concept of masculinity and expressions of that masculinity through examples from fieldwork.

Methodology

There were three elements to the study:

* an ethnography of the social networks of league in Sudthorpe;
* a review of popular literature produced by and for people interested in rugby league. (By 'popular literature' I do not intend to patronise or

belittle these sources, merely to differentiate them from the academic literature.) These sources include specialist newspapers, fan books and match reports.

- a set of semi-structured interviews with key informants from the field such as players, fans and administrators. I asked about their experiences in coming to league, and their perceptions about it: as will be seen, their *maleness* is important.

Sport, men and masculinities

Steel that he was, his courage never failed him, his conquering hand seized many a glorious prize when he came to battle... Thus I salute the hero. — Sweet balm to woman's eyes, yet woman's heart's disease! (Wolfram von Eschenbach, *Parzifal*)

In the poem *Parzifal* the aspiring knight is given an image of what it means to be a man, to be a knight. The hegemonic masculinity portrayed is one of nobility, courage and prowess in battle. It is the tourney ground where the allegorical character of the perfect 13th Century noble man is found. In writing his poem, von Eschenbach drew upon the noble culture of his time, writing about the things his audience held to be important in their everyday life. Hence it comes as no surprise to see the conflation of masculinity and the favoured sport of the 13th Century noble man.

The theoretical site of gender is often lumped together with those other sites for discrimination: race and class. Yet while class has influenced the development of sociology throughout the 20th Century as a primary concept of investigation, both race and gender have been seen as less important or ignored altogether by the meta-theorists. For example, Miliband (1989), although exploring these issues, feels it necessary to subsume them under the banner of class discrimination. This paper addresses the issue of masculinity, which (if pigeon-holed hierarchies are necessary to understand the theoretical field) has arisen from the feminist reassessment of the lack of gender directed social theory (Kimmel, 1987).

In the sociology of sport the impetus to place gender on the agenda came with responses to male dominance in sport and sports theory that reflected that dominance (J. A. Hargreaves, 1990). This has taken the form of highlighting inequalities and attempts to redress imbalances in participation, coverage etc. (Snyder and Spreitzer, 1989), following a liberal feminist agenda (Messner and Sabo, 1990). However, it has been noted that there are more deep rooted social structures that have to be addressed to deal with male dominance of sport. Critical feminists have pointed to a more complex relationship between gender, class, and sport that calls for changes in the social structure (J. A. Hargreaves, 1986, 1990; Talbot, 1988). Connell (1987) has described the "gender order", which describes gender as a process rather than a thing. Thus we are asked to study "a historically constructed pattern of power relations between men and women and definitions of femininity and masculinity" (Connell, 1987: pp. 98-99). This concept fits easily into my own conceptual interest with the processes surrounding the development of the imaginary communities I have described.

Masculinity is tied up with sport and sport's identity (Dunning, 1986; Whitson, 1990; Messner, 1992; Morgan, 1992). As Clarke and Critcher (1985: p. 162) comment, "sport remains an area where existing gender roles are re-established and confirmed". Competitive sport can be said to maintain gender divisions and perpetuate the rituals of masculinity (Bryson, 1990; Morgan, 1992). The historical dominance of men in sport, although ultimately connected to the patriarchal nature of western society, was enforced by the Victorian ideals of muscular Christianity and the belief in sport as a means of "making men" (see Mangan, 1981). Hoch (1972) described sport as a "school for male dominance". The feminist study of sport and masculinity belongs to the wider domain of the study of men and masculinity (Kimmel, 1987) which sees in feminism a way of exploring the male dominance of society, of "developing an analysis of men's problems and limitations... within the context of a feminist critique of male privilege" (Messner and Sabo, 1990: p. 13). Hence, one can describe sport as a social construction which helps to form the hegemonic relationship of men over women. Whitson (1990) argues that sport continues to bolster this hegemonic masculinity by the ritualisation of aggression, strength and skill in the male body and linking it to competitive achievement. Sport becomes a way of reaffirming male identity (Nankervis, 1994). One sees why the Daley advert was pitched to its young (male) target audience in such a way. Jansen and Sabo (1994) take the aggression one step further by exploring the use of war metaphors in sport that maintain the masculine hegemony. Television advertisements for the 1995 Premierships made an explicit connection by referring to Agincourt, Naseby and Waterloo while showing tackles and tries, before linking these scenes of battle to Old Trafford (the site of the matches).

By masculinity I mean the processes and ideas that go towards the construction of male identity. Although it becomes self-evident if we talk about the social construction of masculinity that there can be a number of masculinities (Connell, 1987; Messner and Sabo, 1990), this paper is concerned only with the hegemonic masculinity within rugby league. This relates to the hegemonic masculinity expressed in sport per se, but also to the construction of "the game". As Connell (1987) suggests, there can be competing masculinities, and the cultural setting of the masculine construction must be taken into account. An expression of the hegemonic masculinity from a working class, residual culture (Williams, 1977) will be different to the expressions of masculinity produced in the setting of the public school influenced rugby club (see Sheard and Dunning, 1973; Donnelly and Young, 1985). Craib (1987) observes that masculinity is often organised not in a positive way, but as a reaction to that which is feminine.

Dunning (1986) describes the male dominance of sport that can be seen in the games themselves, which are institutions in which physical strength and fighting skills are celebrated: therefore youngsters are constrained in seeking ways of expressing their maleness. Messner (1992) explores the relationship between learning how to play, the desire to win, and the construction of masculinity. Sabo and Runfola (1980) and Nixon (1993) concentrate on the pain principle as the focus of masculine construction (the Nike advert is can be described as promoting the obliviousness to pain). Gruneau and Whitson (1993) use the idea of masculinity in exploring the rituals of the culture based around ice-hockey, especially the glorification of the brawl which is also evident in rugby league.

In all these studies are a number of themes: masculinity developed through endurance of pain, the game as war/the hardness of the game, the attitude to women/women players and violence fostered by the sporting subculture (Kane and Disch, 1993), the will to win and drug use to achieve success, homophobia as reaffirmation of dominant male identity and enculturation into masculinity through coaching/literature etc. The following section draws upon my fieldwork to show how and where the hegemonic masculinity is developed and reaffirmed.

The field as a site for the production of men

Winning isn't everything — it's the only thing. (Vince Lombardi, American coach)

The Lombardian ethic reached the game of rugby league in 1982, when the Australian Kangaroo touring side swept the British challenge away without breaking sweat (Fitzpatrick, 1994). The shock caused a revolution in British rugby league coaching methods — the trappings of the traditional masculinity of the game, such as the heavy drinking and the overlooked illegal dirty play were thrown out as the game tried to become more professional. Coaching methods were inspired by the Australians (Larder, 1988), who in turn owed their American style ultra professionalism to the working relationship between influential coach Jack Gibson and Vince Lombardi himself (Masters, 1990).

Gibson was the mentor of a new wave of Australian coaches, including John Monie who was responsible for the phenomenal success of Wigan. The new ethic gave the prospective player another way to affirm his masculinity through the will to win and the dedication described as essential to the affirmation of masculinity by American sociologist Michael Messner (1992). The Australianisation of rugby league is. effectively, Americanisation through the back door, and although the ideal masculine type has changed, the importance of sport in maintaining and reproducing hegemonic masculinity in the gender order remains. The extended tour provides an example of an elite site for reaffirmation of masculinity through training, playing and socialising (Belcher, 1991; Caplan and Schofield, 1993).

In Sudthorpe the old working class expressions of masculinity survive as part of the value system of the imaginary community of "the game". It is expressed in the pub culture that surrounds the game in the area — and although the Lombardian ethic has been absorbed into the game it has become a part of this original value system, so that unlike a local union club there is less tension between old beer drinkers and young athletes partaking in "serious leisure" (Stebbins, 1992). One Sudthorpe born player, now an international, is renowned for his love of ale. At one function, "(he) arrived pissed out of his brain with all his drinking mates, and he would've been kicked out if everyone else hadn't been two sheets to the wind too" (Graham Smith). What makes this anecdote more revelatory is that he was playing in a televised cup fixture the next day, in which his team won comfortably.

Drinking and the pub culture remain a strong part of the Sudthorpe rugby league scene. Chemicals are proud of their new clubhouse, which they hope will serve as a watering hole for all their fans, and every other open-age amateur side in the area is a pub team (there are seven others at the moment). Since most of the men of the social network live outside the area, returning to the pubs serves as a return to their past, to the time of the thriving community where the man "always went out on a Saturday after the match for a few, when he could discuss the match and keep out of his wife's hair" (Bill Brown). It is in the pubs as much as the training pitch that the old expressions of masculinity are reinforced and reproduced.

Drinking, where ribald jokes are told and sexual liasions recalled, and where tough matches are remembered, is only one part of the structure supporting the hegemonic masculinity of the imaginary community. As one ex-Chemicals player told me,

> ... rugby's not a game for blokes who are scared of taking knocks...
> if you think you're gonna break your jaw or your arm you shun't be
> out on the pitch.

In other words, it is the sheer physicality of the game that makes it a man's game — one where only the toughest survive. He described how, when an elbow from another player depressed his temple and caused a shockwave to fracture his jaw, he continued playing:

> It hurt fucking bad, but I wanted to stay on. I carried on playing for
> ten minutes until I was dragged off... I wanted to get back on.

Allowing for exaggeration, he demonstrates how the processes behind this affirmation of masculinity work. As Sabo and Runfola (1980) demonstrate, overcoming pain is seen as a sign of manhood. He also wanted to stay on, because the game was important to him. He wanted to give his all for his team: this is what he learnt which makes him a man (Messner, 1992). It also demonstrates the lazy attitude to violence and injury, where it is seen as a vital part of the game. It can also be seen as a strategy in achieving success. The ex-Chemicals player continued:

> [One player I knew was] a five pointer [in the days of three points
> for a try and two for a goal] ... whenever he played we knew we'd
> got an advantage... he went round giving their side a crack... [O]nce
> we were in the Yorkshire Cup against a team from Hull, and they
> had a front row that were knocking the shit out of us, so Clive
> walloped them all through t'game. When we played the next tie [the
> replay] they'd chickened out, and didn't play.

Such violence is also described in an almost celebratory way in some of the
popular literature, such as Clayton and Steele (1993).

Similarly, Johnny Mawdsley, an ex-Sudthorpe player, was routinely
subjected to the violence of the field. Being black, he was seen as an easy
target when he first turned out in the late forties, but the social bonding of
the team supported him when things became rough. Having proved his
manliness by taking his punishment and turning into a good, strong player, he found his team mates acting as minders on the field. On reflecting
on his career, he wrote,

> ... some of the players thought I must be gay [because of his initial
> fear and real name], which is not a reputation anyone would want
> in professional rugby. Yet though they were a tough bunch... I shall
> be indebted to them for the rest of my life. They were hard but
> courageous and generous too. Because they knew I always gave my
> best on the field, they looked after me. A player can easily be hurt
> [if] there is a collision between an opponent's fist and your face, but
> my team mates always protected me from unfair play... twelve of
> my mates would retaliate if I went down. It gave me a hugely com-
> forting feeling. (quoted in Thompson, 1994).

Johnny, coming from a disturbing childhood, found his maleness confirmed by his prowess and his survival on the pitch, and he was accepted
into the masculine network of Sudthorpe by the players who supported
him through their masculinity. Those who felt he was gay felt their own
expressions of masculinity were being challenged — they feared Johnny's
"otherness" and reaffirmed their own masculinity by dismissing his as
effeminate (Whitson, 1990). His move away from the game has allowed him
to take a reflective view. For all the nostalgia for the game that made him a
man, that made him (a black orphan) accepted by the people of Sudthorpe,
he still described it as:

> ...a cruel, inhuman thing... it takes people and rips them up... it is
> so sad seeing what has happened to them [his team mates]... they
> are still in Sudthorpe, they have nothing except constant pain from
> their injuries... it is an injustice to humanity.

Rugby league is seen by the people in the social network as a man's game.
Although women's rugby league is established in Sudthorpe, the club is
small and not supported in the same way as a top amateur club like the
Chemicals. It has had a precarious life in the small Women's Rugby

League, and is seen by many of the Sudthorpe men as something of a joke, a game for "fat women and lesbians", as Jimmy Cross described it. The coach of the professional club, Martin Banks, was more reflective on the women's game, though he had reservations of why women wanted to be involved:

> "Rugby league's a game for everyone... but it's a man's game, the rules were designed with strong blokes in mind, not lasses."

There was a contradiction between his first comment, the 'party line' trotted out regularly by the Rugby Football League, and his fears about the game being too hard for women. In effect, rugby league was, in his eyes, a game for everyone — but everyone didn't include women. Other respondents casually refer to players as lads, or talk about the average fan as "the working man" (Paul Dawson). Prolonged ethnography reveals that women do attend matches and support rugby league, but the proportion of women decreases from pro matches to amateur level. At the latter, women are mainly girlfriends and wives, who serve the same tea making and kit washing function as the ladies committee of a union club. At the professional club women such as Helen Lane are, as supporters, close to the administration of the club, helping to sell lottery tickets and being consulted by the secretary, Frank Silcott, who only joined the club last year. Helen is the longest serving helper at the club, yet as a fan she is denied access to greater control of the club's affairs. The secretary and the board, and the entire coaching staff, are all men. Similarly, the head of the unofficial supporters club, and the club historian/programme editor are men. The pro supporters who are also connected in some way to the amateur scene in the area are all men. This social network can be seen to be maintaining Connell's gender order.

However, it is wrong to assume there is a correlation between the social network of Sudthorpe rugby and the constituency of the Sudthorpe pro team, though there are strong links between the two. One supporter, Gary Sawyer, explained:

> Sudthorpe (the club) don't really represent the place, you don't get the blokes who drink in the Junckie or the Brassie going of a Sunday... you can't expect a Sudthorpe man to watch a team that don't represent Sudthorpe, or even play there anymore.

There is a suspicion that the coach does not care about the Sudthorpe tradition, and only three of the first team squad are Sudthorpe lads. What counts is that both at the pro club and with the amateur sides, control is in the hands of men, and the perception is that "it's a game for the working man, invented by the working man" (Maurice Oldroyd, British Amateur Rugby League Association [BARLA] Chief Executive).

The hardness of the game, the violence and the ability of players to cope with pain, has been established. Following Jansen and Sabo (1994) one can see a pattern of war metaphors throughout the popular literature and the coaching jargon: big hits, killing the attack, digging in, trench warfare, bombs etc. Frank Silcott, the Sudthorpe secretary, spent an entire game next to me in the press box encouraging each player with the ball to "go on, son, straight at 'em, make 'em scared to tackle yer!". This language is reflected in jeers based around softness or questions of a player's masculinity when he produces an error. One Sudthorpe chant is full of violence expressed towards the city rivals, and it is evident from the words that it is a man's song (sung to the tune of *Que Sera, Sera*):

> *When I was just a little boy, I said to my mother,*
> *what should I be?*
> *Should I be Sudthorpe? Should I be [rivals]?*
> *Here's what she said to me...*
> *Wash your mouth out son!*
> *And go get your father's gun!*
> *And shoot the [rival] scum, shoot the [rival] scum.*

The song reflects the rituals of masculinity expressed in the violence, the bravado and the solidarity of the network, as well as supporting the Sudthorpe belief in their 'otherness'.

Mark O'Reilly has been described as the quintessential Sudthorpe man by the Chemicals coach and Maurice Oldroyd of BARLA. He is a coach at the Boys Club, where he can pass down to his charges the values of the game that go towards creating Sudthorpe man. Last season his under-18 side went unbeaten, and Wigan have signed two of their number, whilst half of the others already have their names on contracts for Dewsbury, Castleford, Batley and St. Helens. One, the son of one of the Boys Club hangers on, is close to signing for Sudthorpe — the lack of interest shown in Mark's side by Sudthorpe is another symptom of the rift between the pro club and the social network based around the amateur game. It is at the junior level that the process of masculinising the players is undertaken, where the imaginary community's gender order is reinforced. Boys are taught to "have a laugh with one another, play hard and win" (Mark O'Reilly).

However, there are tensions at this level of enculturation. Exposed to the Australian ideas permeating the game, the young lads now see maleness as being something else: the dedication and professionalism of the Lombardian ethic. This is seen at Chemicals, whose coach has replaced the father of an international. He has introduced more rigorous training and a weights room, and his ambition is to take Chemicals out of the Saturday league in which most of the Sudthorpe clubs play and into the National Conference, where the players and coaching methods resemble those of the professional league. Another issue is the introduction of young girls into the sport at age levels up to and including under-12. The Boys Club have resisted this and have no girls playing for them, but they have been forced by the local council to put in motion a name change to the Club for Boys and Girls.

That said, however, one must realise that the game in Sudthorpe is still a device for shaping and reinforcing the dominant masculinity. Training sessions are full of appeals to hardness, to strength and commitment, and the male dominated pub is still the important focus for the amateurs and the supporters of the pro club. One Sudthorpe player, a black African with a rugby union background and a university education, was described to me by Gary as:

> ...one of us... yeah, funny but he's more like a Sudthorpe lad than some of the others". When I asked him why I realised the question was foolish. "He dunt mind mixing with the fans, he's got a bird who lives in Sudthorpe... he says he loves the place cos of the friendliness and that, in the pubs, *he's a right boozer an' womanizer*, you wun't expect it would you? [my italics].

At a match at the Boys Club, the youngsters were encouraged to "Have some fucking pride in yer jerseys! If they hit you hit them back!". Apart from the appeal to loyalty to the social network, the lads were congratulated for their violence, and when an opposing player was kicked by Darren, a supporter shouted "Stop beefing! He hardly touched yer!". It is in this climate of aggression that the young lads were being turned into men (Messner, 1992). The solitary girl on the pitch (on the opposing side) was not involved in the violence, and when she beat her marker to almost score a try, this marker was shouted at by a fan, who screamed "What's wrong? Can't you tackle a girl?". His masculinity was doubted, though I saw him later in another match "getting stuck in", though I don't know whether the humiliation of letting a girl beat him was still on his mind.

War correspondents? Match reports and reporters as producers and defenders of masculinity

> "Oh... 'e's 'ad a knock, but 'e'll be all right ... just a bit of concussion." (Eddie Waring, commentating for television on the 1965 Challenge Cup)

An important aspect of the connection between rugby league and masculine construction is how the sport is described and defined by the media. Sport is described in explicitly masculine language in an attempt to normalise the dominant masculinity and hence maintain the gender order (Duncan and Hasbrook, 1988). The role of the media in producing and promoting sport is clear (Bourdieu, 1993; Eco, 1986). Jansen and Sabo (1994) and McKay and Rowe (1987) look at the legitimation of masculine modes of thought, of the masculine myth, through the identification of masculinity with sport and war in the cultural sites of the media. Although Lynch (1993) has demonstrated how advertisements for Australian rugby league reflect a cultural repositioning of the sport, the dominant images of rugby league remain masculine (McKay and Rowe, 1987).

Hence the media plays a large role in defining the masculine discourse in rugby league. The masculine myth both supports, and is perpetuated by, the images presented in the media. Berger (1972) has outlined how the language of advertising works to create images of masculine power, while Easthope (1986) describes how the "masculine myth" present in popular culture (and in sports like rugby league) naturalises, normalises and universalises the dominant masculinity.

As a reporter working for one of the trade papers I am aware of the restrictions on structure and style of a match report: editorial policy decides what is a "good" report.

In one of these ('Bram-busters!'. In *Rugby Leaguer*, No. 1909: p. 16), a match between Bramley and Swinton in the Second Division of the Rugby Football League, the report is littered with masculine symbols, and uses an aggressive, confrontational language. Swinton are "a shadow of the side that beat Leigh": here I am criticising them for not winning and being weak. I congratulate Tony Barrow Jr. for "hard work", Ray Ashton is a "tactical genius", equating him with a general at war deciding a plan of action, and the Swinton hooker is "lively", a coded word that meaning tough and able to play beyond the rules. The message for kids learning to be rugby players and men is to maintain a high work rate all the time to win (and become men).

The structure of a rugby league match report stresses the war element of "the game", praising confrontation, rewarding players for their toughness and ability to score. By calling masculine highlights (tries, hard work, fighting) key moments a myth is created over what "the game" is about. Substitutions are ignored unless it is through them that better men arrive on the scene to win the game. The eighty minutes of the match are reduced to a stereotyped view, a "gender advertisement" (Goffman, 1979), that extols the war and conflict aspect inherent in "the game" as the most important. The style and structure reflects Barthes' (1972) myth-making, and produces information on the gender order that is reflected in "the game".

The report is also caught in the tension between different expressions of masculinity that operate in "the game". Editorial control dictates how "the game" is presented to supporters, and to some extent it decides on the symbolic boundaries. At the same time, the myth-making inside the media is informed by tacit signs within the imaginary community. The process of enculturation and enculturating defines what is written: how the dominant masculinity becomes expressed (Easthope, 1986), and the archetypes and metaphors that are used (Lynch, 1993; Jansen and Sabo, 1994).

"The game" is seen as spectacle and sport by opposing discourses (Moorhouse, 1989), but it can also be both, through a reading of match reports. It is a sport for Sudthorpe men, for boys who want to be men, and it is a spectacle of dominant masculinity. Expressions of masculinity identified in American sport (Messner, 1992) come to the fore: game as war, survival of the fittest, dedication, physicality. Older expressions of masculinity are glossed over but referred to through codes drawing upon mutual knowledge (Giddens, 1984), the knowledge of the insider: of white, working class, Sudthorpe man.

Conclusion: masculine constructions and the drug debate

Rugby is a game played by men with odd shaped balls. (Anon., seaside/car sticker pun)

It comes as no surprise to learn that rugby league, like union, is seen as a man's game. At the top level both are dominated by men, and women are denied positions of influence. They serve to maintain and defend the gender order (Connell, 1987), though that order is under strain both from women's desire to have influence and access to the games, and from competing masculinities. The expressions of the dominant masculinity described by Messner (1992) are culturally situated in North American professional sport, yet they are beginning to become part of the culture of both codes of rugby. The old union player's maleness was expressed in the lewdness and drinking contests described by Sheard and Dunning (1973), and this is less prevalent than it was. As Donnelly and Young (1985) describe, English rugby union has become more like the cultural form of sport prevalent in North America. Similarly, the working class maleness that forms part of the values of the Sudthorpe social networks of the imaginary community of "the game" is in tension with the expressions of masculinity in Australian league, and the discourses around Superleague.

This paper emphasises violence. It has been taken as self-evident that this culture causes the bracketing out of women through sexual jokes, boasts of conquest and disbelief in their athletic qualities. Homophobia is also a 'natural' part of this social construction: poor performances on the pitch, as well as inability or undesirability to drink large amounts of alcohol, are ascribed to un-masculine traits. Words that denigrate different masculinities such as "soft bastard", "puff", "queer" are used against those who do not reach the standards of playing, fighting and drinking. The word "woman" is also used as a term of denigration, as in "Get off the floor, you fucking woman", a shout heard at a match. To be a man, the players have to take injuries with a stoic acceptance. Jimmy's story of carrying on playing, true or not, is an expression of this hardness, a desire to prove one's manhood, to show the listener how hard one is. Shaun Edwards of Wigan played most of the 1990 Cup final with a fractured cheekbone and depressed eye socket. Alan Prescott — in a 1958 test match dubbed by rugby league historians as the Battle of Brisbane — stayed on the pitch with a broken arm. These cases are extreme examples of overcoming the pain barrier and fighting on to win, thus reaffirming their masculinity.

The match report operates with shared understandings, leaving unwritten the mutual knowledge that must be drawn upon to understand what it means to be a man and how the report explains this. It is a sign of how dominant Australianised expressions have become that the advertise-

ment for the 1995 Premierships passed without comment. Professionalisation has become equated with globalised masculine expressions of "manly
sport".

I have yet to mention the use of drugs. One player said, "the only drug
round 'ere is Tetley's" ['Tetley's' is both a local beer and ordinary tea].
Nevertheless, rugby league has a drug problem. Steroids and ampheta-
mines were common in Australia in the eighties (Fenech and Fenech,
1993). Although testing has improved, the suspicion is that drugs are still
used. A recent survey of Australian first grade players revealed 51% believed steroids and other performance enhancing drugs were in use (*Rugby
League Week*, Vol. 26, No. 21). Jamie Bloem of Doncaster was banned
recently for steroid use, and promptly claimed its use was rife in rugby
league (*Mail on Sunday*, 22 January 1995). The Rugby Football League
(RFL) recently improved its drug testing. Another player, David Stephen-
son, was caught at the end of the season. The RFL claim that any drug
taking is isolated and in line with what any sport would expect in terms of
positive cases. Painkillers and nutritional supplements are performance
enhancers used throughout the game because of their legality, though
some players object to the use of the former (Caplan and Schofield, 1993).
The RFL has confused the issue, however, by banning players for cannabis
use and allowing the stories to be conflated with the Bloem case (*Independent*, 6 January 1995).

In autumn 1995, the Halifax Rugby League Centenary World Cup took
place in the UK, with routine drug testing for all squad members of the
competing ten nations. This resulted in three positive tests: one for nan-
drolone (a steroid), one for pseudoephredine and one for cannabis. The
punishment — immediate dismissal from the tournament — and condemnation (in public) was the same for each player, though subsequent
punishment was left to national governing bodies. Pierre Grobbelar of
South Africa was the player caught taking steroids, which led to rumours
concerning individuals involved in the South African Rugby League, and
much finger-pointing at the steroid culture in South African rugby (see
Grundlingh, 1994). Syd Eru of New Zealand claimed the pseudoephredine
was the result of a mixup he had made in hospital over branded pharma-
ceuticals. However, the use of this drug enables a player to get mote oxy-
gen through his lungs and last longer: a requisite for the modem game. In
1994, during the Kangaroo tour to the UK, Dean Pay of Australia tested
positive for this drug, but at the time it was not a banned substance by the
Australian Rugby League. It was later revealed that Australian captain
Ricky Stuart also tested positive (Stuart, 1995). As for young French back
Stephane Millet, who had only been called into the squad as a last minute
replacement, he suffered the wrath of the tournament organisers and
the associated media for being "careless". Grobbelar was banned
indefinitely, but Eru and Millet have yet to be punished by their respective
governing bodies. Tournament Director Maurice Lindsay declared the drug
testing procedure a success, though there were criticisms from Welsh

international Kelvin Skerrett about the English squad being forewarned at
their training camp. Clearly, the three positive drugs tests only added to
the innuendo that surrounds rugby league and its (hypothetical or
otherwise) drug culture.

It seems drink driving, assault, and being drunk and disorderly —
although just as illegal as cannabis use — are seen as less of a blight on
the game's image than a second division player having a joint (all the
offences mentioned have involved players). Cannabis use is evidently seen
as un-masculine when compared to the dominant expressions of masculinity, which accommodate alcohol abuse, fighting, and a denigrating
attitude to women.

References

Barthes, R. (1972) *Mythologies*. London: Cape.

Belcher, G. (1991) *Kangaroo confidential*. Rushcutters Bay: Ironbark.

Berger, J. (1972) *Ways of seeing*. Harmondsworth: Penguin.

Bourdieu, P. (1993) 'How can one be a sportsman?', in P. Bourdieu
       Sociology in question. London: Sage.

Bryson, L. (1990) 'Challenges to male hegemony in sport', in J. Messner
       and D. Sabo (eds) *Sport, men and the gender order*. Champaign:
       Human Kinetics.

Caplan, P. and Schofield, G. (1993) *Garry Schofield's season diary 1992-93*.
       Durham: Pentland.

Clarke, J. and Critcher, C. (1985) *The Devil makes work: Leisure in
       capitalist Britain*. London: Macmillan.

Clayton, I. and Steele, M. (1993) *When push comes to shove*. Castleford:
       Yorkshire Arts Circus.

Cohen, A. P. (1985) *The symbolic construction of community*. London:
       Tavistock.

Connell, R. (1987) *Gender and power: Society, the person and sexual
       politics*. Stanford: Stanford University Press.

Craib, I. (1987) 'Masculinity and male dominance', *Sociological Review*,
       Vol.35, No. 4: pp. 721-743.

Donnelly, P. and Young, K. (1985) 'Reproduction and transformation of
       cultural forms in sport: a contextual analysis of rugby', *International
       Review of the Sociology of Sport*, Vol.20, No. 1: pp. 19-38.

Duncan, M. and Hasbrook, C. (1988) 'Denial of power in women's televised
       sports', *Sociology of Sport*, Vol.5, No. 1: pp. 1-21.

Dunning, E. (1986) 'Sport as a male preserve: notes on the social sources
       of masculine identity and its transformation', *Theory, Culture and
       Society*, Vol.3, No. 1: pp. 79-90.

Dunning, E. and Sheard, S. (1979) *Barbarians, gentlemen and players*. Oxford: Martin Robertson.

Easthope, A. (1986) *What a man's gotta do: The masculine myth in popular culture*. London: Paladin.

Eco, U. (1986) 'Sports chatter', in U. Eco *Faith in fakes: travels in hyper-reality*. London: Minerva.

Fenech, M. and Fenech, S. (1993) *Personal best*. Sydney: Pan.

Giddens, A. (1984) *The constitution of society*. Cambridge: Polity.

Goffman, E. (1979) *Gender advertisements*. New York: Harper.

Grundlingh, A. (1994) 'Playing for power? Rugby, Afrikaner nationalism and masculinity in South Africa, c.1900-1970', *International Journal of the History of Sport*, Vol.11, No. 3: pp. 408-430.

Gruneau, R. and Whitson, D. (1993) *Hockey night in Canada*. Toronto: Garamond.

Fitzpatrick, P. (1994) 'A foreign country: Australia 1982', in D. Hadfield (ed) *XIII winters*. London: Mainstream.

Hargreaves, J. A. (1986) 'Where's the virtue? Where's the grace? A discussion of the social reproduction of gender through sport', *Theory, Culture and Society*, Vol.3, No. 1: pp. 109-121.

——— (1990) 'Gender on the sports agenda', *International Review of the Sociology of Sport*, Vol.25, No. 4: pp. 287-308.

Hoch, P. (1972) *Rip off the big game*. New York: Anchor

Jansen, S. and Sabo, D. (1994) 'The sport/war metaphor: hegemonic masculinity, the Persian Gulf war and the new world order', *Sociology of Sport*, Vol.11, No. 1: pp. 1-17.

Kane, M. and Disch, L. (1993) 'Sexual violence and the reproduction of male power in the locker room: The Lisa Olson incident', *Sociology of Sport*, Vol.10, No. 4: pp. 331-353.

Kimmel, M. (ed) (1987) *Changing men: New directions in research on men and masculinity*. Newbury Park: Sage.

Larder, P. (1988) *The Rugby League coaching manual*. London: Heinemann.

Lynch, R. (1993) 'The cultural repositioning of rugby league football and its men', in A. Veal and B. Weiler (eds) *First steps: Leisure and tourism research in Australia and New Zealand*. Sydney: University of Technology.

McKay, J. and Rowe, D. (1987) 'Ideology, the media, and Australian sport', *Sociology of Sport*, Vol.4, No. 3: pp. 258-274.

Mangan, J. (1981) *Athleticism in the Victorian and Edwardian public schools*. Cambridge: Cambridge University Press.

Masters, R. (1990) *Inside league.* Sydney: Pan.

Messner, M. (1992) *Power at play.* Boston: Beacon.

Messner, M. and Sabo, D. (eds) (1990) *Sport, men and the gender order.* Champaign: Human Kinetics.

Miliband, R. (1989) *Divided societies: Class struggle in contemporary capitalism.* Oxford: Oxford University Press.

Morgan, D. (1992) *Discovering man: Sociology and masculinities.* London: Routledge.

Nankervis, B. (1994) *Boys and balls.* Sydney: Allen and Unwin.

Nixon, H. (1993) 'Accepting the risks of pain and injury in sport: mediated cultural influences on playing hurt', *Sociology of Sport,* Vol.10, No. 2: p. 183-197.

Sabo, D. and Runfola, R. (1980) *Jock: Sports and male identity.* Eaglewood Cliffs: Prentice Hall.

Sheard, K. and Dunning, E. (1973) 'The rugby football club as a type of male preserve: some sociological notes', *International Review of the Sociology of Sport,* Vol.8, Nos. 3: p. 5-21.

Snyder, E. and Spreitzer, E. (1989) *Social aspects of sport.* Eaglewood Cliffs: Prentice Hall.

Spink, J. (1989) 'Urban development, leisure facilities, and the inner city: a case study of inner Leeds and Bradford', in P. Bramham, I. Henry, H. Mommaas and H. Van der Poel (eds) *Leisure and urban processes.* London: Routledge.

Stebbins, R. (1992) *Amateurs, professionals and serious leisure.* Montreal: McGill Queen's University Press.

Stuart, R. (1995) *Ashes to ashes.* Rushcutters Bay: Ironbark.

Talbot, M. (1988) 'Understanding the relationship between women and sport: The contribution of British feminist approaches in leisure and cultural studies', *International Review of the Sociology of Sport,* Vol. 23, No. 3: pp. 31-43.

Thompson, C. (1994) *Born on the wrong side.* Unpublished manuscript.

Whitson, D. (1990) 'Sport in the construction of masculinity', in M. Messner and D. Sabo (eds) *Sport, men and the gender order.* Champaign, IL: Human Kinetics.

Williams, R. (1977) *Marxism in literature.* Oxford: Oxford University Press.

Newspaper references

Independent, 6 January 1995.   *Rugby League Week,* Vol.26, No. 4.
Mail on Sunday, 22 January 1995.   *Rugby League Week,* Vol.26, No. 5.
Rugby Leaguer, No. 1909.   *Rugby League Week,* Vol.26, No. 21.

Sport Stars, Youth and Morality in the Print Media

Garry Whannel

Roehampton Institute London

This paper offers an interim report on our research into images of sport, sport stars and fitness in the print media, with specific focus on those titles most read by young people[1]. We have been looking at a range of titles: *Beano*, *Viz*, and *Loaded*; *Sega Power*, *Shoot* and *Match*; *Horse and Pony*, *My Guy*, *Just Seventeen*, and *Smash Hits*; and *FHM*, as well as the *Sun* and the *Mirror*. We focus on changing images of the body, construction of gender differences, portrayal of stars and the ways in which audiences are invited to identify with them, and the presence within such representations of moral and ethical discourses.

Sport stars are commonly assumed to be potentially influential figures. If they are successful and well behaved, they are typically held up as role models, and often used in advertising campaigns targeting young people (e.g. campaigns on anti-smoking, anti-drugs, and on fitness promotion). Sebastian Coe, Kevin Keegan, Duncan Goodhew, Frank Bruno, Steve Davis and Nick Faldo are examples of the type. Robert Atkin, formerly the Minister for Sport, referred, on the first morning of his appointment, to both Davis and Faldo as the kind of figures from whom all young sports-people could learn ("Today", BBC Radio 4, 24 July 1990).

According to the *Daily Mirror*, Ian Sproat, Sports Minister, "believes sports are vital not only to improve the poor fitness of the young, but also to teach them team-work and discipline — values which might also overcome the problem of thuggery in the classroom" (*Daily Mirror,* 4 August, 1994). Sproat recently said "If we had more organised games in schools we'd have fewer little thugs like those who murdered Jamie Bulger. In response, John Evans, Professor of Physical Education at Loughborough, commented that "Sport has as great a capacity for producing bullies and thugs as it has good citizens and saints" (*Guardian*, 1 March, 1994). However the belief that top sports performers can also be moral exemplars is still firmly entrenched.

If, on the other hand, the behaviour of such sports performers is regarded as inadequate or in some way morally reprehensible, the consequent moral concern frequently focuses on the bad influence this may have on the young. Examples include Ben Johnson, John McEnroe, George Best, Ian Botham, Alex Higgins, Eric Cantona and Vinnie Jones. Fallen tennis star Jennifer Capriati allegedly smoked crack in a seedy motel bathroom during a drug-crazed binge. According to *The Sun* "Hers is a tragic morality tale of a child propelled into millionaire celebrity status without any thought of the repercussions". The concern persists beyond the playing days of such figures, fuelled by the provocative lack of moral and social accountability expressed by, for example, George Best: "I'm my own boss. Nobody tells me what to do, when to do it, where to do it or how to do it. That's a nice position to be in. Nobody tells me what to do" (cited in the Robert Chalmers interview, *Sunday Correspondent*, 23 September 1990: p. 27).

But to what extent do sport stars provide role models, and what cultural meanings are produced and consumed in the sport star system? By what process are models of correct and incorrect moral behaviour produced and reproduced ? Sport plays a major role in British cultural life. Its major traditional rituals and broadcasts of them — the Cup Final, the Derby, the Boat Race, the Grand National, Test matches, and Wimbledon — are a significant part of our cultural history and form part of the fabric of "Englishness", contributing to a sense of national identity.

Yet now culture is increasingly dependent upon the mass media — our concept of sport owes as much to images of sport as it does to our own lived experience of participation. So while sport occupies a position of cultural centrality, it does so in part — indeed, in most cases — through forms of representation. The expansion of domestic media (video recording facilities in the home, new satellite channels) means that viewing practices are changing and in many respects expanding (Morley, 1986).

In contributing to the growth in popularity of sport, the media have helped produce a sporting star system (Whannel, 1992). As a consequence top sport stars, being in the public eye, find themselves under pressure from sport organisations concerned with their public image. Much of this concern is expressed in moral terms. Mike Gatting had to give up the England captaincy after a much publicised incident involving a barmaid; Tommy Docherty had to resign as Manager of Manchester United after an affair with the wife of a colleague; Ian Botham and Alex Higgins have frequently been in trouble with the authorities for incidents that took place well away from the field of play; and the tabloid press continued to hound the England soccer manager Bobby Robson to the very end of his time in that post. One theme consistently present in such stories is that stars, being in the public eye, are an influence on the young, and that consequently they must be expected to have higher moral standards than people in everyday life.

Popular fears over the power of the media have been rooted in a crude stimulus-response model, sometimes called the hypodermic model. While it is entirely appropriate to adopt and test a hypothesis of powerful media influence, any adequate model of that influence needs to recognise the complexity of the process (Curran and Gurevitch, 1991; Hall *et al.*, 1980).

In order to understand contemporary society we need to recognise that life is a continuing process of cultural adaptation, starting with entry into language, and socialisation into particular codes of belief and behaviour, and continuing on into adult life. The process of growing up physically is also crucially a process of growing up culturally. A sense of society, its values, attitudes and beliefs and cultural positions in relation to these is crucially formed in the process of growing up. It is undeniable that the family exerts a strong influence as an agent of primary socialisation. The mass media, having now emerged as one of the major agents of secondary socialisation, interconnect with the primary sphere of the home from the very earliest age; and sport is one of the major popular cultural forms in which this process occurs. In particular, many young people in early adolescence go through a period in which identification with public figures — stars of music, film and sport — appears of considerable importance. Evidence of this can be seen in the prominence of pin-up and poster images in magazines bought by this age group. But these images are not empty — they carry connotations and convey meanings, and stand for specific values and attitudes (McRobbie, 1982).

Understanding these processes calls for the development and investigation of a grid of intersecting factors — age, class, gender, race and region. This could show how people are differentially placed, in way which might bring a distinctive cultural repertoire to bear upon their response to media messages. Our own fieldwork, currently underway, has made a small start on this massive task.

Youth, media, sport: the public debate

Youth, Media, Sport: three words that are all associated in public discussion with concern, with fears and with discourses of moral decline. The state of youth has been a cause of perennial anxiety. Precedents go back at least to Ancient Greece and Rome.

However, youth as we now understand it is a relatively recent social category. Youth is not an eternal trans-historic concept. The notion of a period in life, the teenage years, distinct from both childhood and adulthood is primarily a product of the 1950s. Before this, youngsters were expected to make the transition from children to adults rapidly and seamlessly. From the 1950s, adolescence increasingly became a culturally distinct phase of life, rather than a mere biological transition.

If one was writing a history tracing the antecedents of the present sense of moral crisis, the moment of rock and roll marks a significant opening of a gulf between the generations, an escalating of the parental fears of children, in Bob Dylan's memorable phrase, "beyond your command" (Bob Dylan, *The Times They are A Changing*, 1962). Subsequently a whole series of sub-cultures served to generate folk devils and to be the focus of moral panics (Cohen, 1971).

Moral panics over youth became a regular structural feature of the contemporary media. In the 1950s it was teddy boys, rock-and-roll and ripping up cinema seats; in the 1960s mods and rockers and pills, followed closely by hippies, dope, acid and free love. In the 1970s, sex and drugs and rock-and-roll were followed closely by punks, violence, and the icons of deviant sexuality.

During the 1970s, according to Hall *et al.*, such moral panics increasingly became mapped together within the terms of a generalised discourse about law and order, that in turn provided part of the ideological substructure for the emerging discourse that became known as Thatcherism (Hall *et al.*, 1978).

During the 1980s the ideological and political successes of Thatcherism fostered a culture of enterprise and consumption, produced a series of political defeats for the left, and defused the 70s climate of dissent and opposition. Affluent youth became increasingly focused on style, identity and conspicuous consumption (Tomlinson, 1990), whilst the poorer strata of youth supposedly became disaffected but apathetic, dubbed by some *Generation X* — the blank generation, with no ambition, and no discipline.

It is certainly the case that the alternative and oppositional character of subcultures was much less in evidence in the 1980s youth subcultures like the new romantics and the goths, who were far more narcissistic and inward looking. Only with the emergence of the rave scene, the new anarchism, and the increasing militancy of the new travellers towards the end of the 1980s did this oppositional character begin to resurface. For a brief period during the early eighties the spotlight of moral disapproval turned elsewhere (single mothers, welfare scroungers) but then returned to youth to highlight raves, ecstasy and crack, ramraiders and joyriders.

The social concerns over youth during the 1980s increasingly highlighted fitness. The expression "couch potato" served to denote the large number of hours devoted to television watching; computer games increasingly replaced outdoor activities. In a two page spread on school sport, the *Independent on Sunday* (21/11/93) examined these issues. It asserted that the average child watches 27 hours of TV a week. Concern over the decline of school sport, and the impact of a diet of junk food, was heightened by the publicising of the research of Neil Armstrong (Professor of Health and Exercise Sciences at the University of Exeter). Briefly, Armstrong showed that children rarely exercised vigorously enough to improve and build adequate cardio-vascular fitness. According to Armstrong, for example, one third of all girls between 11-16 do not do more strenuous exercise than one brisk 10 minute walk per week.

The low level of intense physical activity amongst children is in turn linked to the decline of school sport, both within- and extra-curricular. Extra-curricular sport never recovered from the impact of the 1985 industrial action by teachers and consequent disillusion amongst the teaching profession, and withdrawal by teachers from extra-curricular activity. Since then there has been a 70% decline in schools football: 80% of football between boys 9-16 now takes place on Sunday morning. At secondary schools, a minimum 2 hours per week Physical Education is recommended. But a survey in 1987 showed that 38% of 14 year olds had less than 2 hours. By 1990 in school plans this had almost doubled to 71%.

The crystallisation of such fears was increasingly linked to other concerns — the Americanisation of society, the weakening of marriage and the family, the declining strength of traditional morality.

Since Major became Prime Minister, those seeking a regeneration of traditional school sport have spoken out with renewed confidence. The *Guardian* (1/3/94) recently suggested that Ian Sproat sometimes gives the impression that a regime of cricket and cold showers would solve all the nation's ills at a stroke, making the campaign for "real" sports in schools a one-man crusade. Sproat is quoted as saying "When I talk about sport in schools I do not mean step aerobics, going for country walks and listening to lessons on the history of diets. These are all right in their way but they are not what I want. I want team games properly organised — competitive team games, preferably those which we invented, such as soccer, rugby, hockey, cricket and netball".

The position of those such as Sproat fails to recognise the changing nature of physical activity amongst the young. It takes no account of the popularity of dance amongst girls, or of martial arts amongst boys. It fails to recognise that the declining popularity of many traditional team games has been matched by a growing interest in new more individualist, narcissistic or dangerous activities — aerobics, weight training, hang gliding, wind surfing etc.

Media

The power of the media has always been a source of concern, indeed literacy itself was historically seen as such a threat by dominant groups that for a long time its spread was rigorously controlled. Every new media innovation has served as the focal point of such fears. It always has to be noted, then, that fears of the power of the media are usually associated with a fear of the loss of power for some other institution, whether it is the ruling class, the state, the church or the family (Curran and Seaton, 1991).

The power and influence of the media has characteristically been linked to deviance and dissidence, whether political, cultural or sexual. Such fears are usually associated with influence on the young, and these fears usually attach themselves to the latest technology. Thus the spread of printing was seen as a threat to the control of the literate clerisy. Film was seen as dangerous because it reached the less literate lower orders, and so needed censorship. Radio entered the home and so required policing. Television has been the focal point of endless debates about the degree of explicit violence and sexuality that should be permitted. Horror comics in the 1950s, porn magazines in the 1960s, video in the 1980s, satellite channels and live sex chat lines in the 1990s, have all been the focus of concerns. Virtual pornography and the distribution of sexually explicit images by computer are currently causing concern. It is noteworthy that one major issue triggered by the growth of the Internet is that it enables exchanges between users that are hard for any power to monitor or control.

Just as the issue of the power of the media is usually connected to the threat it poses to other possessors of power, it is also the case that the media offers an easy scapegoat that can be blamed for problems whose real causes are more deep-rooted, pervasive and harder to address. The rush to blame the media for violence, copy-cat killings, and moral decay, betrays an unwillingness to face up to the multi-factoral complexity of cause and effect in the social world.

Sport

Much analysis of sport, from both left and right wing perspectives, has focused on the concept of commercialisation. For the left, commercialisation has been viewed as evidence that sporting cultures are determined by the societies that sustain them. Sport, like other areas of cultural life are inevitably going to be colonised by capital, becoming integrated into capitalist economic relations. For the right, commercialism has challenged, undermined and destroyed the old corinthian ideals of amateur sport. For both right and left, many of the ills that beset sport — drugs, violence, cheating, corruption — are all, ultimately, effects of this process. Hence the fear, particularly on the right, that the activities of some can constitute a bad influence on the young.

Set against this is the strong desire that sport should be a good influence and the belief that it can ideally fulfil this role. This position only makes sense if we remind ourselves of the role of sport in the 19th century public schools in the formation of the ethics of fair play (McIntosh, 1952, 1964, 1979; Mangan, 1981, 1985). Sport's ideological role here was to offer a metaphor for the supposed fairness of life's competition. As an ideological form, it masked the forms of advantage and exploitation that, even then, underlay sporting practices, and so forged an imaginary unity, the muscular Christianity of the sporting gentlemen.

Team games provided an image of team work — interdependence, mutual support, and working together for the greater good, a process celebrated in literature and verse, most notably in Newbolt's *Vitai Lampada*. In the late nineteenth century in partly in reaction to the bourgeois hegemony of team games, a rather different discourse focused on self-reliant individualism, often counterposed to the conformity of the team game. This can be seen in Kipling's writing, especially *Stalky and Company*, and in the rhetoric of Baden-Powell. The spartan regime of Gordonstoun, the Outward Bound Movement and the Duke of Edinburgh's Award Scheme, can be seen as part of the same discourse. These two discourses, team-work and individualism, together form a contradictory element at the heart of sporting cultures. Football crowds, for example, value the whole-hearted player who runs flat out for the team, but also respond to the gifted individual who, often, is seen as not producing adequate work-rate.

The contemporary sporting hero can be seen in relation to this tension, in which the massive growth in material reward constantly acts as a threat to team loyalty, and national commitments.

Morality

So in "youth", "media" and "sport" we have three terms that refer to fields of contention over moral influence. Youth are vulnerable to influence, whilst sport and the media can supposedly convey good or bad influences. Concern over youth condense broader fears over the concept of a culture in decline. The desire for a good clean sporting hero is a symptom of the desire for magical resolutions.

When England were defeated in the 1990 World Cup, Brian Robson was quoted in the *Sun* as saying "I'm just so sorry for the 50 million people back home crying like us". In an editorial, "Salute our brave lads" *The Sun* saluted the "bulldog spirit" that "has carried this England team through so much", and referred to a chubby cherubic bouncing ball of fun called Gazza. "He lived and cried for England. And we cried with pride" (*The Sun*, July 5 1990).

The press response to death of Bobby Moore spoke of him in eulogistic terms as:

"a captain of grace and vision";

"tall, blond, cool and clean cut";

"the epitome of the England captain, a post he filled with distinction";

"a great person in every sense";

"a footballer of intelligence and vision";

"a man of dignity and stature";

"the perfect English gentleman";

"gentleman of sport";

"he enhanced sport by example, behaviour and skill";

"the most natural leader the national side has ever had";

"a true hero, who'll never be forgotten";

"sense of decency and honour";

"he won respect for the way he played and the manner in which he conducted himself".

As Williams and Taylor (1996) have pointed out, these reactions functioned as the condensing point of a number of complex ideological elements, concerning economic decline, moral crisis, and belief in a generalised decline of standards. Moore's heroic status was counterposed to the perceived sense of moral decline.

When England cricket captain Michael Atherton was accused of cheating, the tabloid press reaction was one of moral outrage that a captain of our national team should be setting a bad example. *The Sun* and the *Mirror* ran banner headlines: "HE DID CHEAT" (*Daily Mirror*) and "QUIT NOW" (*The Sun*). The *Daily Mirror* launched a campaign under the banner headline, "SACK HIM AND LET THE WORLD KNOW WE STAND FOR HONESTY" This anxiety about the appointment of an adequate leader has become a constant theme of sports discourse, with its authoritarian strain (what this sport needs is a supremo) and its construction of managers and captains as figures of power and authority.

Simon Barnes of the *Times* wrote that "Atherton has now realised the strange truth that sports people are expected to have higher moral standards than the people who run the country. People want sport to be an escape from the real world, for sport to be a place in which ideal standards actually exist and they cannot bear the truth that it can never be anything of the kind" (27 July, 1994).

A central paradox of sport is that it is constructed as a world of its own, a bounded universe, which it can never be. In a world of confusion, doubt and moral ambiguity, in which structures are patently unfair and enshrine the power of the privileged, sport offers a protected domain in which impartial rules and officials and respect for fair play are supposed to predominate. Yet sport has never been, cannot be, separate from social structures and processes. In a world of ruthless competitive individualism, the fair play ethos is constantly undermined.

Consumption

In our own work, the relation between magazines and their readers has to be placed in the context of consumption.

Our first step was to examine information about the nature of youth media consumption. According to the youth TGI, 50% of 7-10 year olds and 68% of 11-14 year olds have a television in their bedroom. Over 95% live in households with a VCR. 30% watch satellite or cable television. 97% of 7-10 and 11-14 year olds use a computer. 86% of 11-14 year olds play video games. (TGI, 1993) However television viewing still occupies far more time — 26 hours weekly for 11-14 year olds, as compared to 4. 9 hours playing video games. 31% of 7-10 year olds and 43% of 11-14 year olds had been to the cinema in the last month The evidence supports the notion that young people (not unlike the rest of us) inhabit an image rich world.

Amongst 7-10 year olds *Crystal Maze* and *Gladiators* are the most popular programmes, whilst 11-14 year olds favour *Birds of a Feather* and *Casualty*, and 15-19m year olds prefer *Casualty* and *Home and Away*. Interestingly there is strong evidence of a degree of hostility to sport amongst 7-10 year olds who list boxing, American Football, *Football Italia* and *A Question of Sport* as programmes they don't like. This is possibly because of enforced passive viewing of such choices made by parents or older siblings.

Magazine reading exhibits clear signs of marked gender differentiation Boys between 7-11 read the *Beano*, *Dandy*, *Disney Mirror*, and *Match*, whilst girls read *Disney Mirror*, *Fast Forward*, *My Little Pony and Barbie*. The most popular magazines amongst 11-14 year old boys are *Viz*, *Gamesmaster*, *Beano* and *Sega Power*, whilst girls opt for *Smash Hits*, *Just Seventeen*, *Big*, and *Fast Forward*.

For the age 15-19 bracket there is a marked switch to newspapers: boys read *Viz*, *The Sun*, *News of the World*, and the *Daily Mirror*, whilst girls read *More!*, *Just Seventeen*, *News of the World* and *The Sun*.

Print media: form and content

In general three features, image centered page layout, celebrity focus, and gender differentiation, have been very apparent across the whole field of our analysis. All the magazines had a high number of photographs and pages were generally built around the placement of combinations of images. The text appears as a subordinate element, providing verbal anchorage in elaborated caption form. There was a very clear individual focus, often on star individuals. A relatively small number of stars re-occurred constantly, and typically, the most featured stars, in becoming celebrities, began to appear in a wide range of titles. Ryan Giggs, for example, within a short time appeared in *My Guy*, *Sega Power*, *The Face*, and *Smash Hits*, as well as *Shoot* and *Match*. Just as the readership exhibits gender differentiation, so does the content. It was relatively rare for sport stars to appear in *My Guy*, *Just Seventeen*, or *Smash Hits*, whilst images of or references to girls and women, were almost entirely absent from *Shoot* and *Match*.

One of the most striking features of the material we have been looking at has been the importance of photographs:

Title:	Average number of photos per issue
Sun	113
Mirror	112
Sunday (News of the World)	333
Shoot	119
Horse and Pony	138
Smash Hits	195
Just Seventeen	138

In our sample of the sports pages out of 347 (*The Sun*) and 250 (*Daily Mirror*) separate features, 260 (*The Sun*) and 191 (*Daily Mirror*) included an individual mentioned in the first sentence. Of these, only 8 (*The Sun*) and 3 (*Daily Mirror*) were women. Over 60% of the individuals mentioned in first sentences in the sports section of the *Sun* were associated with football. In the rest of the *Daily Mirror*, where 33 individual sports stars were mentioned, only 3 were women.

Out of all the editions of *Sunday* (*The News of the World* magazine) printed in 1992, 13 separate sporting personalities were photographed In the regular feature 'People'. Of these, Gary Lineker appeared on three separate occasions. Martina Navratilova and Chris Evert were the only female sport stars portrayed and they appeared in the same photograph.

In the *Beano*, 18% of the features had a sport reference. 74% of these related to male sporting activity, and 26% to both sexes. There were no exclusively female sporting references. In our sample of *Viz*, out of 19 sport stars mentioned throughout the magazine, only 1 was of a woman (Joanne Conway, the ice-skater).

In *Shoot*, Paul Gascoigne and Gary Lineker emerged as the most photographed and mentioned in print throughout 1990. Gascoigne featured in an average 4 pictures and 13. 5 mentions per issue.

The absence of the opposite sex was also evident in *Horse and Pony*. Only 14% of photos featured either a male or both sexes together. It can also be noted that the males featured were generally adult and seen in a professional capacity to equestrian pursuits (i.e. rider, groom, vet etc., or father).

As *Smash Hits* is chiefly a 'music paper', the representation of sport was not prominent. Only 2.36% of the total area featured sport and only 1. 8%% of the photographs had a sport reference. Of the 195 photos per issue an average of 3 contained a reference to sport. Out of 17 references to sport, only 2 contained a woman as a central.

In *My Guy* references to sport were typically secondary to the main focus of the feature. 54% of the sport-related features were in the format of a celebrity (film/TV/pop star) identifying or associating with a particular sport. Specific sports were also used to connote style or cultural identity. For example, Les Hill (from *Home and Away*) is pictured with a surfboard even though, in the accompanying article, he claims he never surfs.

In *Just Seventeen* out of an average 138 photos per issue, an average of 8 contained a sporting reference. Overall, the lack of any reference to sport was quite apparent, with an average of just 3 references to sport per issue. This compared to *My Guy* (2) and *Smash Hits* (2.5). Of the sports stars mentioned, there were 20 individual male personalities referred to, whereas the only female mentioned was Karen Dixon (in a competition to win a horse riding weekend).

Meanings and identities

In embarking on textual analyses our central areas of concern have become the relation of ideology and morality and the role of sport in the construction of gendered identities. McRobbie (1982), Betterton (1987), and Winship (1987) have examined the place of magazines and advertising in the construction of female identities. Bolla (1990), Dunne (1982) and Lines (1993) have examined the range of images of sport in magazines read by young people. Jennifer Hargreaves (1994) has analysed the process of sexualisation of the female body in images of sport. The ideological role of sport has been examined by John Hargreaves (1986) and Gruneau (1979, 1983). This work has been continued by Goldlust (1987) and Lawrence and Rowe (1987). Stardom and the forms in which it is represented have been analysed by Dyer (1979) and Gledhill (1991). More recently, there has been a growth in the analysis of images of masculinity (Messner, 1993; Messner and Sabo, 1991; Kirkham and Thumin, 1993).

Sabo and Jansen remind us of the need to examine absences as well as presences:

> What is not said in sports media reveals as much about how hegemonic processes work within the U. S. sports industry as what is said. The socially structured silences that the representational conventions cultivated by these media support, legitimize and police the interests of both profit-driven media organizations and the established gender order. (Sabo and Jansen, 1992)

Those who are not commonly mentioned include the physically unfit: that is, those who do not fit into the 'ideal' body type, gays, people with disabilities, and the unsuccessful.

Such a discursive formation establishes a universe of expectations that organises the ground of common sense. It organises rather inchoate prejudices "poofs don't do sport", "no pain, no gain", into rather more organised ideological elements.

Gender

In our research into the forms of print media most heavily consumed by young people, two absences have been particularly striking — the absence of images of sport in magazines read mostly by girls, and the absence of references to personal relationships and emotions in magazines read mostly by boys.

We have considered the consumption of sport magazines as involving the acquisition of a form of alternative cultural capital. A knowledge of the esoteric details of football, as boys acquire through *Match* and *Shoot*, produces a cultural capital that confers status in the playground. Such cultural capital can be stored away, used to advantage and used as a means to exclude unwanted outsiders. And it is girls and women who seem to constitute a distinct group of unwanted outsiders.

Their almost total absence from *Match* and *Shoot* could be seen as a form of symbolic annihilation (Tuchman, 1978). Apart from adverts, only three photos in our entire sample featured women. Tina Turner featured in a 'look-a-like' feature and there were two separate photos of the wives of Gary Lineker and Ian Rush, each pictured with their husband. Even in a regular feature showing footballers at home — rare acknowledgement of life away from the stadium — there is scarcely any trace of wives, partners, parents or children. In this feature women get a mention, but only as the invisible mothers, wives and girlfriends who make the tea and cook the meals. As compared to the girls magazines, which are rich in discussion of relationships, emotions and problems, this problematic and central area of life is rigidly absent (Whannel, 1994).

By comparison, *Horse and Pony* is based in large part around a discourse of caring and nurturing. The manifest content concerns horse and ponies, but much of the focus is on the work necessary to look after the animals. A typical plot structure of the photo-stories concerns a girl who observes someone else ill-treating an animal. Her responsibility is not only to put matters right, but to do so with tact, so that neither the errant girl or her mother will feel offended. Such content provides a socialisation into the responsibilities of caring, nurturing and managing relationships. By contrast one can look in vain for any advice in *Shoot* and *Match* on how to care for football kit (Whannel, 1994).

Where sport appears in *My Guy*, *Just Seventeen* and *Smash Hits*, it is characteristically used to mark gender difference. One quiz featured the question; "Is your lad football mad?" and posited three possible types of lad — the football mad, the fairly keen on football, and finally the one who is more interested in you, but still has a favourite team. The universe of lads offers no position for a lad who is disinterested in sport, and no position for a girl keen on football herself. As Mary Dunne (1982) pointed out, sport typically appears as a threat — an alternative and competing interest for the boys. Where sport celebrities appeared the frame of reference was generally to do with attractiveness and desirability.

Culture, morality, and ideology

We are trying to place our work in the context of the broader cultural political and economic configurations. The cultural formation of Thatcherism — the new individualism, enterprise culture, fitness chic, work-aholic, no pain no gain, greed is good — is clearly beginning to fragment. Cultural practices, that when in dominance are naturalised, take on an estrangement — they seem distinctly odd:

> I used to get a kick out of whipping out a Powerbook on planes....
> Suddenly the penny dropped: the 80s were over. People who need

to be working even while they're on a plane are not necessarily high powered and successful: quite the opposite. They're sad bastards who clearly have no right to call any of their time their own. (Charles Shaar Murray, *MacUser*, 2 September, 1994)

In place of the thrusting young Thatcherite entrepreneur, we have new figures emerging, such as the new lad (an unashamed hedonist), and the caring capitalist (of whom Anita Roddick seems to be a benchmark). These two themes can be detected in the soccer strips of the two major tabloids, *Striker* and *Scorer*.

Scorer reconciles hedonism and responsibility. He has sex without responsibility, without repercussions, with no sexually transmitted diseases, no unwanted pregnancies, and jealousy only from those he rejects. He works hard, and plays hard; his hedonism never affects his ability to play and train. He offers a magical resolution that is the ultimate vindication of lad culture (Whannel and Wellard, 1994).

Striker is rooted more in the core contradictions around the work place and work relations. Footballing protagonist Nick Jarvis, is an employee in a trade that embodies traditional male working class values — tough, physical, masculine, and involving physical skill and dexterity. By chance he becomes an owner of the club. The dilemmas produced by being both boss and worker prove irreconcilable, he abandons ownership not by selling his shares but by giving them to the fans (Whannel and Wellard, 1994).

While we must be cautious about over-politicising this, it does echo an apparent growing disillusion with the enterprise culture, most notably amongst that very class fraction, upper working class, personified as Essex Man, most crucial to the eventual success of Thatcherism.

Terms like "ethics", "morals" and "values" have their own particular histories. Authoritarian, libertarian, humanistic, and Marxist discourses all locate these terms within different frameworks.

Their significance fluctuates — within liberal relativism there has been a decline in the centrality of "ethics" and "morality" as terms. Their re-emergence on both right and left, since the high water mark of Thatcherism, is another indicator of the growing cracks and fissures in the ideological structure of Thatcherism. The sense of crisis on the right, with its confused appeals for a back-to-basics return to traditional moral values has been mirrored by "new" Labour's current concern with values and ethics.

In the context of Britain's structural economic decline, and its failure to manage the transition from the early industrialised legacy of heavy industry into a new modernised and globalised economic system, post war politics has worked through a range of attempts to reconstruct hegemony. The slow disintegration of Thatcherism's authoritarian populism and the concept of a crisis of morality, point to the potential emergence of a new discursive formation.

Striker and *Scorer* offer magical resolutions to moral problems and can be taken as evidence of the perception within popular language that there are things to be resolved — the narrative structures of these strips contain symptoms of the broader sense of a national malaise.

Our field work is currently in progress. One tentative findings is that young people in the sample appear to have a strong resistance to the very idea of identification. when asked which sport star or celebrity they would like to be, around 80% refuse the question with answers like "none of them", "I just want to be me". In a social context where sport is strongly associated with corruption, it may be that the response of the young is neither to seek to identify or emulate, but rather to become cynical. Cynicism can breed a desire for change or an apathetic disillusion. It is surely important to try and explore this further.

Note

[1]   Research carried out in conjunction with Ian Wellard, between November 1993 and October 1994.

References

Betterton, R. (1987) *Looking on: Images of femininity in the visual arts and media.* London: Pandora.

Bolla, P. A. (1990) 'Media images of women and leisure: an analysis of magazine ads 1964-87', in *Leisure Studies*, Vol. 9 No. 3: pp. 241-252.

Cohen, S. (1971) *Folk devils and moral panics.* London: Paladin.

Curran, J. and M. Gurevitch (eds) (1991) *Mass media and society.* London: Edward Arnold.

Curran, J. and Seaton, J. (1991) *Power without responsibility.* London: Fontana.

Dunne, M. (1982) 'Introduction to some of the images of sport in girls comics and magazines', in C. Jenkins and M. Green (eds) *Sporting fictions.* Birmingham: Birmingham University PE Dept and CCCS, pp. 36-59.

Dyer, R. (1979) *The stars.* (Teachers Study Guide) London: BFI.

Gledhill, C. (ed) (1991) *Stardom: Industry of desire.* London: Routledge.

Goldlust, J. (1987) *Playing for keeps: Sport, the media and society.* Australia: Longman.

Gruneau, R. (1979) *Class, sport and the modern state*. Ontario, Canada: Sports Studies Research Group.

——— (1983) *Class, sports and social development*. Massachusets USA: University of Massachusetts Press.

Hall, Stuart *et al.*, (eds) (1980) *Culture, media, language*. London: Hutchinson.

———(1978) *Policing the crisis*. London: Macmillan.

Hargreaves, Jennifer (1994) *Sporting females*. London: Routledge.

Hargreaves, John (1986) *Sport, power and culture*. London: Polity.

Kirkham, P. and Thumin, J. (eds) (1993) *You Tarzan: Masculinity, movies and men*. London: Lawrence and Wishart.

Lawrence, G. and Rowe, D. (eds) (1987) *Power play: The commercialisation of Australian sport*. Sydney, Australia: Hale and Iremonger.

Lines, G. (1993) 'Media and sporting interests of young people', in G. McFee and A. Tomlinson (eds) *Education, sport and leisure: Connections and controversies*. CSRC Topic Report 3. Eastbourne: University of Brighton, pp. 167-177.

Mangan, J. A. (1981) *Athleticism in the Victorian and Edwardian public school*. London: Cambridge University Press.

——— (1985) *The games ethic and imperialism*. London: Viking.

McIntosh, P. (1952) *Physical education in England since 1800*. London: Bell.

——— (1964) *Sport in society*. London: C. A. Watts.

——— (1979) *Fair play: Ethics in sport and education*. London: Heinemann.

McRobbie, A. (1982) *Jackie: An ideology of adolescent femininity in popular culture: Past and present*. London: Croom Helm.

Messner, M. *et al.* (1993) 'Separating the men from the girls: The gendered language of televised sports', *Gender and Society*, Vol. 7, No. 1.

Messner, M. and Sabo, D. (eds) (1991) *Sport, men and the gender order*. USA: Human Kinetics.

Morley, D. (1986) *Family television: Cultural power and domestic leisure*. London: Comedia.

Sabo, D. and S. C. Jansen(1992) 'Images of men in sports media: The social reproduction of gender order', in Craig, S. (ed) *Men, masculinity and the media*. London: Sage, pp. 169-184.

Tuchman, G. *et al.*, (eds)(1978) *Images of women in the media*. London: Open University Press.

Whannel, G. and I. Wellard (1994) 'Citizenship and morality: Sporting heroes', paper presented at Citizenship and Cultural Frontiers conference, Staffordshire University, 14-17 Sept.

————— (1994) 'Competitive sport versus the emotional and the personal', paper presented at Critical Practices conference, Middlesex University, 14-17 Sept.

————— (1992) *Fields in vision: Television, sport and cultural transformation.* London: Routledge.

Williams, J. and Taylor, R. (1994) 'Boys keep swinging: Masculinity and football culture in England', in T. Newburn and E. Stanko (eds) *Just boys doing business: Men, masculinity and crime.* London: Routledge.

Winship, J. (1987) *Inside women's magazines.* London: Pandora.

Part II

Values in Public and Private Spheres

Market and Non-Market Leisure

Stan Parker

University of Brighton

There are many ways of defining leisure and of dividing it for various purposes. Of the three most frequent ways of defining leisure — as time, activities and experience — I shall here concentrate on the leisure experience. I then want to ask how the leisure experience is made available: is it provided for people by some body external to themselves, or do they do it themselves, individually or collectively?

The other and related distinction I want to make is between market and non-market leisure. Market leisure, like all marketable commodities, implies a buyer and a seller. This is most obvious with commercially-provided leisure: the company or enterprise sells the leisure goods or services, the customer buys them. If there are no paying customers in prospect, there are no commercial providers; if the providers fail to get enough customers, they go out of business, or at least out of that line of business.

Leisure provision, however, is not just commercial. The concept of market leisure includes those leisure experiences (in the shape of facilities, personnel and opportunities) which are provided by various public bodies, where the profit motive is absent or low key, the aim of the provider may simply be to break even, where subsidies may be involved — and even where the customer may have the leisure experience free at the point of consumption. Publicly provided leisure, is in short, a broad church, but always involves a market, even though 'market forces' may be constrained by considerations such as welfare or public service.

Non-market leisure is not provided by anyone or anybody outside of those who have or share in the leisure experience. It takes two forms, which I call mutual aid and individual. There is mutual aid in leisure when people get together in clubs, associations and societies to pursue an interest or pleasurable activity or experience without a financial motive. Some members of the particular mutual aid group are usually more active than others (for example, by being on the organising committee) but they are not really providers because they share with other members in the leisure experience that is 'provided' for all. The other form of non-market leisure is individual, when people 'do their own thing' not in the company or with the help of others.

The four types of leisure experience I am proposing may be depicted thus:

LEISURE EXPERIENCE			
MARKET		NON-MARKET	
Commercially provided	Publicly provided	Mutual aid	Individual

None of these four types is pure, in the sense of never being mixed with any of the others. But each type may be seen to be dominant in a given kind of leisure experience. For example, gambling is predominantly a commercially provided activity and experience, although it is quite possible for individuals to gamble among themselves, and of course the government takes a cut from gambling such as on horses and the national lottery. Again, most sequence dance clubs are primarily mutual aid groups, but their members usually have to pay a public or commercial body for hall hire and have to buy records and sound equipment from commercial suppliers.

The case against market leisure

In this paper I make no claim to be impartial as between the merits and demerits of market and non-market leisure. I am firmly in favour of the latter. I leave it to others who may wish to point out what they see as the advantages of providing leisure through the market or the disadvantages of encouraging people to make and experience leisure for themselves. My criticisms of market leisure are several. They are not just my personal criticisms — they are shared with, and often inspired by, others.

1. Market providers tend to go for creating and supplying the largest possible market, which usually means appealing to the lowest common denominator of taste. I know there are such things as niche or segmented markets in which there is some attempt to cater for different preferences at higher prices than the mass market. But market leisure is generally stereotyped, bland, undemanding and not really satisfying except perhaps in the Chinese meal sense. Allen (1989) writes of how much of what passes for leisure is superficial and insubstantial: "Just as we can work to fill up the emptiness of life, so too can we fill up our free time with movement and noise, especially the latter today. If there is nothing really worthwhile in life, then we can

busy ourselves with distractions... Leisure, then, declines to mere amusement, time-filling and becomes like work, and perhaps even more so, something to be got through...' We may not have to go to a leisure provider to get this feeling, but the offerings of a provider too often seem to lead to it.

2. Market leisure, especially in its form of recreation, is often used as a means to an end, thus subverting one of true leisure's basic characteristics, that of being an end in itself (Stormann, 1989). Customers' golf, as it is sometimes called, is one example. Another is corporate hospitality at race meetings, entertainment events, etc. attended by people there for business purposes rather than for their interest in the event. Reid (1995) writes about leisure in the Corporate Economic (by which he means contemporary capitalist) society:

> ... leisure is the reward for work or an opportunity to reduce stress produced in the work environment. Leisure is utilitarian in that it is an activity engaged in for some ulterior purpose. Escaping from the pressures of life or boredom are often the motivations for recreational activity. Recreation activity also takes the form of self-improvement in the sense of developing practical skills, not necessarily just for enjoyment or creating a different perspective on life, but for enhancing one's marketability. Emphasis is placed on "doing" not on the intrinsic rewards of the experience. (Reid, 1995)

3. Market leisure appears to call the many but, at least in games of competition and chance, few are actually chosen. Britain has recently joined most other countries in organising a national lottery. It is a profit-making enterprise for the promoters and the government, and re-distributes wealth from the poor to the rich by its sponsorship of middle-class cultural activities and its promotion of a tiny few punters to the ranks of the super-rich. Its huge pointing finger and voice intoning 'It's you!' mocks us all. Rojek (1995) approvingly paraphrases Veblen's critique of the leisure class:

> For Veblen the acquisitive need in consumer society is stimulated by the insincere values of advertising and the practices of the leisure class. We have lost contact with the values of craftsmanship and probity that inspired the development of the industrial society. We are hopelessly enmeshed in the values of consumer culture. (Rojek, 1995)

4. Finally, market leisure aids the escape into a dream world by men and women frustrated in the real world. Associated with my last point about lottery fever and our acquisitive culture is the further point that market leisure is to a large extent postmodern leisure. I am very sceptical about the concept of postmodernism, since it has been used by so

many writers to mean so many different things. But one interpretation of postmodernism is relevant here: that it points to the growth of signs and signifiers, to virtual reality as a rival to, if not a replacement of, substantive reality. You could say, if you like, that recreation was modern, and that market leisure is to a large extent postmodern. Or you can see a progression rather than a disjunction. As Lasch (1979) notes,

> The appearance in history of an escapist conception of "leisure" coincides with the organisation of leisure as an extension of commodity production. The same forces that have organised the factory and the office have organised leisure as well, reducing it to an appendage of industry. (Lasch, 1979)

The case for non-market leisure

If there were only market leisure available to us then we might sensibly take the view that we should try to make the best of it, to look on the bright side of capitalist life, to reform market leisure to make it better. But we do have an alternative. In fact many of us already reject many of the leisure experiences that the market offers for sale, and we make our own leisure with minimal contact with any market.

As I said earlier, it is not a matter of choosing only 100 percent pure non-market leisure experiences — there are in present society few if any of those to choose. Rather, it is a matter of seeking out those forms of leisure which not only avoid the disadvantages of market leisure but also offer advantages which the market does not, and probably cannot, offer.

Non-market leisure is a negative, residual term, but it does contain at least two very positive concepts and practices: one is mutual aid in leisure and the other is serious leisure. The first has been drawn to our attention chiefly by Bishop and Hoggett, most notably in their book *Organising Around Enthusiasms* (1986), and the second by Bob Stebbins, who some 20 years ago introduced the concept of serious leisure and has since researched and developed it with colleagues around the world (Stebbins, 1992; Stebbins, 1995).

Mutual aid in leisure is exemplified in the very many groups, clubs and associations that exist to enable us to pursue for pleasure interests and activities as varied as local history and rat-fancying, collecting coins and volunteering as a gallery guide. The meetings of such groups are usually face-to-face but there are exceptions such as radio hams around the world whose contact is normally confined to the airwaves or the mail, electronic or otherwise. Not everyone makes an equal contribution to mutual aid in leisure groups but if some are on the organising committee while others are not it is on the basis not of remuneration but that 'some of us help all of us'.

Seabrook (1988) writes warmly of mutual aid in leisure groups, in words that are a world away from the cold and calculating leisure market:

> ... it is essential to take account of the extraordinary energy and passion, the commitment and skills that people in Britain give voluntarily: whether this is in the form of gift-work — from nature conservation to sitting on committees for the NSPCC or running Oxfam shops — or whether it is the devotion to growing fuchsias, breeding dogs or collecting butterflies. There exists a vast reservoir of knowledge and expertise, much of it highly specialised, often recondite and obscure, which creates a world of detailed special-isms which mean nothing to outsiders. There is a vast channelling of altruism and enthusiasm into activities undertaken for their own sake or for the sake of those who share the same, ordinary pas-sions. Leisure remains an ambiguous idea; what makes it inter-esting is that it represents both an intensifying of marketed experi-ences on the one hand, and growing individual autonomy on the other.

Stebbins is aware of Bishop and Hoggett's research on mutual aid in leisure but his own contribution to the subject of non-market leisure is the concept and practice of serious leisure. He defines serious leisure as 'the systematic pursuit of an amateur, hobbyist or volunteer activity sufficiently substantial and interesting in nature for the participant to find a career there in the acquisition and expression of a combination of its special skills, knowledge and experience.

Serious leisure takes three forms: amateurism, hobbyist activities and career volunteering. I disagree with Stebbins about building 'career' into the definition of serious leisure (though it is certainly an associated varia-ble). But I believe he has done a great deal to develop an area of study that needed to be opened up. Together with Bishop and Hoggett and others, he has drawn attention to the rich variety of non-market leisure that survives and even flourishes, despite the encroachment of market forces on all our lives.

It would be an interesting research project to try to assess the relative strengths of market and non-market leisure in this country — or even more ambitiously in the world — today. But how would we seek to measure those strengths? Obviously, we could not do it in monetary terms: only market leisure is measurable in terms of money spent. Perhaps we could do it in terms of time spent — but that is still a very quantitative evalua-tion, implying that one hour spent as a customer or spectator is the equi-valent of one hour spent as a participant or enthusiast.

In the end it is not a matter of measurement but of judgement. As my philosopher friend Bob Paddick put it when writing on leisure education, (1992): "We are led to consider what kind of people and what kind of society ought to be promoted".

It has been objected that my division of leisure experiences into *market* and *non-market* fails to acknowledge the extent to which some serious leisure activities do require the purchase of items from the market: for example, members of mutual aid dance groups still have to purchase dance shoes in the market. It was also suggested that the voluntary leisure sector was involved in the leisure market.

To reply, I point out that Bishop and Hoggett were not happy (and neither am I) with the term 'the voluntary sector' to describe the myriad activities that people engage in as mutual aid in leisure and as serious leisure. The voluntary sector is more properly regarded as a mixture of paid and unpaid organised effort, sometimes with charitable or government help, to provide leisure for others. The unpaid volunteers may, of course, experience their donated time and effort as leisure, since they choose to give it (non-market) rather than sell it or exchange it (market).

References

Allen, R. T. (1989) 'Leisure: The purpose of life and the nature of philo-sophy', in T. Winnifrith and C. Barrett (eds) *The philosophy of leisure.* New York: St. Martin's Press.

Bishop, J. and Hoggett, P. (1986) *Organising around enthusiasms.* London, Comedia.

Lasch, C. (1979) *The culture of narcissism.* New York: Warner.

Paddick, R. (1982) 'Time on my hands, hands off my time', *Leisure Studies,* Vol. 1, No. 3: pp. 355-364.

Reid, D. (1995) *Work and leisure in the 21st century.* Toronto: Wall and Emerson.

Rojek, C. (1995) Veblen, leisure and human need', *Leisure Studies,* Vol. 14, No. 2: pp. 73-86.

Seabrook, J. (1988) *The leisure society.* Oxford: Blackwell.

Stebbins, R. A. (1992) *Amateurs, professionals and serious leisure.* Montreal: McCall-Queen's University Press.

———(1995) 'Serious leisure', *Newsletter* of RC13 of the International Sociological Association, July.

Stormann, W. (1989) 'Work: True leisure's home?', *Leisure Studies,* Vol. 8, No. 1: pp. 25-34.

Theoretical Limitations in Codes of Ethical Conduct

M. J. McNamee

Cardiff Institute of Higher Education

Introduction

A national automobile association recently called upon the Government to curb the excessive zeal with which car parking wardens were performing their duties by establishing a code of professional conduct, and the Church of England (surely immune from ethical-fad addiction) has found itself looking toward a code of conduct in the wake of its recent outbreak of over-zealous "preaching". "Got yourself a problem?...Get yourself a code" seems to be the public relations solution to the "contemporary" professional moral malaise. What is to be made of all this?

Is the would-be crisis of morals merely confirmation of the smorgas-bord of cultural practices now available? Or is it really, as MacIntyre illustrated so brilliantly in *After Virtue* (1981), the loosening of the moral moorings of our age (postmodernity, late modernity, or whatever you wish to call it). Perhaps it is true that it has never been more difficult to ascer-tain evaluative standards through which to appraise ethical dimensions of conduct. But there appears to be a moral conservatism in codes of con-duct; a flight back to the language of moral certainty, of duties, obligations, principles and rules. And these are certainly not in keeping with the heterogeneity of values central to characterisations of postmodernity. Why should we look to them, then, as a route to moral salvation (if only in professional or occupational life)?

This paper offers but a few ideas. There is nothing so well developed here that it can properly be called an argument. To understand the current vogue for codes of professional or ethical conduct one has to understand the conceptions of moral philosophy that nourish them. But merely to illuminate them is not, of course, to help solve the problems they address. More often the effect is to exacerbate the issues by presenting the array of alternative and at times conflicting theories that attempt both to

145

characterise the field as well as to offer potential routes through which solutions may be approached. Finally, a broader and potentially more rewarding perspective is sketched out in which we may develop future discussions on ethical dimensions of sport and leisure. Before that, however, some words on the ethical roots of codes of conduct; to misquote Berkeley, let us raise some philosophical dust so that we may complain we cannot see.

Codes of ethical conduct

We must first understand the reasons for adopting a code of professional practice. Let us agree that in late modernity there is something of a cafeteria of ethical choices among which evaluational consensus is more than merely *difficult* to achieve. Let us agree also that we desire authoritative support for our evaluations of those acts that are considered permissible and not permissible. Finally, let us agree that articulated rules allow us to point up most clearly the clashes between such acts and their evaluations. We can still ask, though, why we need a code of rules to guide ethical conduct in professional life? Dawson (1994) offers six suggestions for the value of such codes:

(i)   the apparent clarity and simplicity they offer;

(ii) they set out clearly fixed standards for, among other things, provision and expectation;

(iii) they provide independent and pre-determined criteria to minimise ambiguity;

(iv) they reduce litigational conflict resolution and increase satisfaction for all parties;

(v)   they guarantee a standard of practice within the client/professional relationship that is consistent over time and between those persons governed by the authoritative body; and

(vi) they provide of a neutral framework, responsive to different populations.

All of these reasons offer sound justification since their alternatives, ambiguity and confusion, lack of standards or criteria for consistent judgement all appear to open the door to bias, capriciousness, exploitation and subjectivity. Their purposes may, of course, outrun these justifications. Brackenridge (1994) offers two objectives for these codes that move beyond Dawson's justifications; first, codes of conduct offer a degree of control over the professional's behaviour by constraining certain actions and, secondly, they allow exclusion from the professional organisation of members who will not conform to the code. In short, we might say that codes of conduct franchise "blameability" and consequently "punishability" to their respective organisations. The closeness of these quasi-ethical objectives to a legal mind-set is apparent. "Blame", as Williams reminds us, "is the characteristic reaction of the morality system" (Williams, 1985: p. 177); it invites us to think of the whole of ethical life in terms of a series of obligations of increasing power that must be met for fear of incurring blame and possible retribution.

Common sense might have it that what morality is is a rather simple affair. One can well imagine a moralist (not moral philosopher) on some daytime television debate on abortion, terrorism, child abuse or any other social ill shouting "look here, morality is simply about deciding what's right and what's wrong and how to get people to do the former instead of the latter". One can imagine further the crowd's shrieks, whistles and rounds of applause, all of which signals defeat for the high-minded liberal in the audience (usually an invited specialist) who is urging caution, imploring more subtle distinctions and warning of problems of interpretation. This, then, is one common sense view of morality; a set of rules or principles which stop people from doing any old thing in the pursuit of their interests to the detriment of others'. The sum of these rules or principles, both negative and positive, constitute the moral code enshrined in rights, duties and obligations. So much for common sense; reality is rather less comforting.

The sheer range of ethical theories presents a difficulty for anyone who wishes to give a brief summary of the field. In keeping with the brevity of this presentation and the heterogeneity of the audience, we can assert that (albeit following many philosophers before) that we may separate ethical theories into two categories; those that concern themselves with actions and those that concern themselves with agents, or, put another way, those that focus on what it is right to do and those that focus on what sort of agent it is good to be. In keeping with the above, we will eschew felicity for the sake of brevity and generalise further by naming them "rule-based" and "virtue-based" theories of ethics. We must now consider how these caricatured positions underwrite codes of conduct.

"Rule-based" ethical theories

One way in which people consider it valuable to demonstrate the necessity of moral rules is to consider man (it is always *man*) in a pre-ethical state. Hobbes's famous account of man in the state of nature is of a solitary being, poor, short, nasty and brutish; in a condition of a war of every man against every man. Conflict is the order of the day and to save us from this heinous state (how we achieve this rise is of course a contested matter) we need to establish some rules to frustrate the worst of people's desires, rules that are grounded in reason such that they have an authoritative voice. We are faced with a problem of how to decide between competing courses of action in a way that is not merely capricious, that anyone in those shoes would agree is right.

Perhaps the most well-known theories of right actions are deontological (from the Greek word '*deon*' or duty). To act rightly is to refrain from

things that can be known, before the fact, to be wrong. The rules are effectively negative, whether as constraints, proscriptions, prohibitions or
norms. They prevent us from doing, with good conscience, things that are
known to be wrong, irrespective of all consequences, including good ones.
Characteristic of deontological theories is the prioritisation of the right over
the good. The fact that my harming one person may save the lives of several others does not weigh with the strict deontologist; the rules guide his/
her conduct which is good or bad in itself, not the consequences. S/he is
not concerned with maximising happiness or minimising pain. Instead
what informs the rules of conduct is the distinction between the permissible and the not permissible; and these considerations enables agents to
perceive their obligations. Again, this may be stated negatively; we are
obliged not to do that which is not permissible. This negative characterisation of morality is captured well in Mill's *Essay on Liberty* ([1989], quoted
in Warnock, 1962: p. 177):

> Its ideal is negative rather than positive; passive rather than active;
> Innocence rather than Nobleness; Abstinence from evil, rather than
> the energetic Pursuit of the Good; in its precepts (as has been well
> said) "Thou shalt not" predominates unduly over "thou shalt".

Davis (1991) sets out three features of deontological constraints that show
their nature and structure. First, though it is possible to formulate these
rules or constraints positively, (for example one might say "never lie" can
be translated into "always tell the truth") they are negatively formulated
and there is no entailment between them, neither are they equivalent. For
example, even though lying may be considered wrongful, one may withhold
information from another without lying to them; they are different kinds of
acts. Additionally, the rules are narrowly framed and directed. One is not
permitted to act in ways that are wrong. This gives the actions a form of
specificity to the rule; it also puts into context the distinction between actions intended to bring about certain outcomes intentionally and those
where, for example, bad outcomes result from foreseen and unforeseen
consequences from our *prima facie* permissible action. To do wrong one
must do it intentionally.

In many ways the moral value of games and sports has resided in
rather opaque accounts of rule-responsibility. If we can develop children
who follow the rules (moral and non-moral) we will thereby develop moral
maturity. But all this is a far cry from the idea of a moral code, a set of
principles, not merely aggregated but ultimately reducible to one such
principle. Thus we often have reductions from many rules to the "Golden
Rule" instanced in more than one type of ethico-religious system. Consider
the Categorical Imperative of Kant that entreats us to treat persons never
merely as means but as ends, worthy of respect in their own right, or
Hillel's amusing anecdote about the message of the Torah (when asked by
a non-Jew to teach him the entire Torah while he [the questioner] stood on
one foot; Hillel replies 'What you dislike, don't do to others; that is the

whole Torah. The rest is commentary."); or as in Matthew's gospel "always treat others as you would like them to treat you".

What is suggested here, somewhat less than originally, is that at the heart of the rule-based ethics, especially deontological ones, is negative; moral behaviour consists in the avoidance of wrong acts[1]. This is one reason why codes of conduct are framed explicitly or implicitly in rule-like ways (whether negative or positive) but also because of the legalistic nature of rule-formulations and the blameability they offer. Where there are rules we should be able to distinguish right- from wrong-doing and wrong-doers.

Yet there are some obvious weaknesses in this way of thinking. First, we may wish to enquire into the nature of the rules that supposedly distinguish clearly the permissible from the not permissible. Then we may ask some searching questions about rule conflict, scope and interpretation.

Several codes of conduct[2] (for example those of the British Association of Sports and Exercise Scientists, Coachwise, the Association of Professional Sports Massage Therapists and the Chartered Society of Physiotherapists) display a wide variety of rules, principles, duties and more general exhortations. Consider one such principle in the *Code of Practice for Sports Coaches*:

1   The first and paramount responsibility of coaches is to the health, well-being and future participation of the performer.

Let us ask a few questions about this rule, not by way of criticism but rather in the spirit of exploration. We must have some mechanisms to guide the conduct of our performers, coaches and administrators in sport. And this rule seems laudable enough; the health of the performer should rank above the maximisation of his or her athletic potential. Or should it? What is being said here of the relationship between sport, health and well-being? Isn't much of elite sport bad for your health anyway? And who decides what is to constitute the health and well-being of the performer? The coach, or a parent (where the performer is a minor) or the performer his or herself? All three could potentially conflict: how will resolution be reached? What if a parent gives the coach *carte blanche* in order to prepare a young athlete for elite competition, thinking it would be in the interest of the child's long-term financial well-being? What appeared to be at first sight a laudable principle, captured in clear terms, to enable the discernment of exploitative coaches unambiguously, may not be quite that effective. What is particularly praiseworthy in this code, however, is the articulation of duties and responsibilities that correspond to each of their principles. For the principle quoted above, the duties and responsibilities read:

While coaches are concerned with performance improvement, they must constantly exercise judgement in relation to the social, emotional, physical and moral needs of performers. This should take precedence over the pressure to train or compete. Coaches should balance the needs of the person with the development of the sports performer.

Again the spirit of this development is clearly praiseworthy; indeed coaches must exercise judgement though, perhaps, we should note two points. In the first instance, one imagines that it is good judgement they are referring to, where the term "good" is used (possibly primarily) in its ethical rather than the merely technical sense. (There may be plenty of good [i.e. technically good] coaches who are clearly wicked persons[3].) Secondly, as was highlighted above, what happens if and when that judgement brings them to prioritise the role of performer over other aspects of the person?

Having identified some simple problems of interpretation, prioritisation and clarification, we can move to another aspect of rule-guidance that is problematic. What is the scope of the rule? We noted above that deontological rules are narrowly directed, framed and bounded. This in part gives them their purchase and application. Among many sensible attempts to demarcate the responsibility of scientific work in exercise and sport some exceptional comments are made that appear to have rather more to do with institutional powers than ethical conduct *per se*. Consider the following example, again in a genuine spirit of interest, from the BASES code:

6.   Competence

(d) Full members should seek to become *accredited*.

(e) All members *must* be knowledgeable in respect of contemporary practice.

7.   Professional and Personal Conduct

(b) Members must conduct themselves in such a way that brings credit to their specialist areas.

(e) Members must not in any way jeopardise the safety or interests of clients.

One could draw out many other examples of clear, sensitive and sensible principles. For present purposes, however, one might ask whether accreditation is really an ethical issue. Likewise, of course, scientists should be knowledgeable in the areas of their purported professional expertise, but just what constitutes "contemporary" practice? Take for example the traditional practice of using Douglas bags to capture expired gases rather than utilising the more accurate and sophisticated on-line gas analysis systems. Would this mean anyone employing the former, an outmoded experimental method, was in some way being unethical or unprofessional? Additionally, it is not beyond the bounds of sense to imagine a conflict of interests between 7(b) and (e); how does the professional choose? Moreover, the lack of specificity in respect of 7 (b) is self-evidently alarming.

A far more pressing difficulty might be raised however. Of considerably greater concern is the notion that contemporary practice may run counter to any given code, and not merely the practice of the odd individual here or there but of many, even the majority, of a given profession such as coaching. How many elite rugby coaches will entreat their players to "respect all performers equitably", as the sports coaches second principle would have it? How many sports scientists working at maximal values for, say, international swimmers would have their clients well-being (in the bio-medical sense of the term) in mind? Perhaps the apotheosis of this mind-set is coming to light now in stories from the former East Germany. Such issues, as might generally be put under the heading 'the *habitus* of elite sport and sport science' (and there are a plethora of them) are beyond the scope of this paper but are in need of urgent ethical and empirical examination. This is not a crass political exhortation.

Perhaps, though, what people *expect* of codes of conduct in terms of unambiguity, clarity of application, non-conflicting order and specificity is what needs re-addressing. One way to do this would be to consider the range of moral rules. Pincoffs (1986: p. 25) writes:

> Rules may be like general standing commands or like general standing orders; analogously they may be like general standing specific and non-specific prescriptions. They may allow no leeway in compliance or they may allow a great deal of compliance.
>
> Some moral rules are more like general standing orders than like general standing commands: for example, "love they neighbor" or "Do not cause suffering." They say what is wanted but do not say what to do. If, however, we concentrate upon rules that are like commands, such as "Do not kill" or "Never break promises," we are likely to think of moral rules much like criminal laws, in that they will consist for us, largely of specific injunctions and directions. But if we recognize that they can also be like orders, we will be more aware of the discretion they sometimes allow. They do not tell us exactly what to do so much as they indicate what we should struggle toward in our own way.

We can see now, perhaps, the disparity of the kinds of rules that are on offer in codes of conduct. Glossing over problems of interpretation, scope and application, and the crucial distinction between rule-following and acting merely in accordance with the rule, it might be said that people expect too much of rules without attending to their diversity[4]. Some rules will be *constitutive*; they might act like definitions, telling us, for example, what the term "client" is taken to mean. Others might be *regulative* in the strict, command sense; "Coaches must gain the informed agreement of their performers". Others still might be *general orders*: "Coaches should show respect to all performers and treat them equitably" [examples taken from the Coachwise draft sports coaches code of conduct].

What becomes clear from this brief consideration of rules in codes of conduct in addition to the diversity of rules and their action-guiding implications is the need for something beyond mere rule-observance where this means merely the avoidance of not-permissible acts of rule breaking. We can come to imagine, quite wrongly, that rule-responsibility is at the centre of ethical life. It is clear that it is an essential social virtue; how could we get along if there were social anarchy or mere unpredictability and randomness of behaviour? What, of course, does not follow is the idea that ethics and ethical conduct can be simply *reduced* to the idea of rule-re-sponsibility. To see why this is the case, we need to return to our earlier distinction of being and doing; of agency and acts.

One of the central reasons why we need either to replace or augment the notion of rules as exhaustively descriptive of ethical theory and conduct is, so to speak, their underdetermination. Put simply though they commonly tell us what not to do, often what to aim toward and, occasionally, what to do, they leave so much else in the void. Fried (1978: p. 13) captures this point well:

> One cannot live one's life by the demands of the domain of the right. After having avoided wrong and doing one's duty, an infinity of choices is left to be made.

It is at this point we need to focus on the character of the agent; the would-be virtuous coach, sportswoman or manager.

Virtue-based ethical theories

The tendency to think of morality in terms of duties and principles has been challenged recently by a powerful array of philosophers who take their lead from Aristotle[5]. Where the deontologist delivers us a guide to right conduct by deduction from general rules, the virtue theorist looks to the particular that is exemplified in the living of good lives by agents. The pursuit of *eudaimonia* (human well-being or flourishing) is better served by certain sorts of characters rather than others. We morally prefer the just to the unjust, the courageous to the cowardly, the honest to the dishonest, and so forth.

The picture of the good life is one that is lived in accordance with virtue against a background of a proper nature of human being. *Arete* (virtue) is a combination of excellences that enable persons to achieve their *telos* (function, goal) of flourishing yet they are also an ingredient of the attainment of that goal at the same time. The socially and historically embedded character of the particularity is instantiated in the good lives of agents situated in place and time who are possessed of a core of virtues that are acquired, displayed and produced in a variety of shared social practices that are themselves constitutive of broader cultural traditions[6].

On a virtue account, when we are faced with a quandary we cannot simply consult the moral rule-book. We cannot write off the particularity of quandary. It is "us", grounded selves, with particular psychological attributes, histories, social position and so forth. What will we do here in the light of who we conceive ourselves to be; just, cowardly, arrogant, sensitive, untrustworthy.

One of the key points in such a scheme is the notion of a virtue conceived not as an isolated act but as part of a narrative that is my life. This idea works both negatively and positively. In its negative aspect it partially defines virtue; it is unlike rule-based conceptions, and not merely deontological ones. More positively, it points to the fact that virtues are relatively settled dispositions to act in ways with a qualitative dimension. Virtues, or vices of course, are displayed in the manner in which we are disposed to act in regular and interrelated ways. This point is usually developed by remarking, first, that one cannot simply possess a virtue in isolation and secondly, that the moral sphere is thereby extended to include a wider range of acts and appraisals than are found in rule-based accounts.

Of the former, Baier summarises, "The virtues hunt in packs" (Rorty, 1988: p. 316). McDowell (1981: pp. 332-33) develops the point:

> Thus the particular virtues are not a batch of independent sensitivities. Rather, we use the concepts of the particular virtues to mark similarities and dissimilarities among the manifestations of a single sensitivity which is what virtue, in general, is: an ability to recognize requirements which situations impose on one's behaviour. It is a single complex sensitivity of this sort which we are aiming to instil when we aim to inculcate a moral outlook.

Having sketched the rule-based position as one that is, perhaps inherently, reductive, by considering the good life as a narrative of particular agents possessed of unique combinations of virtue we must be wary of a similar move. Some virtue theorists, in parallel to the exaltation of a "Golden Rule," would argue for a master virtue such as justice. We need not discuss this difficulty here. Instead, and without providing the justification, we will simply point to the variety of functionally various virtues. Just as we limited our deontological field to permissible and not-permissible acts of right and wrong conduct, by focusing on character-appraisal the full richness of human conduct is prized open.

Imagine whatever quandary you will in a coaching situation; it may be mundane just as well as a defining moment, crisis-time or humdrum training situation. We are met with a course of competing options; do we finish the session now?; shall "we" try that routine one more time?; is the performer too tired?; have we succeeded in achieving all we wanted to this session?; have we done enough for next week's championship? All these questions are invoked in everyday contexts that commonly fall well outside the rule-governed jurisdiction of the code of conduct (or perhaps better, beyond all but the most comprehensive rule-book whose limits seem almost beyond the horizon) yet in each, as coach, we may have to ask ourselves "what sort of person are we/would we be to act in this way or that?" And the range of replies may range from considerate, sympathetic and supportive, to arrogant, intolerant, vindictive and spiteful. How could any rule-book cover such a range without tearing down all the rain forests in order to attempt to write rules for every possible occasion or eventuality? And yet the exaltation of the rule-book mentality, "moral minimalism" we may call it for want of a better term, is precisely that mentality whose character is raised by the exclamation "we have done nothing wrong or immoral; we have broken no rules", as if the latter entailed the former! On this point specifically, it is worth quoting Pincoffs (1986: p. 42) at length:

> Some moral problems, as has often been recognized, have a quasi-legal character: they presuppose a network of rules, and they concern the rights, duties, responsibilities, liabilities and obligations of those who fall under the rules. ... This temptation leads, by easy steps, to the erection of an ethical theory that will then itself allow, as a moral problem, only what can be described in the appropriate quasi-legal language.

From this he proceeds:

> It can be a moral problem what the benevolent thing to do or to approve is, in the circumstances, or the kind thing, the loyal thing, the honest thing, the just thing. In short, it can be a moral problem whether what I am considering doing or approving is consistent or not with the standards or ideals by which I would like to live. (p. 42)

Lest we are charged with presenting too rosy a picture of virtue ethics by contrast, one important criticism must be raised. From the many possible lines of criticism, here we should focus on what a deontologist might consider a substantial theoretical difficulty. Having made more basic the notion of a life lived with narrative unity, or "aretaic connectedness" as Audi puts it, we may ask the simple question 'What am I to do such that I may become, or further consolidate myself as, this kind of person rather than that?'. I cannot merely act in a vacuum. But the charge, then, becomes one of circularity (Audi, (1995: p. 466):

> ...there is the epistemological difficulty of determining what, or even who, a morally virtuous person is without already knowing what sort of thing such an agent would do.

This raises the great difficulty of how a virtue theory tell us what to do. Rule-based accounts appear, *prima facie* at least, to do this. Audi (p. 466) points out a standard Aristotelian answer that if we know our *telos* (proper end or function) we must exercise the virtues toward the living a life of *eudaimonia* (flourishing or well-being) by choosing wisely between matters of good and bad, pleasure and pain, and strike a mean between excess and deficiency. At this point, a fuller account would have to focus on the notion of *phronesis* (practical wisdom or judgement) in arriving at this reflective equilibrium though there may still be a need to assign a proper place to rules and rule-following in ethical life. And this is beyond the scope of this paper.

The virtue theorist need not banish rules from the moral scene however. Yet this should not imply that rules are generated simply from generalisations of virtuous behaviour. Though this is, I think, precisely what codes of conduct illicitly do (attempting to make rules do the work of virtue requirements by replacing the particularity of judgement to the rule of law). One need not throw the baby out with the bath water:

> Even making virtues conceptually fundamental need not make them indefeasible sources of moral authority. Similarly, if one could specify the types of actions a virtuous agent should in general perform, practical wisdom and a virtuous disposition would be required for applying the relevant rules is particular cases. (Audi, 1995: p. 468)

To focus on this last point may well be to concede too much ground. McDowell notes the inverse point that a place can be made for virtues in rule-based ethics in terms of a secondary notion giving them executive status; they carry us forward to action or inaction that is prescribed or proscribed by the rules. This relegation, I suggest, is unhelpful two principle reasons. First, the scope of rule-based ethics is underdetermined; there is still oftentimes a wide range of options and corresponding dispositions to fill the void after the rule has been laid out. Second, even after the rule is specified, it will only be followed, in the strong sense, by the virtuous agent. Mere robot-like rule-observance is an inappropriate point of departure for our description of ethical lives, professional and otherwise. And, worse, it can lead to an *ethos* of rule-bending in its other extreme — as is characteristic of so much conduct in modern sports.

Conclusion: neither this nor that

This paper has addressed the nature of ethical theories far more than it has grounded itself in substantive discussion to practical situations such as sports coaching. What has not been argued is that codes of conduct for professional associations in sports and leisure is a waste of time. On the contrary, they are valuable, and would become more so if the community of coaches were invited to debate more thoroughly in their construction (a task that is too commonly performed by organisational elites). Expertise is required to be sure. But one must be extremely wary both of the masked elites who would underwrite standards of behaviour in the absence of the population they seek to control, as well as the moral philosophers who deigns to come out of the ivory tower in order to minister theory to the practising minions. Whatever is presented here emanates from a very different conception of the moral and philosophical task that is required to make the practices we love and are committed to more throughgoingly good. But the paper has both negative and positive notes of conclusion. We should similarly be wary of associating morals to closely with a legislative mind-set. This is not a plea for the areas of sports and leisure to be thought of as moral holidays, but rather a plea to consider the full range of ethical considerations in our professional practice, not merely the cultivation of rule responsible dispositions to meet minimal moral obligations.

While the more outstanding and spectacular failings of our sports coaches, administrators and performers will always hit the headlines (and while codes of conduct will allow us in certain circumstances to blame and chastise them,) knee jerk reactions for tighter rules and their more rigorous application will only serve to distract our attention from the more pervasive considerations of character that carry us to action in order to promote the good lives that are bound up with, and in, those practices.

Notes

[1]   Any utilitarian would properly object that this negative characterisation, though it fits the utilitarian rule to minimise pain, misses entirely the corresponding rule to maximise happiness or pleasure. It should be clear that the general target here is the deontological one.

[2]   I am particularly grateful both to BASES and to Coachwise for showing me draft copies of their code of conduct.

[3]   See Brackenridge *op. cit.* for galling evidence of which.

[4]   I address the notion of "rule" and "rule-following" elsewhere: 'Doing the right thing? Virtue versus rule-based conceptions of ethics an their implications for codes of conduct in sport', Philosophic Society for the Study of Sport, 1995 Conference, University of Tsukuba, Japan.

[5]   Examples of prominent works are MacIntyre (1981) and Nussbaum (1986).

[6]   As with the thumbnail sketch of "rule-based" theories so with "virtue based" ones; my account is brief and necessarily selective. The characterisation owes more to MacIntyre (1981) than some philosophers would be happy with, even in so brief an account. For a critical application of MacIntyre's account applied to sport, see McNamee (1995).

References

Audi, R. (1995) 'Acting from virtue', *Mind*, Vol. 104, No. 415: pp.449-471.

Brackenridge, C. (1994) 'Fair play or fair game? Child sexual abuse in sport organisations', *International Review for Sociology of Sport*, Vol. 29, No. 3: pp. 287-99.

Davis, N. (1991) 'Contemporary deontology', in P. Singer (ed) *A companion to ethics*. Oxford: Blackwell, pp. 205-18.

Dawson, A. J. (1994) 'Professional codes of practice and ethical conduct', *Journal of Applied Philosophy*, Vol. 11, No. 2: pp. 145-54.

Fried, C. (1978) *Right and wrong*. Cambridge, Mass.: Harvard University Press.

McDowell, J. (1981) 'Virtue and reason', in S. H. Holtzman and C. M. Leich (eds) *Wittgenstein: To follow a rule*. London: Routledge and Kegan Paul, pp. 332-3.

McIntyre, A. C. (1981) After virtue. London: Duckworth.

McNamee, M. J. (1995) 'Sporting practices, institutions and virtues: A critique and a restatement', *Journal of Philosophy of Sport*, Vol. 22: pp. 61-83.

Mill, J. S. (1859) 'On Liberty', chapter 2 'Of thought and discussion' in M. Warnock (ed.) (1962) *Utilitarianism*. Glasgow: Fontana, p. 177.

Nussbaum, M. (1986) *The fragility of goodness*. Cambridge: Cambridge University Press.

Pincoffs, E. (1986) *Quandaries and ethics: Against reductivism in ethics*. Lawrence, Kansas: University of Kansas Press.

Rorty, A. (1988) *Mind in action: Essays in the philosophy of mind*. Boston: Beacon Press.

Williams, B. (1985) *Ethics and the limits of philosophy*. London: Fontana.

Hustling in Havana: Ethnographic Notes on Everyday Life and Mutual Exploitation between Locals and Tourists in a Socialist Economy under Siege

John Sugden and Alan Tomlinson
University of Brighton

> Once Cuba's famed hospitals made it a destination for so-called health tourism. Now the island is becoming a magnet for body tourism of a different kind. (Freedland, 1995)

This paper emerges as a by-product of research looking at the relationship between sport and society in Cuba (see Sugden *et al.*, 1994). The authors made separate field trips to Cuba in 1989, 1990 and 1994, totalling 12 weeks in the field, based primarily in Cuba's urban capital, Havana. The first two visits were conducted within a semi-official framework and were also prior to the total collapse of the Soviet Union, hitherto Cuba's closest political, military and economic supporter. At this time, despite domestic difficulties, the USSR and her allies were still able to provide a considerable amount of economic assistance to Cuba. Thus, even though the island was clearly beginning to experience a degree of economic hardship, there was no sense that the general population was suffering significantly from subsistence deprivation. Cuba was also establishing economic links with Spain, "with $12.5 million in aid, $100 million in soft loans over the previous four years, and millions more in private investment in tourism" (Hall, D. H., 1992: p. 119): though diplomatic tensions around human rights were soon to lead to Madrid's suspension of such support, demonstrating the fragility of Cuba's new economic partnerships.

Despite such economic policies, there was an obvious difference between the spending power of the increasing numbers of tourists who came to Cuba in the 1980s and 1990s and that of the average Cuban. Even from within our semi-official cocoon we were able to look out and see that these parallel economies were linked by unofficial forms of exchange including money changing, black market trading in cigars and black coral and what seemed to be a limited and strictly controlled amount of prostitution.

In the visits at the turn of the decade the tourist experience was clearly policed. The same smiling armed policewoman patrolled the different hotels in which we stayed during the 1989 and 1990 visits. Tourist guides made disapproving gestures if we suggested walking a block or two away from the hotel to use the unlicensed, cheaper pesos-based taxis; the official taxis charged dollars. Frank yet semi-illicit discussions with young black people in the sea at the Varadero resort were abruptly ended when the tourist police or beach patrol was anywhere near. Personal encounters between visitors and prostitutes in the Piano Bar of the Hotel Presidente in 1990 were promoted by pimps with the privilege of access, but the streets were far from rampant with sex-selling hustlers. Exchanges clearly took place in which sex was the main transaction, but in the sequestered space of the all-tourist, predominantly white Hemingway Marina, where playboy yachts berthed in a corrupt tax-free haven of deals and pleasures of various kinds. The visitor could step outside of this, into an everyday underworld in Old Havana, where imitation Cohiba cigars could be illegally purchased for a few USA dollars (which amounted to the equivalent of several weeks' working wages in Cuban pesos). The trades took place in darkened bars, set up by hustling intermediaries and concluding in exchanges in which it felt like one was acting out a script combining the multi-dealings of a Le Carré narrative or a Hitchcock screenplay, and the farcical inter-cultural confusions of a Bob Hope/Bing Crosby road movie. But despite the relative ease of access to these settings, at the turn of the decade we always felt that, essentially, we were guests in a very controlled society. The lucrative tourist market was under surveillance, directed for the benefits of state-rooted monopolies.

By the time of the 1994 expedition things had changed dramatically. The Soviet Union and many of its client states such as East Germany and Czechoslovakia had ceased to exist and in the face of radical shifts in the balance of world power relations and economic chaos in eastern Europe, material support for Cuba was neither economically possible nor strategically relevant. Despite the thawing of the cold war, the United States was not inclined to lift the economic boycott of Cuba, and kept pressure on NATO allies to follow suit. In the absence of a developed domestic economic infrastructure and devoid of trading partners with sympathetic lines of credit Cuba began to suffer serious material shortages. Along with replacing gas-guzzling ancient cars with cheap Chinese bicycles another response to this 'special period of economic hardship' was to continue the drive to expand the hard-currency earning tourist market. Unable to sell sugar at break-even prices Castro felt that the appeal of Caribbean sun-shine, sea and sand to foreign visitors would help to shore up the island's otherwise failing economy. When USA dollars became legal tender in 1993, the local pesos currency was instantly still further devalued. Freedland, in the Summer of 1995, met a waiter in the Hotel Nacional who was a quali-fied mechanical engineer, and told of a friend of his, a Soviet-trained atomic scientist, who had also switched from his career, to drive a cab or wait at a hotel table. Freedland captures vividly this culture and world of status disruption and confusion, in which "the hotel lift operator can earn more than a university professor" (Freedland, 1995).

By 1994 the relative deprivation between host and tourist which we had observed five years earlier had become extreme. Moreover, our vantage point had changed. The main purpose of the 1994 field trip was to gather information about Cuban boxers. Some of this research necessarily was carried out with the assistance of the Cuban authorities. However, much of it involved becoming immersed in the everyday life of the streets of Havana, getting to know the habitat and the social relations from which come many of the world's finest amateur boxers. Havana from the streets in 1994 was a different place from Havana in the hotel lounges of 1989 and 1990. Particularly striking was the fact that the marginal black economy of the earlier years had exploded into a wholesale cottage industry from which few *Habaneros* (Havana residents) seemed disconnected.

The leading public figures of this illicit industry were young men and women who patrolled the city's tourist quarters, hotels and beaches seek-ing in a variety of ways to gain access to the lucrative tourist economy. These are Havana's hustlers and the remainder of this paper will focus on them and their activities. A brief definition of the social art of the hustler is followed by a series of field reports describing Havana's hustlers at their work. In conclusion, some tentative generalisations, and a preliminary typology, are offered about tourism and hustling.

Hustling was not the prime focus of the research visits, though, and the following narrative and grounded theorisations should be treated not as definitive analysis but as preliminary observations and stimulants for future research.

Hustling and resistance

In popular usage the term "hustling" covers three related sets of activities. Traditionally, it has been used as a descriptor, for example, of the pool player who manipulates his performances in such a way that opponents are 'conned' into losing money through side bets on the outcomes of a series of games (Polsky, 1967). Secondly, as Polsky points out (citing Kingsley Davis, see Polsky, 1967: pp. 184-186), it has long since been evoked to depict the ways through which prostitutes target and interact with those to whom they wish to sell sexual favours. Finally, it has most recently been added to our vocabulary to capture a wide variety of illegitimate buying and selling manoeuvres usually taking place in marginal areas of the inner city — including petty thievery, begging, 'fencing' stolen property, drug dealing and related forms of extortion and vice (Wacquant, 1994).

This paper focuses on the activities of the latter two categories of hustling. It is perhaps more than coincidental that as a by-product of his own research into ghetto boxing clubs in black Chicago, Loic Wacquant becomes fascinated with what he describes as the 'social art' of hustlers. In doing so he provides us with a flexible working definition of hustling which will serve as a good starting point for this paper. The verb "to hustle", he argues:

> ...denotes a field of activities which have in common the fact that they require the mastery of a particular type of symbolic capital, namely the ability to manipulate others, to inveigle and deceive them, if need be by joining violence to chicanery and charm, in the pursuit of immediate pecuniary gain. (Wacquant, 1994: p. 4)

In this regard hustlers live off their wits in combination with physical capacities ranging from beauty to strength, speed and predatory prowess. These street-wise skills represent the only capital they have in a context of scarcity and want. If they do not invest this capital, in other words live out the hustle, then either their largely hand-to-mouth existences are threatened, or, their sense of relative deprivation is deepened. In either case hustling becomes legitimised within the ghetto as a coping strategy and a means of resistance in the face of structured inequalities and a paucity of more generally socially approved opportunities for making a living. As Wacquant observes, not to hustle is a threat to one's survival:

> And thus, owing to the chronically insufficient level of income received from work or from social assistance, nearly all the residents of the ghetto must, at one point or another, rely on some kind of hustle to get by. (Wacquant, 1994: p. 6)

Just as it is with those who dwell in the ghettos of Chicago, there is a sense that hustling is a way of life which touches most people who live in old Havana. In this regard we have attempted to look at hustling in Havana as a normal feature of the city's everyday life, and not as a deviant endeavour. Here we are following the advice of Ned Polsky, who in his classic study of the pool-room hustler, makes the strong methodological point that because hustlers are viewed by the majority as marginal figures, operating outside of the conventions and rules of the mainstream, they are categorised from the outset as a 'social problem'. This, he argues, colours as 'criminologist' the interpretation of researchers, to the extent that they are unable to capture the social logic of the behaviour under scrutiny. He offers this scathing critique of this style of conventional criminology:

Until the criminologist learns to suspend his distaste for the values and life-styles of the untamed savages, until he goes out in the field to the cannibals and head-hunters and observes them without trying to civilize them or to turn them over to colonial officials, he will only be a veranda anthropologist. That is he will only be a jail house or a court house sociologist, unable to produce anything like a genuinely scientific picture of crime. (Polsky, 1967: p. 145)

As with Polsky's own study, in what follows below we deliberately reject a 'social problem' focus, instead trying to understand Havana's hustlers from their own perspectives as people who are trying their best to get by, even to enjoy themselves in a socialist economy under siege.

Havana

Havana is horribly crowded. The population is crammed into a city designed for less than half its 2.5 million inhabitants. In some cases two or three generations of families share a single three or four room apartment. The old, the middle-aged, the mature, the young and the children all live on top of one another. In the words of Cuba's most famous salsa and sol band, '*Los Van Van*', "there is no room in Havana". Apart from the squalor to which such overcrowding inevitably leads, these living conditions force *Habaneros* to live much of their lives, day and night, in public. Public culture may have diminished in the United States and Western Europe, but not in Cuba. Because of the economic crisis, television viewing is limited to two hours in the evening. Cubans are forced to make their own entertainment through socialising in the narrow streets or in the city's parks and squares.

The broad sea wall of the Malecon is the most popular location for *Habaneros* to socialise and is the nearest thing the city has to a public leisure centre. During the day it is dotted with fishermen, sun bathers, courting couples and thousands of children who play in the watery shallows in the rocks at the bottom of the sea wall. But it is at night that the Malecon really comes alive. There is hardly a spot which is not claimed by Cubans in pairs or small groups, chatting, courting, listening to music, dancing, smoking and drinking cheap rum as the waves from the Atlantic crash against the promenade.

One day in old Havana

It is 8.30a.m. in May, the first day of this trip and, armed with a camera, several cigarette lighters, a few bars of soap and a handful of packets of chewing gum (referred to as 'chicklet' by the locals), we set off to walk across the city to Vedado. We head towards the sea front along Paseo del Prado, a formerly grand boulevard with a tree-lined central divide which leads past the former presidential palace to the Malecon.

Today, while Paseo del Prado is still pretty, her elegance has faded. The pavements are cracked and distorted and the cafes, clubs and casinos have all gone. The presidential palace has been turned into a museum in honour of Castro's Revolution. Because del Prado connects 3 or 4 tourist hotels it has become the epicentre of Havana's black market trade. We are no further than 50 yards along the road when we are approached by our first pair of hustlers known locally as *jiniteras* — those who make a living by latching themselves on to tourists and, by fair means or foul, extract in cash or kind the mighty dollar. We later learn that the opening exchanges between tourists and jiniteras has a pattern which goes something like:

"*Ola, senor,* my friend ... where are you from?"

Not deterred by silence, the 'find the place game' begins:

"*Aleman* (German)? *Italiano? Canadese?. ...*"

A novice mistake is to tell him one's nationality, and get hooked:

"Ah, you are English! How long do you come to Cuba, it is beautiful, no?" ... and so on and so forth.

It is an easy skill through which to get rid of *jiniteras* like Roberto and Toni — look them in the eyes, smile broadly and say kindly but firmly "*Gracias, no*" two or three times, simultaneously raising your hand palm out. This, usually works, but you have to know the skill. Otherwise, you will be stuck with them for as long as you are in public and on your journey may be cajoled into making a deal to buy cigars from them, being lined up with a "*chica Cubana*" (Cuban woman), buying them a beer, giving them a couple of dollars to go away, or at least giving them cigarettes.

Feeling more than a little uncomfortable, on our first excursion into the heart of the city we are forced to share the company of Roberto, who despite claiming to be an architect (his friend says he's a sculptor) shuffles along in his beaten baseball boots and scuffed jeans like a man down on his luck. Eventually the facade of old Havana gives way to that of Vedado, the city's commercial district which also housed some of the more prosperous middle classes prior to the revolution. Here the post-colonial skyline is broken by some ugly high rise offices and apartments and several pre-revolutionary luxury hotels. Notable among them are the *Habana Libre* (Free Havana), formerly the Havana Hilton, which towers 40 or more storeys above the horizon and the *Nacional*, a wedding cake of a building overlooking the Malecon. The *Nacional*, like one or two other exclusive hotels, is an oasis for tourists in Havana. When it was built in the early years of the twentieth century it was Havana's finest hotel, but after the revolution it suffered from neglect and fell into disrepair. To this day it is still scarred with bullet holes, relics of the failed *putsch* of 1933 when 300 dissenting army officers were flushed from the hotel by soldiers loyal to Batista's first government (Thomas: 1971).

It is at the latter that we finally shake off Roberto and Toni, using the false pretext that we have some people to meet inside. They cannot come in unless invited by a tourist — an invitation which we do not extend — and our first two hustlers reluctantly disappear with a handful of cigarettes. Most of the best tourist hotels and restaurants have been developed in partnership with foreign capital, usually Spanish or Canadian. In return for its investment, the foreign company gets 49% of any profit, while the Cuban government gets the remaining 51%. Because the total tourist infrastructure in Cuba remains under developed and because of the country's reputation for radicalism on the international stage, insufficient numbers of tourists come to the island, making profit generation a dubious business.

By now it is early afternoon and the sun is high and hot. We elect for an oasis and call into the Hotel Presidente for some pool side refreshment. It is not long before we are approached by a young "white" Cuban with more than a passing resemblance to James Dean. He introduces himself as Willi — short for William and the English translation of Guilermo, his given Spanish name. The significance of his anglicised name will only emerge later. Willi's opening gambit is to tell us that he has arranged to meet somebody who had borrowed some scuba diving equipment (this turns out to be a fiction designed to inveigle him into our company; but it is a familiar fiction. We had been stalked in 1990 by a white-bearded pirate-like figure, often appearing in the Piano Bar at the Hotel Presidente, seeking to tempt us to join him on a diving expedition to relieve an old sunken galleon of its booty of coral and gold). It is certain that Willi is yet another *jinitera* of some kind or complexion, but his pleasant non-pushy manner is comforting and he accepts the offer of a beer, but not before he goes outside to bring in his friend, Raul. In contrast to Willi's fair complexion, Raul's is a deep shade of black. He wears a baseball cap and has a small golden crucifix dangling from his right ear. Yet another pirate. Willi explains that Raul would have been prevented from entering the hotel alone, because he was black and obviously Cuban. Willi gets in and out because he can pass for an "internationale" or tourist, especially since he appears to have inherited most of his clothes from other tourists from Europe or Canada.

Despite claims to the contrary (made by the communist authorities), there is an entrenched, institutionalised form of racism practised in Cuba. Most Cuban people are of mixed race: 60% are of European descent (*criollos* or Creoles) and 22% are a mixture of European and African heritage (mulattos). 12% are of pure African descent. There is a small Chinese community (approx. 1%), made up of descendants of servants shipped from China towards the end of the 19th century (when slavery finally withered away). There is little sign that an indigenous Indian population has survived the persecution of the conquistadors and their successors, other than the veiled presence of Indian features in the faces of some of the Creoles. Despite the egalitarian rhetoric of socialism the ingredients of Cuba's racial and ethnic cooking pot steadfastly refuse to melt.

Marx himself was vague when, in 1843, answering questions regarding forms of status segregation excluding class, he tackled the issue of what would happen to the Jewish question in Europe. He argued that once "society succeeds in abolishing the empirical essence of Judaism — the market and the conditions which give rise to it", then at that transformative point "the Jew will have become *impossible*"; socialism itself would eliminate social prejudice (Marx, 1975: p. 241). This disappearance of prejudice manifestly has not happened in Cuba. Observation tells the visitor that the overwhelming majority of decent jobs are held by paler-skinned Cubans. At the airport all of the officials and police/security are "white". In the hotels, for example, "white Cubans work as receptionists and waiters, while black women make up the bulk of the chamber staff. Similarly, in universities, the army and other important institutions, the whites dominate" (Calder and Hatchwell, 1993: p. 27). With the exception of music and sport — universal receptacles, it seems for talented blacks — there seems to be little room for the heirs of Cuban slaves in mainstream Cuban society.

Also, there is another unwritten global convention in operation in Cuba. Because there are so many of them in and around the streets of Havana, it is particularly noticeable that virtually none of the police is black. Yet most of the Cubans who are bothered by the police are. This is partly through overt racism and partly through the self-fulfilling justification of institutionalised racism. With the blacks getting the worst end of the stick in Cuba they dominate within the country's poorer communities, particularly in the cities and especially in Havana. Following a time-honoured and universal tradition which links poverty and misery to inner-city crime, in Cuba blacks predominate at the fetching and carrying end of the black market (it is less certain whether they actually control and benefit most from the black market), do most of the hassling of tourists and are disproportionately responsible for crime, including the popular hit-and-run bicycle shoulder bag snatch — a favourite method of liberating dollars and other merchandise from tourists. However, it must be stressed that by comparison with other Caribbean resorts, crimes against tourists in Cuba are relatively few and far between.

Willi explains that Raul is a dancer — Raul produces an identification document which, at least on paper, confirms this status. Later in the night Raul gives us a dancing demonstration which leaves us in little doubt that, what ever Raul is, he can certainly dance. However, he has trouble getting work within official circles because he has a criminal record — he did 2 years in a military prison for desertion — something he considers to be better than risking his life in Angola fighting against the South African Defence Forces. Willi has likewise done time. In his case it was 10 months in a civilian prison for trying to escape to Florida with a group of friends when he was 19 (Willi is now 24). After a couple of hours pleasant conversation we arrange to go to Raul's home that night in a suburb of Havana.

For the next three weeks we are to engage in a mutually exploitative/ beneficial relationship with Willi and Raul. They act as our guides and interpreters when we wish to pursue the formal aspects of our research. Perhaps more importantly, they act as our minders and confidants as we gradually explore deeper and deeper into the heart of old Havana. Willi and Raul become our gate keepers to the world of Havana's hustlers. In return, through us they gain access to the tourist life-style. They share our food, live in our hotels (when they choose), share our expeditions into Havana's cultural life and spend time with us on the beaches of Varadero. Very occasionally $10 or $20 changes hands, ostensibly for Raul's girl friend and his child or to help support Willi's grandfather. We are being hustled but in a very benign way and this gives us access to the underbelly of Havana, the cultural heart of the boxing subculture. In this way we exploit Willi and Raul and in their own ways they exploit us. Most importantly, in the process we become 'friends' to the extent that we are able to talk intimately about politics and life in today's Cuba, converse about more personal subjects and engage in mutually deprecating joking relationships — a sure sign of access to a given subculture.

One night in old Havana

Willi turns up at the Hotel Inglatera at about eight o'clock. Only one hour after sun set and the centre of Havana is in virtual darkness. Raul awaits us outside and beckons us towards one of the concertina buses at a nearby bus stop in Parque Central. Willi pays the driver in pesos and we board the bus, squeezing our way along the crowded central isle to find some breathing space near the rear. It seems like all humanity is crammed onto the bus. There is one internal light in the ceiling of the vehicle which has a bad connection. It continues to flicker on and off as we grind our way out of central Havana down a dark street towards the suburbs. Mid way through the 20 minute journey a passer by leaps onto the rear door for a free ride, scaring the daylights out of a fellow traveller. When it comes to our stop we almost get left on the bus. An English queuing tradition lets us down and we feel uncomfortable about pushing our way to the door. Only the intervention of Willi and Raul extracts us from the bowels of the bus a split second before it pulls off.

A trudge down blacked out back streets leads us towards Raul's apartment block which turns out to be a tiny rabbit warren of a place in south Havana. It appears to have no more than 2 rooms with at least 8 people living there, including at least one small child. Raul invites us in and introduces us to his extended family. Apparently he has a steady girl friend some where and a 5 year old daughter of his own, but we do not meet them. One of the women in the house is tidying up. Despite the overcrowding, the Cubans work tirelessly to keep their meagre homes clean.

We sit outside on the pavement. Raul turns on his ghetto blaster and immediately a crowd begins to gather. Then the barter system swings into action to acquire a bottle or two of local rum. Officially, each family is entitled by ration to one bottle of rum per month. Unofficially, rum is one of the neighbourhood's hottest black market items. The production of a couple of dollars speeds the arrival of the first bottle from an apartment above. By now the cigarettes have almost all gone — smoked largely by Raul and his neighbours. Willi borrows a bike and sets off to find some more. He returns with two packs of Popular, a local brand made with rough Havana tobacco which are very strong. We sit and chat until about 11pm watching Raul go through a series of complex dance routines on the pavement. A small crowd congregates around us — which is bad news for our cigarettes! Everybody is very friendly. Inside Raul's house three men sit around drinking a very rough cane-based alcohol. This is entertainment if you live in Cuba. Every now and again the conversation turns to political economy and it soon becomes clear that at this level — lower class Havana — the shine has gone off Castro and his revolution.

Through our presence and the largesse of a few dollars we have provided a night's entertainment for Raul and his neighbours. In return we have not only enjoyed ourselves immensely, but we have also begun to learn things which were hidden from our view on previous visits to the island.

Next we set off to meet "grandfather" who lives around the corner. This man turns out to be a living history of the twentieth century. He is 82 and was born in 1912 in Cuba. His father was a German Jew who sired him during a business trip to the island — he dealt in gems. Although he was never officially recognised by his father, Willi's "grandfather" was taken by him to Germany when he was 6 in about 1918. He spent his formative years there, experiencing Germany after the humiliating defeat of World War I, the rise and fall of the Weimar state and the emergence of Hitler and the Nazis. He fled the country in 1938 on the eve of World War II, escaping underneath a car and travelling through France to Marseilles where he boarded a ship bound for the United States. He went to college in the US and stayed in America until the early 1950s when he returned to Batista's Cuba because of his sister's serious illness and because he wanted to avoid conscription into the US army for the Korean War. He couldn't afford to take care of her properly in the States and Cuba's health care was cheaper. He worked as an accountant up to and beyond Castro's revolution of 1959, finishing his career in a nationalised bank and spending some time working for Ché Guevara.

In the beginning he thought the revolution was a good thing for Cuba, but now, like so many other people, believes that it is failing Cuba and her people. He believes that Castro should have restructured the Cuban economy and political system along free enterprise/democratic lines many years before. Now he believes it's too late. Once his aged and dying sister passes away, Willi's grandfather wants to leave Cuba and believes that this would be the best course of action for his "grandson". He speaks several languages and claims "to know many things" which he will tell us about later. A generalised fear about being informed upon later prevents him from doing so. Presently he is trying to obtain German citizenship on the basis of his illegitimate status. The irony of an aged Cuban-German-Jew hoping to escape back to the country of his teenage persecution seems to speak volumes about civil liberties and human rights in contemporary Cuba.

By now it's past midnight. Willi suggest that we should go and find some way of getting back to the hotel — the buses have stopped running so this proves to be a difficult but fascinating challenge. After walking several blocks we stumble upon what seems to be a house party which, inevitably, has spilled into the street. Willi and Raul begin negotiations which end in us all piling into an early 1950s Buick along with several of the revellers. Eventually we are dropped at the hotel. It is after 1pm but the hotel's roof top bar is still going strong and cannot be resisted. As we step out onto the roof the sound of a live salsa band washes over us. To the accompaniment of an electric piano drums and a brass section an exotically attired woman singer/dancer is blasting out a tale of unfulfilled passion. There are about twenty people in the place spread around half a dozen or so tables. About half are women/girls and most if not all of them appear to be prostitutes of some description. One of us visits the toilet and while he is gone the other is 'hit upon'. On the table is a pack of Marlborough cigarettes acquired en route. This gives the lead hooker the opportunity to ask for a cigarette. Immediately she is joined by two of her friends and one of us is sur-rounded. There seems little option but to let them sit there for a chat. Just like our encounter with the *jiniteras,* this kind of approach is to become a regular feature of this visit. With help from Willi and Raul, we learn to deal with it.

The following verbatim extract from field notes (see Sugden, 1996) illustrates the pervasive nature of prostitution in contemporary Havana:

> There is a stir in the audience with the arrival of Cuba's world heavy weight champion, Felix Savon. He seems to know everybody and as he makes his way to the changing rooms, like the pied piper, he accumulates a growing train of children. I inadvertently break up this scene by producing a packet of chewing gum out of my pocket. Immediately I am surrounded by 6 or 8 children demanding 'chicklets'. I make the near fatal mistake of dividing up my single packet and handing the pieces out. Suddenly every child in the place cascades down out of the stands and I am engulfed by 30-40 urchins chanting 'chicklet, chicklet, chicklet'. This seems to amuse the audience more than the fight taking place in the ring a few yards away. So much for the researcher not disturbing his field.

After about an hour, I step outside the stadium for a break and to take in the scenery. By now it is pitch dark outside and the atmosphere feels slightly more sinister. I have no sooner set foot outside than I am once more set upon by the chicklet-kids. Older youths and men approach me with the standard sales patter about cigars: "Habana cigar ... bery gooood, Monti Cristo? Cohiba?" Ten yards from the stadium door across the street a young girl is smiling at me from her doorway. "My sister" I am informed by a smiling, black youth, "ten dollar?". During such times of extreme economic hardship it seems that there are few things that are not for sale for hard currency in Cuba. I take a deep breath and re-enter the auditorium.

The Paris Cafe[1]

In order to make more sense out of this nether region of Old Havana we are guided by Willi to the Paris Cafe which is in the heart of Old Havana on the corner of *Calle Obispo* and *Calle San Ignacio*. This is a place where old Havana's underworld goes when it's not working. It is no more than 200 metres from *El Bodegeta de Medio*, one of the city's biggest tourist attractions, but it is rare to see foreigners inside the Paris Cafe. Because it is a dollar only establishment it is equally rare to see "ordinary" Cubans there. It is open for 24 hours a day, but the best time to go is between midnight and 6 a.m. during which period many of old Havana's characters and their entourages will pass through.

Initially, the Paris Cafe can feel intimidating to non-Cubans. There is always a heavy police presence outside the large arched entrance and an even larger crowd of locals milling around outside, either waiting for a table or simply interested in watching the social interaction taking place within. The cafe is dominated by a large hardwood bar behind which Cuba's equivalent to a busty British bar-maid serves small draughts of cheap German larger and cans of Hatuey, the almost undrinkable local beer. A small army of waiters scurry about, ferrying drinks and plates of over-done chicken and *patatas fritas* (thin fried potatoes) to customers at the ten or so small tables which take up the rest of the Cafe.

The intimidating atmosphere of the place fades as we realise that we are far less accessible here than in other, more tourist-oriented bars and that most of the clientele are here for their own good time and are not, at this stage of the evening, interested in hustling foreigners. The best place to be is at the bar, especially if you can get the bar stool close to a criss-cross wooded screen which divides the cafe from Calle Obispo. From this vantage point it is possible to watch the comings and goings of the bar as well as keep an eye on the chaotic street life of Old Havana.

On this particular evening the invitation comes to join a table of young Cubans who are obviously in the midst of a good night out. One is wearing a 1994 USA soccer World Cup t-shirt — an immediate point of common interest. His name is Laredo, and he is proud to be named after a town in Texas in the United States. With his mop of curly brown hair and pale olive-brown complexion, Laredo looks more Greek than Cuban. He would like to visit the town which is named after him one day, he informs us with a laugh. Laredo's voice drops to a whisper as he admits that he has been in prison for two years after having been caught trying to escape to Florida.

Laredo is 26, handsome, intelligent and very dissatisfied with his life in Cuba. The fact that he has been in prison for trying to flee the country means that he is unable to get a decent job — not that this would be worth much in terms of salary, but at least he would have some self-respect. He complains about being constantly harassed by the police and produces a piece of paper which tells us that he has had his car confiscated because he acquired it through improper channels — that is, without seeking the permission of the state which would have been denied because of his 'criminal' record. He believes that 30 years ago the revolution was good for Cuba because it got rid of much of the corruption and injustice which had become institutionalised under successive dictatorships. However, he thinks that the revolution has now become stagnant and has failed the people, largely because Castro has stubbornly refused to adapt his view of political economy, despite radical changes in the rest of the world. Even worse, he believes that Castro's Cuba has become as corrupt and dictatorial as the Cuba of Batista. Ché Guevara could see this happening, he tells us, which is why he left to fight and die in Bolivia.

The more beer Laredo drinks the more vociferous he becomes. He insists on an anti-Castro toast and, in close proximity to armed, paramilitary police who are beginning to pay undue attention to the goings on at our table, he finishes his anti-Castro polemic and begins to entertain us with a series of conjuring tricks which he learned in prison. Salsa is blaring from the cafe's hi-fi and some people begin to dance in the aisles between the tables. A young black man approaches our table to whisper with Laredo before leaving. Five minutes later he returns and, with a policeman standing no further than three yards away, surreptitiously slips Laredo a small silver paper package — of what it must be assumed to be drugs of some description. It is an ingenious pass. The dealer has the package concealed beneath his watch strap. He shakes hands with Laredo and as he does so Laredo's middle finger dislodges the drugs from behind the watch strap and flicks them into the palm of his hand. The policeman is looking, but he sees nothing. Nevertheless, it is time for the researcher to leave.

During another visit it is a surprise to meet Tomas, a German staying in the same hotel, who is in the company of a tall, dark Cuban woman called Cardea. The wrong conclusions are quickly reached — that she is a working girl who has struck lucky and picked up a tourist. Once we get talking it turns out that Tomas and a German friend had been on a cycling holiday to Cuba the year before and his friend had met and fallen in love with Cardea in the town of Ceinfuegos. This year Tomas had taken some leave from his bank to return to Cuba in an attempt to bring Cardea back to Germany for a three month trial marriage with his friend. This scenario is not so unusual and in these times of great economic hardship an informal 'lonely hearts club' seems to operate in Cuba. Many women (and indeed men) will do almost anything to get out. Marrying an 'internationale' is one of the more favoured routes to 'freedom'.

Tomas is a dance enthusiast and Cuba's stature in this area is one of the main reasons why he likes to visit the island. He explains that he is excited by the prospect of going out tomorrow evening with one of Cuba's top exponents of modern ballet. Two days later he relates a story of how, after a meal and some time spent in a dancing club his escort offered to spend the night with him for $20. He declined the offer and expressed a sense of both confusion and exasperation over his inability to comprehend relationships with Cuban women in general.

During the first visit of the three visits to Cuba, in 1989, we had arrived on New Year's Eve amidst the celebrations of the thirtieth anniversary of the revolution. The hotel porter misunderstood a question concerning what all the people were doing in the streets. Stepping back aghast, he informed us sternly that there was no prostitution in Cuba. As it turned out, in and around the hotels there was evidence that prostitution was taking place. Very occasionally we were "pssst, pssst" from the shadows and made a variety of offers and in the hotel lounges it was clear that a small number of hookers were allowed to mingle with the tourists. In 1990, while there was a marked increase in this kind of behaviour, it seemed to be strictly controlled and limited to late night hotel cabarets and the like under the watchful eyes of hotel staff and tourist police.

By 1994 it appeared that prostitution in one form or another had become a prolific and acceptable feature of the tourist landscape. The upsurge in this form of hustling is clearly related to the continuing decline in Cuba's economic fortunes taken in concert with restrictions on emigration and a significant increase in the numbers of 'western' tourists. Hustlers of all kinds are cultivated in the fissures of a dual economy. Maria Dolores Espino refers to this duality as 'tourist apartheid' which she feels is responsible for a range of social ills including the rise in rates of prostitution:

> Prostitution is once again rampant in the streets of Havana. Around international hotels and along every main street, one can find young girls eager to trade their services for gifts or a night on the town, including a meal at restaurants where only convertible (hard) currency is accepted. (Espino, 1993: p. 108)

However, it may be a mistake to view this form of hustling in Cuba in the same light as the strictly commercial forms of prostitution which dominate in cities such as London or New York[2]. In Havana, through Willi and Raul we were able to talk, albeit briefly, with a number of young women who in one way or another sought relationships with tourists. It has been noted, too, that female tourists offer opportunities for material gain to young Cuban males. Raymond Reynoldo, a 21 year old art history student, with aspirations to "research the roots of Cuban culture" (Freedland, 1995: p. 8), lives a double life: student and embryonic intellectual by day, street gigolo and occasional pimp for young girls by night. The Malecon and Varadero are his sites of operation by night: shoes, clothes and payouts his rewards: "Clothes are the main thing, and some money. I don't know if this is good or bad for the country. For me, this is the only way" (*op. cit.*). Reynaldo engages in both an emotional dynamic (of his last girl, Louise from Manchester, England, he recalls: "She said I was an animal in bed, that I was the best she'd ever had ... Now she writes to me and sends me money. I tell her I love her. I miss her and want to see her" [*op.cit.*]; and a blatantly commercial transaction when doing the 'dirty work' of providing for male tourists, pimping for girls. Both of these forms of involvement feature in our own tentative fourfold classification of forms of hustling/ prostitution, based mainly upon observations of and exchanges with the hustlers at the Paris Cafe.

There is a visibly high level of *overt prostitution* whereby tourists are offered sexual favours for money. Quite often this is done by the women themselves, but sometimes the offer is made through a male associate ("psssst ... *chica Cubana bonita* ... $10"). To what extent these men are pimps in the conventional sense is difficult to discern. Some women claim to work more or less for themselves, though not necessarily as a full-time occupation.

There also appears to be a kind of informal *escort service* which probably ends up being a more subtle form of prostitution. Regularly in hotels, bars and night clubs foreigners are approached by Cuban women who will strike up a conversation by asking for a light for a cigarette, hoping that this will develop into a conversation, a dance a drink, and perhaps even something to eat. Undoubtedly, many of these encounters end up in an hotel bed room, after which money changes hands.

Slightly different from the escorts are the *good time girls*. This variety hangs around the tourist areas generally looking for entry into the good times which can only be accessed through tourists and their dollars. For instance, a disco which has a $5 cover charge and within which beer or coca cola costs $2 or more is prohibitively expensive for the vast majority of Cubans, yet relatively cheap for a tourist who may be willing to bring in a Cuban girl for company and fun. It is arbitrary as to whether or not this leads to any physical and/or emotional relationship or whether any money changes hands directly.

The critical point here is that tourists are viewed as attractive prospects because, physical contact notwithstanding, they are the gatekeepers to a world of fun not usually available to young Cubans. Indeed, the extent to which these relationships are really fun for both participants is something which is open to question. A related issue is whether or not appeal through access to an otherwise forbidden world of fun and plenty actually affects the long-term perceptions of these young women, becoming embedded in their collective psyche so that foreigners are really more attractive than Cubans. These are sensitive questions which require correspondingly sensitive and detailed researching.

Finally, there are those who belong to the aforementioned *lonely hearts club*. That is they are seeking a relationship with a foreign partner which, they hope, will lead to marriage and 'escape' to a more prosperous life. No doubt there will be Cuban women and foreigners who have a natural and genuine attraction for each other. However, with so many layers of relationships working simultaneously it must be virtually impossible to tell when, if ever, 'romantic love' is in the air.

With regard to the multiple nature of this form of hustling in Havana a comparison between contemporary Cuba and parts of pre-HIV Thailand in the early 1980s could prove to be fruitful. Eric Cohen (1993) in his urban-anthropological study of prostitution in Bangkok in the summers of 1981 and 1982 strongly reinforces the above point that prostitution should not be defined simply. He sees it rather as existing somewhere along a continuum of relationships between visitors and natives. Cohen develops a fourfold typology for relationships between Thai women and *farangs* (foreign visitors) which is not so far away from the informal classification taken from our own notes. They are:

1   mercenary — based on emotionless 'economic exchange';

2   staged — also based on 'economic exchange', but accompanied by faked or staged emotions on the part of the woman;

3   mixed — based on both 'economic exchange' and emotional involvement on the part of the woman; and

4   emotional — based primarily or exclusively on emotional involvement or 'love'. (Cohen, 1993: pp. 414-417)

Cohen also makes two very important points which help to inform the Cuban case. Firstly, the forms of relationship with foreigners have to be studied in the context of the traditions and customs which characterise a given culture. Briefly, Cohen makes the point that women in Thai society have traditionally secured their futures through engaging in a variety of mistress/master relationships and by working the paternal hierarchy to their own advantage. The tourist boom precipitated by the rest and recreation sojourns of American GIs during the Vietnam War enabled certain classes of Thai women to extend this tradition to embrace relatively wealthy foreigners. While once more further detailed research is necessary here, to a casual observer it seems that Cuba is a relatively promiscuous society and that furthermore this is rooted in pre-revolutionary traditions whereby Havana was one of the great playgrounds of the western world and one of the earliest resorts to tolerate if not systematically encourage sex-tourism[3].

Secondly, while accounting for the exploitative nature of what he refers to as 'open ended' prostitution in Thailand, Cohen also stresses the ludic or playful context within which relationships are constructed:

> Open ended prostitution, like all full-time prostitution is work ... however, it is more of a game in which the women compete with skill and daring, and what they consider 'luck', for the prizes which the prospective customers offer. While such an attitude may be foreign to the neutral, professional, Western prostitutes, it very much reflects, in the concrete area of prostitution, a wider Thai cultural attitude emphasising preference for activities which are pleasurable or fun and an aversion to purely neutral, reward oriented, 'work'. (Cohen, 1993: p. 175)

Despite prevailing conditions of economic hardship and political repression, it is obvious that Cubans do their best to enjoy life. It is a very public culture and it soon becomes obvious to the visitor that risqué joking relationships between men and women are central to the patterns of interaction which characterise social life in Cuba. On our 1990 visit, when we were dining in official splendour in the restaurant of an exclusive Soviet hotel, a female translator could tease, in earshot, a world-famous figure in the nation's sports administration: "Oh, [...], he's got a small penis", even if he's got a very big reputation and job. To an outside eye, or ear, some sexual dynamics might certainly look exploitative, but such professional women denied that there was any exploitation of women in such dynamics and exchanges, arguing that women could give as good as they got in a public culture of uninhibited sexual banter and innuendo. Furthermore, public displays of physical affection are commonplace in and around the streets of Havana. At one point, when this was remarked upon to a senior Cuban sports administrator, along with the suggestion that this and not athletics or boxing was the Cuban's favourite pastime, his response was straight to the point: "Cubans, they love to fuck", he said. It is in this context that we should try and make sense of open-ended prostitution in Cuba. This and other forms of hustling may be viewed by some young people as avenues through which they can not only hope to make a living, but also enjoy themselves in ways which are not too far removed from traditional cultural practices[4]. An amoral leisure culture of liberal sexuality in Cuba merges in complex ways with an opportunistic hustling culture, together potentially providing both personal pleasure and much-needed material benefits.

Conclusion

It is obvious that an influx of tourists has disturbed the cultural equilibrium of socialist Cuba and has stirred up patterns of interaction between tourist and locals which are redolent of an era of pre-revolutionary vice and decadence. As we approach the fortieth anniversary of Castro's revolution it is very difficult to predict what is likely to happen there. Shortly after our last visit there was a massive exodus of Cubans across the treacherous and shark infested Florida straits in a wide variety of ramshackle and very unseaworthy craft. We have not heard from Willi or Raul since we last left the island — in all probability they were part of this desperate flotilla. While the indigenous population appears to be increasingly desperate to leave, more frequently Cuba appears in the glossy magazines of the package tourist operators, advertised as a cut-priced Caribbean paradise — which it can be with plenty of dollars in your pocket and so long as you remain in the tourist bubble. However, the very presence of the tourist economy and all that flows from it encourages the growth of Cuba's black market and the proliferation of those who hustle to make a living by wheeling and dealing between the domestic and the tourist economies.

The above narrative alludes to layers of complex and often very exploitative relationships between locals and tourists. To some extent, when you have a research mission such as our own which requires an element of giving to gain access to subcultural networks, elements of this exploitation can be mutual with costs and benefits for both parties.

It is an anthropologically complex dynamic, in which the role of researcher is a long way removed from that of objective and disinterested observer of some authentic but un-affected real world. It was in the interests of Willi and Raul to be both interested in and interesting to the researchers. We knew that. It would be a naive — yet certainly not un-common — ethnographic mistake indeed to believe at face value all that is related to the newcomer. But openness combined with worldliness gained a degree of acceptance within the everyday worlds of Willi and Raul. At the same time, as Burgess rightly points out in his discussion of Polsky's position on participant observation, "it is essential for participant observers constantly to monitor the differences between themselves and their informants" (Burgess, 1984: p. 93). But the researcher cannot stand back until having first got close to the subjects.

In accomplishing this, the ethnographer's role itself becomes one of a hustling kind, the researcher-subject dynamic one between hustlers. Subcultural research demands this kind of hustling investigative methodology, in which the worthy professional codes of ethics of social science are as much use as the clipboard of the market researcher, or the tally-sheet of the social psychologist of human interactions. Sociologically imaginative research and interpretation cannot proceed only by the rules of the professional ethical book. Researching sport and boxing during these Cuban field trips, it would have been interpretively dishonest not to have sought some informed understanding of the wider context of those cultural phenomena. How we survived the tensions, dilemmas, threats, and pleasures of the situations typical of those contexts was a matter of recognising the integrity of the research mission and the methodological and interpretive imperatives pointed to by the research process itself.

There were costs and benefits for both parties within the Willi-Raul/ researcher relationship. But it was always clear what was in it for whom. We also witnessed, though, more prevalent forms of local/tourist relations in which the mutuality of the exploitation was less pronounced, and where there was little doubt that, if prevailing trends continue, it will increasingly be the locals who are exploited by the tourists rather than vice versa.

Notes

1   A version of this account of the Paris Cafe is also presented in another article, dealing with ethical issues around ethnography, and the dangerous and threatening situations which can arise in the field (Sugden, 1995).

2   Or, indeed, in parts of the Third World such as South-East Asia. C. M. Hall (1992: p. 64ff) identifies three major forms of prostitution in an overview of sex-tourism in South-East Asia: the freelance casual prostitute, led by financial need; more formalized prostitution, with call-girls and call-boys accessed via intermediaries, and clubs and brothels providing what amounts to an institutional infrastructure for the trade; and bonded prostitutes, sold to pay debts and reduce loans. Interestingly, Hall makes no mention of Cuba in her review of sources of prostitution in the Third World beyond South-East Asia.

3   D. H. Hall (1992) provides useful data on this. In 1938 Cuba attracted 37% of all tourists visiting the Caribbean, and Havana was a focus; even in 1915, 27 out of the island's 72 hotels were located in Havana. Between 1951 and 1958, hotel capacity increased by one third. Most commentators recognise that forms of sex-trade featured as an attraction to non-Cuban tourists.

4   Huge issues exist here concerning the spread of sexually-transmitted diseases, most notably HIV and AIDS. It is absurd that Cuba should operate a policy via which Cubans who are discovered to be HIV-positive are quarantined for an indefinite period while the authorities at best turn a blind eye to sex tourism.

References

Burgess, R. G. (1984) *In the field: An introduction to field research.* London: Unwin Hyman.

Calder, S. and Hatchwell, E. (1993) *Cuba: Travellers survival kit.* Old Woking: Unwin Brothers.

Cohen, E. (1993) 'Open ended prostitution as a skilful game of luck: Opportunity, risk and security among tourist-oriented prostitutes in a Bangkok *soi*', in M. Hitchcock, V. T. King and M. J. G. Parnwell (eds) *Tourism in South-East Asia.* London: Routledge, pp. 155-178.

Espino, M. D. (1993) 'Tourism in Socialist Cuba', in D. J. Gayle and J. N. Goodrich (eds) *Tourism, marketing and management in the Caribbean*. London: Routledge, pp. 100-110.

Freedland, J. (1995) 'Body tourism booms again in Havana', *The Guardian*, Thursday August 24: p. 8.

Hall, C. M. (1992) 'Sex-tourism in South-East Asia', in D. Harrison (ed) *Tourism in the less developed countries*. London: Belhaven Press, pp. 64-74.

Hall, D. H. (1992) 'Tourism development in Cuba', in D. Harrison (ed) *Tourism in the less developed countries*. London: Belhaven Press, pp. 102-120.

Marx, K. (1975) 'On the Jewish question', in *Early writings* (Introduced by Lucio Colletti). Harmondsworth: Penguin Books, pp. 212-241.

Polsky, N. (1967) *Hustlers, beats and others*. Harmondsworth: Pelican.

Sugden, J. (1995) 'Fieldworkers rush in ... The perils of ethnography', in A. Tomlinson and S. Fleming (eds) *Ethics, sport and leisure: Crises and critiques*. CSRC Topic Report 5, Eastbourne: University of Brighton, pp. 223-244.

Sugden, J. (1996) *Boxing and society: An international analysis*. Manchester: Manchester University Press (forthcoming).

Sugden, J., Tomlinson, A. and McCartan, E. (1994) 'The making and remaking of White Lightning in Cuba: Politics, sport and physical education 30 years after the revolution', in A. Yiannakis, T. P. McIntyre and M. J. Melnick (eds) *Sport sociology — contemporary themes* [4th Ed.]. Dubuque, IA: Kendal Hunt Publishing Company, pp. 197-205.

Thomas, H. (1971) *Cuba, or the pursuit of freedom*. London: Eyre and Spottiswoode.

Wacquant, L. (1994) *Inside the zone. The social art of the hustler in the contemporary ghetto*. Working Paper 49. New York: Russell Sage Foundation.

The National Lottery — the Acceptable Face of Gambling?

Clare Brindley and Richard Hudson-Davies
Manchester Metropolitan University

Introduction

"Lottery mania" has swept Britain since the National Lottery started full operation in November 1994. Few will have escaped the high profile launch, organised by Camelot PLC who run the National Lottery, and the sustained media coverage. Beyond the "hype" and headlines is a serious strategy to raise revenue for the State and five "good causes" — Sports, the Arts, Charities, Heritage and the "Millennium Fund". The implementation of this strategy has required legislation, in the form of the National Lottery Act 1993, to set up a controlled framework for the National Lottery to operate within. Broad support was given to the Act despite the chequered history of UK nation-wide lotteries which saw their abolition in 1826 and several subsequent attempts at reintroduction, earlier in the 20th Century, rejected (Fitzherbert, 1995).

This paper assesses the National Lottery's principal product, the weekly lotto game (hereinafter called the UK lotto game for the purposes of distinguishing it from the National Lottery's "Instants" scratch card games, the National Lottery "umbrella" brand and similar games played in other countries), as a form of gambling. Its market position and consumer profile are assessed relative to other segments of the UK gambling industry prior to reaching a judgement as to whether the UK lotto game is the acceptable face of gambling.

Gambling in the UK

Gambling takes a variety of forms and is defined for the purposes of this paper as the UK lotto game, scratch cards, betting (horse racing etc.), the pools, bingo, gaming machines, casinos and lotteries (approved by the

Gaming Board only). The distinctive characteristics of gambling involve the staking of money and engagement with risk and uncertainty (Cornish, 1978). The gambling industry in the UK is big business with a net market size of £4.379 billion (Home Office, 1995) in 1993/4 — approximately 1% of consumer expenditure (Central Statistical Office, (CSO), 1995) (Table 1). Figures for 1994/95 are not yet available, however, significant change is expected with the addition of the National Lottery's products, which had already produced a net turnover (stakes less winnings) of £628 million by March 31st 1995. On top of this there will be new sales generated from the launch of other new scratch card games.

Total sales of National Lottery products for 1995/96 are forecast by Camelot to be £5 billion gross (approximately £2.5 billion net). Based on current levels of activity, this would be split 60:40 between the UK lotto game and the "Instants" scratch card game (Camelot, 1995) giving a projected market size in 1995/96 of £1.5 billion and £1 billion respectively. Under the assumption that the market size of all other gambling sectors would remain static at best because of the substitute effect of the new segments, this forecast suggests the UK lotto game will be the largest market segment in the UK gambling industry in 1995/6 — less than two years after its launch.

Distinctive attributes of the UK lotto game

The tremendous impact the UK lotto game has made in Britain since its launch can be explained by identifying the commercial attributes the game has in comparison to other traditional sectors. First and foremost, the product fulfils three vital criteria that have been identified as crucial for a gaming product (Henley Centre for Forecasting and GAH Partnership Strategy Consultants, 1995). It is simple and easy to understand, it has a huge jackpot payout and has a large number of other smaller prizes. Its unique selling point is the size and number of its prizes where it offers 25 times greater prizes than its nearest competitor — the pools. This has the "knock on" benefit of winners attracting greater levels of publicity than its rivals which helps strengthen its market position.

The UK lotto game also benefits from a number of other attributes that help support it as a product in the marketplace. It is distributed widely (see Table 2), and in convenient retail outlets such as supermarkets and newsagents which have low barriers to entry in that they are used regularly by all social groups. Moreover, they do not have the stigma that some gambling premises have attached to them, and do not require an entrance fee or membership card. The UK lotto game also receives regular prime time television coverage on Saturday evenings with the broadcast of the game itself. Furthermore, the product is augmented by its attachment to a social purpose in the sense of it being used to contribute to the funding of five "good causes" (28% of turnover). While some have argued that the contribution should be higher, the scale of contribution that has been

Table 1: Estimated Net Turnover on Gambling in the UK 1993/94

Estimated Net Turnover (£ millions)	
Betting	1,330
Amusement-with-prizes machines	1,000
Jackpot machines	800
Pools	730
Casinos	411
Bingo	76
Lotteries	32
(Gaming Board only)	
TOTAL	**4,379**

Source: Home Office, 1995

Table 2: Estimated distribution of UK lotto game and other gambling sectors - March 1995

No. of outlets	
UK lotto game	14,000
"Instants" only*	6,000
Betting Shops	9,300
Bingo Halls	927
Casinos	118
* Instants game also sold in many UK lotto game outlets	

Source: Keynote 1994, Home Office, 1995 and Camelot, 1995

possible to date has a further positive "spin off" for the product as many grant awards have been of a size that attract supportive and high profile local publicity.

The product attributes identified have all combined to provide the UK lotto game with excellent opportunities for attracting mass participation. Competing segments within the UK gambling industry do not possess comparable attributes. This is mainly because despite recent relaxation in controls (Home Office, 1995; Jones and Turner, 1993) they have less freedom than the UK lotto game enjoys (The Economist, 1995). For example, while betting shops can now be open to the street to attract passers-by and offer refreshments, they are not allowed to advertise their location or use broadcast media (Fitzherbert, 1995). The UK lotto game has thus been able to benefit from a position of competitive advantage within the industry (Porter, 1985).

It is, therefore, not so surprising that this relatively new game is set to become the largest market segment within the UK gambling industry so soon after its launch. Less obvious is what underlying factors in terms of consumer profile lie beneath the surface of this significant development. Is the population of Britain turning into serious and compulsive gamblers? Do consumers just have a small "flutter" on an impulsive basis as part of a shopping trip? How sustainable is the initial success of the UK lotto game? Does the UK lotto game represent the acceptable face of gambling?

Consumer profile surveys

As the UK lotto game is relatively new, evidence about the consumer profile of participants is scarce. The largest independent survey to date was conducted by the Henley Centre for Forecasting and GAH Partnership Strategy Consultants on a sample of 1,006 people during the tenth week of the lotto game in early 1995. Since then, evidence of participation is mainly limited to figures released by Camelot. The regulatory body responsible for the National Lottery (OFLOT) has its own research into consumer profiles underway but this has not yet been completed. In order to provide a more up to date and independent survey — and build upon existing research into participation levels — further research was carried out in June 1995.

Methodology

The survey (hereafter referred to as the MMU survey) was undertaken on a stratified sample of staff and students at Manchester Metropolitan University's Crewe and Alsager Faculty. The Faculty provided a diverse group of people from 18 year old students to academic, administrative and other support staff including cleaning and catering staff in a readily accessible environment to the researchers. It is acknowledged that such a sample is not wholly representative of the UK population in that it has a regional focus, does not cover the extremes of socio economic group classifications namely, As and Es — as categorised under the Joint Industry Committee for National Readership Surveys (JICNARS) (Macdonald, 1994) — and does not include 16 and 17 year olds.

Nevertheless, through using the JICNARS system of linking occupation to social economic group and by targeting specific occupational groups and age ranges through assessment of the University's personnel records, it was possible to stratify the sample by occupation. In this way occupational groups within the University were able to be included in the sample and the various occupational groups identified as targets for the sample were kept in proportion according to their total representation in the Faculty. This process prevented, for example, lecturers forming a disproportionate part of the total sample thus enabling bias to be limited. The approach also provided for differences in purchase behaviour between more common socio economic groups to be assessed, thus giving a worthwhile basis for comparing findings with existing research.

Semi-structured questionnaires (see Appendix) were used for the research and administered by the researchers over a period of two weeks. The aim of the questionnaire was to provide up to date and additional information on consumer behaviour in regard to the UK lotto game. An anonymous questionnaire was used in order to elicit more honest responses. The questionnaire included several types of question style in order to obtain effective and meaningful responses. Dichotomous questions were used to determine points of fact (Webb, 1992). These questions provided a base from which to carry out quantitative analysis. The other question style used involved the adoption of Likert scales as a measuring instrument of attitudes and behaviour. This provided a basis for qualitative analysis of consumer behaviour.

Questions ranged from collecting information concerning gender, age and occupation to finding out detailed purchasing behaviour such as frequency of purchase, point of purchase, and size of purchase. Questions which were designed to provide new insights that had not yet been covered in previous published research included the reasons for people deciding not to play, motivations for purchase and past and present gambling activity in other areas. All questions about past and present gambling behaviour were designed to distinguish between participants playing weekly, monthly, quarterly and yearly. Questionnaires were pre-tested at a Research Committee meeting of lecturing staff of the Department of Business and Management. A copy of the questionnaire is attached. The MMU survey received a response rate of 92% evenly distributed across all occupational categories within the Faculty.

Consumer profile findings

a) Participation

With 89% of the population having tried the UK lotto game and 65% playing it regularly, (Camelot, 1995) the game has clearly achieved mass participation unlike traditional segments where the highest regular participation rate in 1994 was the pools at 28% — along way ahead of betting and bingo at 8.2% and 5.8% respectively (Keynote, 1994). This marked contrast demonstrates that the UK lotto game has attracted people who have never gambled regularly before. Indeed, the research showed that of those people that had tried the UK lotto game 30% had never tried any other form of gambling.

Evidence of mass participation is supported by the research undertaken by the Henley Centre for Forecasting and GAH Partnership Strategy Consultants, see Table 3 below, and the MMU survey carried out in its 31st week which indicated regular weekly participation, across all occupation groups, at levels ranging from 40% to 87%. Mass participation has,

Table 3: Demographic Profiles for UK Lotto game, Betting, Pools and Bingo

% of sample playing the game				
Game:	**UK lotto**	**Betting***	**Pools**	**Bingo**
Gender				
Men	71	10	38	2
Women	73	2	24	7
Age Group				
16-24	71	5	12	2
24-34	81	4	23	5
35-44	69	4	44	-
45-64	77	5	38	5
65+	64	10	32	11
Social Grade				
AB	63	2	23	-
C1	74	3	26	2
C2	81	9	34	5
DE	70	6	36	6
* Horse Racing only				
# Henley Centre/GAH Survey of a representative sample of 1006 people in December 1994. Other figures from Gallup Poll/Key Note survey in 1993 of 1,102 people.				

therefore, outlasted the initial marketing campaign and intense publicity associated with the launch of the game in November 1994. The extent to which participation levels are likely to be sustained is discussed towards the end of the paper where reference is made to the experience of lotteries in Canada and the United States.

Table 3 also shows a further distinction of the UK lotto game with other forms of gambling in that it has attracted high levels of participation across gender, age and social groups (Henley Centre for Forecasting and GAH Partnership Strategy Consultants, 1995). This is unlike traditional sectors where, for example, betting and the pools are most popular with men and those aged above 34 and bingo is more popular with women aged above 45 (Keynote, 1994 & Mintel, 1984).

A parallel between the UK lotto game and other traditional sectors is, however, that people within the A and B social grades participate less than other social groups. Nevertheless, the UK lotto game still has a 63% parti-cipation rate amongst As and Bs, see Table 3. The MMU survey confirmed the trend of lower participation rates for the higher social groups. It also showed 40% of lecturers (Bs) played the game regularly in contrast to 87% of support staff (C2s and Ds).

b) Reasons for non-participation

The MMU survey found that the minority who do not play the UK lotto game (16%) decided not to chiefly because of objections to gambling on moral grounds (45%). It is suggested the ethical and moral objections to gambling stem from the fact that it undermines "disciplined work habits, prudence and thrift." (Dixey and Talbot, 1982). Furthermore, some reli-gious groups morally object because gambling is perceived to appeal "to an outside force — fate — whereas only God, within Protestantism, is in a position to bestow favours" (Dixey and Talbot, 1982: p. 9).

The "long odds" of winning a prize was the next most popular reason for people deciding not to play the game (37% of objectors). This is under-standable given that the odds of becoming a jackpot winner have been widely quoted by the media as fourteen million to one.

c) Scale of activity in the UK lotto game by participants

Important measures of consumer profile patterns are the size of stakes and any trend indicating an escalation in the size of stakes. The MMU survey illustrated that 56% of stakes were of £1 and 40% between £2 and £5. This shows that the majority of people place the absolute minimum stake possible and that 96% of the sample spend no more on the UK lotto game each week than what equates to less than the price of the cheapest ticket for entry to most professional football matches in Britain. Interestingly, the small minority of participants (4%) in the MMU survey that placed stakes above £5 per week were from the support staff who represented the lower social income group. Nobody in the survey placed stakes above £20 per week.

d) Distribution

The convenient distribution system has certainly supported the product's success with 48% of participants using a newsagent and 27% using a supermarket (MMU survey). Petrol stations and post offices were the next most popular purchase points.

e) Motivating forces

The findings of the MMU survey confirmed that the main motivating influ-ence for playing the UK lotto game was the same force shown by parti-cipants in the betting sector, (Bruce and Johnson, 1992) namely, that financial gain (90%) was the primary reason for playing the UK lotto game. Importance was also attached to the "dream factor" (86%) and excitement (65%) highlighting the entertainment qualities of the UK lotto game.

Excitement and enjoyment needs have also been cited as being important motivators in betting and bingo (Market Line International, 1995).

18% of participants felt the game fulfilled a need for social interaction. Nobody felt the game provided an intellectual challenge, reinforcing its simplicity, and emphasising a distinction between the UK lotto game and betting where knowledge of "form" is desirable, and greater judgement exercised (Filbey and Harvey, 1988 and Bruce and Johnson, 1992).

f) Experience in other sectors before and after the start of the UK lotto game

The final area the MMU survey covered was gambling experience in other sectors before and after the launch of the UK lotto game. This showed that participants in the UK lotto game have continued to participate in other forms of gambling, the most popular sectors being the pools (32%) and betting (18%). Of these, the pools mainly attracts weekly activity. In contrast betting is undertaken mainly on a yearly basis. Based on reports that turnover in both these segments has been affected by the UK lotto game, it seems reasonable to conclude that while people appear to be staying loyal to traditional segments, they are spending less.

The MMU survey also revealed that 28% of participants in the UK lotto game had played the scratch card "Instants" games and 21% of participants had become regular participants playing it weekly. All these participants also played the UK lotto game weekly. In contrast to the UK lotto game, there is a marked difference in participation levels for scratch cards according to age group. 35% of the 18-24 year age range participated in the scratch card game weekly, whereas only 19% of the support staff participated weekly — all of whom were aged over 25. The lowest level of weekly participation was by lecturers, where only 10% played scratch cards weekly. As with support staff, all lecturers were aged over 25.

The acceptable face of gambling?

A number of factors from the above analysis suggest the UK lotto game does represent an acceptable form of gambling. Firstly, high participation amongst all categories of the population has enabled this form of gambling to be perceived to be the norm, rather than an activity undertaken by particular social groups. Evidence demonstrating the proportion of new gamblers prepared to try the UK lotto game gives further support to its acceptable nature.

Indeed, it has been argued that the game has become a national event "adding to the gaiety of the nation." (*Daily Telegraph*, 26th August 1995). The level of participation supports this claim, together with the fact that the game has the advantage of being broadcast every week nationally on television at peak viewing time. This national profile reinforces the UK lotto game's mass participation characteristic and further adds to its acceptability.

Secondly, the UK lotto game is taking place in premises which are more accessible than those needed for traditional areas of gambling. Distribution outlets such as supermarkets and newsagents are used by all social groups and thus encourage the perception that participation can be available to everyone of the permitted age and can, for example, simply be an adjunct to the regular shopping trip.

Thirdly, based on the relatively low stake levels, it would appear that activity is largely at an entertainment and "fun" level, rather than at a serious and controlled level. Therefore, if spending patterns were to continue, it would seem unlikely that weekly budgets of the vast majority of households would be seriously threatened by the UK lotto game itself. This is supported from experience in the United States where a Government funded study concluded that lotteries do little damage to the average purchaser's finances (Industrial Market Research Ltd, 1976).

Finally, it is suggested that the UK lotto game has an additional more acceptable characteristic than many other forms of gambling: namely that it is regarded as being at the least addictive end of the gambling spectrum (Fitzherbert, 1995). This is because its features include a low chance of winning and a wait until the outcome of buying a ticket is known. As a result, the game is more likely to be played at an entertainment level with low stakes. In contrast, research conducted in the United States has shown that games which have short arousing spans of play, a higher frequency of wins and the opportunity for immediate replay are more likely to be associated with compulsive gambling. This state is described as:

> A high similar to the effect of a stimulant drug and also as a feeling of dissociation permitting an escape from worries. As the disorder progresses the pathological gambler is increasingly preoccupied with betting; needs to increase the size of wagers to achieve desired psychological effects; and finds that efforts to control, reduce or stop gambling are unsuccessful. The pathological gambler characteristically gambles increasing amounts to try to win back lost money. (Blume, 1995: p. 522)

Scratch card games therefore appear to pose more of a concern. This is confirmed by feedback from Gamblers Anonymous who reported in May 1995 that the majority of the calls they received relating to the National Lottery (20% of all calls) were connected with the "Instants" scratch card game.

While these factors have contributed to the UK lotto game being perceived as an acceptable form of gambling at present, research of both primary and secondary sources point to several concerns about the game. Firstly, it can be argued that the UK lotto game in its current form can pctentially lead to adverse social consequences in a number of ways. The MMU survey demonstrated that 21% of participants in the UK lotto game have also taken up the more addictive "Instants" scratch card game on a weekly basis. It can therefore be argued that the UK lotto game has provided a "gateway" to a more addictive form of gambling. This has the danger of turning both new and largely entertainment seeking gamblers into more serious participants, or even ultimately pathological gamblers, leading to a very different state for the consumer in comparison to gambling for fun. Escalating gambling levels by individuals would lead to pressures on the weekly budgets of households and concerns about the social consequences of such a trend would inevitably be widespread. Indeed, it has already been suggested that public health consequences should be monitored in order to check that the health of participants is not being jeopardised by their expenditure on the National Lottery's products (McKee and Sassi, 1995).

Another potentially adverse social consequence of the UK lotto game is its effect on children (under 16's) in light of the fact that they are exposed to the nature of the game through high profile publicity and its accessible distribution system. The Independent Television Commission reported that 27% of children watched the broadcast of the game each week at the end of 1994. While those under 16 are not permitted to play the game, the access they have to the details of the game raises the question as to whether it will increase their chances of becoming regular gamblers in the UK lotto game or other more addictive forms of gambling such as gaming machines or scratch cards. This is another area that warrants regular monitoring. Potentially negative affects like these also raise the question as to whether it is morally right for the government to support the UK lotto game by enabling it to be perceived, and broadcast, as a national event.

The likelihood of participants turning into pathological gamblers should, however, be kept in proportion and not over-estimated. Research from the United States, where many states have had a more deregulated gambling industry than Britain for several years, shows that the current prevalence of pathological or addictive gambling is between 1.4% and 2.8% (Volberg, in press). These are not high levels especially when compared to other forms of addiction, such as smoking (CSO, 1995).

The second main factor which suggests that the UK lotto game could lose its acceptable form comes from research on North American lotteries which indicates that the characteristic of mass participation across all social groups declines as lotteries mature. In the United States the high spenders tend to come from ethnic minority populations, urban locations and lower income groups (Clotfelter and Cook, 1989). From Canada it is reported that two thirds of lottery tickets are sold to low income, less educated players (Lampeter, 1989). These findings have been supported by more recent research of American experience which found that the poor spent more of their income on lottery tickets than the middle class and sales increased with rising unemployment (McKee and Sassi, 1995). Whether the UK lotto game will follow this trend remains to be seen. If the UK lotto game did follow the trend in North America, it could lose the mass participation characteristic it holds across all social groups, that currently contributes to it being perceived as acceptable. Also, it would become an unfair method of raising tax because it would affect the lower social income groups the most.

The final area of concern about the UK lotto game which has attracted much media coverage is the equity of the distribution of funds to "good causes." This does attract negative media comment as examples such as the £13.5 million grant for acquisition of the Churchill Archives, the £55 million grant towards the Royal Opera House and the proportionately fewer grants being awarded to inner city areas (Lottery Link, 1995) in the first batch of grants awarded by the Sports Council, have shown. However, there is no evidence to suggest this has had a negative impact on participation in the game. It does, though, raise a warning signal when taken in conjunction with the point already made about high participation by lower income groups. This indicates how the UK lotto game can come close to fulfilling a prediction made in an article in the *Economist* in 1994, namely, that "the National Lottery will gather money from the poor to spend on the amusements for the wealthy."

There are, therefore, several pitfalls that could potentially seriously damage the UK lotto game's image and ultimately its widespread acceptance. There is insufficient evidence to date to suggest any of the factors identified have seriously affected UK lotto ticket sales. The partial information available from the MMU survey and experience from overseas does, however, seem to justify regular monitoring by independent bodies and the taking of appropriate action to keep these factors in check.

Conclusion

The UK lotto game is a strong gambling product which benefits from convenient and mass distribution and high profile publicity. This has enabled it to become a leading market segment within the UK's gambling industry. Consumer profile studies show that unlike traditional forms of gambling the UK lotto game has succeeded in achieving weekly mass participation across gender, permitted age ranges and social groups. The MMU survey has confirmed that higher income social groups participate less than lower income social groups and that paradoxically lower income groups have a greater propensity to place higher stakes than higher income groups.

The prime motivator for playing the UK lotto game is financial gain followed by the "dream factor". Current expenditure on the UK lotto game is mostly at a level that would not seriously affect the weekly budgets of households and would indicate the game is played for fun rather than as a compulsive form of gambling. At this level the UK lotto game can be seen to be an acceptable form of gambling. Mass participation, weekly television coverage and distribution in convenience related outlets, rather than gambling related outlets, has also contributed to the game's acceptable form. These factors have also given the game a strong position for building upon its initial success. However, whether the UK lotto game will represent the acceptable face of gambling in the longer term is open to question given the concerns raised by its "gateway" effect to other more addictive forms of gambling, the narrowing of its customer base as the UK lotto game matures and evidence demonstrating inequitable distribution of the proceeds. Provided OFLOT and ultimately the Government take action to avoid problems that have been highlighted such as the participation in other more addictive forms of gambling, one is inclined to conclude that the game's acceptability can be sustainable — and perhaps the chequered history of UK nation-wide lotteries will not be repeated.

References

Blume, S. (1995) 'Pathological gambling', *British Medical Journal*, Vol. 311: pp. 522-523.

Bruce A. C., and Johnson, J. E. V. (1992) 'Towards an explanation of betting as a leisure pursuit', *Leisure Studies*, Vol. 3, No. 12: pp. 201-218.

Camelot PLC (1995) *Annual Report and Accounts*.

Camelot PLC (1995) *National Lottery News*.

Central Statistical Office. (1995) *Social Survey*.

Clotfelter C. T., and Cook P. J. (1989) *Selling hope*. HUP.

Cornish, D. B. (1978) *Gambling: A review of the literature*. London: HMSO, London.

Daily Telegraph (26th August, 1995).

Dixey R. and Talbot M. (1982) *Women, leisure and bingo*. Leeds: Trinity and All Saints College.

Filbey M. P. and Harvey L. (1988) 'Recreational betting: everyday activity and strategies', *Leisure Studies*, Vol. 2, No. 7: pp. 159-172.

Filbey M. P. and Harvey L. (1989) 'Recreational betting: Individual betting profiles', *Leisure Studies*, Vol. 3, No. 8: pp. 219-227.

Fitzherbert, L. (1995) *Winners and losers. The impact of the National Lottery*. York Publishing Services.

Home Office (1995) *Deregulation: Gaming machines and facilities in betting offices*. A consultation paper. London: HMSO.

Henley Centre for Forecasting and GAH Partnership Strategy Consultants. (1995) *Lottery fallout*. London: Henley Centre for Forecasting.

Industrial Market Research Ltd. (1976) *Lotteries in overseas countries*.

Jones, P. and Turner, D. 'The betting shop business', *Business Education*, Vol. 6, No. 2: pp. 16-18

Keynote Report (1994) *Betting and gaming.* Keynote Publications.

Lampeter. (1989) *Analysis of the costs and benefits of public lotteries, The Canadian experience.* Mellen Press.

Macdonald, M. and Leppard, J. (1994) *The marketing audit.* London: Butterworth-Heinemann.

Market Line International. (1995) *Betting and gaming survey.*

McKee, M. and Sassi, F. (1995) *British Medical Journal,* Vol. 311: pp. 521-522.

Porter, M. E. (1985) *Competitive advantage.* Free Press.

Sports Council (1995) *Lottery link.* London: The Sports Council.

The Economist (August 5th 1995) 'Fair play for bingo'.

Volberg, R. A. Prevalence studies of problem gambling in the United States. *Journal of Gambling Studies.* (in press).

Webb, J. R. (1992) *Understanding and designing marketing research.* Academic Press.

Appendix

QUESTIONNAIRE

THE NATIONAL LOTTERY — A STUDY OF CONSUMER BEHAVIOUR

The aim of this questionnaire is to provide information on consumer behaviour in relation to the National Lottery. This will be used to support research activity in this area. Your time in completing the questions would much appreciated.

Please answer questions by ticking the relevant box provided

1. PERSONAL DETAILS

Age

☐ 15-24   ☐ 45-54
☐ 25-34   ☐ 55-64
☐ 35-44   ☐ 65+

Sex

☐ Male   ☐ Female

Occupation

☐ Lecturer   ☐ Administration Assistant
☐ Manager   ☐ Support staff
☐ Student   ☐ Other (please specify)

2. PARTICIPATION

Have you participated in the National Lottery ?

(NB This does not include the Instants game) If no, please complete questions10 and 11 only. If yes, please answer all the questions

☐ Yes   ☐ No

3. FREQUENCY OF PURCHASE

How often do you buy a lottery ticket ?

☐ Weekly   ☐ Every six months
☐ Monthly   ☐ Rollover week only
☐ Quarterly

4. DATE OF LAST PURCHASE

When did you last buy a lottery ticket ?

☐ Nov 94 - Jan 95
☐ Feb 95 - Apr 95
☐ May 95 onwards

Appendix (cont.)

5. METHOD/APPROACH

Which of the following approaches do you use most often in buying lottery tickets?

☐ Individual

☐ Syndicate

☐ Informal group (e.g. with family, partner/friends)

6. AMOUNT

How much do you usually spend when buying a lottery ticket/s?

☐ £1   ☐ £11-20

☐ £2-£5   ☐ £21+

☐ £6-£10

7. POINT OF PURCHASE

Where do you usually buy lottery tickets?

☐ Post Office   ☐ Newsagent/grocery shop

☐ Supermarket   ☐ Petrol station

☐ Multiple store   ☐ Other (Please specify) _____

8. MOTIVATION

Please tick relevant box to illustrate the influence you feel the factors below have on your decision to participate.

	Strongly Agree	Don't Know	Disagree	Strongly Disagree
Financial gain	☐	☐	☐	☐
Intellectual challenge	☐	☐	☐	☐
Social interaction	☐	☐	☐	☐
Excitement	☐	☐	☐	☐
Dream factor	☐	☐	☐	☐
Other (Please specify)..........	☐	☐	☐	☐

Appendix (cont.)

9. CURRENT PARTICIPATION IN ABOVE

Please tick relevant box(es) according to your current activity.

	Weekly	Monthly	Quarterly	Yearly
Betting	☐	☐	☐	☐
Charity Lotteries	☐	☐	☐	☐
Bingo	☐	☐	☐	☐
Casino	☐	☐	☐	☐
Gaming machines	☐	☐	☐	☐
Premium Bonds	☐	☐	☐	☐
Pools	☐	☐	☐	☐
Scratch card (Non Instants)	☐	☐	☐	☐
Scratch card (Instants)	☐	☐	☐	☐

10. PAST NON NATIONAL LOTTERY GAMBLING EXPERIENCE

Please tick relevant box.

None

If none, please proceed to question 11. Otherwise, tick relevant boxes below according to past activity.

	Weekly	Monthly	Quarterly	Yearly
Betting	☐	☐	☐	☐
Charity Lotteries	☐	☐	☐	☐
Bingo	☐	☐	☐	☐
Casino	☐	☐	☐	☐
Gaming machines	☐	☐	☐	☐
Premium Bonds	☐	☐	☐	☐
Pools	☐	☐	☐	☐
Scratch card	☐	☐	☐	☐

11. REASONS FOR NON PARTICIPATION

If you have not played the game please indicate the main reason below. *Please only tick one box.*

☐ Objections on moral grounds
☐ "Long" odds
☐ Participation in other gambling sectors
☐ Cannot afford it

Thank you for your co-operation.

Cultural Determinants and the Demand for Professional Team Sports: A Study of Rugby League Clubs

Brian Davies, Paul Downward and Ian Jackson
Staffordshire University Business School

Introduction

The factors which influence people to attend the matches of professional team sports are both complex and varied. These influences range from the purely economic — for example, admission price; to the cultural — for example, place of birth or residency. As a consequence, the demand for professional team sports can be problematic to identify and forecast.

This paper focuses upon the pattern of demand for one particular professional team sport: Rugby League Football. Three pivotal questions will be highlighted. Firstly, which determinants drive the demand for Rugby League? Secondly, why do Rugby League supporters follow this sport in preference to other sports? Finally, to what extent can future levels of support be predicted? Bourdieu (1978) generalises those issues as the demand for 'sports products':

> ... how is the demand for 'sports products' produced, how do people acquire the 'taste' for sport and for one sport rather than another, whether as an activity or as a spectacle? (p. 340)

In sum, the economic factors and the cultural determinants of the demand for Rugby League are each considered as important and will be fully explored.

The plan of the paper is twofold. The first section will touch upon the existing literature on the patterns and behaviour of support known as spectatorship from both an economic and cultural perspective. Unlike the well-documented axiomatic structure of economic determinants of demand, the section does not presuppose the precise cultural determinants. It is offered simply to highlight the potential complexity of the matrix of determinants of spectatorship.

Page 196

The second section will present the results of a postal questionnaire conducted on Rugby League supporters clubs during the 1994-95 season.

The spectatorship of games

Physical contact sports, such as Rugby League, have a twin function according to Calhoun (1987). The first function is to generate 'cultural learning', where important attitudes are formed through the symbolism of the game. For example, group-work and co-operation are in part developed by team games. The second function is to create 'emotional expression' along the lines of folk tales or music. Moreover, it became increasingly clear from the mid-Victorian era onwards, as crowds got larger at British football matches[1], that the twin function of games, applied equally to the spectator and the participant alike. Therefore, the concept of a spectator, generating support for one team or another and providing a sense of occasion at the match, is referred to as "spectatorship".

The historical reasons why people engage in the spectatorship of sport is highly varied. Based on Midwinter (1986) at least three types of spectator can be identified:

The Spectator-Gambler. The original intention of most spectators before 1850 was to gamble at the sporting event. The common element for those who attended was, a priori, to bet on the uncertainty of the result. The main examples were prize fighting, cricket and horse racing, the latter of which remains heavily patronised by the spectator-gambler to this day.

The Spectator-Consumer. As team sports developed in the late Victorian era, it became apparent that the games themselves actually generated intrinsic enjoyment. Thus, people actually 'consumed' episodes of sporting events for the fun of it.

Two types of spectator-consumers can be shown to exist. One is the loyal spectator who is dedicated to a particular sport, team or an individual. The other is the casual supporter who will attend matches rather infrequently depending on such factors as the weather conditions, quality of opposition or the appearance of a named player, for example. This generates both bedrock and transient support respectively and accounts in part for the fluctuation in attendances.

The Armchair-Spectator. Prior to the development of television and radio, the only way to be instantly involved in a game was to attend the match itself. Reading match reports in newspapers was *ex post facto*. Coverage of games on radio and, in particular, 'live' matches on television have changed this situation over the last generation or so. As media coverage becomes more widespread, the armchair-spectator, in the comfort of the home, has become a paradoxical figure. On the one hand, spectators at home using modern technology to 'view' games are not providing gate revenue or atmosphere at the venue of the game. However, on the other hand, these spectators can potentially boost media coverage and therein sponsorship money, which is filtered down to the clubs. The current turmoil in world Rugby, League and Union alike, is solely aimed at winning the hearts and minds of the armchair-spectator, in order to secure revenue for multi-media companies, such as News Corporation and their advertisers.

It is worth noting that many casual spectators are also armchair-spectators from time to time; and doubtless some loyal spectators are at some time also armchair-spectators. The latter is true because in an economic sense, the expense and time incurred by attending every game in a season is usually prohibitive for most people.

From an economic viewpoint the spectators at professional team sports can be modelled in terms of supply and demand. Essentially, two separate markets exist. A labour market for players or participants, and a goods market for the spectators. This is represented in Table 1.

Table 1   Two Markets: Participants and Spectators

	Participation (Labour Market)	Spectatorship (Goods Market)
Supply	Players	Clubs
Demand	Clubs	Spectators

Therefore, clubs both demand players and supply games to watch, usually under the auspices of a governing body, the Football Association or Rugby Football League, for example. Players supply their labour for financial remuneration and spectators have effective demand when they pay the admission price at the turnstile.

The literature around each of the four components is growing. For example, Dabscheck (1993) has researched the labour market for Australian Rugby League players associations. Nevertheless, the objective of this paper remains the analysis of demand from spectators (not clubs) for professional Rugby League. This will be achieved firstly by placing team games within a cultural context; and secondly by specific reference to our questionnaire.

The cultural context of team games

The economic analysis of the demand for professional team sports is well documented. The seminal article by Jennett (1984), for example, develops the concept of uncertainly of outcome as being important for the level of attendance. In general, economic theory views spectators as discerning consumers, who decide upon levels of consumption in a rational manner. Price, the price of substitutes, complimentary goods, and income are all vital in this respect. This is, however, only part of the analysis. Demand for a 'sports product' is also dependent upon cultural determinants.

Culture and sport create a complex matrix. Games such as football and rugby can be considered as an integral part of mass society and popular culture. This recognises the interdependency of organically developed communities rather than the market relationship between individuals, characterised by 'atomistic' behaviour (see Billington *et al.*, 1991). Therefore, this paper will follow the Durkheimian tradition of culture, which emphasises the collective nature of society and its capacity for integrating the individual into the wider group. This view of culture will be developed with the specific reference point of Rugby League, as well as sport in general.

The game of Rugby League stems from the bifurcation of Rugby Football in 1895 into two codes: namely League and Union. The details surrounding this event are extremely well-documented (see, for example: Delaney, 1984 and 1993; Latham and Mather, 1993; Williams, 1994). The hostility between the two codes has remained ever since and is dubbed by Dunning and Sheard (1979) as 'Rugby Apartheid'.

Rugby League has a number of defining cultural traits. Firstly, it is hitherto an overtly working -class game in origin and historical development, not unlike speedway and (until recently) Association Football (see Clayton and Steele, 1994). Secondly, the laws of the game (i.e. product development) are with spectators directly in mind and not necessarily players (unlike Rugby Union, which is a highly technical game). As Midwinter (1986) states:

> Rugby league, from its earliest days, was programmed to attract
> spectators, its refusal to allow line-outs or rucks and its reluctance
> to permit scrums is a testimony to this. (p. 105)

Thirdly, professional Rugby League has specific geographical links with the industrial heartlands of the former boundaries of Lancashire and Yorkshire[2] (and Cumbria in the post-war period). This stems from a power struggle between the clubs in the North of England and the South of the country, over bona-fide broken-time payments, the creation of cup competitions and leagues, the taking of gate money and the venue for Annual General Meetings amongst other issues which relate to professionalism. However, this schism did not spread elsewhere. South Wales, for example, has a similar socio-economic milieu as Lancashire and Yorkshire, but remained loyal to Rugby Union, because it was largely allowed to govern its own affairs, within strict amateur rules. Thus, whilst professional Rugby League has spread overseas principally to Australia, France, New Zealand and Papua New Guinea, it has only spread throughout the rest of Britain at an amateur level. Overall, professional Rugby League can therefore be viewed in terms of its deep roots, which are both culturally and geographically specific.

It is now possible to identify the cultural determinants which, along with economic factors, form the basis of our questionnaire.

A.   Cultural Determinants

(i) **Community Representation**:   A sports team usually derives its name from the local community out of which it operates. Rugby Union provides some interesting exceptions: Harlequins and Wasps, for example. Rugby League can provide no similar examples, except in Australia. This local identity can augment both interest and pride in a club often from within its immediate surroundings (and sometimes from beyond). According to Stone (1981): "Sports teams, bearing the community name (or totum) have become this kind of collective representation, as have players and sports themselves" (p. 221). Thus, the area in which a person is born or resides can be considered important in determining support for a sport or a club, although this is not necessarily so in Association football, where some teams command support nationally, for example, Manchester United or Glasgow Rangers.

(ii) **Overlapping Generations**:   Continuity in any spectator sport is important. Parents and other family members are often the first to take children to a sports match and colleagues at work can also help to generate interest in a club or a particular sport.

(iii) **Cultural Identity**:   As we have shown, Rugby League is a working class game described by Clayton and Steele (1994) as "The peoples game". Geoffrey Moorhouse, fellow of the Royal Society of Literature, goes a stage further and describes Rugby League as: "... embodying not only a certain preference in athletic skills but also the way and the where and from what I was reared, the history of the British class system, and persistent cultural differences between North and South". (Moorhouse, 1989: p. 75).

Therefore, for many people, Rugby League is an 'action frame of reference' (see Billington *et al.*, 1991).

B.   Economic Factors

(i) **Financial Considerations**:   Price, income and travel costs (loosely, transaction costs) are all standard measures of determining the likelihood of a person consuming a particular good or service. This applies equally to spectatorship at professional team sports as with all other goods and services.

(ii) **Quality of Goods or Service**:   Success or failure in previous encounters can act as a proxy for the quality of a 'sports product'. This is likely to apply most to the casual or infrequent spectator.

(iii) **Substitutes**:   Many towns and cities have a variety of sporting activities, which compete for spectator income. For example, Carlisle, Doncaster and York all have a professional rugby league club, a football club and a race course. Bradford, Kingston-upon-Hull, and Sheffield all have at least one rugby league club, at least one football club and a speedway team.

At this stage, three outcomes can potentially exist. The spectator forms a social relationship with the club; or attends matches as part of a wider diet of leisure; or in an economic sense the interaction is purely a market encounter (see Davies, Downward and Jackson, 1995).

The study

This survey on Rugby League support is part of an on-going research project on professional team sports. As previously stated, during the 1994-95 season all 32 professional Rugby League supporters clubs in Britain were invited to ask members to complete the questionnaire. By our own definitions of spectatorship, this confines the study to the loyal spectator type. This was done deliberately to spotlight the bedrock support for Rugby League, which we consider to form the majority of the 50,000 people who attend all professional Rugby League matches on a weekly basis.

Over 130 completed questionnaires were returned from 12 clubs, see Appendix 1. The spread of teams is from both divisions and throughout Cheshire, Greater Manchester, Humberside, Merseyside, South and West Yorkshire (none from Cumbria or London). Spectator comments on specific issues are summarised as Appendix 2.

This questionnaire forms part of a wider study on the demand for professional team sports. Thus, spectator profiles are important; together with the main area of interest in this paper namely the respective importance of cultural as well as economic factor, which determine the spectatorship of Rugby League clubs.

The results

The results from the questionnaire were analysed using factor analysis. This is a mathematical model which can identify the statistical relationship or correlation between a large set of variables specifically in terms of a smaller set of underlying factors. Factor analysis allows non-continuous variables such as economic and socio-cultural influences, used in this study, to be considered. The overall conclusion appears to be that socio-cultural factors have a major influence upon the reasons for attendance at professional Rugby League matches. See Table 2 below. However, economic factors are also significant as factor 1 indicates.

The combinations in factor 1 accounted for 25% of the sample and show that although family, area of residence, and success or failure in previous games influence attendance, even more so do admission prices, the size of income and costs of travel.

Factor 2 at 12% of the sample gives a mixed picture of both economic and cultural factors. Not only are admission price and travel costs influential, but so also are the influence of friends, colleagues, area of residence and the pattern of previous results and perceived quality of the opposition. Factor 2 would appear to describe casual supporters.

In Factor 3 (at 9% of the sample) two cultural features would appear to dominate. These are influences of the supporters' locality — the area born in and residing in and peer pressure from family and friends — and a qualitative appreciation of future games — based on quality of the opposition and previous success or failure of the team supported.

Both Factors 4 and 5 (at 8% and 7% respectively) suggest cultural reasons for the length of support (namely age of first attendance, area of birth, and the longer the years of support the more likely of continued support), and active involvement in having played the game at school and/or as an amateur.

Clearly Factor 6 (5%) indicates the cultural characteristics of a bedrock home supporter with age of first attendance, length of support and family membership as strong influences. However, this type of supporter is not greatly interested in attending away games.

The truly fully committed supporter is shown in Factor 7 (5%) with strong cultural influences from area of birth, family and media influence being committed to both home and away support with little regard for the success or failure of the team.

Only Factor 1 would seem to be influenced by economic issues but even here not totally. Most supporters of whatever degree of commitment overwhelmingly respond to cultural factors.

A summary of the factors is found in Table 2.

Table 2   Socio-economic and cultural factors which influence attendance

Factor	Type
1	Mainly economic influence
2	Mixed casual support identified
3	Cultural mainly locality
4	Cultural mainly length of time supporting
5	Cultural mainly active involvement
6	Solid home support only
7	Solid support home and away

Using these results it is possible to offer tentative answers to the three questions which were initially asked in the Introduction to this paper. The demand for Rugby League appears to be driven more by cultural factors, such as locality of residence and birth than economic theory would suggest. Economic factors such as price have a much weaker effect on demand. Rugby League supporters follow their sport in preference to others because of involvement at amateur levels and intergenerational ties. Many people identify Rugby League football as the game of their own community. Future levels of support are more difficult to pinpoint. However, it is likely that the Rugby Football League will have to be loyal to its existing spectators before plans of expansion to areas where the game does not traditionally exist.

Conclusion

The relationship between a professional team sport and spectators is shown to be both economic and cultural. The demand for professional Rugby League is a complex mix of strong cultural determinants and weaker economic influences.

Overall, this has at least two policy implications. Expansion of the Rugby League may not be possible without sufficient infrastructure and 'grass-roots' support. This will require investment in facilities and developing teams at all levels, not just professional teams. Bedrock supporters must be consulted before any significant changes in the organisation of the game. The game must be loyal to the spectators and true to its traditions. This is true for many aspects including kick-off times, team colours and club venues.

Rugby League football does have some unique and defining characteristics as shown in this paper. However, it does share some characteristics such as continuity and community identity with other sports: for example, Rugby Union football in South Wales and Association football in the West Midlands of England. This may allow some of our findings to be generalised, rather than be specific to Rugby League.

Whilst this study is based on surveys of supporters' clubs it has identified that cultural as well as economic determinants are important in specatorship. It could be argued that concentrating on supporters clubs has created an in-built bias towards certain cultural factors. This is recognised. It is also recognised that not all cultural factors have been included. Whether this specific approach can be extended to a wider population of Rugby League consumers could also be debatable, but this study has identified the need to give greater consideration to cultural factors — an issue poorly addressed by the literature.

Notes

1   Football in the widest definition — that is, rugby and association football.

2   An interesting case study in this area is the city of Leeds, which has seen the development of many football clubs over the past 150 years, League, Union and Association alike. See Green, 1993).

References

Billington, R., Strawbridge, S., Greensides, L., and Fitzsimons, A. (1991) *Culture and society*. Basingstoke: British Sociological Association.

Bourdieu, P. (1978) 'How can one be a sports fan?', in S. During (ed) (1993) *The cultural studies reader*. London: Routledge, pp. 339-356.

Calhoun, D. W. (1987) *Sport, culture and personality* (Second Edition). Champaign, IL: Human Kinetics Publishers.

Clayton, I., and Steele, M. (1993) *When push comes to shove: Rugby League the people's game*. Castleford:Yorkshire Art Circus.

Dabscheck, B. (1993) 'Rugby League and the Union Game', *Journal of Industrial Relations*, Vol. 35, No. 2: pp. 242-273.

Davies, B. (1988) 'Bifurcation in sport: Some preliminary thoughts on the case of Rugby Football', *The Journal of Regional and Local Studies*, Vol. 8, No. 1, Spring: pp.2329.

Davies, B., Downward, P., and Jackson, I. (1995) 'The demand for Rugby League: Evidence from causality tests', *Applied Economics* , Vol. 27: pp. 1003-1007.

Delaney, T. (1984) *The roots of Rugby League*. Keighley: Trevor R. Delaney Publisher.

———— (1991) *The grounds of Rugby League*. Keighley: Trevor R. Delaney Publisher.

———— (1993) *Rugby disunion volume one — broken time*. Keighley: Trevor R. Delaney Publisher.

Dunning, E., and Sheard, K. (1979) *Barbarians, gentlemen and players: A sociological study of the development of Rugby Football*. London: Martin Robertson.

Dunning, E., *et al.* (1993) *The sports process*. Champaign, IL: Human Kinetics Publishers.

During, S. (ed) (1993) *The cultural studies reader*. London: Routledge.

Gate, R. (1991) *The Rugby League fact book*. London: Guinness Publishers.

Green, M. (1993) *The origin and development of football in Leeds*. Mike Green Publishers.

Hadfield, D. (1994) XIII Winters. Edinburgh: Mainstream Publishing.

Jenks, C. (1993) *Culture: Key ideas*. London: Routledge.

Jennett, N. (1984) 'Attendances, uncertainty of outcome and policy in Scottish Football League', *Scottish Journal of Political Economy*, Vol. 32, No. 2: pp. 176-198.

Latham, M., and Mather, T. (1993) *The Rugby League myth: The forgotten clubs of Lancashire, Cheshire and Furness*. Preston: Mike R L Publications.

Lüschen, G. F., and Sage, G. H. (1981) *Handbook of social science of sport*. Illinois: Stipes Publishing Company.

Mangan, J. A., and Small, R. B. (eds) (1986) *Sport, culture and society*. London: Spon Publishers.

Mardia, K. V. *et al.* (1979) *Multivariate analysis*. London: Academic Press.

Midwinter, E. (1986) *Fair game: Myth and reality in sport*. London: George Allen and Unwin.

Moorhouse, G. (1989) *At the George and other essays on Rugby League*. London: Hodder and Stoughton.

Stone, G. P. (1981) 'Sport as a community representation', in G. F. Lüschen and G. H. Sage (eds) *Handbook of social science of sport*. Stipes Publishing Company, pp. 214-245.

Taylor, R. (1992) *Football and its fans*. Leicester: Leicester University Press.

Walvin, J. (1975) *The people's game*. London: Allen Lane Publishers.

Williams, G. (1994) *The code war: English Football under the historical spotlight*. Uxbridge: Yore Publications.

Appendix 1: The Participating Supporters Clubs (1994-95 season)

	Team	County	Division
1	Batley	West Yorkshire	2
2	Bradford Northern	West Yorkshire	1
3	Dewsbury	West Yorkshire	2
4	Halifax	West Yorkshire	1
5	Hull FC	Humberside	1
6	Hull KR	Humberside	2
7	Leigh	Greater Manchester	2
8	St. Helens	Merseyside	1
9	Sheffield Eagles	South Yorkshire	1
10	Swinton	Greater Manchester	2
11	Warrington	Cheshire	1
12	Widnes	Cheshire	1

Appendix 2: Views from the Supporters

I.   On the game itself

Refereeing	*"Appalling standards of refereeing".*	Warrington supporter
Rule changes	*"The game is great, but would be even better if certain rule changes were re-introduced, i.e. scrummaging, [and] allowing of ball stealing".*	Halifax supporter
Australian influence	*"We pay too much attention to the Australian game [of Rugby League football]. Most of the [Australian] games on video are boring.*	Leigh supporter

II.   On the image of the game

Grounds and facilities	*"... the paramount need of all Rugby League clubs [is] to upgrade their Stadia.*	Batley supporter
Links with BARLA and RFU	*"Professional [RFL] and Amateur (BARLA) should work together."*	Halifax supporter
Publicity	*"Greater media coverage (as Rugby Union perhaps)."*	Sheffield Eagles supporter
	"We do not promote the game enough. We should show more games in development areas".	Hull Football Club supporter

III.   On the future of the game

The dominance of Wigan RL	*"I think all rugby club supporters agree that until Wigan start losing, we have all had it".*	Halifax supporter
Summer rugby	*"Summer rugby would be the biggest improvement of all".*	Hull Football Club supporter
Possible expansion	*"There is nothing wrong with the sport itself, in fact it is now better than ever from a spectator point of view; [expansion] must therefore come down to grass roots and national recognition and exposure".*	Hull Kingston Rovers supporter
	"British Rugby League requires a strong leadership from Leeds HQ and a clear plan to spread to gospel".	Swinton supporter

Back to Basics:
The Ethics of Leisure

Alan Clarke
University of Derby

The Leisure Studies Association has moved a long way since its original formation and much of the history has been revisited in the run up to its 20th birthday celebrations. It seems that this might be a good time to return to basics and consider where leisure studies is positioned in relation to some of the core debates in contemporary ethics. It is also appropriate as the attempts at definitions of leisure, which have been debated in the Association's Journal *Leisure Studies* and at LSA conferences, have sought to focus around issues of personal, cultural and community development. One collection of writings extracted from LSA Publications even bore the title *Freedom and constraint* (Coalter, 1989) to crystallise one dimension of the debate. The current changes in the leisure scene further contribute to the importance of these ethical issues as they challenge the traditional parameters which have surrounded leisure in the United Kingdom.

The essence of leisure was established in its earliest oppositions to work. Work which we were told was a central life interest:

> Since the industrial revolution the predominant view has been that work and economic activity in general is the main focus of life, the principal organising force, the main provider of satisfactions and dissatisfactions. Leisure has been considered to have a more peripheral function. Its role has been seen to be essentially one of recreation and recuperation, with entertainment subserving these functions. Recently, however, this view has been challenged. It has been suggested that there has been a decline in work as a 'central life interest' and that increasingly significance and meaning are being sought in leisure. Leisure, it is suggested, is crucial to the development of self identity and self realisation. There is a quest for

new sensations, new experiences, and fulfilment through fun. The fashion revolution, the growth of minority cultures, the cult of the eccentric and the exotic, the acceptance of revolution as a way of life, have all been cited as examples of the rejection of work as a central organising force and the pivotal link between the self and society. (Haworth and Smith: 1975: p. 8)

Work gave us the ethic that leisure was defined in opposition to as it was inscribed within much of the early writings of leisure theory. It was difficult to think of leisure without first accounting for the importance of work. The central issues dominated and dictated the peripheral ones of leisure. Moreover the discussion not only inscribed leisure within the realm of work but it also inscribed the moral code of leisure. As students of leisure, we were engaged in the study of the effects of the Protestant Work ethic away from the place of work. The affinity between capitalist accumulation and the Calvinist ethic of Puritanism and predestination has shaped many of the attitudes towards leisure and identified the deadly sins of leisure in capitalist societies. As Weber observes, the behaviour of the entrepreneur dedicated to the pursuit of profit is presaged by the attitude of the Puritan who recognised that "not leisure and enjoyment, but only activity serves to increase the glory of God" (Weber, 1976: p. 157). As Rojek (1985) observed: "Impulsive enjoyment, killing time, voluptuous pleasure seeking — these are the deadly sins of capitalist leisure time" (Rojek, 1985: p. 67).

Much has been said about the development of leisure as a serious subject — the progress through pluralism, Marxism and feminism is now a familiar core for undergraduate studies. The central concern to catch the dialectic of leisure has remained — the charge of reductionist social control pitched against naive statements of consumer sovereignty may help to re-capture the joy of the debates. Underpinning these sometimes vitriolic debates has been a belief common to all writers that leisure is important in itself as a legitimate object of study. It has been differently constructed within different positions but these definitions and treatments have a number of elements which are held in common, to be considered in what follows.

Leisure — the lowest common denominators

Leisure is about self expression. Leisure is a point where people can strive for self expression and self determination. This idea is found in the early writings and implicitly recognised in the critiques of those early writings, as the critiques demonstrate that leisure fails to fulfil this promise within the constraints of patriarchal and capitalist society. Nevertheless properly addressed and developed leisure recast still contains this kernel of self actualisation.

Leisure is about choice. Within the realms of non-obligated time, people can make choices about how they use their leisure. There may be debate about the extent and range of choices available to different individuals as determined by gender, class, education, culture and income but there is the recognition of discretion in the selection of activities and inactivities undertaken.

Leisure is about re-creation. The core idea here is either expressed in the creation of positive citizens, good role models for the rest of society or in the ability of the labour force to recover enough strength for another days toil. There is a strong commitment to the moral development of the individual within leisure and through leisure, although this can be expressed either as a positive process of self actualisation or a negative sense of regulation and repression.

Leisure and ethics

There has always been an ethical core recognised in the study of leisure. This has often been an implicit code which nonetheless determines the position adopted by the writers. It is a version of a humanist code with a strong commitment to the utilitarian notions of maximising opportunities and minimising negative impacts on others. It has followed essentially 'civilising' patterns, positioning itself against at least the nasty and the brutish if not the short.

There has been little concern shown for explicitly discussing the morality of leisure. Comments have been made about the attempts of puritan revivalists and muscular Christians to dictate a moral agenda through leisure. This leaves a gap in the writing which is difficult to fill as there is no single moral doctrine which would unite the writers on leisure.

Sport: the playing fields of Eton

If the moral code of leisure has been allowed to remain explicitly unchallenged, it has not gone uncriticised. The implications of the moral code have been analysed and critiqued in relation to sport and to the moral and ethical beliefs which can be read into sport. Sport has the capacity to act as the site of cultural reproduction, with ideological values being written into and read off from sports, sporting events and results. It is important to note that there is not necessarily any given morality within sport. It is a site capable of infinite revisiting. The recent attempts to promote team sports through the compulsory reintroduction of 'games' into the national Curriculum has pointed up the importance of sport once again. The nation's flagging spirit must be lifted and the Government's chosen vehicle to achieve this is team sports. This championing of sport as a national figurehead speaks to the dominant construction of sport as a saviour. There may a strong sense of a dominant construction of sport as a moral educator for the good of the young, the delinquent and the unemployed but this is by no means to be accepted uncritically. These topics were debated throughout the conference, to which a version of this paper was initially presented (see, especially, Parker, 1995), but it is worth making passing reference to at least two of the critiques. Mangan (1995) has argued that athleticism can be seen as a codified form of aggression, and Hargreaves (1995) has rightly condemned the middle-aged public-school male conspiracy which has determined the range of competitive team sports to be included in the school curriculum, as a narrow selection of male sports with a token nod in the direction of netball to 'appease' the girls!

But can we speak of ethics in this context? And where would the ethics be derived from? It is clear that sports are based on an ethical principal of fair play and respect for authority. It is arguable that without the notion of fair play all sports become unplayable. Therefore it has to be recognised that sports contain a strong moral core which will benefit our children to learn. It is less clear how we are to learn these moral principles in practice. We see growing pressures to win at all costs reflected in behaviour which would not be tolerated any where other than on the playing field. We have recent evidence of the moral depths which sport has achieved in bribery, drug taking, violence, racism and sexism. The catalogue of tales which can be laid at sports door is more reminiscent of a chamber of horrors rather than a morality fable. There are more examples of Cantonas than Linekers in contemporary sport — even before Lineker was reduced to stealing crisps. There is at best the opportunity for contradictory messages to arise around the parameters of approved leisure. The question which the rest of this paper must address is how far sport is applicable to leisure — whether we hold it to be a positive or a negative influence.

It could be you — it could be all of us

The National Lottery has been far more successful than expected — producing profit figures far in advance of Camelot's wildest avarice. The consequences of this growth are still being debated. We have also seen the relaxation of the licensing laws and the Sunday Trading laws, making Sunday just another day in the week for those with the leisure time to enjoy it. With racing on a Sunday and the betting shops open, life continues as normal.

This expansion of opportunities — voluntary and forced — has been undertaken without a rigorous questioning of the *basics* involved. No one has asked what values are are being brought into play by these changes and these appeals to the general public. There does not appear to be a conception of the ethics of leisure involved in the discussions, despite the 'high moral ground' taken by many of the participants.

A more careful consideration of these debates will help to illustrate this more fully. We are *told* that compulsory team games are good for our children — employers have not yet been urged to institute similar practices for their workforce. Team games are good because they establish core levels of fitness and cooperation amongst the players. We have also been *told* that they teach respect for authority and obedience to the rules of the game.

The abolition of restrictions to Sunday trading have been based on extending freedom of choice to the individual and the rights of the religious have been protected by protective clauses within the legislation. The values of the free market and the freedom of the individual have replaced the religious concern for the restriction of competition to their rights as sole traders on a Sunday.

Gambling is of course more complex still. The debate over the lottery is much more keenly contested, even than the Sunday Trading issue. We have the vision of a Government pledged to uphold family values and individual responsibility welcoming the advent of a gambling boom, based on an appeal to the most basic of instincts — getting something for (relatively) nothing, and certainly not by working for it. The moral dilemma is starkly encapsulated here. The get-rich-quick mentality of free market competition, so warmly succoured by Thatcherism, has prepared the way for the successful to prosper and the unsuccessful to become even poorer. The lottery now goes one stage further and promises — in its advertising at least — the glory of riches to everyone and anyone. It could be you becomes it is you. It could indeed be all of us — except it cannot be all of us all of the time.

The ethics of the free market however are not far removed from the '*win at all costs, just do not get caught*' mentality which pervades a growing number of sports. The fine line between *evasion* (which is illegal) and *avoidance* (which is legal but may not be ethical) is one which would be instantly recognisable to sports players and tax payers alike. We are concerned to become individual winners and to avoid being losers.

A Leisure Ethic

The content of leisure are clearly derived from complex sources and subject to great contestation. Leisure, no matter which definition is taken, does not exist within a moral vacuum. It is produced and consumed within morally determined and morally challenged conditions. The whole debate around time within leisure and within contemporary society is founded on notions of moral obligation and the negotiation of moral obligations. Free time has to be constructed from all the obligations which determine our lives and such negotiations involve complex power relations within both micro and macro levels of society. Non-obligated time, although a favourite term amongst some leisure scholars, is difficult to operationalise as the leisure experience is constructed within a nexus of enduring moral obligations. Even the simplest forms of leisure are subjected to he processes of consumerism, commodification and globalisation, all of which processes have significant consequences for the experience of leisure.

There can be no moral vacuum in attitudes towards leisure. Although writings in the Leisure Studies Association conference papers and journal have never sought to be prescriptive, a moral consensus underpins the writings. There are therefore commitments to moral principles which underpin leisure and set parameters on the definitions of leisure. These core values appear to be around establishing and promoting higher thresholds of tolerance about activities and the diversity of actions, based on the premise that such activities demonstrate respect for the rights of expression of others. There are conflicts here and some of the writing around drug taking as leisure, rather than the criminalising literature, demonstrates this tension clearly. For these writings have sought to establish an appreciation of all activities rather than a condemnation, to facilitate the development of leisure rather than repress it. There is a basis of respect for others in practices and in the understanding of the consequences of those practices.

This is no claim to a higher moral ground of consensus in this paper and certainly no call for a return to moral certainties of a Victorian Puritanism. There never has been a moral consensus in leisure and the changing opportunities, the shifts in the balance of power within society, from religion to the free market, from the community to the individual make one ever more unlikely. These are not uncontested changes and nor do they go unchallenged. The growth of small-scale community festivals, the development of local facilities through the village hall programmes in rural areas and the re-emergence of a 'right to roam' campaign demonstrate that alternatives to the monolith of privatised shared provision of the free market are still possible.

What I am arguing for is not the elaboration of a Protestant Leisure Ethic or a Hedonists' Charter. However it does appear that the construction of a moral agenda for leisure is being attempted which does not recognise the complexities and contradictions of the leisure experiences being put forward. The version of contradictory individualism which is being propounded by the Government is finding favour because there is little consistent opposition to it. The triumph of anonymous charity and the reinforcement of an imagined community, not to mention the national glory claimed for recent developments, is at odds with the radical critiques. However the critiques appear fragmented and are not generalisable, as they address the specific weaknesses of specific proposals. At the heart of these critiques, I believe, there is a leisure ethic. It is a core which seems to approximate to the moral core found in the writings around the sustainability movement and the Agenda 21 declaration from the Rio Earth Summit. The leisure ethic must take heed of sustaining not only the environment, but also of the culture and the local communities. It is an agenda to which the Leisure Studies Association can make a major contribution through continuing its traditions of critical analysis and developmental writing.

References

Coalter, F. (1989) *Freedom and constraint: The paradoxes of leisure.* London: Comedia/Routledge.

de Grazia, S. (1962) *Of time, work and leisure.* The Twentieth Century Fund.

Hargreaves, J. (1995) 'Gender, morality and the national physical education curriculum', in L. Lawrence, E. Murdoch and S. R. Parker (eds) *Professional and development issues in leisure, sport and education.* LSA Publication No. 56. Eastbourne: Leisure Studies Association, pp. 23-40.

Haworth, J. T. and Smith, M. A. (eds) (1975) *Work and leisure.* London: Lepus Books.

Heeley, J. (1986) 'Leisure and moral reform', *Leisure Studies*, Vol. 5, No. 1: pp. 57-67.

Jarvie, G. and Maguire, J. (1994) *Sport and leisure in social thought.* London: Routledge.

Mangan, J. A. (1995) 'Athleticism: Origins, diffusion, and legacy in the specific context of militarism, masculinity, and mythology', this volume: pp. 23-46.

Parker, S. (1995) 'Market and non-market leisure', this volume: pp. 139-144.

Rojek, C. (1985) *Capitalism and leisure theory.* London: Tavistock.

Shand, A. H. (1990) *Free market morality.* London: Routledge.

Weber, M. (1976) *The Protestant Ethic and the spirit of capitalism.* London: Allen and Unwin.

Part III

Lifestyles, Citizenship and Change

Social Stratification, Lifestyle, and Leisure Choice: The Case of Switzerland

Hanspeter Stamm and Markus Lamprecht

University of Zürich[1]

1.   Introduction

Explaining the choice of leisure activities has traditionally been an important area of interest in leisure research. In the past, two main approaches
were used: : on the one hand, conventional stratification models were used
to estimate the effect of formal education, income and occupation etc. on
leisure behaviour. On the other hand, various hypotheses concerning the
relationship between work and leisure experience have been suggested.

It was argued that leisure may *compensate* adverse work conditions in
the sense that, for example, people experiencing stress at work would
primarily seek relaxation, whereas boredom and a lack of involvement at
work would be compensated with exciting and active leisure pursuits.
Another position argues that the work experience is being *generalized* into
leisure, i.e. that bad work conditions also lead to an impoverishment of
leisure pursuits. Conversely, interesting jobs would coincide with more
exciting leisure activities. A somewhat similar hypothesis states that the
work experience is *continued* during free time in the sense that leisure
activities similar to one's job are chosen. Finally, there are hypotheses
assuming a *neutral* relationship (independence) between leisure and work,
or a two-way *interaction* between leisure and work in the sense that the
leisure experience also influences job involvement. In the past, there have
been several attempts to test these hypotheses, but conclusive evidence is
still lacking. Evidence, at best, indicates that leisure may indeed be quite
independent of work (for overviews see, for example, Zuzanek and Mannell,
1983; Hecker and Grunwald, 1981; Roberts *et al.*, 1989; Bamberg, 1991;
Brook, 1993).

Somewhat the same applies for stratification-oriented research. During the 1960s and 1970s various studies have shown a relationship between leisure activity and variables such as education, occupation and income (see Wippler, 1973; Scheuch and Scherhorn, 1977; Wilson, 1980; Giegler, 1982; Lalive d'Epinay *et al.*, 1982; Kelly, 1983; Stockdale, 1987). Yet, on the one hand, other variables such as age, gender or position in the life cycle had an even stronger effect, and, on the other hand, during the 1980s it became increasingly difficult to demonstrate effects of stratification variables.

Against this background, one might be tempted to conclude that leisure has become independent of structural background. To some extent, this assessment is certainly correct: Leisure is no longer the exclusive domain of a "leisure class" (Veblen) but has become open to almost everyone. The extension of free time, rising income levels, the diffusion of entertainment technologies etc. have to some extent "democratized" the choice of leisure activities and leisure consumption. To the extent that leisure activities have become cheaper and less exclusive, there may indeed be an important element of freedom in chosing one's leisure pursuits.

At the same time, however, there has been increasing suspicion that it was no longer possible to describe society and leisure choice in terms of conventional stratification theory or work-centered approaches (Beck, 1983; Berger, 1987; Hradil, 1987a; Kreckel, 1987). In fact, leisure is not the only field of research encountering difficulties in its attempt to demonstrate the linkage of social stratification and behavioural patterns (e.g. voting behaviour and political attitudes). One conclusion was that social inequality had either become irrelevant, de-structured or that it had at least been complicated in a way that challenged the relevance of conventional approaches. As a consequence, new approaches appeared that either opted for a micro-sociological reorientation of research or introduced "new" inequalities into the theoretical framework (Hradil, 1987b; Lüdtke, 1989; Hörning and Michailow, 1990; Bornschier, 1991; Kreckel, 1992; Müller, 1992). These approaches were successful in showing that everyday behaviour is in fact more complicated than was suggested by conventional research. Yet, they frequently offered only partial explanations and (implicitly) often refered back to conventional theories.

The present study summarizes some arguments and results from an attempt to combine the "best of both worlds" (Lamprecht and Stamm, 1994). It is argued, that traditional inequalities based on the occupational system still play a major role in explaining the choice of leisure pursuits, but that a more complete explanation can only be achieved by also integrating "new" inequalities and micro-sociological perspectives into the framework of analysis. In the following section, such a framework is sketched out. The remainder of the paper is dedicated to a discussion of measurement problems and empirical findings from a study of 1,103 workers and employees in a mid-size Swiss town.

2.   A multi-level model for explaining leisure choice

The discussion of social inequality in modern societies has traditionally focused on occupational inequality. Even so-called multi-dimensional models that also take into account variables such as social origin, education, income and formal authority at the workplace always refer back to the occupational system, because these additional dimensions of inequality either have an effect on occupational status or are — as is the case with income and formal authority — affected by one's occupational position.

In the light of the, at best, mixed evidence for the effects of such models on everyday behaviour, an extensive critical discussion of conventional and new approaches has emerged since the early 1980s. In short, three proposals for the lack of explanatory power of conventional models of stratification were advanced.

The *first* proposal was primarily founded on methodological considerations, and stated that measurement of variables and statistical techniques used so far were far from perfect. In fact, a lot of earlier research — particularly in the field of leisure studies — had been working with very crude variables or only tested effects at the bivariate level. Consequently, there was a call for more sophisticated measurement and the use of multivariate statistical techniques (see Prahl, 1977; Stockdale, 1987).

This empirical point of view found some theoretical support in a *second* perspective, which suggested that social stratification had become more complicated and differentiated during the post-war era. Status inconsistency, for example, earlier defined as a deviant and marginal feature of stratification (Lenski, 1954) had become a normal feature of social stratification and increasingly started to superimpose on conventionally assumed effects (Landecker, 1981, Bornschier, 1991). In addition, it was argued that some of the effects may have changed or have become less pronounced in connection with the long-term improvement of incomes as well as educational expansion. In this perspective, a more realistic model of stratification would have to take into account non-linear interactions of various dimensions of social inequality as well as changes in their relative importance.

A *third* line of reasoning suggested that the long-term process of social change had not only changed the overall pattern of stratification, but also the fundamental structure of inequality in modern societies. In this perspective, work situation and occupational status had lost their centrality for a large part of the population (see, for example, Beck, 1983; Hradil, 1987a). Instead, new inequalities had emerged which were at least as important as work-related dimensions. Under the heading of "new" inequalities the effects of variables such as gender, age, one's place within public social security networks, job security, ethnic origin, housing conditions or access to new technologies have been discussed. In this perspective, failure to demonstrate the effects of stratification was due to its decreasing relevance relative to new inequalities. As different social groups may be affected by different inequalities, there was also a call for a closer, i.e. more micro-sociological and qualitative examination of the processes that transform objective inequalities into *life-styles*, i.e. behavioural attitudes and patterns in everyday life (Hradil, 1992; Hörning and Michailow, 1990; Müller, 1992; Kreckel, 1992; Warde, 1995).

It is evident, that most of the "new" inequalities are not really new. Rather, they have always played a role in explaining social behaviour. Yet, under the assumption that modern industrial society was developing towards an open or strongly meritocratic society, these variables have increasingly been neglected or only been included as "control" variables into the analysis. Thus, the "new" inequalities discussion has not only focussed on contemporary changes in social structure but also brought ascribed inequalities back into inequality research.

Still, "new" inequalities alone do not explain more of the variations in behaviour than "old" inequalities. In fact, the other two positions mentioned above still have a strong case. Too often measurement has been very rudimentary in the past and various studies have shown that contemporary stratification processes are indeed very complex (see Bornschier, 1986, Buchmann, 1991, Ruschetti and Stamm, 1991). Consequently, combining the three perspectives into one single approach is very promising. German and French scholars in particular have brought forward a variety of such models and also first attempts to empirically test them. In the following paragraphs we shall therefore briefly sketch out such an extended model which has been inspired by the seminal contributions of Beck (1986), Bornschier (1991), Bourdieu (1987), Hradil (1987b), Lüdtke (1989), Kreckel (1992) as well as some of the more recent studies on the relationships between work, personality and leisure (Parker, 1983; Hoff, 1986; Kohn and Schuler, 1983).

Figure 1 summarizes our model that is characterized by four inter-related, analytical levels of explanation for life-style and the choice of leisure activites: the general level of development of a given society, the structure of inequality, internalized attitudes and the interaction context. The dependent variable in the model is life-style, i.e. specific behavioural patterns, of which leisure activity is only one dimension. As can be seen from Figure 1, leisure as a special aspect of life-style has been decomposed into two different components: leisure activity and leisure style. Whereas the term leisure activity refers to the choice of single activities or groups of similar activities as, for example, reading, gardening, dancing or sports, the term leisure style refers to the overall pattern of leisure activities, i.e. the weighting of different kinds of activities in one's free time. For space reasons, the discussion in this paper will only deal with leisure activities.

The most general level of independent influences on leisure in our model refers to *general cultural, economic, technological, political and legal conditions* which may differ in time as well as between different societies. What we have termed *level of development* thus gives an indication of how

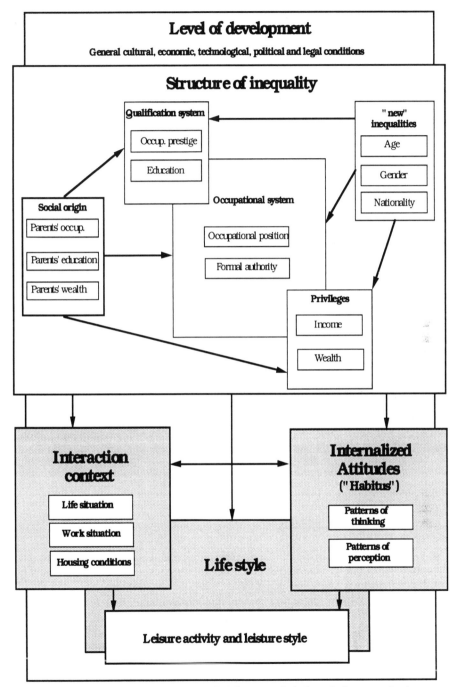

Figure 1:   A multi-level model for explaining leisure choice

Source: Lamprecht and Stamm (1994: ch.8)

social life is organized at a general level and which kind of activities are possible and legitimate in a given society. With respect to leisure activities, there are differences between societies with respect to general levels of wealth (and thus leisure consumption) and free time available as well as with respect to the technologies which can be used during free time (e.g. cars, airplanes, tv sets, computers etc.). In addition, there are cultural and historical differences with respect to how many normative constraints are imposed on leisure activities. For example, until some decades ago, sport involvement was not regarded as a suitable pasttime for women except in some well-defined areas. Church attendance on sunday mornings, on the other hand, has ceased to be a normative imperative for large proportions of the population.

The general level of development has an impact on the next analytical level in our model: the *structure of inequality or social positions*. The over-arching cultural, economic, technological and political structure broadly determines how societal power and privileges are distributed. As can be seen from Figure 1, for modern industrial societies the structure of inequality is still assumed to be organized around the occupational system and the dimensions leading to (social origin, formal qualifications) and being affected (privileges) by occupational position. In addition, the model has been enriched by some of the more important "new" inequalities, i.e. age, sex and nationality which are assumed to have independent influences on educational, occupational and income status.

It should be noted, however, that the arrows in Figure 1 do not imply perfect linkages of the different dimensions of inequality. As stated above, the linkages between the qualification, occupational and reward systems are not perfect and further "blurred" by the effects of social origin and "new" inequalities. Of course, income is still dependent on occupational position which in turn is influenced by educational and social background. But in contemporary society these linkages are far from perfect and are also influenced by "new" inequalities in the sense that women generally earn less, that salaries and jobs in the core sector of the economy are better and more secure, that older persons and people enjoying internal training are prone to move up in the occupational hierarchy and that people from foreign countries are often found in subordinated jobs. In addition, large parts of the population are characterized by incomplete sets of variables, as is the case with housewives, pensioners or the unemployed. As a consequence, there are systematic deviations from the model of equili-brated status linkage. But exactly because these deviations are systematic, they lead to the evolution of a pattern of social positions which may not be equilibrated or complete but which are nevertheless normal in the sense that many people experience similar deviations. Therefore, status incon-sistencies become a normal feature of modern society. It is important to note that the occurence of status inconsistency is not equal to a total de-structuration of the inequality structure. Rather, it is assumed that there are still distinctive groups with similar status configurations but that these configurations no longer need to be connected in a linear way (Ruschetti and Stamm, 1991). As a result we do no longer find clear cut "strata" but rather "social locations" or "social positions" ("soziale Lagen" in German).

If there is no longer a clear linear linkage pattern of inequality dimensions, it becomes difficult to clearly distinguish between groups characterized by clear preferences because different dimensions may compete with each other and lead to mixed preferences. In addition, it has often been assumed that objective positions in the inequality structure influence behaviour directly. This assumption only holds with respect to the inequality structure shaping the overall space of action possibilities. The outer boundaries for leisure consumption, for example, are determined by income constraints as well as by one's work time and educational background. Yet, in view of generally decreasing levels of work time and improving incomes, there is still quite a lot of room for action within the space opened up by the various dimensions of inequality.

For that reason, two more analytical levels have been included in our explanatory model. On the one hand, the dimension of *internalized, subjective attitudes* refers to patterns of perception which influence one's life-style and leisure activities. In addition to direct effects of social position there are also specific predispositions that have been internalized during class, cohort or gender specific socialization as well as in one's work context. While the position in the inequality structure determines the outer boundaries of the space of opportunities, internalized attitudes indicate preferences within this space. It is important to note, that this analytical level is very similar to Bourdieu's (1987) *habitus* concept. As we will not be able to operationalize this dimension adequately, we are not using the term habitus, however.

Whereas internalized attitudes refer to relatively stable long-term dispositions, the *interaction context*, on the other hand, refers to the impact of social relationships and networks in everyday life (particularly at work and in the family, see Kohn and Schuler, 1983, Nave-Herz and Nauck, 1978, Hoff *et al.*, 1991). Membership in formal and informal groups opens up possibilites but also imposes additional constraints upon the actor. A good example is the family: children claim a lot of their parents' time but they also offer them special opportunities for leisure experience not open to people without kids (playing, trips to the zoo, spectating children's sports etc.). Another example is the work context: the work experience may not only affect one's leisure preferences, colleagues at work may also suggest new leisure activities and become leisure partners. In addition, leisure may itself constitute special interaction contexts as is often the case in sports clubs which frequently extend their influence on participants beyond the mere sphere of sports to political behaviour and other leisure activities.

As shown in Figure 1, subjective attitudes as well as the interaction context are both assumed to have effects on life-style and leisure choice. Yet, as both are also influenced by the structure of inequality, they also mediate effects of the overarching structure. One of the important questions to be answered by empirical research is whether the direct effect of the inequality structure or the effects mediated by attitudes and interaction contexts are stronger. It should be noted, however, that subjective attitudes and interaction context are not fully determined by the structure of inequality. With respect to subjective attitudes there are psychological dimensions not fully accounted for in the model. The various interaction contexts, on the other hand, are also subject to some degree of free choice and luck in finding convenient partners.

Of course, effects on leisure choice are not expected to be perfect. As already mentioned in the introduction to this paper, it is plausible to assume that modern leisure indeed involves a high degree of free choice. Many leisure activities such as the use of the media, sports or eating out have become "democratized" during the post-war era. Yet, leisure has also become differentiated in the sense that there are still differences in the kind of restaurants and sports that are preferred by different social groups. Such differences cannot be examined with our data (see below), however. Thus, it is suggested, that the influence of social background is overshadowed by a relatively high degree of freedom of choice by individuals and social groups at the level of general types of leisure activities. Against this background, the interesting question is not, how social structure determines leisure choice but rather to which degree and in which way it (still) has an impact on leisure choice.

3. Research strategy, measurement and operationalization

It is difficult to derive exact hypotheses regarding the choice of leisure activities from the model presented in section 2. Even though it is possible to make assumptions about patterns of status linkage, the establishment of specific attitudes and the effects of interaction contexts at work and in the family, the interactions of the different levels of the model would also have to be taken into account. As a result, one would have to derive dozens of special hypotheses regarding leisure consequences for, for example, women from rural contexts who are married to small farmers as opposed to single male urban professionals with a working class background etc..

As working out and discussing such a set of hypotheses would go beyond the scope of this study we have decided to use an exploratory research design that only focusses on the question whether the different levels of our model are indeed related in the way indicated by the arrows in Figure 1. In a first step, we are concerned with modeling the interplay of our independent variables. Subsequently, we shall go on to test whether these levels influence leisure choice at all or whether leisure is indeed a field of completely free choice as has often been claimed.

The *data* used in this study have been gathered during summer 1992. A written questionaire concerning work, leisure, sport and social background was answered by 1103 workers and employees in five industrial and services enterprises in a mid-size Swiss town. The data describe quite well the unequal structure of this segment of the working population as well as its leisure preferences. The intermediate levels of the interaction context and subjective attitudes, however, have not been fully addressed by the questionaire. Apart from restrictions in the length of the questionaire, a more complete survey of these dimensions would call for the use of qualitative methods of data gathering. Consequently, our data only include some crude measures of life and work contexts as well as some dimensions of attitudes towards work.

Even our restricted set of variables involves several problems, however. As discussed in section 2, every single analytical level of our model is composed of a set of interrelated dimensions. It would be highly problematic and also quite confusing to introduce dozens of variables into the analysis. Therefore the number of variables had to be reduced before estimating the interplay of analytical levels and their effect on leisure activities. The operationalization of the different analytical levels of our model as well as the subsequent empirical tests therefore involves several *statistical procedures*.[2] To reduce the number of variables, principal components analysis was used in the operationalization of work situation, work attitudes and leisure activities. With respect to social stratification and general life situation we were interested in a closer examination of the relationships of the different variables involved. Thus, in a first step, the interplay of these variables is analyzed on the basis of regression analysis and path models. As status inconsistencies are assumed to play a major role in stratification and life context, these two dimensions are operationalized by clustering observations on the basis of important variables.[3] For modeling the interplay of the different independent levels of our model, regression analysis as well as hierarchical log-linear models are used. The final test of effects on leisure involves multiple regression analysis as well as multiple classification analysis (MCA).[4] For reasons of space we have to confine our discussion of the *operationalization* process to some general remarks, however (for more details see Lamprecht and Stamm, 1994: ch.10-13).

Structure of inequality/social position. A first step in the operationalization of the structure of inequality involved the estimation of a path-model of the Blau-Duncan type (see Blau and Duncan, 1967, Müller, 1972, Bornschier, 1986) to see whether conventional approaches to stratification research still made sense for our segment of the working population. The path-model was restricted to fully employed people aged more than 24 years old and included the following six variables: Father's and mother's formal education, respondent's formal education, occupational prestige[5], income and formal authority[6]. In addition, the model included the two "new" inequalities age and gender as control variables. As could be expected, for the core segment of the working population, conventional approaches still are very powerful. All variables showed highly significant effects and 72.0% of variance in income was explained by the model.

Formal education (20.2%), occupational prestige (26.5%) and formal authority (38.5%) did worse but explained variance was still comparatively high (see also Lamprecht and Graf, 1991). Yet, even in the quite homogenous group under study, the linkage of different status positions is far from perfect thus indicating the occurence of status inconsistencies. In addition, the analysis also shows substantial effects of the "new" inequalities age and gender.

To get a more precise picture of the stratification structure and to see whether status inconsistency indeed occurs in a "regular" fashion, the linear assumptions behind the regression model were loosened in a further step. A cluster analysis involving the four variables formal education, occupational position, income and formal authority at the workplace was calculated. A stable solution explaining 81.0% of variance was achieved if the sample was divided into eight different clusters.

This solution, graphically represented as patterns of cluster means in Figure 2, indicates that status inconsistency indeed plays a major role in contemporary stratification: as could be expected on the basis of the results of the path analysis the linkages between occupation and income are frequently equilibrated (i.e. horizontal), but deviations from such linkages frequently occur with respect to education and formal authority. Without going into details, the eight clusters could be classified into five groups: one consistent "upper class" cluster encompassing 19.8% of the sample (cluster 6), a "class of experts" (cluster 8, 14.5%) characterized by low values on formal authority, a cluster of "loosers" (cluster 1, 9.0%) characterized by consistently low values except on the educational dimension, a consistent "lower class" cluster (cluster 7, 17.6%) and four, at times inconsistent groups in the middle range of the stratification continuum (clusters 2-5, 39.2%).

An additional analysis examining the internal composition of the clusters once more showed that new inequalities play a significant role in contemporary stratification: People from foreign countries, women and younger respondents were primarily found in the lower or loosing configurations. Against this background it makes sense to include these new inequalities in the further analyses as more than mere control variables.

Interaction context: The available data only render possible the modelling of two interaction contexts, namely work situation and general housing and life situation. With respect to *work situation,* ten variables including various assessments of the work context were available.[7] In order to reduce the number of variables, two alternative operationalizations were used. On the one hand, a simple additive index was constructed by adding positive and negative assessments of the work situation. On the other hand, a principle components analysis explaining 56.2% of variance was carried out which revealed three distinctive components of the work context. A first dimension refered to *autonomous control and decision-making possibilities,* a second one to the *use of general and social competence* and a third one to *stress.*

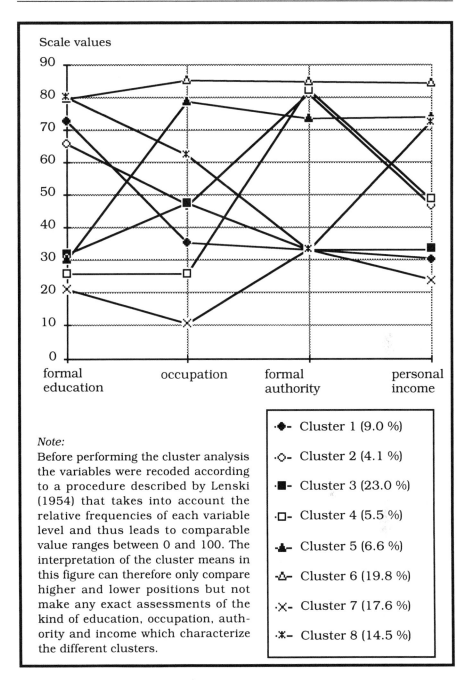

Figure 2: **Graphical representation of the structure of social positions as found on the basis of a cluster analysis (8 cluster means, n=1007)**

Housing conditions and general life situation involve several dimensions. After prior evaluation and to keep the operationalization simple, we have selected the following five variables which *roughly* describe life situation, wealth and housing conditions: marital status, housing space per person (rooms per person), availability of durable consumer goods[8], ownership of appartment/house[9], and household income. These variables were submitted to a cluster analysis and revealed a pattern of eight clusters explaining 64% of variance. Even though the emerging pattern cannot be discussed here, it is very plausible in the sense that people owning their appartments are usually married and doing somewhat better on the dimensions of material wealth (housing space, consumer goods, household income) than the unmarried and those renting appartments. Once again, it was found that age matters quite a lot in the sense that older people whose children have already moved out and young people without children or still living at home, are doing best.

Subjective attitudes. As stated above, the dimension of subjective attitudes has only marginally been adressed in the questionaire. With respect to *work attitudes,* however, eleven items which give a rough indication of respondents' orientation towards work have been included.[10] Once again, the variables were used to construct a simple additive index taking into account positive and negative attitudes. In addition, a principal components analysis explaining 55.4% of variance was performed, which revealed four dimensions describing work (1) as a *necessary evil,* (2) as *fundamental to life,* (3) as a *strenuous experience* and (4) as a *positive activity.* It should be noted, however, that this operationalization of subjective attitudes is very crude and does not reflect general patterns of perception as described by Bourdieu's *habitus* concept.

Our independent variable *leisure activity* also had to be "treated" beforehand. Respondents had given frequencies of involvement in 28 different activities. As can be seen from Table 1, most of leisure is passed in a regenerative or consumptive way (television, reading etc.) at home. Yet, activities such as sports, social contacts and going out also are very popular. Finally, cultural or sports events are only attended in an irregular fashion. This finding is not due to a lack of interest on the part of the respondents but rather reflects financial constraints and an inadequate supply. In fact, the mentioned activities are among the most popular if people are asked, what they would like to do more frequently.

To reduce the number of variables for the subsequent analyses, leisure activities were subjected to a principal components analysis extracting seven components of similar activities (see the last column Table 1) which compare very well to other such attempts (Giegler, 1982; Meier-Dallach *et al.*, 1991). The first principal component summarizes various sociable and entertaining activities such as eating out, meeting friends and going to the movies. Accordingly, it has been termed *sociability and entertainment.* A second factor is mostly made up by *sport,* club activities and taking part in local parties and festivals. The third component, *high culture,* includes

Table 1 Frequencies of 28 different leisure activities (percentages)

Leisure activity	at least once a week	at least once a year	very rarely	Main PC Load-ing*
Reading newspapers and journals	95.4	2.4	2.3	PC5
Watching television	85.5	4.1	10.4	PC5
Listening to radio	81.8	6.4	11.8	PC5
Being together with one's family	81.1	9.8	9.2	PC6
Relaxation, resting	75.1	11.2	13.7	PC5
Sports, fitness, physical activities	61.4	21.9	16.7	PC2
Making repairs, tidying up	53.8	34.8	11.4	PC4
Arts and crafts at home	46.8	25.8	27.4	PC4
Reading books	46.8	25.5	27.7	PC3
Social contacts outside of home	43.5	49.8	6.7	PC1
Social contacts at home	37.5	48.8	13.7	PC1
Gardening and yard care	36.6	13.2	50.1	PC4
Outdoor activities (hiking)	35.6	56.1	8.3	PC6
Club and organized group activities	34.7	27.0	38.3	PC2
Going out	31.7	43.9	24.4	PC1
Animal care	30.0	4.9	65.1	PC7**
Adult education	23.9	42.9	33.2	PC3
Eating out	19.7	64.1	16.2	PC1
Playing games at home	14.2	29.6	56.3	PC5
Cultural activities (choirs, orchestras, theatre)	9.1	4.0	86.9	***
Spectating big sports events	5.4	33.6	61.0	PC2
Excursions	5.3	81.8	12.9	PC6
Hobby courses (arts, crafts, cooking etc.)	2.5	9.1	88.4	PC4
Contemporary musical events and dancing	2.3	38.5	59.2	PC1
Cinema	1.2	45.1	53.7	PC1
Political action	0.7	17.2	82.1	PC7
Events of classical culture (opera, concerts, theatre)	0.6	50.4	49.0	PC3
Attending local parties and festivals	0.3	47.7	52.0	PC2

Note: Number of cases in the range between 1004 and 1091 for different activities

* "Main PC loading" refers to the principal component on which the respective variable loads strongest; Numbers in the last column refer to the following principal components of leisure activity: Leisure activities (principal components): PC1: Sociability and entertainment, PC2: Sport, PC3: High culture, PC4: Do-It-Yourself, PC5: Media and Regeneration, PC6: Nature, PC7: Politics. **Strong negative loading; *** Excluded from principal components analysis for statistical reasons.

reading books, spectating operas and theatres as well as educational activities, whereas a somewhat opposing, fourth factor includes *do-it-yourself* activities at home (arts and crafts, gardening etc.). *Media consumption and regeneration* are making up a dimension of their own, as do family outings and *excursions*. Finally, there is a residual factor characterized by *political activities* and a strong negative loading of animal care.

4.   Leisure and social context: some results

Before analyzing the effects on leisure activity, several tests have been performed to examine whether the independent levels of our model are in fact related as suggested in section 2. In Table 2, the results of a summarizing hierarchical log-linear analysis involving the four previously constructed indicators of social position, life situation, work situation and work attitudes are presented. In addition, age and gender were included in the analysis as independent measures of "new" inequalities.[11] Nationality and geographical origin have been omitted as these dimensions do not affect social position, life and work situation in a substantial way. The upper half of Table 2 shows that a simple model (model 2), involving only the main effects already explains 83% more than the independence model

Table 2   Hierarchical log linear models relating the independent model variables (tests of fit and effect)

	LR-Chi^2	df	p	Eta^2
Models				
1. Independence model	625.4	88	.00	.00
2. Model involving main effects two-way effects)	107.1	68	.00	.83
3. Model involving all three-way effects	37.8	38	.48	.94
4. Model involving main and important three-way effects	67.6	67	.46	.89
Effects in model 4				
{Social position/Life situation/Gender}	17.4	2	.00	—
{Social position/Life situation/Age}	13.5	2	.00	—
{Social position/Work situation /Age}	5.4	1	.02	—
{Social position/Gender/Age}	6.3	1	.01	—
{Work situation/Work attitudes}	66.3	1	.00	—
{Work situation/Gender}	3.9	1	.05	—
{Life situation/Work attitudes}	14.8	2	.00	—

Note: n = 742; LR-Chi^2: Likelihood-Chi^2; Eta^2: "explained variance" in comparison to independence model.

(Knoke and Burke, 1980). If important three-way effects are also included (see model 4), Eta2 rises to .89 thus providing a very good fit. The structure of effects in model 4 is presented in the lower half of Table 2 and indicates that the levels of our model are related in the expected way. Age, gender, social position, life and work situation are closely related, even though the latter two are not connected. Thus, social position and "new" inequalities bind previously unrelated interaction contexts together. Work attitudes, on their part, are related to interaction contexts, but not to the overarching inequality structure. This finding at first sight seems to contradict our model that also expected a connection between social position and work attitudes. Yet, as already mentioned, work attitudes are only a crude approximation of Bourdieu's habitus concept which refers to general views and dispositions rather than to mere work attitudes which could be expected to be influenced primarily by daily work and general life experiences.

Against this background, effects on leisure activities were tested. As mentioned above, the analysis would become very hard to follow if all of our 28 leisure activities were to be related to our independent variables. For that reason, the statistical test was restricted to the seven general principal components of leisure activity constructed in section 3. For two reasons, such a strategy is somewhat problematic: on the one hand, principal components are artificial variables mixing various dimensions which reflect "real life" only to a limited degree. Therefore, results should be interpreted with some caution. On the other hand, performing a principal components analysis (or similar dimension reducing techniques) always involves a loss of information. Consequently, it should be kept in mind that estimates based on principal components may be weaker than if the original variables had been used.

In a first step, only bivariate correlations between leisure components and independent variables were calculated (see Table 3 overleaf). The independent variables included some of the original variables of the questionnaire as well as our summarizing measures of the different levels of the theoretical model which have, in some instances, been converted into simple aggregate indices to further simplify the analysis.[12] As can be seen from Table 3, the effects of the aggregate indices summarize the confusing overall pattern quite nicely. Even though correlations are generally weak, old and new inequalities as well as general life situation are more closely related to leisure preferences than are work situation and work attitudes. Thus, stratification and particularly "new" inequalities appear to play a more important role in leisure choice than work-related dimensions. In addition, the effect of social inequality on leisure only seems to be partially mediated by the intervening levels of our model.

To sum up, the findings suggest that social stratification still matters in the explanation of leisure choice. Work-related approaches, on the other hand, only appear to be of limited relevance. This finding suggests a neutral relationship between work and leisure that is even more striking if one keeps in mind, that the analysis only involved working people for which it

Table 3   **Summary of bivariate relationships between leisure activity and the independent model variable**

	PC 1	PC 2	PC 3	PC 4	PC 5	PC 6	PC 7
Social position:							
Formal education	-.08		.23	-.12	-.08		.20
Occupation	-.25	-.11.	.09			.11	.19
Formal authority	-.16					.09	.19
Personal income	-.32	-.09				.10	.21
Aggr. index of social position*	-.24		.20			.09	.23
Gender	-.20	.14	-.21	-.19		.07	.24
Age	-.54	-.17		.17		.17	.20
Nationality		-.10					-.08
Life and housing situation							
Marital status	-.51	-.12	-.08	.17	.08	.23	.15
No. of children	.44	.08	-.14	.15		.18	.18
No. of persons in household	-.21	.13	-.09			.11	
Household income			.18				.07
Living space	.10		.11	.08			.08
Ownership of house/appartment	-.28	.09		.28			.16
Ownership of consumer goods	-.11			.09		.10	.07
Aggr. index of life situation*	-.39			.23		.15	.14
Work situation:							
No. of work hours				-.20			.11
Autonomous control and decisions**	-.10						.10
General and social competence**		.09					
Stress**						.07	.11
Aggr. index of work situation***				.09			.09
Work attitudes:							
Work satisfaction							
Work as a necessary evil**	.18		-.17				-.11
Work as fundamental to life**	-.11					.11	.18
Work as a strenuous experience**		-.08					
Work as a positive experince**	.12						-.10
Aggr. index of work attitudes***	-.13		.13	.09			.13

Note: n between 825 and 1085; only coefficients significant at the 99%-level are shown; * Results of cluster analysis, ordinal scale according to the mean of average values; ** Principal component values; *** Additive index; PC1 to PC7: Leisure activities (principal components): PC1: Sociability and entertainment, PC2: Sport, PC3: High culture, PC4: Do-It-Yourself, PC5: Media and Regeneration, PC6: Nature, PC7: Politics.

was plausible to assume such effects.

To test whether our assumption concerning the effect of social strati-fication and new inequalities also holds if the effects of the other levels are controlled simultaneously, separate multiple regression models for each dimension of leisure activity were estimated. As independent variables, the four aggregate indices of social position, life and work situation, and work attitudes as well as age and gender were included into the models.

Figure 3 graphically summarizes the main findings from our seven regression analyses which confirm our expectations.

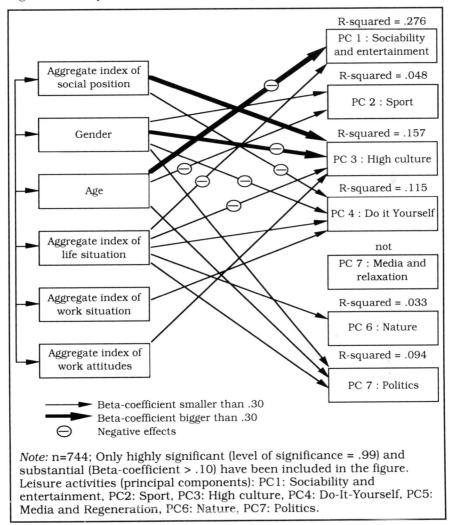

Note: n=744; Only highly significant (level of significance = .99) and substantial (Beta-coefficient > .10) have been included in the figure. Leisure activities (principal components): PC1: Sociability and entertainment, PC2: Sport, PC3: High culture, PC4: Do-It-Yourself, PC5: Media and Regeneration, PC6: Nature, PC7: Politics.

Figure 3:   Summary of relationships between social position, life and work situation and leisure activities (regression estimates)

Position in social stratification, "new" inequalities and general life situation are better predictors of leisure activities than work situation and work attitues. The latter two dimensions only show one significant effect each: A good work situation positively influences creative pasttimes whereas positive work attitudes induce higher levels of involvement in "high culture". Consequently, there is some support for the generalization hypothesis mentioned in section 1, but neutrality still seems to describe the linkage of work and leisure best.

Figure 3 also shows that there is no simple causal structure. Some activities are more dependent upon age and life situation (as, for example, sociability and politics) whereas the impact of social position and gender is strongest with regard to participation in events of high culture. Thus, leisure choice does not follow a simple explanatory pattern but is linked in a complicated way to various dimensions of one's social background.

It should be noted, however, that our models only explain relatively small proportions of variance. On the basis of one's age and life situation, somewhat more than a quarter of variance of the component "sociability and entertainment" can be explained, whereas there are no significant effects for "media and relaxation". The results for "sports" and "nature" are also very weak. With regard to sport, only the well known age and gender effects seem to matter, whereas people in a favorable life situation are more prone to leave their home for "excursions". The remaining two dimensions of leisure have the most complex explanatory patterns: Apart from the already mentioned effects of work attitudes and work situation, social position, gender and general life situation all affect involvement in "high culture" (R^2=.16) and in "do-it-yourself" activites (R^2=.12).

There are four interrelated explanations for the comparatively low degree of explanation of variance. *First*, the use of principal components instead of original variables may have resulted in a "blurring" of effects. Still, even though a test involving the original variables indeed leads to better results in some instances, explained variance generally remains low. A *second* explanation aims at the linear assumption behind the regression model. It is possible that some of the effects are not strictly linear: there might, for example, be a curvilinear relationship between social position and the use of media in the sense that the lower classes experience constraints that force them to spend more time with low cost leisure pursuits, whereas the higher classes have a high use of the media for information purposes. In order to examine this assumption, the linear assumption was relaxed in a further test involving multiple classification analysis. The test revealed a substantial increase in the proportion of explained variance showing various non-linear relationships.[13]

A *third*, and very straightforward explanation for the weak findings refers to the characteristics of modern leisure. In some instances there is just not much variance to be explained: The use of mass media for entertainment purposes, for example, is generally popular and therefore differences are only gradual. Thus, the results also reflect a certain degree of homogeneity in leisure pursuits already demonstrated by other studies (Lüdtke, 1984). *Finally,* our results suggest that leisure indeed involves a high degree of freedom of choice and is not fully determined by one's social status or work experience. Against this background, there is an alternative, more positive assessment of our findings: they show that leisure choice is *not* independent of social background as has been suggested by the advocates of the leisure society. Even though leisure is not fully determined by structural variables, we are still far from a true leisure society where there are no longer systematic linkages between decision-making and social context.

Concluding remarks

The present study has attempted to show that the lack of empirical evidence regarding the relationship between leisure activity and social status is only partly due to a de-structuration of society or the increasing independence of leisure from "normal life". Rather, recent research has been characterized by the use of out of date theories as well as problems of empirical measurement. For that reason, we have suggested a multi-level explanatory model based on the recent discussion of changes in stratification patterns and life-styles that integrates and systematically links various dimensions of socio-economic position, life and work situation.

Our results show, on the one hand, that stratification still plays a significant role in determining life chances. On the other hand, however, the relationship between leisure pursuits and social background cannot adequately be described in terms of conventional stratification research or work-centered approaches. With regard to the latter, our study indicates that work situation and work attitudes no longer play an important role in determining the choice of leisure activities. "New" inequalities, status inconsistencies and the partly independent dimension of one's general life situation have a more substantial effect on life-style and leisure choice.

Overall, however, the relationships are relatively weak, thus suggesting a high degree of freedom in the choice of general leisure activities. As is the case in other reaches of modern life, leisure is not fully determined by social background variables. Yet, there is evidence that leisure remains closely linked to the overarching social order. Leisure choice is not only affected by one's social position or work experience but it is embedded in different spheres of life. Further research has to consider the interplay of these additional dimensions of social structure in order to achieve better explanations of leisure's role in contemporary society. In addition, the internal differentiation of leisure activities has to be addressed: there may only be small social differences with regard to eating out, watching tv or playing sports, yet within these general activities there may well be specific patterns that have closer ties to social background than can be found at the general level.

Notes

[1] An earlier version of this paper was presented at a meeting of ISA's RC 28 on "Dynamics of Social Stratification: Macro and Micro Approaches", Zurich, May 25-27, 1995.
Send mail to: H.P. Stamm, Sociological Institute, University of Zürich, Rämistrasse 69, CH-8001 Zürich /
e-mail: hpstamm@soziologie.unizh.ch

[2] The general level of development. As our study of the working population in a mid-size Swiss town neither involves a dynamic analysis nor a cross-cultural comparison, the level of development can be taken as a constant.

[3] An iterated version of MacQueen's k-means algorithm (Hartigan, 1975) was used in the calculations. The cluster analysis was calculated for various numbers of clusters and the solutions compared with respect to stability, homogenity and comparative optimality.

[4] MCA is a special kind of analysis of variance which estimates effects similar to those in regression but does not rely on linear assumptions. MCA is thus useful to detect non-linear relationships (Andrews et al., 1971).

[5] The questionaire only recorded a number of broad occupational categories. Average prestige score were assigned to the different levels of the variable on the basis of Treiman's (1977) tables.

[6] According to Bornschier's (1984) suggestions, the number of subordinates was transformed into number of hierarchic levels.

[7] Approval of the following statements was measured with a four-point scale (assignement to the principal components of work situation in brackets): "I am under constant control" (1, negative loading); "I can organize and plan my work by myself" (1); "I can make decisions on my own" (1); "I can introduce my own ideas" (1); "My work is clearly structured" (1, negative loading); "I work closely with other people" (2); "In my work I can improve myself" (2); "I can use my knowledge and capabilities well" (2); "I am under pressure" (3); "It is difficult to substitute me by other persons" (3).

[8] The list included TV and VCR equipment, computers, cars, campers, musical instruments, gardens and week-end houses.

[9] In Switzerland, more than two thirds of the population live in rented flats or houses. Thus, the ownership dimension may be more important than, for example, in the United States.

[10] Approval to the following statements was measured with a four-point scale (assignement to the principal components of work orientation in brackets): "Money is the only reason I work" (1); "On Mondays I am already looking forward to Friday" (1); "My work is often dull" (1); "I

am missing my work during vacations" (2); "My job is my hobby" (2); "The meaning of my life is determined by my work" (2); "My work is very fullfilling" (2); "After work I feel tired and exhausted" (3); "Outside of work I have hardly any time to do other things" (3); "My colleagues are my friends" (4); "Good working conditions are more important than money" (4).

11   To keep the analyis simple, all variables except life situation were dichotomized to indicate "high" and "low" positions. Life situation has three levels: not married, married with medium standard, and married with high standard.

12   The aggregate indices of work situation and work attitudes are based on the simple additive indices described in section 3. The aggregate indices of social position and life situation where constructed by hierarchically ordering the clusters solutions according to the average variable values in each cluster. With respect to life situation, marital status was excluded from this calculation.

13   Values for explained variance in the MCA were as follows: Sociability and entertainment: .33; Sport: .10; High culture: .22; Do-It-Yourself: .19; Media and relaxation: .07; Nature: .08; Politics: .12.

References

Andrews, F., Morgan, J. and Sonquist J. (1971) *Multiple classification analysis: A report on a computer program for multiple regression using categorical predictors.* Ann Arbor, Michigan: Survey Research Center, Institute for Social Research, The University of Michigan.

Bamberg, E. (1991) 'Arbeit, Freizeit und Familie', in S. Greif, E. Bamberg and N. Semmer (eds) *Psychischer Stress am Arbeitsplatz.* Göttingen, Toronto, Zürich: Hogrefe, pp. 201-221.

Beck, U. (1983) 'Jenseits von Stand und Klasse? Soziale Ungleichheit, gesellschaftliche Individualisierungsprozesse und die Entstehung neuer sozialer Formationen und Identitäten', in R. Kreckel (ed) *Soziale Ungleichheiten.* Göttingen: Schwartz, pp. 35-74.

Beck, U. (1986) *Risikogesellschaft. Auf dem Weg in eine andere Moderne.* Frankfurt a. M.: Suhrkamp.

Berger, P. A. (1987) 'Klassen und Klassifikationen: Zur neuen Unübersichtlichkeit in der soziologischen Ungleichheitsdiskussion', *Kölner Zeitschrift für Soziologie und Sozialpsychologie,* Vol. 39: pp. 59-85.

Blau, P. M. and Duncan, O. D. (1967) *The american occupational structure.* New York: John Wiley.

Bornschier, V. (1984) 'Zur sozialen Schichtung in der Schweiz', *Schweizerische Zeitschrift für Soziologie,* Vol. 10, No. 3: pp. 647-688.

——— (1986) 'Social stratification in six western societies: the general pattern and some differences', *Social Science Information,* Vol. 25, No. 4: pp. 797-824.

——— (1991) 'Soziale Schichtung im keynesianischen Gesellschaftsmodell', in V. Bornschier (ed) *Das Ende der sozialen Schichtung? Zürcher Arbeiten zur gesellschaftlichen Konstruktion von sozialer Lage und Bewusstsein in der westlichen Zentrumsgesellschaft.* Zürich: Seismo, pp. 37-72.

Bourdieu, P. (1987) *Die feinen Unterschiede: Kritik der gesellschaftlichen Urteilskraft.* Frankfurt a. M.: Suhrkamp.

Brook, J. A. (1993) 'Leisure meanings and comparisons with work', *Leisure Studies,* Vol. 12: pp. 149-162.

Buchmann, M. (1991) 'Soziale Schichtung im Wandel. Zur Differenzierung der Struktur sozialer Ungleichheit', in V. Bornschier (ed): *Das Ende der sozialen Schichtung? Zürcher Arbeiten zur gesellschaftlichen Konstruktion von sozialer Lage und Bewusstsein in der westlichen Zentrumsgesellschaft.* Zürich: Seismo, pp. 215-231.

Giegler, H. (1982) *Dimensionen und Determinanten der Freizeit: Eine Bestandesaufnahme der sozialwissenschaftichen Freizeitforschung.* Opladen: Westdeutscher Verlag.

Hartigan, J. A. (1975) *Clustering algorithms.* New York: John Wiley.

Hecker, K. and Grunwald, W. (1981) 'Über die Beziehung zwischen Arbeits- und Freizeitzufriedenheit', *Soziale Welt,* Vol. 32, No. 3: pp. 353-368.

Hoff, E.-H. (1986) *Arbeit, Freizeit und Persönlichkeit: Wissenschaftliche und alltägliche Vorstellungsmuster.* Bern, Stuttgart, Toronto: Huber.

Hoff, E.-H., Lempert, W. and Lappe, L. (1991) *Persönlichkeitsentwicklung in Facharbeiterbiographien.* Bern, Stuttgart, Toronto: Huber.

Hörning, K. H. and Michailow, M. (1990) 'Lebensstil als Vergesellschaftungsform: Zum Wandel von Sozialstuktur und sozialer Integration', in P. A. Berger and S. Hradil (eds): *Lebenslagen, Lebensläufe, Lebensstile.* Göttingen: Schwartz, pp. 501-522.

Hradil, S. (1987a) *Sozialstrukturanalyse in einer fortgeschrittenen Gesellschaft — Von Klassen und Schichten zu Lagen und Milieus.* Opladen: Leske und Budrich.

——— (1987b) 'Die "neuen sozialen Ungleichheiten" — und wie man mit ihnen (nicht) theoretisch zurechtkommt', in B. Giesen and H. Haferkamp (eds) *Soziologie der sozialen Ungleichheit.* Opladen: Westdeutscher Verlag, pp. 115-144.

——— (ed) (1992) *Zwischen Bewusstsein und Sein: Die Vermittlung "objektiver" Lebensbedingungen und "subjektiver" Lebensweisen.* Opladen: Leske + Budrich.

Kelly, J. R. (1983) *Leisure identities and interactions*. London: George Allen & Unwin.

Kohn, M. L. and Schooler, C. (1983) *Work and personality: An inquiry into the impact of social stratification*. Norwood, N.J.: Ablex.

Knoke, D. and Burke, P.J. (1980) *Log-linear models*. Beverly Hills: Sage.

Kreckel, R. (1987) 'Neue Ungleicheiten und alte Deutungsmuster. Über die Kritikresistenz des vertikalen Gesellschaftsmodells in der Soziologie', in B. Giesen and H. Haferkamp (eds): *Soziologie der sozialen Ungleichheit*. Opladen: Westdeutscher Verlag, pp. 93-114.

—— (1992) *Politische Soziologie der sozialen Ungleichheit.*. Frankfurt a. M., New York: Campus.

Lalive d'Epinay, C., Bassand, M., Christe, E. and Gros, D. (1982) *Temps libre. Culture de masse et cultures de classe aujourd'hui*. Lausanne: Favre.

Lamprecht, M. and Graf, M. (1991) 'Statuszuweisung in den siebziger und achtziger Jahren', in V. Bornschier (ed) *Das Ende der sozialen Schichtung? Zürcher Arbeiten zur gesellschaftlichen Konstruktion von sozialer Lage und Bewusstsein in der westlichen Zentrumsgesellschaft*. Zürich: Seismo, pp. 189-214.

Lamprecht, M. and Stamm, H. (1994) *Die soziale Ordnung der Freizeit*. Zürich: Seismo.

Landecker, W. S. (1981) *Class crystallization*. New Brunswick: Rutgers University Press.

Lenski, G. (1954) 'Status crystallization: A non-vertical dimension of social status', *American Sociological Review*, Vol. 19: pp. 405-413.

Lüdtke, H. (1985) 'Gleichförmigkeiten im alltäglichen Freizeitverhalten: eine Analyse von Zeitbudget-Daten aus zwei norddeutschen Grossstädten', *Zeitschrift für Soziologie*, Vol. 13, No. 4: pp.346-362.

—— (1989) *Expressive Ungleichheit: Zur Soziologie der Lebensstile*. Opladen: Leske and Budrich.

Meier-Dallach, H., Gloor, D., Hohermuth, S. and Nef, R. (1991) *Die Kulturlawine. Daten, Bilder, Deutungen*. Chur, Zürich: Rüegger.

Müller, H. (1992) *Sozialstruktur und Lebensstile: Der neuere theoretische Diskurs über soziale Ungleichheit*. Frankfurt a. M.: Suhrkamp.

Müller, W. (1972) 'Bildung und Mobilitätsprozess — Eine Anwendung der Pfadanalyse', *Zeitschrift für Soziologie*, Vol. 1, No. 1: pp. 65-84.

Nave-Herz, R. and Nauck, B. (1978) *Familie und Freizeit. Eine empirische Studie*. München: Juventa.

Parker, S. R. (1983) *Leisure and work*. London: Allen & Unwin.

Prahl, H.-W. (1977) *Freizeitsoziologie: Entwicklungen, Konzepte, Perspektiven.* München: Kösel.

Roberts, K., Lamb, K. L., Dench, S. and Brodie, D. A. (1989) 'Leisure patterns, health status and employment status', *Leisure Studies*, Vol. 8: No. 2: pp. 229-235.

Ruschetti, P. and Stamm, H. (1991) 'Muster der Statusverknüpfung in sechs westlichen Ländern', in V. Bornschier (ed) *Das Ende der sozialen Schichtung?*. Zürich: Seismo, pp. 99-125.

Scheuch, E. K. and Scherhorn, G. (1977) *Freizeit, Konsum.* Stuttgart: Enke.

Stockdale, J. E. (1987) *Methodological techinques in leisure research.* London: Sports Council and Economic & Social Research.

Treiman, D. J. (1977) *Occupational prestige in comparative perspective.* New York: Academic Press.

Warde, Alan (1995) 'Cultural change and class differentiation: Distinction and taste in the british middle classes 1968-88', in K. Roberts (ed) *Leisure and social stratification.* LSA Publication No. 53. Eastbourne: LSA, pp. 27-47.

Wilson, J. (1980) 'Sociology of leisure'. *Annual Review of Sociology*, Vol. 6: pp. 21-40.

Wippler, R. (1973) 'Freizeitverhalten: ein multivariater Ansatz', in R. Schmitz-Scherzer (ed): *Freizeit.* Frankfurt a. M.: Akademische Verlagsanstalt, pp. 91-107.

Zuzanek, J., and Mannell, R. C. (1983) 'Work-leisure-relationships from a sociological and social psychological perspective'. *Leisure Studies,* Vol. 2, No. 3: pp. 327-344.

Leisure, Sport and Active Citizenship

Neil Ravenscroft
University of Reading

Introduction

In the years since Mrs. Thatcher's first general election victory in 1979 Britain has experienced what amounts to a cultural and economic revolution. This has involved the replacement of the social democracy of the post-World War II years with a new bourgeois liberalism based on the primacy of markets and with a concomitant shift in emphasis from welfare rights to consumer rights (Bramham *et al.*, 1993). This has been accompanied by the restructuring of government intervention in the economy, particularly in terms of welfare, where there has been a shift from direct provision towards more of an 'enabling' role (Henry, 1993).

Within this 'revolution', the construction of leisure has been a significant element. This has been particularly so in its complex relationship with work, where it has become a major source of employment as well as a primary incentive to seek and retain employment (Ravenscroft, 1993). Also important has been the changing socio-political signification of leisure (see Baudrillard, 1981, Clarke and Critcher, 1985, and Rojek, 1985). While the significance of the work/leisure dualism is a predictable concern of a post-industrialising society, the recent emphasis on '
' perhaps implies a more complex shift than is first apparent. An important element of body culture has undoubtedly been a renewed interest in, and emphasis on, 'active living', both in terms of its semiotic affirmation of the new economic and political imperative, as well its more general input to the welfare of an increasingly ageing Western population. The persistence and longevity of leisure-related welfare concerns are well documented (see, for example Coalter, 1990; Glyptis, 1989). Their emphasis on ameliorating urban deprivation, promoting physical and mental health and developing social integration has led Clarke to comment that:

> The driving motivation in nearly all the policies has been to move people into active leisure lives. The feeling is that the general principle of the argument about the benefits of leisure has been accepted but that participation is lagging behind the received wisdom about its benefits. (Clarke, 1995: p. 223)

This concern is brought to the fore by the findings of the Allied Dunbar national fitness survey (Activity and Health Research, 1992) which found that notwithstanding significant increases in active leisure participation over the last 30 years, very few Britons currently attain activity levels appropriate to improving, or even maintaining, their physical fitness. While publicity campaigns and general practitioner-related referrals can have some impact on participation levels, there is growing support for the view that the primary determinants of participation are the habits formed during school age years (Sports Council, 1988). As Houlihan states:

> The school years are an obviously important period in introducing children to the enjoyment and satisfaction to be gained from active participation in sport. In addition ... the profits of many leisure centres ... rest on the steady flow of enthusiastic older pupils and school leavers. (Houlihan, 1992: p. 59)

Notwithstanding the use of the term 'profits' to describe sports centre income, it is clear that the provision of public leisure facilities plays a pivotal function, for regardless of the attitudes and habits bred at school, a lack of appropriately managed facilities will certainly hinder future participation. While some facilities will be, and already are, supplied by the private sector, the majority of the burden of provision has fallen and, for the foreseeable future must continue to fall, on the public sector. Yet the very future of direct public sector leisure provision is now in doubt.

At a time when there has never been clearer evidence of both the welfare benefits of active leisure and the most appropriate types and levels of activity, therefore, the restructuring of the Welfare State threatens crucially to undermine the very future of public leisure facilities. Perhaps even more critically, this restructuring has already affected the nature of the public interest in access to leisure activities. This has been principally through its emphasis on the market, rather than any construction of social rights, as the principal forum for determining resource allocation, thus posing critical questions about the (re)construction of the notion of citizenship and its attendant rights and liabilities.

This paper therefore seeks to examine the legacy of Thatcherism with respect to leisure provision. In so doing, the paper will review the principal elements of the economic and social restructuring in Britain, considering in particular, the ways in which 'active' citizenship has been reconstructed. The paper will conclude with an analysis of the significance of the changing construction of leisure for the future of the citizen project in Britain.

Sport, leisure and the restructuring of the Welfare State

Founded unequivocally on the basis of equity and social welfare, the Welfare State was developed to rectify perceived market imperfections rather than to compete with existing private suppliers. As such, its major orientation has traditionally been towards service provision, with scant attention paid to quantifying or justifying its services in terms other than those upon which they are provided. As such, it has conformed to a broadly liberal construct of citizenship, characterised by the passive receipt of rights and the general protection of the law (Mouffe, 1993 and Twine, 1994).

Although public sector sports and leisure provision has never formally been part of the Welfare State, urban sports provision, in particular, became thought of as such during the 1960s and 1970s (Henry and Bramham, 1993). But rather than justification through legal mandate, the continuation of public leisure provision has been based largely upon vague and discretionary powers granted to local authorities by central government (see Department of the Environment Local Government Review, 1992). Although apparently an easy target for budget reduction, therefore, it has become apparent that this has ultimately applied less to leisure than to some areas of the Welfare State proper (Bramham and Henry, 1985).

At its most basic level the restructuring of the Welfare State focused on the way in which the political community was conceptualised, particularly in questioning the underlying paradigm of liberal passivity. As far as public leisure provision or, indeed, any element of the Welfare State, was concerned, the critique centred on the extent to which their existence could be justified on service grounds alone. By effectively calling into question the efficacy of the neo-classical construct of externalities, the government was able to assert that the provision of opportunities for enjoyment was essentially a matter for the market (Ravenscroft, 1993).

Through this process of replacing local democracy with the market imperative the early Thatcher government was therefore less concerned with dismantling welfare provision than it was with restructuring it away from its roots in social democracy towards a new model of authoritarian populism, with the dual promotion of social order and self reliance (Henry, 1993).

The full agenda of the New Right, as the apotheosis of Thatcherism, emerged in the mid-1980s. It featured a strong emphasis on the sale of erstwhile public assets, including some sports grounds and school playing fields (Spink, 1994), together with the imposition of competition and 'internal' markets on those services remaining in the public domain. Central to this project have been the Compulsory Competitive Tendering (CCT) of public services such as leisure provision and, following Mrs. Thatcher's demise as leader of the Conservative Party in 1991, the reorientation and restructuring of leisure policy around the formation of the Department of National Heritage.

I have argued elsewhere (Ravenscroft, 1996) that, whatever else CCT is about, it has certainly involved an attempt to 'depoliticise' public sector resource allocation and facility management. At its extreme this may lead to elected councillors assuming the role of 'business people' rather than politicians, administering their control through contract rather than the bureaucratic process. By so doing, this 'commercialisation' of the public sector has effectively institutionalised the discretionary dysfunction of bureaucracy by replacing it with a form of regulated autonomy, limited to areas in which contracts can be monitored and controlled. While presenting problems enough for relatively straightforward areas of service such as refuse collection and park maintenance, the position for sport and leisure management has proved quite insurmountable, largely due to the lack of standard comparative performance data (Bovaird, 1992).

While these difficulties may have contributed to a poor initial response from the commercial sector to the opportunities to manage public contracts, it is increasingly clear that the main concerns of the New Right were less in attracting the private sector into the public domain as they were in commercialising the existing public sector management (Henry, 1993). To this extent the policy has proved successful, with evidence that many local authority managers have welcomed their increasing autonomy (Ravenscroft and Tolley, 1993) and suggestions that this new initiative empowers citizens in ways in which the old bureaucratic model never could (Clarke, 1995).

Empowerment has also been one of the cornerstones in the creation of the Department of National Heritage, with its mandate for translating the nation's "... increased leisure time, energy and money..." into an "improved quality of life" (Conservative Party, 1992: p. 44). With a portfolio drawn from five existing Departments of State, together with the creation of some new functions, the Department of National Heritage spans a sector ranging from the commercialism of the tourist industry to the preservation of built heritage. This has moved Henry (1993) to suggest that its development has been based on reconstructing 'one-nation' conservatism around the New Right strategy of commodification. Indeed, it is apparent that in selecting its title the government has attempted to link heritage with consumption, thereby attempting to shift the construction of heritage from that of the collective inheritance of all to that of a primary signifier of a new citizenship of consumerism (Ravenscroft, 1994).

The outward fostering of an image of the 'new' Britain as a wealthy, energetic, caring and empowered society therefore conceals overriding aims which are somewhat less prosaic. For rather than the supposed social empowerment of New Rightism, the aim has been to regenerate 'free' time, one of the cornerstones of liberal citizenship, away from its roots towards the ubiquitous market model of exchange. Leisure, sport and cultural opportunities are therefore in the vanguard of social transformation, in reconstructing notions of citizenship away from passive receipt towards more active involvement. Thus access to sport and leisure opportunities becomes a 'reward' for those who achieve financial success, just as denial becomes a 'penalty' for those who do not. Similarly, opportunities for access to sport and leisure act as an incentive to achieve success and, thereby, affirm the hegemony of bourgeois liberalism (Ravenscroft, 1993). While subsidised access can be viewed as a remaining vestige of social democracy, it has little part to play in this new version of active citizenship.

This, arguably, lies at the very heart of the debate about the impact of New Right policies. Data from the General Household Survey (GHS) indicate increasing rates of participation in active leisure (Gratton and Tice, 1994, and Stabler and Ravenscroft, 1994). There is, however, growing concern that these increases are neither spread evenly across the population, nor representative of the impact of recent policies on socially and financially disadvantaged groups, such as those targeted by the Sports Council (1988). This has particular implications for the continued promotion of sports activities to school leavers, especially at a time when paid employment for this sector is at a premium.

That the formerly politically-peripheral arena of leisure should be chosen as a central vehicle for this project is no coincidence for, as Clarke and Critcher (1985) suggest, leisure demonstrates clearly why capitalism works:

> The ability of consumer-orientated capitalism to deliver leisure goods is used as its political validation ... This ideological use of leisure equates the public interest with the pursuit of private gain by both seller and buyer. Leisure is the perfect model of the free play of market forces ... In such ways has the market become the major institution and ideology of leisure. Far from being the antithesis of freedom, it has been represented as its realisation. (p. 232)

Given this emphasis on markets as the rational medium of resource allocation, with concepts of freedom and control constrained by the discourse of consumer choice, it is tempting to conclude that the market itself has been appropriated by the New Right as a surrogate for public policy. If this is the case then former policy areas such as leisure virtually define, or at least assume, their own metanarratives of capitalism. However, while this may be part of the ultimate project, the emphasis on market allocation signifies not so much an end to notions of public policy being superordinate to individual choice as a redirection of the means by which public policy initiatives are implemented.

In the place of the broad concepts of welfarism implicit in the old Sport for All campaigns (see McIntosh and Charlton, 1985), therefore, is the concentratedly reductionist emphasis on participation and achievement evident in more recent policy statements (Department of Education and Science, 1991). This really marks the retreat from the notions of social expenditure evoked by the early Thatcherite concentration on self reliance and social control (see Henry and Bramham, 1993, and Monnington 1993). Rather than a policy vacuum, however, its place has been assumed by the concept of social investment (see Henry and Bramham, 1993). This has been in terms of both the unprecedented government financial support for events such as the Manchester Olympics bid (see Ravenscroft, 1994) and, increasingly, the emphasis placed on the relationship between active leisure, preventative health care and the post-modern identity of the nation; the citizen responsibility for 'investing' in Britain's future.

In both cases public policy seemingly remains evident. The support for the Olympics bid, for example, fits squarely within government initiatives to use leisure and tourism as the basis for social and economic regener-ation. Equally, in the latter case the Sports Council, in organising the first national fitness survey (Activity and Health Research, 1992), has contri-buted to active leisure and fitness becoming a legitimate social issue, to the extent at least of the General Practitioner referral scheme. However, unlike the case of the government promotion of social and economic regeneration which has always, in general, relied on a pluralistic partnership of public and private interests, the case of apparent pluralism in active leisure and health promotion is a new initiative.

That participation in active leisure pursuits has been rising since the end of World War II is without doubt, although it has been questioned to what extent this has been due to central government policy (McIntosh and Charlton, 1985). Rather, it has probably had as much to do with the pro-vision of opportunities for participation, as with promotion per se. In Britain this has fallen mostly to local government, implying that the public policy initiative has been more a local than a national concern, even if the benefits have had a wider impact. Recent analysis of participation in active leisure pursuits between 1977 and 1987 (Gratton and Tice, 1994) supports these assertions, making the point that not only did participation increased rapidly during that time, but the average age of participants also increased. Gratton and Tice (1994) suggest that this rise in age is associated with a 'sports literacy' factor which tends to keep already active people active for a longer period of their lives. While this may well be the case, a further contributory factor could be a relative decline in participants of school-leaving age. Not only would this contribute to the increasing average age of participants but, according to the sports literacy factor, could have impli-cations for participation in the longer term.

Analysis of the most recent information on participation, from the 1990 General Household Survey (Stabler and Ravenscroft, 1994), confirms that the trends are continuing, with increases in the national rates of participation, particularly for indoor sports. What remains far from clear, however, is the distribution of those increases, particularly with respect to national target groups such as school leavers. It is therefore difficult to determine from the national figures quite what effect CCT is having on the use of leisure facilities and, consequently, how well local authorities are able to manage their new leisure contracts to ensure that they achieve their intended results.

Public provision for sport and leisure: a case study

The venue for the case study is Reading, some 60 kms west of London. Historically, Reading's employment base has been manual, concentrated in the railway industry and biscuit making. Neither of these are now major employers, with a present-day concentration in service industries such as insurance and professional services. Many of the 100,000 residents commute daily to work in London. As a consequence, the population is socio-economically mixed, with a growing number of young managerial people replacing the traditional 'working class' families.

Labour-controlled Reading Borough Council retains a strong commitment to local service provision with a particular emphasis on leisure, which has become a central plank of political power in the town. The council's leisure service aims have therefore tended to concentrate on the Sport for All ideals of providing for physical and mental health and well-being, with a particular emphasis on certain target groups including school leavers. The leisure management contract was won by the DSO and is now subject to a proactive Arts and Leisure Policy.

From previous survey work it is clear that up to the time of CCT, Reading Borough Council had a good record in leisure provision, with participation rates in line with the national GHS data and a population satisfied with the level and type of provision on offer (Stabler and Ravenscroft, 1994). It is equally clear that increases in participation have continued post-CCT, with many of the town's participation rates now well ahead of the GHS figures. However, what is less clear is how effectively Reading Borough Council has been able to protect its wider social concerns, particularly relating to its target populations. Although the contractor has generally been performing well, a household survey concerning public leisure provision conducted some 18 months ago raised doubts (Stabler and Ravenscroft, 1994). In particular, it pointed to a continuing disparity in participation, with young middle class white males continuing to dominate usage of leisure facilities:

> On average, those on lower incomes, as signified by the manual socio-economic groups, accounted for just over one tenth of total participation although they constitute almost two fifths of the population. The elderly, defined as those over 55, were found to have participation rates of little more than 5%, although they form 25% of the town's population. Ethnic minorities ... had very low participation rates of only 1% to 2%, but make up 10% of the population. (Stabler and Ravenscroft, 1994: p. 118)

In order to substantiate these findings, some preliminary secondary analysis of public facility user surveys (NOP Social and Political, 1990-95) has recently been undertaken, with the results shown in Figures 1, 2 and 3.

The first survey took place at the end of 1990, with subsequent quarterly surveys now available up to the first quarter of 1995. As a time series it is, therefore, rather short, with the longest consistent period being the first quarters of the years 1991 to 1995, which form the basis of the analysis. For each of the quarters a total of approximately 1,000 users were interviewed at the main public leisure facilities in Reading.

The preliminary analysis has attempted to delineate trends in the relationship between participation and age. Figure 1(opposite), relating to all users, indicates that in general there is an increase in participation levels up to a peak at the 25-34 age group, followed by a steady decline with increasing age. It also indicates that the general shape of this curve has not altered over the five years of the survey, although the 1994 peak of participation for the 25-34 age group does stand out.

Of particular interest, however, are the participation rates for the 18-24 school-leaver age group. While around 23 per cent of this group in Reading claim to exercise regularly (Stabler and Ravenscroft, 1994), only about half do so in the public indoor facilities. Equally, while 18 to 24 year olds are a prime target group for the council, participation has not altered since the start of CCT, with the highest rate of participation being in year 1, March 1991.

In considering the gender differential, in Figures 2 and 3 (following pages), the semblance of a trend begins to emerge. For while participation rates in the 18-24 category have remained largely static for men, it is apparent that they may be declining for women. Indeed, while the participation rate for men in the 18-24 group reached it highest level in March 1995, for women 1994 and 1995 were the poorest years yet, with participation falling to just over ten per cent of the population.

Contrary to national trends to 1987, therefore, Reading appears to be witnessing the intensification of participation around the 25-34 age range, to the detriment certainly of school-leavers, along with older people in general. Indeed, of its primary target populations, only women seem to have benefited from CCT; and these beneficiaries are limited to the group of those already active prior to CCT.

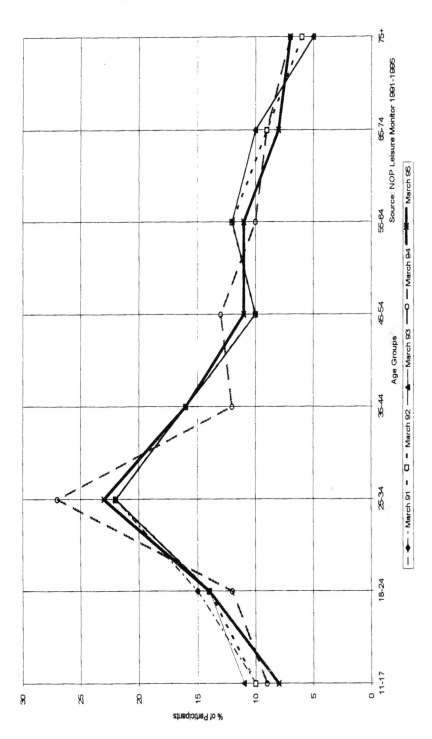

Figure 1   Participation at Public Leisure Facilities

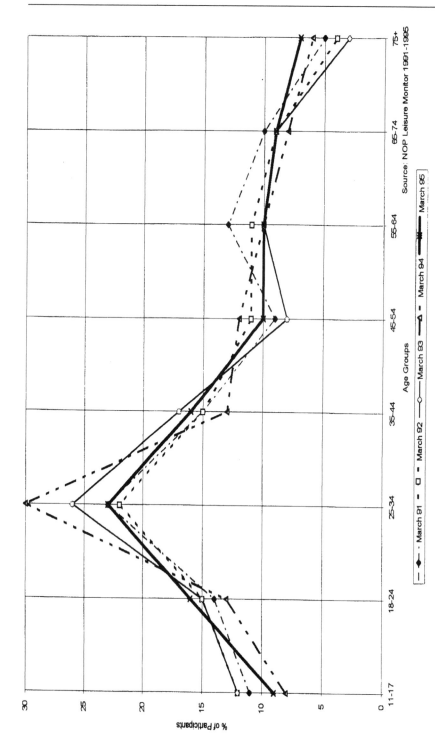

Figure 2   Participation at Public Leisure Facilities: Men

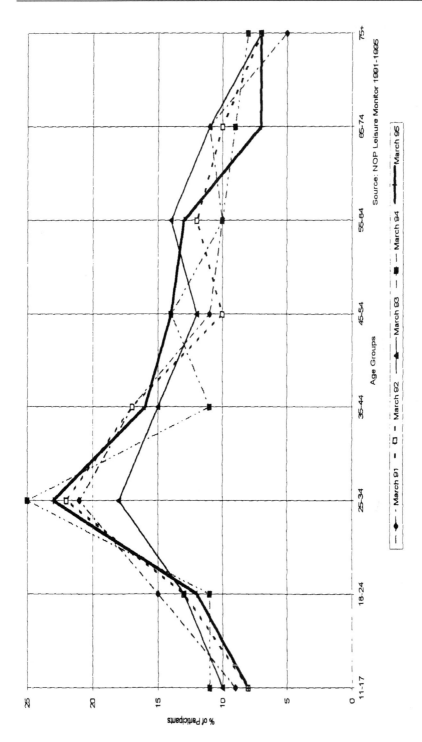

Figure 3   **Participation at Public Leisure Facilities: Women**

Discussion

That UK leisure policy is at a critical point cannot seriously be questioned. For where, over the past 30 years, it has evolved into a vague, and largely unsupported, set of principles designed to overcome perceived market failings, the recent consumerist 'revolution' has sought to overturn this orthodoxy; to convince the public that commercialising the public sector is a legitimate public policy, even when the overwhelming evidence indicates otherwise.

For sport and leisure, at least, this duplicity ended with the 1994 review of sports administration in Britain, where it was made clear that it will no longer be national policy to support mass participation in active leisure:

> ... the new body (*the English Sports Council*) will withdraw from the promotion of mass participation, informal recreation and leisure pursuits and from health promotion. Those are laudable aims, but they are secondary to the pursuit of high standards of sporting excellence. (Sproat, 1994: p. 585)

As the Minister indicated, the focus of the new English Sports Council will be firmly on the support of sporting excellence. A new UK Sports Council will be responsible for co-ordinating British interests in international competition, including policy for bringing international events to Britain. As a result, any residual support for the non-market benefits of sport and leisure will become the preserve of local authorities already so cash-starved that they are more concerned with budget restrictions than additional responsibilities.

In the wake of this most recent policy shift it is pertinent to question what place leisure plays in people's lives and, hence, the reconstruction of citizenship: is leisure a merit good worthy of government intervention in the allocation of resources? Or, is it, as the current philosophy indicates, essentially only for pleasure, a discretionary and conspicuous form of consumption? In terms of citizenship, the question appears to hinge on the degree to which people may retain rights which they have not earned — that is, the degree to which the former passivity has been usurped by a right-wing normative construct of 'active' citizen.

In developing an epistemology of leisure it is essential to appreciate its empirical relationship with work and, in particular, to the industrialisation of work processes (Rojek, 1993). In recognising Marx's separation of the 'ethic' of labour from the 'aesthetic' of non-labour, labour was constructed as the principal foundation of the dialectic of fulfilment, supported by the implied self-actualising qualities of non-labour, or leisure (Rojek, 1993). In this context leisure was viewed as 'other', what work was not. This connotes an unproductivity or vicariousness (Veblen, 1957) which imbued leisure with an element of frivolity or prestige. However, it further constructed leisure as 'activity', in contradistinction to the 'activity' of work, thereby effectively enhancing the centrality of the industrialised basis of Western capitalism.

This associated 'otherness' from work has infused the vernacular of leisure with a strongly bourgeois construction, based on liberal concepts such as 'freedom', 'choice' and 'self-development' (Rojek, 1993). As such, the work-related notion of activity, combined with the aesthetic notion of free, uncommitted or 'disposable' time, has provided the basis for populist definitions of leisure which combine elements of time, activity and attitude of mind (see, for example, Patmore, 1983). It is this bourgeois and vicarious construction of 'leisure for pleasure' that has been seized upon by the New Right as the vindication of its consumerist project, safe in the knowledge that the notions of self-determination and self-actualisation have constructed leisure as both the signification and the legitimation of an 'acceptable' alternative to the former welfarist notions of social democracy.

However, to associate leisure with the 'naturalness' of freedom is to misinterpret, or misrepresent, the relationship between freedom and power. As Foucault (1991) points out, rather than being natural, freedom is an outcome of the organisation and exercise of power. Rather than the formalist construction of leisure as freedom, therefore, it should more properly understood as a form of power. In contradistinction to the New Right position, leisure in Foucauldian terms is not 'natural' but socially constructed; and is not a separately identifiable, but an interdependent, area of social life.

Similarly, Adorno posits the existence of a 'culture industry' which systematically denies people the "... happiness which it deceitfully projects" and which is used as a means of "... fettering consciousness" (1991: p. 91). This theme is developed by a number of authors, including Baudrillard, who sees the primary significance of leisure in its role as a sign connoting "... the repressive desublimation of labour power ..." (1988: p. 110). As such, Baudrillard makes explicit the commodity form of leisure, emphasising its semiotic, if not functional, relationship to work.

Against these essentially modernist metanarratives, Rojek (1993) challenges the continuing validity of the work/leisure dichotomy and, with it, arguments of class domination and sexual repression. While there is evident logic in this deconstruction, particularly in view of the inherently elitist shortcomings of the high modernist epistemology of writers such as Adorno, it is equally important to recognise its limitations. This is essentially about power and scarcity. While postmodernity may be championed by the New Right as an age of post-scarcity, where work can and is being replaced by vicarious leisure, Clarke and Critcher evoke Marxist sentiment on the impact of capital:

> The economic logic of social change is ... clear: not leisure but 'enforced idleness'; not more free time, but the creation of 'competition' between the employed and the unemployed; not the abolition of drudgery, but a 'means of enriching' capital. (Clarke and Critcher, 1985: p. 194)

Leisure is, therefore, the subject of two opposing discourses. The first of these constructs it as a site of struggle, an hegemonic project of the dominant class imbued with a work-orientated rhetoric of conformity and relative worth. The latter discourse deconstructs leisure in the alternative, as a site of identity free from "the modernist quest for authenticity and self-realisation" (Rojek, 1993: p. 133). Power is a central feature of both discourses, with the second expressing it primarily in atomised terms just as the former concentrates on the hegemonic project of distinct class fractions. Both discourses therefore identify leisure with freedom, one with the purpose of casting off the former distinctions of class, gender and ethnicity in favour of a politics of difference (Urry, 1993) and the other seeking to show that this is predominantly another form of hegemony, but associated with new and different identity groups.

Concern must remain, however, about the extent to which leisure's increasingly culturally-constructed 'myth' of freedom is being reinterpreted in the establishment of a 'mute ground' through which socially dominant groups can assimilate inferior groups into the economic imperative, if not the ideology, of their politics (see Fitzpatrick, 1992). This ideologically constructed form of dominance has become one of the core tenets of liberal democracy, for where dominant groups used to legitimate their power through a mixture of fear and benevolence (Hay, 1975), they now require "... a culture shared by rulers and ruled, ways of doing things and seeing the world so ingrained as to have become "common sense" ..." (Horne, 1984: p. 3).

But fear still exists and is still used by governments to maintain their power. The primary, constructed, fears in a liberal democracy are, I would argue, the decline of status associated with job-loss and with ill-health, together with, in most cases, ensuing or concomitant economic deprivation. When associated with social policies which undermine the 'safety net' of citizen rights, as has been the case in Britain, those fears become a major driving force for the populous. Yet just as the relationship between exercise and health becomes more widely accepted, the emphasis on public provision for mass participation is withdrawn, just as surely as has the public support for active leisure programmes for the unemployed. Thus, not only has the status of the unemployed and infirm been called into question, but also has the validity of their former citizen 'rights'.

Concluding remarks

This paper has attempted to illustrate that rather than being of peripheral social concern, the problematic of leisure is central to the emerging project of the New Right. For where, once, leisure was appropriated, by both class fractions and the state, as a form of social conditioning and control, it is increasingly the focus of a new contemporary lifestyle, particularly through its association with consumption and experience.

Leisure, founded on this mythology of a new cultural identity through consumption, is very much part of the process of social reconstruction. Rather than its functionalist connection to assimilation and absorption, Baudrillard views consumption very much as "an active mode of relations" (1988: p. 21) concerned with signification. It is, in MacCannell's (1992) view, a fetishism of acquisition that equates to the valorisation of the superficial — the subsumption of lifestyle in the reification of image. This has the inevitable consequence of superimposing atomised mythical 'truths' on the former constructions of mass culture (Jameson, 1984). It is also the very defence of leisure; that rather than its political significance being subsumed by public sector managerialist rhetoric, it is the market which can and does provide the context and discourse of legitimation. Through the appropriation of leisure as a consumer durable, therefore, the argument is that aspects of negative integration can be rejected in favour of the apparently limitless rhetoric of market-orientated consumer citizenship.

As Cooper (1993) suggests, the notion of conflict, as inferred by the sporting metaphor of 'winners' and 'losers', is assuming increasing centrality in civil society, based largely on the market discourse of buyers and sellers. Rather than being the much-vaunted site of identity and self-fulfilment, therefore, the market represents the extension of a new and, arguably, more divisive metanarrative of atomised 'citizens' as largely 'uncritical' consumers. Now divorced from their work and class origins and, thereby, separated from their own history, people are at the mercy, rather than in command, of a 'consumerised' citizenship based not on activity, nor residence, nor territoriality, but on the ultimate ephemerality of market-based consumption.

Here, then, are the elements of this new metanarrative: atomism as the safeguard of class power (Debord, 1987); the self-parody of a putative freedom beyond social logic (Adorno, 1991); and the ultimate 'banalisation' of a lifestyle subjugated to the constructed needs of acquisition. In effect, therefore, this new metanarrative signals the demise of any form of social democratic, or 'active', citizenship and, in the process, its replacement with a form of 'post-citizenship' based on the creation of the 'perfect consumer' (Featherstone, 1991). However, rather than being a signification of the liberation of consumerism and the concomitant shift from oppression to identity, the perfect consumer must be the apotheosis of fetishism, an idealised incarnation of the human species (Baudrillard, 1988), replete with a market-defined allocation of rights, rewards and power.

Similarly, this new post-citizenship is hardly the discursive surface suitable for the continuing development of the political community, but more an empirical referent of its demise (Mouffe, 1993). Indeed, the very idea of empowerment now seems to be attached to maximising market choice, with rights reinterpreted as the maintenance of consumer sovereignty (Harvey, 1993). And so it is with leisure. Where once 'Sport for All' was a consensus aim, part of the discursive surface of social development, it is now the primary referent for exclusion and exit from that social development, as Twine observes towards the end of his recent book:

> In industrial societies where individuals and their families are dependent upon selling their labour power as a commodity, it is incumbent upon society to either provide forms of employment that make human development possible, or provide social rights that allow for the human development of their members. If this is not done, then the ability of many members of the society to develop their 'self' will be adversely affected. (Twine, 1994: p. 175)

As a consequence it is clear that leisure cannot represent the market-defined site of identity championed by the New Right. Even for those able to exercise their economic status in this forum it must be debatable how far their freedom is other than illusory. While the hegemonic neuroses of high modernity may have been cast-off in the de-differentiated world of the postmodern, therefore, it is far from clear what has been gained. For, in many ways, rather than defining a new active and experiential citizenship, the New Right has achieved no more than a diminished cultural reflection of what went before.

References

Activity and Health Research (1992) *Allied Dunbar national fitness survey.* Summary report. London: Sports Council and Health Education Authority.

Adorno, T. W. (1991) *The culture industry: selected essays on mass culture* (edited by J. M. Bernstein). London: Routledge.

Baudrillard, J. (1981) *For a critique of the political economy of the sign* (trans. by C. Levin). St. Louis: Telos Press.

—— (1988) Selected *writings* (edited by M. Poster). Cambridge: Polity Press.

Bovaird, A. (1992) 'Evaluation, performance assessment and objective led management in public sector leisure services', in J. Sugden and C. Knox (eds) *Leisure in the 1990s: Rolling back the Welfare State* (LSA Publication No. 46). Eastbourne: Leisure Studies Association, pp. 145-165.

Bramham, P. and Henry, I. P. (1985) 'Political ideology and leisure policy in the United Kingdom', *Leisure Studies,* Vol. 4: No. 1: pp. 1-19.

Bramham, P. , Henry, I., Mommaas, H. and van der Poel, H. (1993) 'Leisure policy: Supranational issues in Europe', in P. Bramham, I. Henry, H. Mommaas and H. van der Poel (eds) *Leisure policies in Europe.* Wallingford, Oxon: CAB International, pp. 231-254.

Clarke, A. (1995) 'Farewell to welfare? The changing rationales for leisure and tourism policies in Europe', in D. Leslie (ed) *Tourism and leisure — perspectives on provision* ((LSA Publication No. 52). Eastbourne: Leisure Studies Association, pp. 215-226.

Clarke, J. and Critcher, C. (1985) *The devil makes work. Leisure in capitalist Britain.* Basingstoke: Macmillan.

Coalter, F. (1990) 'The mixed economy of leisure', in I. Henry (ed) *Management and planning in the leisure industries.* Basingstoke: Macmillan.

Conservative Party (1992) *The best future for Britain. The Conservative manifesto 1992.* London: Conservative Central Office.

Cooper, D. (1993) 'The Citizen's Charter and radical democracy: Empowerment and exclusion within citizen discourse', *Social and Legal Studies*, Vol. 2: pp. 149-171.

Debord, G. (1987) *Society of the spectacle.* New York: Rebel Press/Aim Publications.

Department of Education and Science (1991) *Sport and active recreation.* London: Department of Education and Science.

Department of the Environment Local Government Review (1992) *The functions of local authorities in England.* London: HMSO.

Featherstone, M. (1991) *Consumer culture and postmodernism.* London: SAGE.

Fitzpatrick, P. (1992) *The mythology of modern law.* London: Routledge.

Foucault, M. (1991) 'Space, knowledge and power', in P. Rabinow (ed) *The Foucault reader.* London: Penguin, pp. 239-256.

Glyptis, S. (1989) *Leisure and unemployment.* Milton Keynes: Open University Press.

Gratton, C. and Tice, A. (1994) 'Trends in sports participation in Britain: 1977–1987'. *Leisure Studies*, Vol. 13, No. 1: pp. 49-66.

Harvey, D. (1993) 'Class relations, social justice and the politics of difference', in J. Squires (ed) *Principled positions: Postmodernism and the rediscovery of value.* London: Lawrence and Wishart, pp. 85-120.

Hay, D. (1975) 'Property, authority and the criminal law', in D. Hay, P. Linebaugh, J. G. Rule, E. P. Thompson and C. Winslow (eds) *Albion's fatal tree. Crime and society in Eighteenth Century England.* London: Allen Lane, pp. 17-63.

Henry, I. P. (1993) *The politics of leisure policy.* Basingstoke: Macmillan.

Henry, I. and Bramham, P. 1993. 'Leisure policy in Britain', in P. Bramham, I. Henry, H. Mommaas and H. van der Poel (eds) *Leisure policies in Europe.* Wallingford, Oxon: CAB International, pp. 101-128.

Horne, D. (1984) *The great museum. The re-presentation of history*. London: Pluto Press.

Houlihan, B. (1992) 'The politics of school sport', in J. Sugden and C. Knox (eds) *Leisure in the 1990s: Rolling back the Welfare State*. (LSA Publication No 46). Eastbourne: Leisure Studies Association, pp. 59-80.

Jameson, F. (1984) 'Postmodernism, or the logic of late capitalism'. *New Left Review*, Vol. 146: pp. 53-92.

McCannell, D. (1992) *Empty meeting grounds: The tourist papers*. London: Routledge.

McIntosh, P. and Charlton, V. (1985) *The impact of Sport for All policy 1966-1984 and a way forward*. London: Sports Council.

Monnington, T. (1993) 'Politicians and sport: Uses and abuses', in L. Allison (ed) *The changing politics of sport*. Manchester: Manchester University Press, pp. 125-150.

Mouffe, C. (1993) 'Liberal socialism and pluralism: which citizenship?', in J. Squires (ed) *Principled positions: Postmodernism and the rediscovery of value*. London: Lawrence and Wishart, pp. 69-84.

NOP Social and Political (1990-95) *Leisure monitor, waves 1-13*. Technical reports to Reading Borough Council. London: NOP.

Patmore, J. A. (1983) *Recreation and resources*. Oxford: Blackwell.

Ravenscroft, N. (1993) 'Public leisure provision and the good citizen', *Leisure Studies*, Vol. 12, No. 1: pp. 33-44.

—— (1994) 'Paradise postponed? The Department of National Heritage and political hegemony', *Critical Social Policy*, Issue 41, Vol. 14, No. 2: pp. 5-17.

—— (1996) 'Leisure, consumerism and active citizenship in the UK', *Managing Leisure: An International Journal*, Vol. 1 (forthcoming).

Ravenscroft, N. and Tolley, J. (1993) 'The response of local authorities in Britain to Compulsory Competitive Tendering', *World Leisure and Recreation*, Vol. 35, No. 4: pp. 40-44.

Rojek, C. (1985) *Capitalism and leisure theory*. London: Tavistock.

—— (1993) *Ways of escape*. Basingstoke: Macmillan.

Spink, J. (1994) *Leisure and the environment*. Oxford: Butterworth-Heinemann.

Sports Council (1988) *Sport in the community: into the 90s*. London: Sports Council.

Sproat, I. (1994) 'Sports Council'. *Parliamentary Debates*, Vol. 246, No. 127: pp. 584-586.

Stabler, M. and Ravenscroft, N. (1994) 'The economic evaluation of output in public leisure services', *Leisure Studies*, Vol. 13, No. 1: pp. 111-132.

Twine, F. (1994) *Citizenship and social rights*. London: Sage.

Urry, J. (1993) 'Cultural change and contemporary tourism'. Paper presented at the Third International Conference of the Leisure Studies Association: *Leisure in different worlds*. Loughborough University, 9-13 July 1993.

Veblen, T. (1957) *The theory of the leisure class* (third impression). London: George Allen & Unwin.

The Price of Progress: Trends in Leisure Development in Japan

Yohji Iwamoto

Gyosei International College (Reading)

Over the past ten years, Japan has experienced a period of the most active leisure development in its history. This paper examines the unique style of Japanese leisure participation, and discusses some of the problems which result. My approaches are, firstly, to situate today's leisure development activities in the historical context of the industrial policy of the government for the Japanese business sector; and, secondly, to examine the relationship between Japanese leisure and our changing life-styles.

A brief history of Japanese industrial/leisure policies in the industrial age

For the Japanese ruling classes of the nineteenth century, national power was measured by military strength. Only six years after the end of the Shogun dynasty and the Meiji Restoration in 1868, the Japanese army invaded Taiwan. And they invaded neighbouring countries in almost every decade since, until fifty years ago. Our government compelled the nation to endure lower living standards in order to pursue wars, and the promotion of leisure activities was a sort of taboo in those days. After the defeat in the second World War, economic power, instead of military strength, came to be regarded as the new measure of national power, and its establishment was regarded as the first priority. Free competition by domestic companies was eliminated by means of socialistic/bureaucratic control of the government, especially through the Ministry of International Trade and Industry.

Japanese modern industrialisation was made top priority by the Liberal Democrat government which started in 1955, and for almost 40 years this government relied on rural farm villages for support.

Industrialisation was completed during the 1960s in a 'high economic development policy'. It became a international truism that Japan was an industrial state with a manufacturing and trading base which depended on raw materials from overseas and foreign markets.

Concern for leisure activities began to arise only during the late 1960s. Two research and promotional bodies were established as semi-governmental bodies — one in the Ministry of International Trade and Industry (MITI), and the other in the Ministry of Education. A dominant optimistic image for the future at that stage was that introducing the computer would enable us to work at home, reduce working hours, and save paper. Beautiful pictures of the coming age were conjured from this image, but most of them proved to be wrong. During this period there were several 'booms' in leisure activities such as fishing, travelling and bowling. But the economic influence of the leisure industries was relatively low-level as a whole.

Then a 'New General National Development Scheme' was launched in 1969 when economic development encountered difficulties in growth. The scheme resulted in an amazing fever for land speculation which was accelerated by a book by Prime Minister Tanaka entitled *Re-organisation of Japanese Islands*. (The recent 'bubble land' fever was foreshadowed, which I will examine later.) Another incident was 'Expo '70' at Osaka, which had an unexpected economic influence on the domestic market. This also worked as a model case for the exhibition boom, of which I will give some examples later. Japan is said to have become a 'rich society' during the 1970s, following the USA in the 1950s and European countries in the 1960s.

The Japanese economy was damaged by world-wide recession after the oil shocks in 1973 and 1974. Due to this recession, key industries in the manufacturing sector tried to scrap and re-build themselves and also concentrated resources into car-making, which had reached a superior position within the sector. This development was followed by a trading conflict with foreign countries — especially the US.

The post industrial age and the new movement for leisure development

In these circumstances, the shift of Japanese economic structure from a foreign market base to an expanding domestic market was given top priority. Leisure activity was now regarded as a social device which was to convert pastime activities into a money-making structure on a mass scale. This tendency was encouraged by a strong Japanese currency and the structural recession since 1985.

But before 1985 there had already been published the most important policy documents preparing for the Japanese post-industry stage. These were the so-called 'Soft-nomics' reports, published in a series of 37 books in 1983 by strategic policy planning research groups commissioned by the Ministry of Finance during the time of Prime Minister Ohira. ('Soft-nomics' is an artificially composed word stressing 'soft' as different from 'hard' products plus economics.) The series consisted of:

Part 1   Analysis of Structural Change (by 10 teams/reports)

Part 2   Science & Technology and Economy (by 5 teams/reports)

Part 3   Structural Change and Economic Management (by 10 teams/ reports)

Part 4   Structural Change and Financial Policies (by 5 teams/reports)

Part 5   Structural Change and Finance (by 3 teams/reports)

Part 6   Structural Changes and World Economy (by 4 teams/reports)

These policy documents were most influential and they were put into practice during the time of the next Prime Minister Nakasone, who was well-known for policies which were similar to those of his contemporaries Ronald Reagan and Margaret Thatcher. As a result of these policies, several key expressions were created to mobilise public opinion, such as: 'Re-organisation of the Government'; 'Re-organisation of Education System'; 'Loosening of Governmental Control'; 'Application of Private Sector Power' (incidentally the term 'private' in Japanese automatically means 'big companies'); 'Free trade/import'; 'Information Society'; 'Internationalisation'; and 'Coming of an Ageing Society'.

Until now the concept of 'culture' had not been included in the thinking of business development but it was now actively said to help money-making. As a result (under such social circumstances) certain social categories that had been outside the market system — like education, welfare and culture — were put into the market mechanism for profit-making. Thus the 1980s saw the birth of Japanese 'leisure', in the contemporary context.

Another important policy document was the "Maekawa report" in 1985 and the "New Maekawa Report" in 1986. Mr. Maekawa was the former president of the Japanese Bank; he chaired the policy planning group which was privately set up by Prime Minister Nakasone. The first report became the internationally official 'promise document' for a balanced trade relationship with the USA. This led to the re-organisation of the working group. The group was put under the direct supervision of the Prime Minister, and the new group publicised the final report in the following year, 1987. According to the New Report, a comparison of annual working hours at that time showed over 1900 hours in the UK and US, over 1600 in France and Germany, and over 2100 in Japan. The New Report pointed out that "a reduction of the number of working hours should be important not only for the better life of the nation but also for raising domestic consumption". The Report also indicated to our leisure industry that it was expected to promote high growth. It estimated that the leisure industry would have 5,410,000 employees (8.6% of the total labour population) and would contribute 5.5% of the GDP.

The Industrial Structure Council, the biggest (130 members) and most important council of the MITI, published a report entitled "An Outlook for Japan's Industrial Society Toward the 21st Century" and proposed:

1   Expanding domestic consumption;

2   Stabilisation of foreign currency rate;

3   Internationally arranged industrial structure policy.

Generally speaking, the reduction of working hours seems to be difficult to achieve. Actual circumstances in the companies would not permit this reduction. One example from my classmate is as follows: he comes to the office at half past eight, has no coffee break, 45 minutes lunch time and usually works until 9 or 10 p.m. There is a saying "*Shukyu Futsuka Sei*" which means that the two days off per week system is still in effect. This system was introduced so as to reduce the number of working hours, whereas in reality it seems to work to enhance severe working conditions and to expand the number of working hours during weekdays. The paid-holiday system is also available by law, but it is also difficult to use if employees are concerned about promotion in the company.

The final and the most crucial incident in the recent leisure development boom was the enactment of the 1987 General Resort Area Development Act, the so-called "Resort Act". This Act was twinned with the Fourth General National Development Scheme launched in the same year. The resulting changes created new business opportunities by loosening governmental control/regulation, including legal restriction for the protection of water-source forest areas. This legislation was previously established for the public health and welfare and the lobby group which succeeded in this enactment said that the "Leisure industry is now a new national key industry".

The Japanese leisure market was 52,200 million yen (approx. £372million) in 1985. MITI estimated in that year that the scale of this market in the year 2000 would be 106,900 million yen on the grounds that the annual growth would be an average 4.2%. They changed this estimate figure into 163,000 million yen (approx. £1,160 million pounds) after this enactment.

The resort industries were also estimated to net 12,000 million yen between them. Resort holidays are expensive because it is difficult to get long-term holidays. One figure estimated by the government for the year 2000 is that the average Japanese person enjoys tourism 1.61 times per year, for 2.00 days, and this costs 52,770 yen per person (approx. £377).

As a result of supplier-based leisure development, we will have to enjoy very intensive holidays.

Rural leisure facility development

Many local authorities, especially in the rural areas, decided to support leisure projects by developers from Tokyo because they had already suffered from the striking dismantling of local communities during the industrial period by industry-centred policies such as 'Double income scheme', which attracted the labour force away from the countryside into the cities. As a result, only 3% of the population today lives in the mountainous village area, and over 60% of the Japanese population lives in city areas which cover only 2.8% of the land.

The Japanese enclosure movement was completed during the 1970s by the economic gap created by the government and business sector, drastically changing policy for the rural development. As a result, there was a fever of activity in almost all parts of the islands. 850 big projects were planned in two years after the enactment, covering almost 20% of the national land area. In Kyushu Island, with eight prefectures, there was a most intense development fever. The total cost of investment for 135 projects, which covered over a quarter of the area, was 2,800 million yen (approx. £20million). Besides these projects, over 100 golf course developments, ten theme parks, and 5 car racing circuits had been planned. Over 1% of Hukuoka prefectural area (the northern end of the island) had been converted into golf courses. Some of these are still open in 1995, but most of closed before or soon after completion. They left huge derelict areas of land when the development fever had gone.

Developers also rushed to construct similar resort facilities for active sports — ski slopes, tennis courts, marinas, resort hotels, and so-called resort mansions. Furthermore, such facilities constructed by Tokyo developers were often accused of playing destructive roles in the interests of conventional rural communities. I have to point out that leisure development at this stage often comes with the manipulation of information or 'mind control' to mobilise public opinion to support the physical facilities, with huge investment and often with huge-scale environmental destruction. At the same time, the destruction of archaeological heritage was at its peak during this period. There were over 20,000 annual excavations during these years that led to destruction of many of the 290,000 archaeological sites recorded in the islands.

Investment by Tokyo developers required that the profit would be sent back to the headquarters. Traditional small economies in the rural village communities were vulnerable to such leisure development. Extravagant use of water and water pollution caused by certain kinds of big facilities were reported as new environmental problems.

Exhibitions

Let me describe another example to characterise this stage of leisure development in Japan. Exhibitions organised by local governments were started by 'Port Pia' by Kobe City Office at the beginning of the 1980s. This exhibition was taken to be a great success. Then other local governments sent staff to Kobe to learn and they organised similar events, one after another. Dozens of exhibitions have taken place during the 1980s to the early 1990s, such as "MM21" at Yokohama, "World Festival of Food" at Hokkaido, "Yokatopia" at Hukuoka, "Travelling Expo" at Nagasaki and so on.

The most common development method for such expositions was the use of 'commercial power'; however the organiser was the public authority. The government, which has the power to authorise development activities such as 'reclamation' by 'landfilling' in coastal areas, creates huge areas, utilising its own authority and budget. Companies were then induced to come and construct pavilions. They were given a chance and place for promotion but it was expensive because they were often asked to pay for the cost of the road tarmac, as well as selling the tickets using their own network. After the exposition, the land was often sold by the local governments, who then made a profit. Well done! These exhibitions became less popular after several years because they were too frequent. In fact the Governor of Tokyo, Mr. Aoshima, decided to cancel the metropolitan's project 'Word City Expo' planned for next year. It was an unusual case because government would prefer to continue the policy.

Theme parks

The first example of theme parks was Nagasaki-Holland Village, which had 2,000,000 annual visitors. Local business circles, including banks, totally took over the development. Following this came Tokyo Disney Land, Rainbow English Village, Space World (set up by Japan's largest steel maker, Tama-Sanrio), Communication World, Tokyo Culture Village and so on.

Other examples

These include huge scale re-development in the city centres and seaside/water front areas such as aquariums and museums (without curators but with 'companion girls') were constructed, one after another, among the commercial facilities. These were introduced to ensure that the re-developments maintained a certain permanent atmosphere of festival as well as the commercial side.

We now had a new sort of leisure space with huge investment and less environmental care around the area during the late 1980s and early 1990s.

Changing life-style and shared sense of loss

The current tendency is for the target population of the leisure market to become diversified and, especially, to get younger. Formerly, certain modern leisure activities like golf had become closely associated with authentic Japanese business culture. But it seems that the important part of today's leisure market is mainly directed at the younger generation, especially students and single people.

The generation which experienced World War II supported the high economic growth since the 1960s. At the same time, the spread of higher education in quantity was introduced for their children's generation during the 1960s and 1970s. As a result, over 50% of the generation enters Universities and Colleges nowadays. During this period, the school education system became highly selective, contributing to the business sector by generating a top elite in small numbers, and at the same time creating a massive cheap labour force. This put the children into a very hard survival game in the school education system, and brought into existence several other symptoms, especially after the 1980s — including violence in schools, abuse, a rejection of school by pupils and so on.

One important thing which I could point out is that there has been a common background amongst the parents' generation who left schools before the expansion of higher education. Better school and university careers for their children is one of the main personal objectives. It is believed that this will ensure better family status in the future. It is expensive to try to compete with classmates in passing entrance exams for the better schools because they usually need to get home-tutors and to enter 'Juku' (night preparatory schools). Some Japanese mothers would not mind sacrificing their own pleasure for their children if the children or the circumstances require it. They often find part-time jobs at low pay to get extra financial support for children's' tuition fees.

Most of the university students have difficulty in finding clear academic objectives to pursue after the popularisation of higher education. Most of them, once entering university or college, feel that they can relax and enjoy themselves for several years of moratorium, because of the credit system adopted by the Japanese universities. This moratorium is often regarded by parents as a sort of reward for their hard work during former years. As a result, most of them live on the money sent by parents for necessary expenses like education and accommodation fees. Most of the students find part-time jobs so as to get their own pocket money which is mainly spent on their leisure activities. An average student is said to spend a total of 2.6 million to 3 million yen per year (approx. £17,300 to £21,400).

This is one of the most important factors to understand about the Japanese domestic consumer structure and especially the leisure market nowadays. Generally speaking, the Japanese economy has an excellent shock-absorber for the labour market because of the existence of a student part-time labour force which is available during both prosperous times and recession. They also reduce unemployment figures among the younger generation because of their status as students. In terms of the consumer market, students' share has a very serious repercussion effect. These include the construction of fashionable flats with air conditioning or so called one-room mansions (because University accommodation is neither sufficient nor popular nowadays) and so-called 'Fashion Hotels' for the young couple; convenience stores, take away restaurants; video shops whose staff are often the students themselves; and many electronics products which are popular among young people such as cameras, radio, music and video products. Over 50 million Japanese have a driver's licence nowadays which costs around 300,000 yen (approx. £2,140). The younger generation prefers to drive fashionable vehicles, like small 'two-box' cars and bigger 4-wheel drive cars, appropriately called 'leisure vehicles'. They enjoy trips abroad relatively often — probably you have seen living examples in London. It is also suggested by critics that the Japanese university itself has become a 'leisure-land'.

Through the Japanese education system, the younger generation forms a considerable domestic market also with considerable repercussion effect. They are now regarded as the 'tracting part' of the domestic economy. The impact is not only on the leisure market, but it is the leisure market that mostly profits from them.

This highly-consuming youth culture continues after marriage, until couples have the first baby. The average age for marriage has been pushed up in recent years, and also the number of babies has decreased. When it was realised that the average woman had 1.57 babies at the beginning of 1990s, Japanese capitalists felt deeply shocked. Now the central government have started a campaign to encourage more births.

Japanese policy documents identified that the state image in the future should be a highly technological one, providing the most advanced expertise to other countries, even if the domestic manufacturing industry ceases to exist. In fact, the largest percentage of university candidates have begun to prefer humanities and social sciences to scientific subjects. The Ministry of Education is trying to attract children to science and technology. Certain kinds of leisure sites and facilities with computer machines are expected to work as a sort of educational place to contribute to such a national policy by promoting and demonstrating computer technology and electronics for children. Not only by the hardware, but also through its hidden curriculum, leisure facilities are often used for mind control as a tool for manipulating public opinion.

On the other hand, the older (and especially the elderly) generation live in rather miserable socio-economic circumstances. Welfare standards for the elderly decline during this time because of their low priority. The elderly are encouraged to buy word processors so as to typewrite seasonal greeting cards instead of hand writing if they do not want to become out-of-date in these fast-changing days. Their communities have been dismantled not only in the rural area but also in urban areas because of the land tax increased by the astronomical price of land, especially after 1983. It has become difficult to buy land in Tokyo's 23 districts for their own family. Only companies could buy the land as assets and for investment. Even in the local cities, authorities have started to close schools in the old city centres (like my home city, Hukuoka) because of the drift of the population. For the local people, a certain sense of loss and hopelessness is shared commonly.

From environmental illiteracy to re-creation of a new way of life

I have explained so far that Japanese leisure development nowadays has a close relationship with the mega-trend of Japanese capitalism, prospecting for its post-industry stage, and also that its most potential target population, the youth, has converted its culture to fit it. I would like now to comment on this topic from another point of view.

At the same time as the industrialisation and urbanisation after the second world war, countryside leisure activities have disappeared one after another because of the dismantling of rural communities. Traditionally, Japan had certain kinds of seasonal leisure activities, common to the neighbouring countries in Far East Asia. For example, a custom named *Kagai* — an open countryside singing festival, during which people assembled in certain areas in the mountains or seaside, and sang love songs to encourage courting. This was well known in the world's oldest anthology *Man-yo Shu*, edited by an aristocrat/poet in the late 8th century. The same custom was known to the people in Okinawa Islands, in the pacific, and as far as the Miao tribe living in the boundary mountain area between China and Burma.

Other traditional occasions and activities include:

Nanakusa. According to the calendar, people pick up the seven wild plants/vegetables in the field and cook them to celebrate the season in the spring. We now buy these seven cultivated vegetables on the day at department stores and super stores.

Kinokogari. In the autumn people collected *Matsu-take* mushrooms in the pine forest, which used to be common in the Islands. The landscape of the forest was often used as a background of *Ukiyoe* (Yedo period wood prints), especially in Hiroshige's prints. This mushroom became very rare because the change of eco-system of the forest. It also became expensive. It is now imported from Korea and from as far away as Canada. Such leisure activities were popular for medieval aristocrats as well as ordinary people.

Hiyoshigari. At the seaside, people would go to the shore to collect shellfish at low tide in the spring. This custom is widely common to the East Asian countries.

Such activities might seem similar to food-gathering in a former age, but they were actually different from everyday work. We have lost most of these leisure activities in the countryside — not only the activities themselves as phenomena, but also the venues for such activities. We have lost over half of the Japanese natural coastline, mainly in the last 50 years. There is only 42% left. This includes coastline around 7,000 islands. We can therefore, imagine the degree of the loss around the main islands.

Let me describe a typical example. Our local government at Hukuoka city started a huge-scale project of 'reclamation' of coastal areas by 'landfilling' (thereby creating so-called 'bubble land'): in this case, an artificial island of 401 hectares in the bay, off Wajiro Higata (Higata tidal flat). It is the worst environmental destruction in Asia at the moment. One hundred thousand signatures were sent from all over the world to stop the project because it is planned in the centre of a wildlife paradise.

The project threatens, for example, the elegant 'Spooney', a Black Faced Spoon-Bill which looks like a heron, but actually is a relative of the stork and one of the rarest birds — only 199 survive in the world. This species is a seasonal visitor to this bay during summer. Another species of heron has a world population of around 1,000. Also threatened is a sort of small duck which makes a flock of around 20,000 on the surface of the sea. We have two hundred wild bird species in this area during the year, including several rare ones listed on the Red Data Book. There are also some of the rarest plant life and other animals.

This area is also remembered in connection with some of the poems included in the Japanese classic I mentioned, *Man-yo Shu*. The seascape about which ancient governors/poets wrote poems during the Nara period has survived unspoilt until the first landfill work was started by the local government. (I cannot but remember that the Victorian British fought and saved the Lake District.)

The Mayor has explained that a so-called 'Eco-Park Zone' will be created for wildlife and environmental education in certain areas of the artificial island. Such a way of thinking is typical of the Japanese ruling class. They have no sense of environmental crime.

It is only one example. We have lost so many places which not only represented our great cultural life in the past age but also should be a part of world common heritage. The loss caused during these 50 years cannot be estimated.

I will use one particular term to describe the Japanese characteristic which permits such environmental disasters — "environmental illiteracy". This has already been revealed by an international survey (conducted around 1980) about peoples' consciousness and the forest (i.e. environment), that we Japanese have less affection for the environment, less contact with the environment, and less knowledge and information about the environment — contrary to official/conventional reports.

Finally, my own data (collected in 1991) illustrates the progress of environmental illiteracy. The method was simply to ask how many different kinds of plants and animals had been noticed on a particular day by a number of pupils in two age groups (12 and 15). The results are tabulated by individual and by group.

In this data (as shown in the table below), primary school pupils (age 12), living around the Wajiro area east of Hukuoka city, could record the names of around 11 plant and animal species in a day. Junior high students (age 15) from the same area counted under 8 plant and animal species on average. What this reveals is a narrowing grasp of the natural world as the children become older.

Average number of animal and plant species seen by each person		
12 years old	Animal/insect	Plant
Boys (group of 26)	6.4	4.6
Girls (group of 22)	5.9	5.7
Average (group of 48)	6.2	5.1
15 years old		
Boys (group of 27)	3.7	2.7
Girls (group of 22)	4.1	5.1
Average (group of 49	3.9	3.8
Total number of animal and plant species seen by each group		
12 years old	Animal/insect	Plant
Boys (group of 26)	37	48
Girls (group of 22)	35	50
*Total (group of 48)	50	76
15 years old		
Boys (group of 27)	24	30
Girls (group of 22)	20	46
*Total (group of 49)	30	59

* not a sum because of overlapping responses

Conclusion

Japan requires rich and diversified natural resources to ensure better leisure activities and better life for its people — not only for existing generations but also for future generations, and for the environment. Unfortunately, innumerable environmental heritage factors in the Japanese islands have been lost during the decades discussed in this paper. But we also have reached a new stage where we can see the need to share this sense of loss. This could be converted to the creation of a counter-movement against the destructive leisure development that occurs under conventional ideology, and encourage the creation of a more human leisure lifestyle. I conclude that it is essential for Japan to construct a new framework for leisure studies for both the people and the environment by sharing interests and a sense of crisis with other academic disciplines such as educational sciences for human development, especially environmental education, politics and economics for de-centralisation and local autonomy.

Editor's note:

Since the publications cited in this chapter are available only in Japanese, references have not been included. The author invites interested persons to contact him directly for further information:

Mr. Yohji Iwamoto, Lecturer in Education
Gyosei International College
London Road, Reading RG1 5AQ (UK)

A Lifetime of Inactivity to a Lifestyle of Activity:

The Extent to which General Practitioner (GP) Referral Schemes Encourage Long-term Behavioural Change

Sarah-Louise Prime
Cotswold District Council

Vic Kerton
Cheltenham & Gloucester College of Higher Education

Introduction and rationale for GP referral schemes

The health benefits of regular physical activity are well documented (Sharkey, 1990; Sharpe *et al.*, 1995). According to the Allied Dunbar National Fitness Survey, 80% of the adult population in England recognises that regular participation in physical activity reduces the risk of developing coronary heart disease, stroke, hypertension, obesity, diabetes and osteoporosis (Health Education Authority & Sports Council, 1992). This survey, the first of its kind to measure the nation's fitness levels, physical activity patterns and attitudes towards fitness and exercise, revealed that 70% of men and 80% of women are insufficiently active to keep themselves healthy. These findings, along with the publication of The Health of the Nation White Paper (Department of Health, 1992), have provided a theoretical foundation upon which much of today's health promotion activity is based. In an effort to link theory with practice The Physical Activity Task Force proposed a number of strategies for improving the health of the nation (Department of Health, 1995). These strategies are underpinned by the following guidelines:

- The overall aim should be to increase regular lifelong participation in physical activity; to improve health.

- Activities should include a wide variety of population groups.

- Activities should have clearly defined goals, and be based on interventions known to be effective, and well evaluated.

- The principle target group should be people currently taking little or no physical activity and their needs should be taken into account when designing the activities.
- Activities should encourage alliances between different organisations.

This paper critically examines one such strategy for improving the health of individuals who in this case have been prescribed exercise by their GP. Using data from GP referral schemes, questiona re raised concerning their effectiveness in promoting active lifestyles. As a result this examination, the paper suggests firstly that GP referral schemes could be more effective if they are founded first upon an understanding of the objectives and motivations of the major agents or stakeholders involved, and secondly upon on an understanding of the constraints which people face when undertaking exercise programmes.

Once these factors are understood, it is anticipated that more effective programmes can be designed to promote and encourage long term behavioural change to an active lifestyle. The paper concludes by suggesting a model that may assist practitioners in their efforts to provide effective physical activity programmes which encourage and facilitate long-term behavioural change among previously sedentary individuals.

General Practitioner Referral Schemes

Health promotion is commonly understood to be "the combination of health education and related organisational, economic or political interventions designed to facilitate behavioural or environmental changes conclusive to health" (Green, 1980, cited in Patton *et al.* 1986: p. 14). Health Promotion materialises in diverse forms, from no smoking campaigns and healthy eating Heart Beat Awards, to corporate leisure facility membership and the provision of exercise programmes and changing facilities in the workplace and the increasingly-popular GP referral schemes. GP referral schemes typically take the form of the general practitioner referring patients to a leisure facility for a course of prescribed exercise.

The concept of 'exercise on prescription', and the development of alliances between the health and leisure services, is commonly attributed to the Lagoon Leisure Centre in Hailsham. The Oasis Programme set out, in 1990, to reach the 76% of the local population who were not utilising the leisure facilities. Mass media coverage rapidly spread the enlightening news that previously sedentary individuals participating in the scheme were adhering to 10 week exercise programmes and experiencing physiological changes such as reduced blood pressure, reduced resting pulse rates and weight loss. The GP referral scheme was hailed as a revolutionary means of reaching a previously untapped sedentary market and motivating the inactive to adopt a more active lifestyle. As a result of the publicity from the Oasis Programme there are now over 200 GP referral schemes throughout England (Biddle *et al.*, 1994) and the principle has been adopted or at least considered by the vast majority of local authorities (Simmonds, 1994).

In light of the Physical Activity Task Force's guidelines, it might appear that the GP referral scheme concept is a model example of an 'appropriate physical activity programme'. Researchers, local government officials, leisure professionals and health practitioners alike have, until now, been presented with statistical 'evidence' which has highlighted the apparent success of GP referral schemes: the term 'success' being determined by the number of patients who complete a 10 week course of exercise and who continue to attend exercise sessions at the leisure centre thereafter. The Sports Council, in February 1995, commissioned a detailed evaluation of the adherence rates to the pioneering GP referral scheme — the Oasis Programme (Horsfall Turner, 1995). The results of this evaluation raise questions about the effectiveness of GP referral schemes in encouraging and facilitating previously sedentary individuals to adopt active lifestyles and in sustaining increased levels of physical activity. In order to answer these questions an examination of the political framework upon which many GP referral schemes are founded is required, as well as an understanding, and in some cases questioning, of the motivations of the various stakeholders. GP referral schemes commonly operate through a partnership between two or more agents, or stakeholders, who have an interest in promoting a healthy lifestyle through physical activity. Typically these stakeholders may include General Practitioners, Leisure Centre managers, Local Authorities, Lifestyle Consultants and the referred patients. As discussed later, these stakeholders bring to the partnership a range of different, and possibly conflicting, motivations and objectives. A recognition of, and an allowance for, these differing objectives is crucial to the success of a GP referral scheme, but rarely are they considered at the initiation of a scheme.

An evaluation of the Oasis Programme

The results of the Oasis Programme evaluation are summarised in Table 1 (overleaf) which represents the number of patients who attended the Oasis Programme over a 6 month period. The number of prescriptions written by the referring GPs is not known, although figures from a similar referral scheme in Stockport reveal that 60% of referred patients attended their initial consultation with the lifestyle consultant (Lord, 1994). The base figure upon which the percentages have been calculated in this paper is 729, that is the number of referred patients who attended their initial consultation at the leisure facility. It can be seen that 445 patients (61%) began their exercise programme. Of this number 160 patients (36%) completed their 10 weeks of exercise and 66 patients (9%) were still attending the Leisure Centre after 6 months. By focusing on the non-adherers, or drop-outs, the evaluation statistics can be seen in a different and perhaps somewhat controversial light. These figures indicate that 39% of the patients who attended their initial consultation at the leisure facility failed to begin their exercise programme. 64% of those who began their exercise programme failed to complete the 10 weeks of exercise and 91% of the

Table 1   The Oasis Programme Evaluation Results

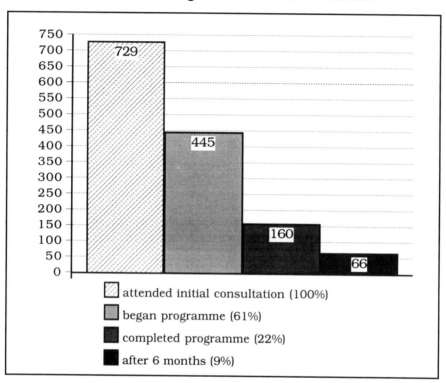

people who attended their initial consultation were not exercising after 6 months. By focusing on non-adherence it is possible to conclude that the Oasis Programme, and many similar schemes, are ineffective in facilitating sustained increases in levels of physical activity.

Model 1 (opposite) links the Oasis Programme evaluation results with the key decision-making processes and influencing factors which referred patients face. Unless providers can identify and understand these influencing factors, GP referral schemes will continue to be largely ineffective in promoting long-term behavioural change. At the base of the model is Stage 1 — the inactive or sedentary adult, who on visiting the GP (Stage 2) may or may not, decide to attend an initial consultation at the leisure centre. Having attended the initial consultation (Stage 3), 445 patients (61%) began their exercise programme (Stage 4), while the remaining 284 (39%) decided against beginning the programme and returned to stage 1 — 'sedentary adulthood'. Of the 445 patients who began the exercise programme, only 66 (9%) continued exercising regularly (Stage 5), while 663 (91%) regressed to 'sedentary adulthood (Stage 1)'.

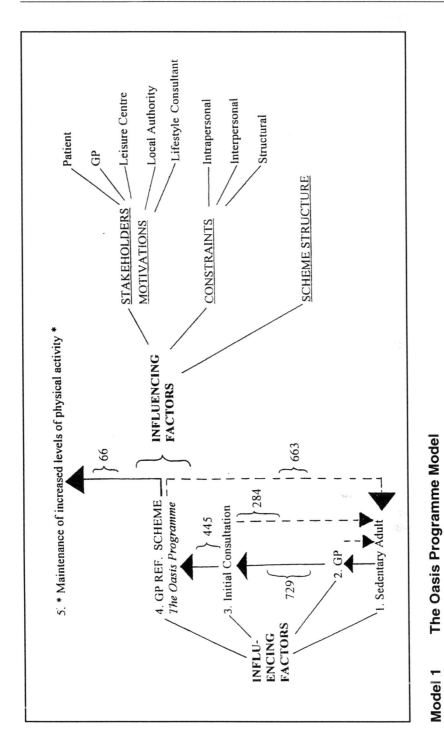

Model 1   **The Oasis Programme Model**

The figures from e Oasis programme raise the following critical questions for providers of GP referral schemes:

1. Why did 39% of those who attended their initial consultation not begin their exercise programme?

2. Why did 65% of those who began their exercise programme not complete it?

3. Why did 91% of those who attended their initial consultation not adhere to the exercise programme?

This evaluation suggests that GP referral schemes are ineffective in promoting long-term behavioural change if they fail to take account of stakeholder objectives, fail to understand the underpinning theories of constraints to participation and fail to provide flexible pathways within the programme structure. This paper considers each of the variables, identifying each stakeholder's objectives and the factors which influence the patient's decision not to begin, or not to adhere to, the prescribed exercise programme. Three categories of influencing factors have been identified:

1. The constraints experienced by the patients

2. The contrasting motivations and objectives of the stakeholders

3. The design and structure of the scheme and whether it facilitates long-term behavioural change by encouraging patients to move from one activity to another and from one level to another.

Constraints to participation

Investigation into the factors affecting participation and non-participation in physical activity and the barriers and constraints which influence people's behaviour is a theoretically important, practical and growing area of research (Jackson and Dunn, 1991). Exercise behaviour has attracted increasing attention from researchers in recent years both in the collection of empirical data and in the development of conceptual models that can be applied in the development of effective programmes (Crawford *et al.*, 1991). Prior to the advance of constraints research in the late 1980s it was assumed that lack of facilities, time, money and access to facilities were the main barriers to leisure participation (Torkildsen, 1992). These barriers to participation are commonly recognised as structural constraints (Crawford *et al.*, 1991). The general consensus was that, if individuals could overcome these barriers, participation would take place. Some twenty years after the leisure facility building boom, participation levels in physical activity are still low among some groups and alternative reasons for lack of participation are being suggested.

Constraints research is based on the assumption that people do not have equal access or opportunity to participate and that there are factors (constraints) that are "perceived by the researchers or individuals to inhibit or prohibit participation or enjoyment" (Jackson 1991: p. 279). According to Jackson, constraints research can fulfil three important functions:

1. It can enhance our understanding of the ways in which activities are constrained.

2. It can shed new light on aspects such as participation, motivations and satisfactions.

3. It can serve as a device to assist in perceiving new connections among apparently discrete facets of activities.

Research into the constraints that restrict people's participation in exercise programmes is therefore essential if effective programmes are to be designed and implemented.

Early constraints research adopted a natural science approach, was positivistic in its assumptions and its methodologies and was largely atheoretical, generating purely descriptive results (Crawford *et al.*, 1991; Raymore *et al.*, 1993). Raymore *et al.* (1993) suggest that investigations into the nature of constraints have traditionally focused on issues such as lack of interest, facilities, time, funds, ability, awareness, or opportunity. Mannell and Zuzaneck (1991) identify the shortcomings of survey methods in their inability to provide information on the nature of constraints as they operate in the context of daily life. Jackson (1991) called for the use of alternative methodologies for studying leisure participation and constraints, and in recent years there has been a growing body of research that has adopted an interpretive paradigm.

The advancements brought by these methodological changes have marked a shift in the underlying theory whereby the term 'barriers to participation' has been replaced by the term 'constraints to partici-pation' due to the growing recognition that the study of 'barriers' has tended to lead researchers to focus on one type of constraint commonly referred to as 'structural constraints'. Crawford and Godbey (1987) suggested that the term 'barrier' was naive because it was based on the assumption that "a leisure preference exists and then a barrier intervenes and results in non-participation or if no barriers exist the individual will participate" (p. 119).

Wright and Goodale (1991) explain the importance of sub-dividing 'participants' and 'non participants' into smaller sub-groups. They argue that only by doing so will the providers be able to effectively target different groups of people, who have different needs and who face different con-straints, with a greater chance of attracting them to, or adhering to, physical activity. They concluded that providers must recognise that those interested in participating face constraints which must be identified, and strategies developed, to alleviate those constraints. Because of the assumption that constraints operate between preference and participation,

Crawford and Godbey (1987) argue that researchers have neglected to look at the way in which constraints relate to the formation of preferences and hence participation. Earlier studies that have focused on 'barriers' have led researchers to look for 'structural constraints' or those inherent within the structure of society. Structural constraints therefore represent constraints as they are commonly conceptualised as intervening factors between preference and participation. For example, the removal of structural constraints to participation does not necessarily result in participation. Some people who have the time, money and access to facilities do not always participate (that is they have not formed the preference, so structural constraints are irrelevant to them). There are other, stronger, constraints which operate to influence preference. These constraints may include negative experiences of exercise, exercise image and socialisation. Crawford *et al.* (1991) identified three types of constraints which affect participation:

1. Structural constraints represent the constraints as they are commonly conceptualised intervening between preference and participation.

2. Intrapersonal constraints involve the psychological states of individuals which influence preference.

3. Interpersonal constraints are the result of the relationships between people that influence both preference and participation.

Crawford and Godbey's (1987) findings are important for those responsible for designing GP referral schemes. Often the referred patients have been inactive for many years, possibly discouraged from participating at an early age through negative experiences or through socialisation. Their negative attitude towards exercise is likely to be a far stronger constraint, and encountered earlier, than the structural constraint of inaccessibility to an affordable programme. Crawford *et al.*'s (1991) integrated model suggests that constraints affect the preference/participation relationship to form a hierarchy of constraints which individuals must negotiate and overcome before they become participants in, for example, an exercise programme .

Crawford *et al.*'s (1991) model (see Model 2 opposite) may be usefully applied to the practical situation of GP referral schemes. Unlike previous research it demonstrates the complex nature of constraints and how they operate to affect participation. It identifies that constraints influence preference for activities, as well as intervening between preference andparticipation. Crawford *et al.* propose that constraints are encountered hierarchically, firstly at the intrapersonal level, secondly at the interpersonal level and thirdly at the structural level. Thus participation is dependent upon the successful negotiation of an alignment of constraints which are arranged from the most proximal (intrapersonal) to the most distal (structural). The model is important because it illustrates that intrapersonal constraints (such as attitudes towards physical activity and perceived skill levels) need to be identified and overcome before

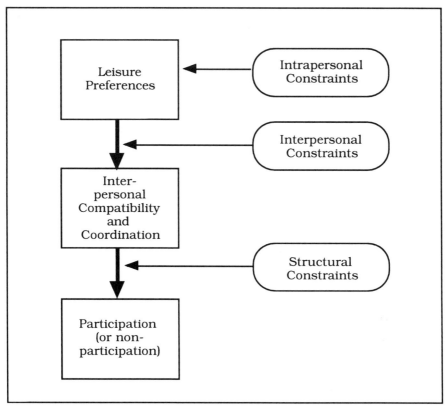

Model 2   Hierarchical model of constraints (Crawford *et al.*, 1991)

interpersonal constraints (such as the absence of people with whom to participate) and structural constraints (such as the availability of resources and programmes) can be dealt with. Only when these inter-personal and intrapersonal constraints have been overcome do structural constraints come into force.

Recent constraints research therefore has implication for the providers of exercise programmes whose strategies would be more effective if they were aimed at reducing the most influential constraints (Kay and Jackson, 1991). As mentioned earlier, traditional provision has been based on satisfying time, finance and access constraints and has not been effective for a large proportion of the population. By assessing the extent to which a person is constrained, it is possible to design programmes to remove, or reduce, the constraints, thereby increasing participation and improving the effectiveness of the provision (McGuire *et al.*, 1989).

Godbey (1985) suggests that differentiating between constraints can assist in defining the most cost-effective strategies for reaching non-participants. Searle and Jackson (1985) suggests that an understanding of the constraints on participation can provide benefits to the provider on four levels — philosophy, policy, programme planning and marketing. Additionally the results of constraints research can be applied directly, through staff training and education, and indirectly through activity programming (Iso-Ahola and Mannell 1985). Therefore providers of exercise programmes have much to learn from current research on constraints and how they operate to affect participation. Although constraints research assists in explaining the factors which influence the decision to participate in an exercise programme, providers also need to understand the factors which influence adherence to the programme. It is where Social Exchange Theory may provide the answers.

Social Exchange Theory

Social Exchange Theory provides the conceptual framework which may be useful in helping to understand and explain the decisions made by individuals when they cease to participate in an activity. It suggests that people continue to participate in an activity if there is a reward or benefit and that the reward or benefit is valued and evolves over time. Participation will also continue if the rewards or benefits are perceived as desirable and fair in relation to others and if the probability of receiving the desired reward or benefit is high (Searle, 1991). Through applying Social Exchange Theory to exercise programmes it is possible to make the following assumptions:

- individuals will cease participation if they do not receive the rewards or benefits they seek.

- individuals will cease participation if the rewards of benefits do not change and expand as the duration of the participation increases.

- individuals will cease participation in the absence of a reciprocal relationship with the provider.

- individuals will cease participation if the rewards or benefits they receive are perceived to be of less value than those received by others.

- individuals will cease participation if the costs are in excess of the benefits.

- individuals will cease participation if they have no power over the form of the programme.

- individuals will cease participation if a power imbalance exists and alternatives are available.

- individuals will cease participation if the probability of receiving the desired rewards of benefits are low. (Searle, 1991)

These assumptions are based on the provider ensuring that the perceived rewards or benefits outweigh the costs of the activity, then making sure that individuals are rewarded in a fair, progressive and cumulative manner. The reward, or lack of reward, may act as a constraint to continued participation. The influencing factors are within the control of the provider and, as such, can be manipulated to prolong participation in an activity or to encourage people to return to an activity. These assumptions have implications for the general practitioner for ensuring that the benefits are realistic and tangible for those patients they refer to the scheme. They have implications for the leisure centre staff for the way in which the exercise programmes are designed and delivered and implications for patients in the way in which the exercise programmes are perceived. Exercise programmes must also reflect the changing benefits sought by individuals. For example, a patient who has been referred by the general practitioner for weight loss may need to identify other benefits once weight loss has been achieved if the individual is to remain active.

The contrasting motivations of the stakeholders

Empirical research has shown that the patient adopts an exercise programme for a number of reasons, including the experience of health benefits, to meet people, to have fun and to learn new skills (Prime, 1994). The other stakeholders in the GP referral scheme partnership may have other objectives and motivations for participating in the scheme. The GP's motivation for involvement is four-fold;

- to reduce practice spending on traditional drug therapy;

- to contribute to potential savings made by the NHS in reducing the number of drug prescriptions written;

- to be actively involved in health promotion activities in accordance with Band 3 of the General Practitioner Contract 1990.

- to have an alternative outlet for the vast number of 'heart sink' patients each GP has, that is those patients whose appearance at the surgery makes the GPs heart sink! (Simmonds, 1994: p. 76)

The leisure centre manager's motivations are often financially driven. The GP referral scheme is often seen by the manager as a means of reaching a previously untapped market — the sedentary adult population, or as a means of increasing revenue during off-peak times. Those managers who are governed by Compulsory Competitive Tendering may find that implementing a GP referral scheme is written into their contract. In these circumstances the provision of a scheme may be viewed purely as something to be done for the sole purpose of adhering to the contract. The evaluation of existing GP referral schemes suggests that there is little long-term financial benefit to the leisure centre in providing exercise programmes for GP referral schemes since only 9% of individuals remain active once the prescription ends. This may only go to reinforce the short-term strategies of the leisure centre. However, this need not always be so. By adapting the programmes to ensure that patients' motivations and needs are recognised, and taken into account, better retention rates may be achieved and thereby improved financial returns for the leisure centre.

With the emergence of the Health of the Nation White Paper, local authority councillors may have altruistic motives for supporting a community health promotions such as the GP referral scheme, that is to be seen to be providing for the community's health needs, 'doing their bit' towards meeting Health of the Nation targets and being seen to be a caring local authority.

The lifestyle consultant who, although governed by the objectives of the employer, may also be concerned with trying to remove the constraints which prevent the majority of the population from participating in sufficient physical activity to experience health benefits. The lifestyle consultant is often the catalyst for ensuring stakeholder motivations are complementary and compatible, and that the design and delivery of the exercise programmes have patients' changing needs as central. The lifestyle consultant must also ensure that the likely constraints to continued exercise participation are understood and removed and that the programme is flexible enough to satisfy the changing rewards of the participants.

From the above it can be seen that there is a range of objectives and motivations for being involved in a GP referral scheme by the various stakeholders. Unless care is taken when establishing alliances these differing objectives and motivations may conflict. If this situation occurs, coupled with a lack of understanding of the constraints which people face, it may not be surprising that many GP referral schemes are, in their present form, ineffective in encouraging long-term behavioural change.

The Cotswold Way

The Cotswold District Council's GP referral scheme is founded on current research in progress and attempts to incorporate the theories and models presented in this paper. Model 3 explains the structure of the Cotswold GP referral scheme. It is based on two existing models, that of Prochaska and DiClemente's model of changing behaviour (1988) and the Sports Development Model (Eady, 1993). Models of health behaviour change recognise that people pass through several stages before achieving a lasting change in health-related behaviour (Health Education Authority, 1995). The precontemplative stage in Model 3 (opposite) represents the sedentary adult who may be unaware of the health benefits associated with physical activity or may not perceive these benefits to be able to influence their current health status. The contemplative stage is represented by the patient, who having contacted the GP, personalises the benefits of increased activity and makes a decision whether or not to participate in the referral scheme: a decision based on the balance of perceived benefits and costs. Once a patient has made the decision to participate in the GP referral scheme, attended the initial consultation and begins the exercise

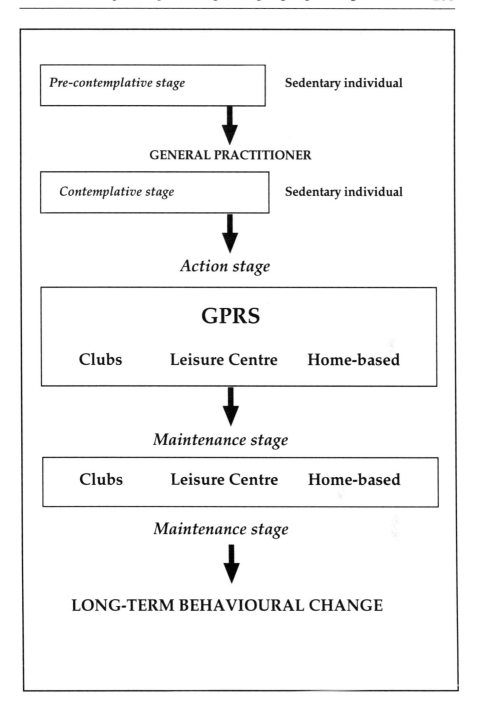

Model 3 — The Cotswold Way

programme they enter the action stage. The Sports Development Model encourages people to move easily between the different levels and intensity of activity according to their personal abilities, expectations and circumstances. By linking the properties of both models it is possible to develop a model that can be usefully applied to the design and implementation of GP referral schemes.

The Cotswold GP referral scheme is designed to take into account both the Prochaska and DiClementi (1986) models of changing behaviour and the Sports Development model. It is designed to operate in the leisure centre, through aerobic classes, adult swim sessions and exercise studio sessions as well as through home-based activities such as walking and the use of exercise videos. The scheme encourages patients to join local clubs to support and encourage long-term participation once the initial prescription has expired. There are indications from research in progress that if the transition from patient to exerciser is made as early as possible within the referral scheme structure it is not necessary for the patient to make major changes to their exercise routines on completing the 10 week programme. Implementation of this flexible structure may well result in greater retention rates on GP referral schemes.

Conclusion

The object of this paper has been to critically review the effectiveness of GP referral schemes. Although there is currently little empirical evidence about such schemes, this investigation concludes that GP referral schemes are largely ineffective in promoting long-term behavioural change among sedentary adults. This critical review identifies and challenges the conflicting objectives and motivations behind GP referral schemes. It also suggests that such schemes need to be founded on an understanding of the constraints which people face in their quest to adopt a healthy lifestyle. GP referral schemes have the potential to make a valuable contribution to the health promotional work of the leisure and medical professions by reaching large segments of the inactive population.

If GP referral schemes are to achieve their potential then the leisure professionals, local authorities and GP's involved in the alliance must all have common objectives, must design programmes that meet the needs of the patients and that remove the identified constraints to participation. Schemes need to be designed so that they are patient-driven as well as being safe, effective and well taught whilst encouraging enjoyment, personal choice and individual effort (Department of Health,1995). If a lifetime of inactivity is to be changed to a lifestyle of activity then personal attitudes towards exercise, personal choice and enjoyment need to be viewed as fundamental criteria by GP's, leisure managers, leisure centre employees and local authorities when designing and implementing GP referral schemes.

References

Allied Dunbar, Health Education Authority, Sports Council (1992) *Allied Dunbar National Fitness Survey: A report on activity patterns and fitness levels. Main findings and summary document.* London: Sports Council, Health Education Authority.

Biddle, S. Fox, L. and Edmonds, L. (1994) *Physical activity promotion in primary health care in England.* University of Exeter & Health Education Authority.

Crawford, D. and Godbey, G. (1987) 'Reconceptualising barriers to family leisure', *Leisure Sciences*, Vol. 9: pp. 119-127.

Crawford, D., Godbey, G., and Jackson, E. (1991) 'A hierarchical model of leisure constraints', *Leisure Sciences*, Vol. 13, pp. 309-320.

Department of Health (1992) *The health of the nation: A strategy for health in England.* London: DOH.

Department of Health (1995) *More people, more active, more often: A consultation paper.* London: DOH.

Eady, J. (1993) *Practical sports development.* Harlow: Longman

Godbey, G. (1985) 'Non-participation in public leisure services: A model', *Journal of Park and Recreation Administration.* Vol. 3: pp. 1-13.

Health Education Authority (1995) *Promoting physical activity: Guidance for commissioners, purchasers and providers.* London: HEA.

Horsfall Turner, I. (1995) *The Oasis Programme Evaluation.* Wealdon District Council. London: Sports Council.

Iso-Ahola, S., and Mannell, R. (1985) 'Social and psychological constraints on leisure', in M. Wade (ed) *Constraints on leisure.* Springfield, Ill: Charles Thomas. pp. 111-151.

Jackson, E. (1991) 'Leisure constraints: Constrained leisure. Special issue. Introduction', *Journal of Leisure Research,* Vol. 23. No. 4: pp. 279-285.

Jackson, E. and Dunn, E. (1991) 'Is constrained leisure an internally homogeneous concept?', *Leisure Sciences* Vol. 13: pp. 167-184.

Kay, T. and Jackson, G. (1991) 'Leisure despite constraint: The impact of leisure constraint on participation', *Journal of Leisure Research,* Vol. 23. No. 4: pp. 301-313.

Lord, J. (1994) *Exercise on prescription: Does it work?.* Stockport: East Lancashire Health Authority.

Mannell, R. and Zuzaneck, J. (1991) 'The nature and variability of leisure constraints in daily life: The case of physically active leisure of older adults', *Leisure Sciences,* Vol. 13: pp. 337-351.

McGuire, F., O'Leary, J., Yeh, C., and Dottavio, E. (1989) 'Integrating ceasing participation with other aspects of leisure behaviour: A replication and extension', *Journal of Leisure Research*, Vol. 21. No. 4: pp. 316-326.

Patton, R., Carry, J., Gettman, L. and Graf, J. (1986) *Implementing health and fitness programmes*. Illinois: Human Kinetics Books.

Prime, S-L. (1994) 'Swimming into old age', *Leisure Studies Association Newsletter*, No. 38: pp. 21-33.

Prochaska, J. and DiClemente, C. (1986) 'Toward a comprehensive model of change', W. Miller and N. Heather (eds) *Treating addictive behaviours*. New York: Plenum Press.

Raymore, L., Godbey, G., Crawford, D., and Von Eye, A. (1993) 'Nature and process of leisure constraints', *Leisure Sciences*, Vol. 15: pp. 99-113.

Searle, M. (1991) 'Propositions for testing social exchange theory in the context of ceasing leisure participation', *Leisure Sciences*, Vol. 13: pp. 279-284.

Searle, M. and Jackson, E. (1985) 'Recreation non-participation and barriers to participation: Considerations for the management of recreation delivery systems', *Journal of Park and Recreation Administration*, Vol. 3: pp. 23-36.

Sharkey, B. (1990) *Physiology of fitness*. Illinois: Human Kinetics Books.

Sharpe, I., White, J., and Rogers, L. (1995) *Physical activity: An agenda for action*. London: National Forum for Coronary Heart Disease Prevention.

Simmonds, B. (1994) *Developing partnerships in sport & leisure: A practical guide*. Norwich: Longman.

Torkildsen, G. (1991) *Leisure & recreation management*. London: Spon.

Wright, B. and Goodale, T. (1991) 'Beyond participation: Validation of interest and frequency of participation categories in constraints research', *Journal of Leisure Research*, Vol. 23. No. 4: pp. 314-331.

Culture, Social Difference and the Leisure Experience: The Example of Consuming Countryside

David Crouch
Anglia University

Neil Ravenscroft
University of Reading

Introduction

As Jameson (1984) stated over a decade ago, life is becoming increasingly dominated by space and spatial logic. This theme has been taken up more recently by Lash and Urry in their work on economies of signs and space. Here they make the point that the circulation implicit in production and consumption processes "... takes place in real, substantial geographical and social spaces" (1994: p. 1).

Countryside is one such space, in which a multitextuality of practices and processes occur. However, it is neither solely nor simply a space, assuming also a particular semiotic significance in late modernity (Halfacree, 1993). 'Countryside' therefore comprises at least a duality of identities, being both a product presented for consumption (social representation) as well as a place where many different practices occur (space). This dichotomy is referred to by Lefebvre (1991) as the distinction between the 'conceived' representation of space and the 'lived' space of representation.

We argue this in terms of leisure in two dimensions. The first of these is that leisure happens in particular 'real' (spaces) places. Thus, the way in which we come to know places is contextualised through practices of leisure. We will call this process of knowing 'geographical knowledge'. Hence, we construct our own unique signification of place. As leisure practices are frequently shared, this knowledge may also contain a strong dimension that is shared and may exist in relation to social differences and cultural distinction. In this process, 'countryside' is no exception.

Second, leisure practices have been subject to neglect in terms of being 'practices', that is, in terms of their significance in the context of social relations and meaning in the practice of everyday life; in lived cultural practices. A coherent understanding of the meaning of these practices in turn illuminates how we make sense of places where these practices occur; in short, what we understand 'countryside' to be. These two dimensions are discussed through reference to predominant institutional claims for the countryside. Following our theoretical section, the arguments presented are worked through preliminary evidence from two examples of consuming countryside: rambling and caravanning. Each of these is subject to commodification, which is aligned, it is argued, to one particular construction of countryside, which this paper contests.

Geographical knowledge

While even a multiplicity of constructions does not necessarily present difficulties, the essential problematic of the countryside, as discussed by Halfacree (1993), is that causal spatial determinism becomes juxtaposed with the "... malleability of the symbolic role of landscape" (Keith and Pile, 1993a: p. 25). Rather than seeing the countryside purely, or even predominantly, as a site or place where practices and processes happen *for all sorts of reasons*, therefore, it is all too often appropriated as a signification of certain social or cultural values — *it is reified as both product and location.*

Consequently, agencies like the Countryside Commission continue to construct the countryside as largely 'unpeopled', utilising highly contestable notions such as 'quality' and 'our finest countryside" (Countryside Commission, 1995) to maintain stasis. Stasis in this case involves the retention of existing land use and tenure patterns, both denying any room for alternatives as well as ensuring that outsiders, the 'non-landed', are viewed as 'other', requiring both tutelage and management:

> People are more able to enjoy the countryside ... when they have the knowledge and confidence to explore it for themselves. (Countryside Commission, 1995: p. 17)

Yet space is neither an object nor *a priori*; it is a frame of reference for actions (Werlen, 1993). Since the social world is produced not by space but by social actions and practices, it is these actions and practices which must constitute it. Accordingly space, such as the countryside, cannot be empirical in a deterministic sense, but can only be a classificatory concept within which the problems and possibilities of practice can be examined (Werlen, 1993).

Rather than being causal, in the spatially deterministic sense, therefore, space — the countryside — is fundamentally political (Massey, 1993). That is, it is not so much space which determines practice, but practice which fills, and gives meaning, to space. Consequently, rather than space itself being a source of power, it is the possibility and actuality of practice

which generates power. Space, or territoriality, thus becomes a metaphorical arena in which the effects of power can be analysed and
determined (Foucault, 1980), but according to the uses of that space rather
than the space itself.

Rather than appropriated to an abstract power, signification in our
everyday lives is not simply detached. As events in everyday lived cultural
practice occur in particular places, these places become meaningful
through the practice itself. Central to this are the social relationships and
cultural meaning that those practices embody, made and reworked
through individual and shared, often collective, practice. These may be
informed by more removed significance but that again will be recontextualised through the lived culture as well. The use of place for this series of
actions, relationships and cultural meaning — (practice) — produces a
hybridity of meaning and identity that does not simply transfer from anywhere else (Rose, 1994).

Therefore rather than only use someone else's iconography, this complex process of practice participates in making geographical knowledge.
Space becomes embedded in the meaning of the phenomena themselves,
including 'borrowed' meaning that is recontextualised in the process. Part
of that borrowing will be the appropriation of commodified and hegemonic
meanings (Crouch, 1992; Gramsci, 1971; Warren, 1993). This includes
tourism material, wider media, national identities and other dominant
forms increasingly utilised in the rationalisation (Rojek, 1993 and Heywood, 1994). Indeed, we return home from a visit to a highly commodified,
signified, event and bring that experience into our everyday life; our everyday relations are not severed as we enter even a World's Fair, as Ley and
Oulds discovered (Ley and Oulds, 1988). *How* we gaze is similarly contextualised and each of these examples is interpenetrated by collective memory
(Smith, 1993).

However this circularity, disruption, recontextualising and contesting
of meaning operates within an hegemonic assertion of Countryside
(Crouch, 1992). As such, our concern remains about the availability of
channels of alternative construction of 'countryside' through available
leisure practices. This concern extends to the means by which these channels can be sustained, changed or appropriated through the contemporary
extension of commodification, together with the notions of countryside and
of leisure through which this happens.

Included in the 'situated' geographical knowledge is a raft of resistant,
transgressive meanings of 'countryside' (Urry, 1995). Urry argues this
alternative especially in terms of the new sociations of green countryside
movements. However, we will argue that these are only a part of a more
complex diversity of meanings grounded in practice.

Leisure practices provide one profound means through which we make
geographical knowledge; test and contest it; remake and reproduce it; that
is situated in a fragmented and fracturing of knowledge, but nonetheless
there. This can be considered in relation to Fiske's notion of Popular Cul-

ture, as a process (Fiske, 1989). What are the content and context of leisure practice that give these dimensions of place?

Leisure practices

Like Charlie Chaplin, de Certau writes, "the walker transforms each spatial signifier into something else" (de Certau, 1984). This proffers neither a Modernist view of leisure, if that view ever held such a unified vision, nor is it a detached Gaze in an 'imagined' de-differentiated, abstracted Post-modern 'space'. What happens in the practice is, we suggest, something much more complex. Here we turn the 'flâneur' to the person walking in the countryside, or just simply 'being there'.

Hot-rodding is an unlikely topic for countryside recreation, but should not be, unless it exposes our narrow thinking. In his study of hot-rodding in the USA, Moorhouse emphasises a desire for intense collective interest; in community, hard work, skill and 'action' (Moorhouse, 1991). This activity is strongly underwritten by club literature and commodification. However, in reading this account, this typical 'enthusiasm' reflects more the content of practices that Gorz noted as "communicating, giving, creating, aesthetic enjoyment... tenderness, the realisation of physical, sensual and intellectual capacities; the creation of non commodity use values" (Gorz, 1985). These observations and interpretations mirror the work by Finnegan on city-based music making (Finnegan, 1989). These authors do not take the practice into geographical knowledge and recontextualise notions of city or country, although each may legitimately do so (Crouch and Tomlinson, 1994).

Our argument is that in each example, and numerous others — we may list angling, caravanning, four-wheel driving, paintballing, historical enactments, allotment holding and car boot sales — the spaces where they occur are contextualised through the practice, as well as in relation to club literature and other sources of signification. Leisure practices happen in 'bits' of the countryside, not isolated inside some great notion of 'country-side'.

The details of the physicality and materiality of the site are recognised as important by the people who take part. These features are embedded in the values and practices themselves and the place where these phenomena occur become part of the metaphor itself — angling and caravanning, allotment holding and paintball are obvious examples. This combination of metaphor and materiality are crucial in making the geographical knowledge (Keith and Pile, 1993). That knowledge is not limited to the hard material dimensions of the site. Moreover, the metaphorical value of the place is not prescribed by a process of commodification, the media or other (semi-detached) iconography (Crouch and Matless, 1995). Geographical knowledge of a site is constituted through the practice, the site's features inscribed in the memory, reinvoked at each occasion and drawn upon in subsequent celebration.

In turn, the metaphorical power of particular sites of leisure consumption and practice are influenced by distinctive social and cultural differences. This produces a complexity of cultural capital and identity through leisure practices in particular kinds of place (Crouch and Tomlinson, 1994), working at the intersections of gender, age, ethnicity and class. These differences are mobilised in the transgression and celebration of the contestation of prevailing norms and orthodoxies about countryside and leisure practices, about power over their enforcement and about commodification and its resistance.

Public access to private land

A prime example of the exercise of this power relationship in the countryside concerns public access to private land. At the centre of the political debate have been arguments about the accessibility, in legal and social terms, of the countryside. While it is argued that walkers have never enjoyed a greater range of opportunities for legal access (Royal Institution of Chartered Surveyors, 1989), it is clear that in most respects the actual experience has declined, with much greater *de facto* freedom to roam prior to nineteenth century industrialisation, land enclosure and the associated 'privatisation' of property rights (Bonyhady, 1987).

Although it is convenient to blame the enclosure of land in a spatially deterministic fashion for the growing dissociation between ownership and usage, the issue is more cultural and contextual. For rather than the regulation of access being of incidental concern to the ownership and management of land, it has been a central element of its legitimation (Ravenscroft, 1995). Thus, public access to private land has been 'protected' as an allowance or dispensation for those 'unsuited' to the ownership of rural property (Thompson, 1993).

Consequently, the legal construction of countryside recreation has been much more closely associated with a 'civilising' mission than it has with the narrower legal definition of rights of access. By constructing those demanding greater rights of access to private space as 'other', what the rural landed are not, the power of the territoriality implicit in the tenure structure effectively decentres the debate from questions about the nature and use of space, to those about the power and signification of ownership. As Baudrillard (1981) suggests, this signification centres on new forms of power and discrimination which go beyond mere possession, into social organisation and usage. Where once it was sufficient for landowners and farmers simply to own land, it is now a significant element of social classification to be able to demonstrate control over it:

> In the good old days when ramblers wore cloth caps and carried their lunch in an old gas mask bag, the issues seemed clearer. It was 'them and us', the 'haves and have-nots'. Now there are rural 'haves' and urban 'haves' still arguing about the same problems,

still presenting the same polarised views, and tending to forget both
the urban and rural 'have-nots'. (Williamson, 1992: p. 87)

In common with the 'unpeopled' spatial determinism of the Countryside
Commission, landowners and farmers have been forceful in attempting to
construct the access issue as technical rather than social. Thus they claim
to be able to accommodate visitors to 'their' land, but through management
rather than as a result of 'uncontrolled' free access. This demonstrates
clearly a politically-legitimised appropriation of power relations, with
property ownership posited as a responsibility unsuited to the evident
ephemerality of 'ordinary' people: they may visit the countryside, but
only under supervision and only to participate in 'approved' activities
(Ravenscroft, 1995).

The issue of access to the countryside further demonstrates the centrality of leisure and leisure practices to questions of space. While countryside sites can feature a multiplicity of uses, it is only really in the case of
leisure that the uses or practices are beyond the 'control' of the owner or
manager. Equally, countryside sites are viewed, in a deterministic sense,
as unique in leisure terms, thereby embuing them with a semiotic meaning
somehow lacking from other sites.

The separation of the leisure practice from the site of consumption is,
therefore, essentially concerned with what Lefebvre (1991) sees as the shift
from a construct of absolute space to that of abstract space. In the former
the characteristics of the space assume a significance which is independent of its use — the country park, for example. The latter, abstract space,
on the other hand is, theoretically at least, capable of being 'emptied', of
deriving its meaning from the practices which it accommodates, as Warren
suggests:

> Landscapes of leisure and entertainment ... seem to have taken on
> entirely new dimensions in recent years. What were once treated as
> separate, self-contained places ... now are seen as not so much
> segregated sites but modes of representation that permeate
> virtually all landscapes and hence are inseparable from daily life.
> (1993: p. 173)

It is this construct of abstract space which is at the centre of a new reading
of leisure in the countryside. For rather than deterministic ideas of the
territory preceding the map and the manager, the opposite is increasingly
the case, as Baudrillard suggests:

> Abstraction today is no longer that of the map, the double, the
> mirror or the concept. Simulation is no longer that of the territory,
> a referential being or a substance. It is the generation by models of
> a real without origin or reality: a hyperreal. The territory no longer
> precedes the map, nor survives it. Henceforth, it is the map that
> precedes the territory — *precession of the simulacra* — it is the map
> that engenders the territory .... (1988: p. 166)

It is the notion of the simulacrum which is at the centre of much leisure provision, creating models of realities that never existed, designed to be consumed by largely 'uncritical' consumers. While such provision is usually thought of in commercial terms, such as theme parks and 'living history' museums, the notion of hyperreality is just as applicable to the 'open' countryside. One example of this is the Definitive Map system which indicates the existence and routes of all legal footpaths and bridleways. Since there is no necessity for the right of way to exist on the ground (and many do not), the Definitive Map is essentially creating the territory. Without the Map there would be no indication of the route; the map therefore, in Baudrillard's (1988) terms, engenders the route.

However, perhaps the epitome of hyperreal leisure sites is not so much the rights of way network as it is the access areas created under the Countryside Commission's Countryside Stewardship Scheme (see Countryside Commission, 1991). The scheme was introduced in 1991 as a voluntary experimental pilot scheme designed to produce conservation benefits or "... improve access and enjoyment of the countryside" (Countryside Commission, 1994: p. 2). It involves some farmers (about 1,000 so far) being paid to allow the public onto predetermined areas of their land for the purposes, usually, of 'quiet' recreation (see Ravenscroft, *et al*, 1995).

Since, in order to qualify for the payments (roughly £50 per hectare per year for ten years), access had to be an addition to what was already available, no maps or representations of the access sites were readily available at the start of the scheme. As a consequence, agreements were reached with, and payments made to, farmers prior to the public having any knowledge of where they could walk (Ramblers' Association, 1993). Initially, therefore, access sites were invisible, if not also abstract, with no impact as potential sites of leisure practice. Subsequently maps and plans were produced, providing the hitherto unavailable reality — a hyperreality created only by the design and distribution of the map. Equally, at the end of the agreement the maps will, presumably, be withdrawn, so effectively denying the reality and delegitimising the site.

Since these access sites have been promulgated solely to suit the needs of farmers and landowners, there is very little evidence of what, if any, leisure practices occur on them, nor how people see and experience them. Evidence from a recent study indicates that few sites receive much use at all, with one in the north of England having about 200 visitors in each of its first two years (Ravenscroft, *et al*, 1995). Evidence from the Ramblers' Association (1993, 1994) confirms this, with many potential users unable to find the sites (an existential reality?) and others culturally 'unable' to use them, when faced with inadequate information about their rights and opportunities. Indeed, it is pertinent to note that although the common rallying cry from rambler organisations is for 'freedom to roam' (see Ramblers' Association, 1993a), the 'demand' within the Stewardship scheme has been for linear rather than open access.

In essence, therefore, paid access sites such as those in the Country-side Stewardship scheme feature a theoretical interface between the abso-lutist spatial determinism of the suppliers and the abstract hyperreality of the potential users. The suppliers claim to be creating, through manage-ment, new sites for new leisure practices which are both delineated on a map and are legally accessible. The potential user, on the other hand, sees none of this. Consulting an Ordnance Survey Map will not yield the infor-mation, while nowhere is it made clear what is either allowed or expected of them should they happen across this land. Rather than new sites for new practices, therefore, the experience is fraught with difficulty, uncertainty and eventually, ephemerality.

Caravanning

In the literature on leisure and countryside, caravanning is problematised in relation to prevailing, dominant, versions of countryside. One hundred years ago, the caravan was first represented as the realisation of Nature, Freedom, and associated bourgeois values, in 'The Voyage of the Land-yacht Wanderer', an autobiographical account of the journey by horse-drawn caravan through Great Britain by a Naval gentleman, with children and valet, but no wife. This inspiration influenced the forbears of the Cara-van Club. However, its popularisation over a century has changed this view.

Sections of the 'conservation' lobby have sought to outlaw caravans as inappropriate in the countryside; the professional response has been to seek their 'landscaping' (concealment). Combined with commercial oppor-tunism, this has included proposals for 'theming' caravan sites. Once themed, the collection of 'vans ceases to be an eyesore and becomes a manageable section of space.

The caravan, as physical object, and caravanning, as people who do this activity and as a way of using the countryside, are archetypal 'others', as in the case of allotment holding (Crouch, 1994). Together, they are constructed in relation to dominant notions of countryside as a 'problem'. The act of caravanning is to transgress 'proper' notions of countryside (Macnaghten, 1993). However much this may be argued in terms of the 'peace and quiet' threatened by their presence, or visual 'disturbance' being a result of their positioning in the view, these are social rather than aes-thetic constructions. The institutional response to them amounts to what Foucault terms 'the aesthetics of existence' (Foucault, 1972), that is a problematisation of the place of the aesthetic in social and political life; a disturbance of hegemonic realms of ethics and aesthetics (Thacker, 1993).

Caravanning has enabled millions of families to get into the 'country-side' and get a little closer to sites of diverse leisure practices. One half a million households each year spend time away from home at weekends on rallies. Many of the millions of people who spend their holidays caravan-ning actually do so with other families, and many more make friends with people they meet on holiday.

For those who take part in rallies the exercise is, resembling Moorhouse's hot-rods, social (Crouch, 1994). This is a leisure practice that has numerous other practices attached to it, as rallies coincide with local events, while many activities are also staged as part of the rally itself. This can include walks and games, while many who rally simply enjoy sitting in the site with a pint of beer. Being able to 'let your hair down' and its value as a 'leveller' are key attractions of this way of being together in the countryside. People who go rallying usually own their own 'van.

Caravanning happens in particular spaces; bits of the countryside. Rather than be alien to the countryside, the availability of small areas to stop is crucial to this activity. People who rally become familiar with sites that become their favourites. These are associated with particular physical qualities, but also with memories of events and activities; a collective memory of the group. 'Even' large sites with caravans that people rent for the summer holiday can become valued places in family, and group, memory, returned to each year and friendships renewed. The experience of place is rooted in the social, where the site becomes important in cultural identity.

The site is more than an adjunct of the practice, but endowed with meaning that is embodied in the practice. The site becomes 'known' as part of a process of geographical knowledge. It is no longer just 'countryside'.

Part of the attraction of caravanning is the escape: *'being away from the phone'*; *'we never talk about work when we are rallying, that is one unwritten rule'*; this includes some signification of countryside as 'peace and quiet'. However, this is not aligned with a sense of countryside emptied of human contact, because exactly the reverse is valued in the caravan experience.

To legislate against this leisure practice is to fail to comprehend the ways in which it is important in people's lives. The legal construction of 'caravanning' has been part of the assertion of an elitist and exclusive version of cultural capital. Its exercise through legal power translates human rights to practice leisure and makes our own identity into unproblematised questions of aesthetics and the technical; when in actuality it is a powerful exercise of moral rights that is being asserted (Rojek, 1993).

Turning caravan sites into 'themed' places regulates and obscures the complexity of cultural identities and social relations that are contained in this leisure practice. 'Commodification' itself does not eradicate the exercise of hegemony and may indeed make its achievement more effective. Regulations about countryside become reaffirmed as they are transferred from permitted rights and access to ownership and 'Styling'.

The commercialisation of the countryside has followed familiar preexisting, rather than alternative, pathways of social and moral order, with the few exceptions kept to acknowledged 'liminal zones' (Shields, 1991). Accompanying this there has been a repackaging of a familiar Heritage that is archetypal of Baudrillard's abstraction (Baudrillard, 1981). This shrinks the scope for absolute space, although as we observed in the World's Fair, people subvert.

Moreover, there is an underlying concern about the legitimacy of this abstraction in terms of a democratic ideal of 'countryside' and claims for its moralistic virtue. Commodification is seen to appropriate choice. It is able to remove sites from one kind of use, for example wayside caravanning and small 'unlandscaped' [sic] locations, to 'properly landscaped' sites. In parts of Cornwall it is necessary for individual householders to have planning permission to site *one* caravan on their property (Crouch, 1995). The planning system legitimises commercial sites that reach an 'approved' aesthetic standard, pursuing notions of 'countryside', so creating territory and extinguishing the possibilities of others. This becomes the more so as 'public' policy relies upon implementation by commercial operators.

Conclusions

What is apparent in this analysis is that the construction of the 'problem' and, hence, the solution, is very much determined by the relative power of the parties to the debate. The dominant construction of this power is in terms of 'values'; that rather than relating to differential power, differences can be explained by reference to relative values:

> The whole access issue has to do with values accorded to areas by those who do not own them, and to do with the values and atti- tudes of the parties involved towards each other, be it the plan- ner's, landowner's or farmer's attitude to the activity, the views of competing users, such as ... recreationists, or the views of one set of recreational users about another. (Glyptis, 1992: p. 7)

However, the discourse on values is far from neutral. Values themselves have little credibility without the means of legitimation. It may suit certain groups or associations to construct the relative positions in terms of values, but the relativity is more associated with the power to substantiate those value claims than it is with values *per se*. It is clear that the domi- nant values associated with access to the countryside have little to do with the abstract and social construction of space and everything to do with the continuation of the spatial determinism upon which land tenure is based.

Any representation of the access 'problem' as one of values, or even rights, is, then, an obfuscation of what is more fundamentally a mechan- ism of alienation and control. This is based on deceptive notions of social process promulgated by the dominant ideological forces associated with property. This dominance has even reached the stage of achieving the acquiescence of the rural 'landless' in the deception that access claims have been materially substantiated, when any 'improvement' is limited to the ephemerality of hyperreality.

Rather than 'freedom to roam' or some similar evocation, therefore, what the Stewardship scheme has promoted is the reinvention of the countryside as a sanitised, safe, site where recreation is allowed or even encouraged, and where people's respect for the countryside can be developed. Rather than a recognition of abstract space, however, this is more a corollary of past managerialism, with specific sites 'sacrificed' to the needs of leisure as a diversion from more 'valuable' or 'high quality' land elsewhere. Now, however, the diversion is not from other land, but from wider and more deeply philosophical issues about the relationship between diverse leisure practices and the spatial determinism of land ownership and management.

Similarly, the claim to assert a preferred aesthetics upon the country-side through the selective permitting and disallowing of caravan sites mobilises a dominant aesthetics that also has its roots in landownership and class power. This occurs conspicuously without mobilising a debate about alternative versions of the countryside. Sustained within a familiar structure of land and investment control, the provision and use of sites for caravanning also replicates existing relations of power over the country-side.

To argue that commodification of this process of leisure development expands choice misunderstands the perpetuation of the ways of thinking that most commercial development embodies. In so doing, it withdraws opportunity for diversity further and makes transgression actually more difficult, except within the structures of 'marketed' countryside (Crouch, 1992). What masquerades as an 'increase' in choice is actually formulaic hyperreality, where the iconography lends little to the practice itself.

Instead of releasing new spaces for recontextualisation through leisure practices, this shift to commodification augers to secure land for uses other than leisure activities such as caravanning, cleansed of the Other and restored to a particular pattern of both land ownership and the control of commodification. This process may offer new choice, but it can also appropriate choices already there.

There has been little opening of a debate over the alternatives that may exist to hegemonic versions of countryside leisure, or alternative means through which we might make sense of the rural (Crouch, 1992). 'New leisure' is understood simply in terms of new stylisations, increasing commodification as extension of 'choice' (also hence as 'disturbance') and new kinds of social relationship grounded in 'playfulness'; its context, meaning and value systems are ignored (Urry, 1995).

For the most part, these are challenges within a system of capital, rather than offering alternatives to it, save in the form of certain 'green', often middle class, sociations. This has as yet ignored the possibility of what Gorz (1985) identified as 'the creation of non-commodity use values' — opportunities for love, care, giving, sensuality and self-realisation. Our initial findings suggest that there are more complex forms and grounds of identity; ways of making sense of our lives, of home, of escape from it, and that leisure and place are important in their construction.

Just as the development of leisure in the countryside has complied with old patterns of ownership and politics, so 'new' kinds of leisure practice do the same. 'Managerialism' and 'new postmodern' leisure possibilities operate to the same notions of both. It remains for a rigorous and critical practice to demonstrate that the future is not foreclosed.

References

Baudrillard, J. (1981) *For a critique of the political economy of the sign* (trans. C. Levin). St. Louis: Telos Press.

—— (1988) *Selected writings* (ed. M. Poster). Stanford, USA: Stanford University Press.

Bonyhady, T. (1987) *The law of the countryside. The rights of the public.* Abingdon: Professional Books.

Countryside Commission (1991) *Countryside stewardship: An outline.* Publication CCP 346. Cheltenham: Countryside Commission.

—— (1994) *Countryside stewardship: Handbook and application forms.* Publication CCP 453. Cheltenham: Countryside Commission.

—— 1995) *Quality of countryside: Quality of life.* Publication CCP 470. Cheltenham: Countryside Commission.

Crouch, D. (1992) 'Popular culture and what we make of the rural', *Journal of Rural Studies* Vol. 8, No. 3.

—— (1994) *Signs, places, lives.* Working Paper, Odense University.

—— (1995) 'Others in the rural: leisure practices and geographical knowledge', in P. Milbourne (ed) *Revealing rural others: Diverse voices in the countryside.* London: Mansell (forthcoming).

Crouch, D. and Matless, D. (1995) 'Refiguring geography: the Parish Maps of Common Ground', *Transactions of the Institute of British Geographers* (forthcoming).

Crouch, D. and Tomlinson, A. (1994) 'Collective self-generated consumption: leisure, space and cultural identity in late modernity', in I. Henry (ed) *Leisure, modernity, postmodernity and lifestyles.* LSA Publication No. 48. Eastbourne: Leisure Studies Association, pp. 309-322.

de Certau, M. (1984) *The practice of everyday life.* Berkeley: University of California Press.

Finnegan, R. (1989) *Music making in an English town.* Milton Keynes: Open University Press.

Fiske, J. (1989) *Understanding popular culture.* London: Routledge.

Foucault, M. (1972) *The archeology of knowledge.* New York: Colophon.

—— (1980) *Power/knowledge: selected interviews and other writings 1972-1977.* New York: Pantheon Books.

Glyptis, S. (1992) 'Setting the scene', in K. Bishop (ed) *Off the beaten track: Access to open land in the UK*. Proceedings of the 1992 Countryside Recreation Conference, Cardiff: Countryside Recreation Network, pp. 4-18.

Gorz, A. (1985) *Paths to paradise*. London: Pluto.

Gramsci, A. (1971) *Selections from the prison notebooks*. London: Lawrence and Wishart.

Halfacree, K. (1993) 'Locality and social representation: space, discourse and alternative definitions of the rural', *Journal of Rural Studies*, Vol. 9, No. 1: pp. 23-37.

Heywood, I. (1995) 'Urgent dreams: climbing, rationalisation and ambivalence', *Leisure Studies* Vol. 13, pp. 179-194.

Jameson, F. (1984) 'Postmodernism, or the logic of late capitalism', *New Left Review* No. 146: pp. 53-92.

Keith, M. and Pile, S. (eds) *(1993) Place and the politics of identity*. London: Routledge.

Keith, M. and Pile, S. (1993a) 'Introduction to part 2: the place of politics, in M. Keith and S. Pile (eds) *Place and the politics of identity*. London: Routledge, 22-40.

Lash, S. and Urry, J. (1994) *Economies of signs and space*. London: SAGE.

Lefebvre, H. (1991) *The production of space*. Oxford: Blackwell.

Ley, D., and Oulds, K. (1988) 'Landscape as spectacle: World's fairs and the culture of heroic consumption', *Environment and Planning D: Society and Space*, Vol. 6, pp. 191-212.

Macnaghten, P. (1993) *Landscapes of discipline and transgression*. Paper presented at the De-traditionalisation Conference, University of Lancaster.

Massey, D. (1993) 'Politics and space/time', in M. Keith and S. Pile (eds) *Place and the politics of identity*. London: Routledge, pp. 141-161.

Moorhouse, B. (1991) *Driving ambitions*. Manchester: Manchester University Press.

Ramblers' Association (1993) *CSS — survey by the Ramblers' Association of public access sites*. London: Ramblers' Association.

Ramblers' Association (1993a) *Harmony in the hills*. London: Ramblers' Association.

———— (1994) *CSS public access sites. Survey report on access provisions at second-year public access sites*. London: Ramblers' Association.

Ravenscroft, N. (1995) 'Recreational access to the countryside of England and Wales: Popular leisure as the legitimation of private property', *Journal of Property Research* Vol. 12: pp. 63-74.

Ravenscroft, N., Prag, P. A. B., Gibbard, R. and Markwell, S. S. (1995) *The financial implications to landowners and farmers of the Countryside Stewardship Scheme*. Research Series 95/1. Centre for Environment and Land Tenure Studies, The University of Reading.

Rojek, C. (1993) *Ways of escape*. Basingstoke: Macmillan.

Rose, G. (1994) 'The cultural politics of place: Local representation and oppositional discourse in two films', *Transactions of the Institute of British Geographers* Vol. 19, No. 1: pp. 46-60.

Royal Institution of Chartered Surveyors (1989) *Managing the countryside. Access, recreation and tourism*. London: Royal Institution of Chartered Surveyors.

Shields, R. (1991) *Places on the margin*. London: Routledge.

Smith, S. (1993) 'Bounding the Borders: Claiming space and making place in rural Scotland', *Transactions of the Institute of British Geographers* Vol. 18, No. 3: pp. 291-308.

Thacker, A. (1993) 'Foucault's aesthetics of existence', *Radical Philosophy*, Vol. 63: pp. 13-21.

Thompson, E. P. (1993) *Customs in common*. Harmondsworth, Middlesex: Penguin Books.

Urry, J. (1995) *Consuming places*. London: Routledge.

Warren, S. (1993) '"This heaven gives me migraines", the problems and promise of landscapes of leisure', in J. Duncan and D. Ley (eds) *Place/culture/representation*. London: Routledge.

Werlen, B. (1993) *Society, action and space: An alternative human geography* (trans. by G. Wells). London: Routledge.

Williamson, R. (1992) 'Opportunities and constraints for landowners', in K. Bishop (ed) *Off the beaten track: Access to open land in the UK*. Proceedings of the 1992 Countryside Recreation Conference, Cardiff: Countryside Recreation Network, pp. 86-90.

Index

Note: No claim is made that this index is either comprehensive or exhaustive. Its modest aim is to provide sign-posts to the extensive range of topics — both discussed in depth and mentioned in passing — in this volume. For example, some authors who have been discussed, quoted and/or extensively cited in a particular chapter are indexed; but no concerted attempt has been made at cross-referencing.